OXFORD THEOLOGICAL MONOGRAPHS

Editorial Committee

J. DAY
P. S. FIDDES
O. M. T. O'DONOVAN

M. J. EDWARDS
D. N. J. MACCULLOCH
C. C. ROWLAND

OXFORD THEOLOGICAL MONOGRAPHS

PETER MARTYR VERMIGLI AND PREDESTINATION
The Augustinian Inheritance of an Italian Reformer
Frank A. James III (1998)

EARLY ISRAELITE WISDOM
Stuart Weeks (Paperback: 1999)

ZADOK'S HEIRS
The Role and Development of the High
Priesthood in Ancient Israel
Deborah W. Rooke (2000)

UNIVERSAL SALVATION
Eschatology in the Thought of Gregory of Nyssa and Karl Rahner
Morwenna Ludlow (2000)

ANGLICAN EVANGELICALS
Protestant Secessions from the Via Media, c.1800–1850
Grayson Carter (2001)

CHRISTIAN MORAL REALISM
Natural Law, Narrative, Virtue, and the Gospel
Rufus Black (2001)

KARL RAHNER AND IGNATIAN SPIRITUALITY
Philip Endean (2001)

EZEKIEL AND THE ETHICS OF EXILE
Andrew Mein (2001)

THEODORE THE STOUDITE
The Ordering of Holiness
Roman Cholij (2002)

HIPPOLYTUS BETWEEN EAST AND WEST
The Commentaries and the Provenance of the Corpus
J. A. Cerrato (2002)

FAITH, REASON, AND REVELATION IN THE
THOUGHT OF THEODORE BEZA
Jeffrey Mallinson (2003)

RICHARD HOOKER AND REFORMED THEOLOGY
A Study of Reason, Will, and Grace
Nigel Voak (2003)

The Countess of Huntingdon's Connexion

A Sect in Action in Eighteenth-Century England

ALAN HARDING

OXFORD
UNIVERSITY PRESS

Great Clarendon Street, Oxford OX2 6DP
Oxford University Press is a department of the University of Oxford.
It furthers the University's objective of excellence in research, scholarship,
and education by publishing worldwide in
Oxford New York
Auckland Bangkok Buenos Aires Cape Town Chennai
Dar es Salaam Delhi Hong Kong Istanbul Karachi Kolkata
Kuala Lumpur Madrid Melbourne Mexico City Mumbai Nairobi
São Paulo Shanghai Taipei Tokyo Toronto

Oxford is a registered trade mark of Oxford University Press
in the UK and in certain other countries

Published in the United States
by Oxford University Press Inc., New York

© Alan Harding 2003

The moral rights of the author have been asserted
Database right Oxford University Press (maker)

First published 2003

All rights reserved. No part of this publication may be reproduced,
stored in a retrieval system, or transmitted, in any form or by any means,
without the prior permission in writing of Oxford University Press,
or as expressly permitted by law, or under terms agreed with the appropriate
reprographics rights organization. Enquiries concerning reproduction
outside the scope of the above should be sent to the Rights Department,
Oxford University Press, at the address above

You must not circulate this book in any other binding or cover
and you must impose this same condition on any acquirer

British Library Cataloguing in Publication Data
Data available
Library of Congress Cataloging in Publication Data
Data available

ISBN 0–19–826369–4 (hbk.)

1 3 5 7 9 10 8 6 4 2

Typeset by Newgen Imaging Systems (P) Ltd., Chennai, India
Printed in Great Britain
on acid-free paper by
T. J. International,
Padstow, Cornwall

For
Sharon—and for Nick, Sophia, and Robin

PREFACE

This book is a development of the doctoral thesis upon which I first began working more than thirty years ago. Any such work of research is bound to incur many debts of gratitude, and that is especially the case with one that has been so long in gestation. Over the years many people have supplied me with information, given advice, or pointed me in the direction of material or profitable lines of enquiry: some of these I have mentioned in the notes, but to all of them, acknowledged or not, I express my very sincere thanks. I hope that all those who have helped me will understand why I have not attempted to list everyone.

Some debts must, however, be acknowledged explicitly. In particular, I wish to thank the owners of the various archive sources I have consulted for permission to use their material, viz: Bath Central Library, Bath; Cheshunt Foundation, Westminster College, Cambridge; Cheshire and Chester Archives and Local Studies, Cheshire Record Office, Chester; Dr Williams's Library, London; Robert W. Woodruff Library, Emory University, Atlanta; Essex Record Office, Chelmsford; Gainsborough United Reformed (John Robinson Memorial) Church, Gainsborough; Gloucestershire County Record Office, Gloucester; Huntington Library, San Marino, California; Leicestershire Record Office, Leicester; National Library of Wales, Aberystwyth; West Sussex Record Office, Chichester. For permission to cite material, I am also grateful to the Historical Society of the Presbyterian Church of Wales, the Congregational Memorial Hall Trust (1978) Limited; the Director and University Librarian of the John Rylands Library, University of Manchester; the Archives and History Committee of the Methodist Church; and the Center for Methodist Studies at Bridwell Library, Perkins School of Theology, Southern Methodist University, Dallas.

Some personal debts must also be made explicit. One such is to the late Dr Edwin Welch, the former honorary archivist of the Cheshunt Foundation (one should perhaps say 'archivist to the Countess of Huntingdon', so great was his zeal in tracking down her scattered correspondence), who gave me much early help and advice. All who work in this or related fields will be in Edwin's debt for many years to come. I wish also to express my gratitude to Dr Geoffrey Nuttall, doyen of Nonconformist history, who treated me so kindly and supportively when I was a callow research student. Above all, I must thank Dr John Walsh, who first drew my attention to Lady Huntingdon and her Connexion, all those years ago, who supervised me during the many years of my initial researches, and who has continued as adviser and friend during the further lengthy stage of turning that work into this book. John's generosity in sharing his time and unparalleled knowledge of the eighteenth-century Revival is legendary: I count myself fortunate indeed in being among the recipients of it. Needless to say, the faults that remain in this text are wholly down to me.

On an important practical level, my thanks are due to Mrs Sheila Blake, who so skilfully typed the whole of the present manuscript, and who doubtless now knows rather more about Lady Huntingdon than she might have wished. And I am grateful, also, both to the Oxford University Theological Monographs Committee, and to the OUP, for their seemingly endless patience and help.

My final thanks are due to my family, to whom this book is dedicated—whether they deserve to be saddled with it, or not! They are (under God) my greatest joy in this life. They have never known me without the companionship of Lady Huntingdon, and their tolerance has been immense; I hope that it will not end with the completion of this work.

Alan Harding

South Mymms
Trinity Sunday 2002

CONTENTS

Abbreviations	x
Map of the chapels of the Countess of Huntingdon's Connexion as given in the Plan of Association of 1790	xiv
1. Introduction	1
2. The Eighteenth-Century Religious Background	5
3. Selina, Countess of Huntingdon: Early Life and the Start of the Connexion	21
4. The Life of the Countess of Huntingdon's Connexion	62
5. Trevecca College	173
6. Doctrines and Divisions	233
7. The Connexion, the Church of England and Dissent	296
8. The Connexion in the Last Years of Lady Huntingdon's Life	358
Annex A. Students of Trevecca College	375
Annex B. The Plan of Association (1790)	377
Annex C. The Articles of the Countess of Huntingdon's Connexion	378
Bibliography	385
Index	395

ABBREVIATIONS

INDIVIDUALS

CW	Charles Wesley
JW	John Wesley
Lady AE	Lady Anne Erskine
LH	Selina, Countess of Huntingdon
Lord H	Theophilus, 9th Earl of Huntingdon

PRIMARY SOURCES

Bridwell MS	Countess of Huntingdon correspondence in the Center for Methodist Studies at Bridwell Library, Perkins School of Theology, Southern Methodist University, Dallas.
A Brief Historick Record	'A Brief Historick Record of Events Relating to the Independent Church Assembling in Caskgate Lane Chapel.' Manuscript in the possession of the United Reformed (John Robinson Memorial) Church, Gainsborough.
CF	Archives of the Cheshunt Foundation, Westminster and Cheshunt Colleges, Cambridge.
Curnock	*The Journal of the Revd John Wesley, A.M.*, ed. N. Curnock (Bicentenary Issue, London, 1938).
CW's *Journal*	*The Journal of the Revd Charles Wesley*, ed. T. Jackson (London, 1849).
Doddridge	*Calendar of the Correspondence of Philip Doddridge, D.D.*, ed. G. F. Nuttall (Historical Manuscripts Commission, HMSO, London 1979).

Abbreviations

Harris's Diary	Manuscript Diary of Howel Harris, in the National Library of Wales, Aberystwyth.
Hastings MS	Hastings family papers in the Henry E. Huntington Library, San Marino, California.
HMC	*Report on the Manuscripts of the late Reginald Rawdon Hastings Esq.* (Historical Manuscripts Commission, London, 1928–47).
HMC (Dartmouth)	*Manuscripts of the Earl of Dartmouth* (Historical Manuscripts Commission, London, 1887–96).
LRO	Hastings family papers in the Leicestershire Record Office.
Meth. Arch. (LH)	Methodist Connexional Archives in the John Rylands Library, Manchester: letters of Lady Huntingdon.
Meth. Arch. (Fletcher)	Methodist Connexional Archives in the John Rylands Library, Manchester: letters of John Fletcher.
Meth. Arch. (Ingham)	Methodist Connexional Archives in the John Rylands Library, Manchester: letters of Benjamin Ingham.
Meth. Arch. (Letters to CW)	Methodist Connexional Archives in the John Rylands Library, Manchester: letters to Charles Wesley.
Rylands MS	Other manuscripts held by the John Rylands Library, Manchester.
Trevecka Letters	Trevecka Letter Collection, National Library of Wales, Aberystwyth.
Wesley, *Letters*	*The Letters of the Revd John Wesley, A.M.*, ed. J. Telford (Standard edn., London, 1931).

Wesley, *Works*	The Bicentennial edition of the *Works of John Wesley*, vols. xx–xxiii, ed. R. P. Heitzenrater and F. Baker (Nashville, 1991–5); vols. xxv–xxvi, ed. F. Baker (Oxford, 1980, 1982).

SECONDARY SOURCES

Alum. Cant.	*Alumni Cantabrigiensis*, ed. J. and J. A. Venn (Cambridge, 1922–54).
Alum. Oxon.	*Alumni Oxoniensis*, ed. J. Foster (Oxford, 1886–91).
Baker, *Wesley*	F. Baker, *John Wesley and the Church of England* (London, 1970).
Baker, 'Polity'	F. Baker, 'The People called Methodists: Polity', in R. Davies and G. Rupp (eds.), *A History of the Methodist Church in Great Britain* (London, 1965).
Blackwell	D. M. Lewis (ed.), *The Blackwell Dictionary of Evangelical Biography: 1730–1860* (Oxford, 1995).
Curnock	*The Journal of the Revd John Wesley, A.M.*, ed. N. Curnock, (Standard edn., London, 1938).
DNB	*Dictionary of National Biography*.
Rack, *Wesley*	H. Rack, *Reasonable Enthusiast: John Wesley and the Rise of Methodism* (London, 1989).
Seymour	A. C. H. Seymour, *The Life and Times of the Countess of Huntingdon* (London, 1839).
Schlenther	B. S. Schlenther, *Queen of the Methodists: The Countess of Huntingdon and the Eighteenth Century Crisis of Faith and Society* (Durham, 1997).
Tyerman, *Wesley*	L. Tyerman, *The Life and Times of the Revd John Wesley* (London, 1880).
Tyerman, *Whitefield*	L. Tyerman, *The Life of the Revd George Whitefield* (London, 1876/7).

Tyerman, *Fletcher*	L. Tyerman, *Wesley's Designated Successor: The Life, Letters and Literary Labours of J. W. Fletcher* (London, 1882).
Welch	E. Welch, *Spiritual Pilgrim: A Reassessment of the Life of the Countess of Huntingdon* (Cardiff, 1995).

Map of the chapels of the Countess of Huntingdon's Connexion as given in the Plan of Association of 1790

1
Introduction

There is something quaint, almost picaresque, about the notion of a titled woman founding her own denomination. It seems the stuff of the historical aside, not of serious mainstream research. Possibly this somewhat eccentric image has been partly responsible for denying the Countess's Connexion its rightful place in the study of the eighteenth-century Revival. Nor was the Connexion helped by the fact that the principal nineteenth-century biography of the Countess (A. C. H. Seymour, *The Life and Times of the Countess of Huntingdon* (London, 1839)) is lengthy, complex and notoriously confused, while at the same time giving the appearance of having said all that could be said on the subject. For the 150 years following the publication of Seymour's *Life and Times*, there was no significant new work published on the Countess or her Connexion, although a number of academic theses on aspects of her work started to appear from the 1950s.

The position began to change significantly after the archives of Cheshunt College, the successor institution to Lady Huntingdon's own foundation, Trevecca College, became available to scholars from the later 1960s. There had hitherto been no shortage of manuscript material on the Countess and her Connexion, but most of it was scattered and fragmentary, each collection reflecting only individual aspects of her life and work. The Cheshunt archive, however, is of a different order. Although there are some discernible gaps, the collection contains a major part of the correspondence that Lady Huntingdon received during the last twenty-five years of her life, and reflects a wide range of her contacts, interests, and activities. Much of it is repetitive, and that is its strength, since it allows clear patterns to emerge, and shows what life was like day-to-day for the Countess and those associated with her. It provides a central core into which material from other manuscript sources can be fitted.

Two major studies of the Countess have been published in the last decade. The first was Edwin Welch, *Spiritual Pilgrim: A Reassessment of the Life of the Countess of Huntingdon* (Cardiff, 1995) which provides the most detailed account we are likely to get of the Countess's family and of her own life. Dr Welch was the archivist who first catalogued the Cheshunt archives and he made it his job to identify as many as possible of the surviving Countess manuscripts in depositories around the world. In addition to his life of Lady Huntingdon, he published a number of valuable monographs on specific aspects of the Connexion's work. Taken together, Welch's various publications represented a significant start to modern studies of the Countess. Then came Boyd Stanley Schlenther, *Queen of the Methodists: The Countess of Huntingdon and the Eighteenth-Century Crisis of Faith and Society* (Durham, 1997). This provides an extensive and challenging account of the Countess's life, but in addition explores more of her inner motivation and seeks, as the title foreshadowed, to link her life and work to the intellectual climate of the later eighteenth century. His work, too, represented a major step in the restoration of the Countess to her rightful place in the study of the Evangelical Revival.

My own focus is rather different from that of Welch or Schlenther, though I hope that my work will complement theirs. I have been concerned less with the Countess herself—fascinating individual though she was—than with her Connexion. I wanted to trace how a new denomination came into being on the ground: who its preachers and congregations were; how preaching was financed and organized; and how it related, nationally and locally, to other evangelical groups and to the established Church and traditional Dissent. I have sought to show both the similarities between the Connexion and other parts of the Revival, and also those aspects in which it differed, both organizationally, in the extent of its activities and influence, and in its theology and ecclesiology. The great strength of the available sources is that they show a connexion at work: the processes by which congregations formed, the reactions they occasioned, their fears and aspirations, and the factors that determined their subsequent development. All in all, the Connexion's records shed a bright spotlight not only on a neglected section of the Revival, but also on aspects of local religious life in eighteenth-century England. It is this that I have attempted to demonstrate in what follows.

The Countess's Connexion was not one of the largest groupings within the evangelical movement. It did not compare in size to Wesleyan Methodism, Welsh Calvinistic Methodism, or the Evangelical party in the Church of England. Yet its influence was considerable. Though the Connexion itself remained quite small, it had a substantial impact particularly upon Dissent, for whom it provided many congregations and ministers. It also offered a powerful example of the possibilities of itinerant evangelism and of ministerial training, both of which had an important influence on Dissent in the late eighteenth and early nineteenth centuries. Derek Lovegrove's valuable book, *Established Church, Sectarian People: Itinerancy and the Transformation of English Dissent, 1780–1830* (Cambridge, 1988), which appeared during the course of my work on the Connexion, is fascinating in illustrating the wide-ranging effects upon Nonconformity of the pioneering example of the Connexion, in the generations following the period with which I have been concerned.

A comment is needed on Seymour's *Life and Times* of the Countess. In an appendix to *Spiritual Pilgrim*, Edwin Welch listed a number of areas in which Seymour's account of events was demonstrably inaccurate; he concluded that he should discount everything in the book that was not supported by independent evidence. Seymour's work is certainly infuriating. Quite apart from his inaccuracies, it is often difficult to determine when the incidents he is describing are supposed to have happened, and he has a tendency to link anecdotes together virtually at random. At the same time, Seymour clearly had access to a great deal of original material. Some of the items he used have survived in manuscript collections (or had appeared in earlier printed versions), but others are known only from him. It has seemed to me wrong to refuse to quote any of his material, since this would be an unnecessary denial of potentially useful information. (It is also the case that copies of the *Life and Times* are comparatively common, making this an easier means for readers to access those texts that otherwise exist only in manuscript or in more obscure printed sources.) Occasionally I have gone further and referred to statements in Seymour that appear to me to provide a useful explanation of the events under consideration. When doing so, I have been careful to signal that fact, so that the reader can make appropriate allowances: an unsupported Seymour statement should be treated as at best suggestive rather than definitive.

Finally, a few words are necessary on usage and spellings. It is difficult to find an appropriate generic term to describe *everyone* involved in, or influenced by, the Revival. Outsiders tended to dub them all 'Methodists', but use of that word can cause confusion when one wishes to distinguish between Wesley's followers and other groups. Accordingly I have opted for the term 'evangelical' to describe the totality of the Revival, reserving 'Evangelical' for members of the Church of England. (The latter is simply for convenience, and is not due to Anglican *amour propre*.)

So far as Welsh spellings are concerned, I have referred to the Harris settlement in South Wales as 'Trevecka', since that is the spelling used for the title of the Harris archive at the National Library of Wales. But I have called the Countess's college 'Trevecca'—the spelling generally used by her and her correspondents. Secondly, I have spelled Harris's Christian name 'Howel' (rather than 'Howell' which also occurs), for what seems to me the excellent reason that this is the form used by Dr Nuttall—for example, in *Howel Harris, the Last Enthusiast* (Cardiff, 1965).

2
The Eighteenth-Century Religious Background

The religious life of England in 1700 was as diverse as at the start of any new century since Christianity was first introduced to the country. After the ejection of Puritan ministers from the Church of England in 1662, Protestant Dissent had been split between those who still hoped to become again part of the Established Church of the nation, and those whose principal objective was the freedom to practise their religion on their own. For the former, the Presbyterians, who at the start of the new century constituted more than half the Dissenting body in England, and some 3 per cent of the total population,[1] the early years of the eighteenth century were ones of adjustment to their position as a tolerated minority. Neither for them, nor for their fellow Dissenters (Independents, Baptists, and Quakers) was the continuation of toleration yet wholly beyond question—as moves to restrict Dissenting freedoms during the reign of Queen Anne demonstrated. For all the Dissenting churches the main object as the century developed was to maintain their strength, and to make the best of their position on the margins of a society in which their role remained circumscribed— and from some of whose institutions, like the universities, they remained excluded. The high standards attained by some of the academies established by the Dissenters indicated how determined they were to create a separate life for themselves when forced to do so.

---

[1] Michael R. Watts, *The Dissenters, from the Reformation to the French Revolution* (Oxford, 1978), 270. There are signs that Dissent was in decay by the 1730s, but that its position had improved significantly by the end of the century (D. W. Bebbington, *Evangelicalism in Modern Britain* (London, 1989), 21).

For Roman Catholics, whose return to the mainstream of English life under James II had been short indeed, the eighteenth century saw no formal toleration, and witnessed brief outbursts of fear and hostility. Yet they were able to preserve a corporate existence and a surprisingly active church structure, particularly in London where they were sustained by the ministrations of the embassy chapels. In 1741 John Wesley wrote of the Catholic converts 'constantly being made by the gentleman who preaches in Swallow Street three days in every week'; and when the young Edward Gibbon converted to Rome a decade later, he appears to have found little difficulty in finding a priest in the capital to receive him.[2] At the start of the century there were some 60,000 Catholics in England and Wales, which made them only a little smaller than the combined number of General and Particular Baptists. They had increased by a third again by 1770.[3]

The Church of England was apparently the victor of the struggles of the seventeenth century, but it bore the scars of those events in a number of ways. For one thing, the Act of Toleration of 1689, though technically concerned simply to relieve Protestant Dissenters from the rigours of the penal laws enacted after 1662, proved an important staging post on the road to religious pluralism in English society. Effectively, thereafter, church attendance was to become a voluntary activity.[4] Another factor was that the Restoration Settlement had not restored the ecclesiastical machinery that might have reformed some of the Church's remaining organizational abuses—for example, pluralism (holding more than one benefice), trading in patronage, and inequalities of church wealth. Further, the Restoration Church gave

---

[2] Wesley's Journal for 14 Aug. 1741, *Works*, xix. 209; Edward Gibbon, *Autobiography* (World's Classics edn., Oxford, 1962), 48–9.

[3] John Bossy, *The English Catholic Community, 1570–1850* (London, 1975), 188, 186.

[4] The impact of this varied across the country: in the Oxford Diocese, presentments for non-attendance continued to be important until the 1730s. (John Walsh and Stephen Taylor, 'Introduction: The Church and Anglicanism in the "Long" Eighteenth Century', in John Walsh, Colin Haydon, and Stephen Taylor (eds.), *The Church of England, c.1689–c.1833: From Toleration to Tractarianism* (Cambridge, 1993), 5. The Walsh/Taylor essay provides the best overview of recent work on the eighteenth-century Church.)

up the right of self-taxation, abandoning in the process any incentive there might have been for the secular power to keep Convocation in being. Convocation was in abeyance for almost all the eighteenth century, leaving the Church with no forum for determining its future development or for tackling issues of reform. Finally, there were the losses that the Church had suffered after 1660, and again after 1689. Some 2,000 clergy left or were ejected after the Restoration, weakening thereby the Calvinist reformed tradition within the Church's ranks. Then, after the accession of William and Mary, an archbishop, eight bishops, and some three to four hundred other nonjuring clergy, left the Church of England over their refusal to abjure their oaths of allegiance to James II. These included some of the Church's most spiritual and scholarly clergy, and made more difficult the survival of Laudian traditions.

It is easy to overemphasize a view of the eighteenth-century Church as lethargic and corrupt, her administrative apparatus incapable of exercising any effective control over the life of the parishes. The truth is more complex, with evidence of a good deal more life in her institutions than that caricature would suggest; recent detailed work on diocesan and other records, indeed, while confirming some aspects of the traditional picture, has shown how diverse was the actual position. Amongst the yardsticks by which the state of the eighteenth-century Church has often been judged are the extent to which incumbents resided in their parishes, the amount of pluralism, and the type and frequency of services. Non-residence certainly appears to have got worse over the centuries. Immediately before the Reformation, 75 per cent of parishes were held by resident incumbents; by 1820 that figure had fallen to 40 per cent, with a good deal of the deterioration occurring in the eighteenth century.[5] Non-residence did not necessarily mean that the cycle of worship in parishes was given up, however; care was generally taken

---

[5] Ibid. 8; Peter Virgin, *The Church in an Age of Negligence* (Cambridge, 1989), 260; Arthur Warne, *Church and Society in Eighteenth Century Devon* (Newton Abbot, 1969), 38–9.

to maintain services, whether through the appointment of curates or by incumbents living near to their parishes, even though not actually in them.[6]

Pluralism, probably the single most important reason for non-residence, also increased.[7] It may have been the case, as apologists claimed, that pluralism was the inevitable consequence of poor livings, itself the result of the unequal distribution of the Church's wealth—although pluralism actually seems to have been greater in those areas where livings were richer.[8] Undoubtedly there were a few hugely affluent benefices, coupled with wide regional variations in average incomes and some very poor parishes.[9] It was to the credit of the Georgian Church that these disparities did not get worse during the course of the century; if anything, it was the poorer clergy who did best out of the general increase in clerical incomes that occurred during the century. The bishops, like some of their seventeenth-century predecessors, set an uncertain personal example in respect of pluralism. Their failure to have a significant impact upon pluralism, despite making frequent exhortations, witnessed to the Church's lack of an effective system for reform or renewal. Nor was the poverty of livings much of a defence for non-residents, when the curates appointed in their stead were expected to exist on an average annual stipend of no more than £35, even at the end of the century.[10]

---

[6] In 33 out of 100 cases of non-residence in Oxford Diocese in 1778, the incumbent lived nearby, and performed duty himself (Walsh and Taylor, 'The Church in the "Long" Eighteenth Century', 8; Stephen Taylor, 'Church and State in the mid-Eighteenth Century: The Newcastle Years 1742–1762', Ph.D. thesis (Cambridge, 1987), 18).

[7] Peter Virgin found that only 16% of a sample of 445 clergy in the first decade of the century held more than one living, but that this had increased to around 36% by the 1770s (Virgin, *Age of Negligence*, 192, 259).

[8] Walsh and Taylor, 'The Church in the "Long" Eighteenth Century', 9.

[9] In 1835, 76 of the 7,500 beneficed clergy were found to earn more than £2,000, and a further 310 more than £1,000. The same survey showed that the typical Norfolk income was £395, while that for Cumbria was £108. £150 was regarded as a reasonable minimum income, but even in affluent Norfolk more than 10% of incumbents received £100 or less (Virgin, *Act of Negligence*, 253–5, 279).

[10] Lancelot Andrewes had been a pluralist on a grand scale. In the eighteenth century, James Cornwallis held the deanery of Durham in plurality with his see of Lichfield for nearly 30 years (Walsh and Taylor, 'The Church in the "Long" Eighteenth

So far as patterns of public worship were concerned, the picture also varied. The traditional view is that a single Sunday (morning) service became increasingly the norm, though there is evidence of a two-service pattern occurring in many areas, particularly in the North and Wales, and in the towns.[11] Daily services were rare, generally speaking, but did occur in a number of major centres as well as London,[12] and weekday services were by no means uncommon.[13] There appears no strong correlation between general service patterns and the frequency of Communion services. The general assumption has been that quarterly Communions were the best that could be hoped for outside the larger towns, but here too more recent work has underlined the diversity of the picture, with evidence of more frequent (often monthly) celebrations in many small towns and populous villages.[14] In the light of this, it would clearly be wrong to conclude of the Georgian Church in general that it had little regard for the sacraments. In fact, no easy generalizations can be made about the spirituality of Anglican laity in eighteenth-century England, or the devotion of the clergy.[15] It is undoubtedly true that there were abuses,

---

Century', 2, 4, 9; Virgin, *Age of Negligence*, 224–5). Robert Drummond, later to be Archbishop of York, held the living of Bothall in Northumberland throughout his time as bishop of St Asaph. The living was worth £280 a year: his curate received £34. 10s. (Judith Jago, *Aspects of the Georgian Church* (London, 1997), 42).

[11] F. C. Mather, 'Georgian Churchmanship Reconsidered: Some Variations in Anglican Public Worship, 1714–1830', *Journal of Ecclesiastical History*, 36/2 (April 1985), 266. As an example of the breadth of variation, 96% of parishes held two Sunday services in St Asaph diocese in 1738, while the comparable figure for Lincoln in 1744 was only 28% (Taylor, 'Church and State', 30). In York diocese in 1764, the figure was just over 40% (Jago, *Aspects*, 90).

[12] For example, Manchester, Newcastle, Leeds, Liverpool, and Southampton (Mather, 'Georgian Churchmanship', 276).

[13] 20% of the 514 parishes in the Lincoln diocese recorded a weekday service every week in 1744 (ibid. 277).

[14] Ibid. 270–1. Roughly 10% of York Diocese had monthly Communions in 1764 (Jago, *Aspects*, 102).

[15] In some areas a very small proportion of the laity took Communion. This could imply a limited degree of personal religious commitment, or disregard for mystery and transcendence in worship—or it could be indicative of reverence for the sacraments and a fear of unworthy reception (Walsh and Taylor, 'The Church in the "Long" Eighteenth Century', 23).

and that some ministers acted in ways that implied no very deep commitment to the spiritual nurture of their congregations, let alone to spreading the faith. It is clear that the expressed desire for reform was seldom translated—whether because of the lack of visionary leadership or the absence of sufficient external stimuli—into effective change. It was also the case, as the century went on, that the Church of England became increasingly enmeshed in the social hierarchies of local communities, thereby weakening its ability to speak distinctively and prophetically to the whole of society.[16] Nevertheless, it would be wrong to assume a general picture of neglect, or that English devotional life was uniformly impoverished. The high sales of popular religious literature in the eighteenth century (to quote one small but not insignificant indicator)[17] strongly suggests that this was not so.

The early years of the eighteenth century were ones of continuing intellectual excitement, which were to have a significant influence upon religious thought. The scientific revolution of the seventeenth century appeared to have confirmed the hypothesis upon which it had been founded, that a world made by a wise creator must be governed by rational and discernible laws. The world seemed obviously in the hands of a beneficent creator, as it ticked effortlessly on like the mechanism of some celestial timepiece. The problem theologically about this image was that the more skilful a watchmaker, the less he subsequently needed to attend to his creation. Thus scientific thought led some to deism, the belief that though God may have initiated the process, there is no subsequent role for him within it. Revelation had no part in such a system, and there was no place for a priesthood as the channel of truth. Christianity, in the titles of two of the most influential deist tracts, was 'not mysterious' and 'as old as creation'.[18] Man, by his natural reason, could discover all he needed to know of God.

---

[16] Walsh and Taylor, 'The Church in the "Long" Eighteenth Century', 28–9.   [17] Taylor, 'Church and State', 37.
[18] J. Toland, *Christianity Not Mysterious* (1696); M. Tindal, *Christianity as Old as the Creation* (1730).

The Eighteenth-Century Religious Background 11

The high tide of deist thought was during the first three decades of the eighteenth century. Against it the apologists of orthodoxy, of whom Bishop Butler of Durham was among the foremost, mounted what proved to be a largely effective counter-attack. Arguments for evidence of a divine hand at work in the design of the universe maintained the defence against atheism, while for most people it proved difficult to contemplate a God who, having bothered to create the world, then took no further interest in it. But nerves had been shaken. On the one hand, the veracity of Scripture was to come under attack as at no previous time. On the other, there developed a tendency to avoid emphasis upon those aspects of Christianity—the Sonship of Christ in particular, and the Trinity—whose biblical basis was thought to be problematical. Attempts to modify the Trinitarian elements in Anglican doctrine occurred throughout the period. Early in the century, for example, the Reverend Samuel Clarke, a royal chaplain and rector of St James's, Piccadilly, argued from Scripture for the supremacy of the Father, as against the other persons of the Trinity, and produced a revised liturgy shorn of all Trinitarian features. Half a century later the Feathers Tavern Petition pressed for clerical relief from subscription to the Thirty-Nine Articles—though the limited support the petition received, and its decisive rejection by the House of Commons, put a check on the advance of doctrinal liberalism.[19]

Although the arguments just described took place largely within the Established Church, Dissent did not escape their impact. Significant numbers of Dissenters adopted forms of Arian or Socinian theology, the denial that Christ had equal (or even any) status within the Godhead. Sometimes whole congregations modified their theology in this way, while at other times doctrinal differences led to secession and regrouping—at which point orthodox Dissent was frequently to draw upon the inspiration and resources of the Evangelical Revival, as will be seen. Denominational designations are

---

[19] Walsh and Taylor, 'The Church in the "Long" Eighteenth Century', 39–40.

of limited relevance in this period, though in general it is true to say that by the end of the century those who by then termed themselves 'Presbyterian' had adopted an Arian position.

Paradoxically, the absence of Convocation meant that the Church of England had no formal setting in which doctrinal issues could be corporately addressed and changes agreed. Only a few of the clergy found that difficulties with the historic formulas of the Church were such as to drive them out altogether. Yet the impact of religious liberalism, combined with reaction against the perceived extremism of the previous century, did have a pervasive influence on parts of the Church of England. A theme of much preaching was God as beneficent creator, to whom reason and nature bore abundant testimony. The Church might have faced persecutions in earlier centuries, some argued, but in a rational and well-ordered world that stage had passed. The commandments of God, in a much-quoted text, were 'not grievous', since God clearly willed the well-being and happiness of his people.

The term used to describe the tenor of much eighteenth-century Churchmanship is 'latitudinarian'—although the word itself was seldom used by contemporaries. It embraced widely different shades of opinion. For some it implied a low-key approach to piety, rational and ethical, rather than emotional and mystical. For others, it spoke of the need for further Church reform to remove the residual traces of medieval sacerdotalism and superstition. For others, it promised moderation, combined with charity to other shades of Protestantism; others located the Church's moderation midway between the extremes of Rome and Geneva. For others, again, it meant belief in the simplicity and sufficiency of the Bible, private judgement, and a faith that was consistent with reason and natural religion.[20]

Despite its varied elements, this faith was essentially comfortable and reassuring. But alongside it lay other traditions which were less so. There was the spiritual inheritance of seventeenth-century Puritanism, preserved outside the

---

[20] Walsh and Taylor, 'The Church in the "Long" Eighteenth Century', 36–8.

Established Church and, though to a lesser extent after 1660, within it. And there was the tradition of dedication to God and the pursuit of holiness that had been a hallmark of the first flowering of High Anglicanism in the early decades of the seventeenth century. This was a feature of the Church of England as re-established at the Restoration, if perhaps with more emphasis on moral duty and less on joy in the worship of God than had been the case earlier. The titles of some of the most influential seventeenth-century works in the tradition—*The Rule and Exercise of Holy Living* by Jeremy Taylor, a future Bishop of Down and Connor, and the anonymous *The Whole Duty of Man*, both written during the Commonwealth period, give a flavour of its rigour. It was a theme picked up in its sternest form in a celebrated eighteenth-century contribution to the genre, the nonjuror William Law's *A Serious Call to a Devout and Holy Life* of 1728. The Christian calling, for such writers, was one of total commitment: as Law put it, 'no condition of life is for enjoyment, but for trial'.[21] It was not, however, a religion concerned only with individual piety and discipline. The value of shared spiritual experience, for example, was recognized in the last years of the seventeenth century, first in London and then more widely, in the development of religious societies—groups of like-minded individuals who bound themselves, generally under clerical leadership, to a routine of daily prayer and regular meeting. These flourished into the early decades of the eighteenth century, but waned later—though their legacy was to be built upon, in varied ways, by sections of the Evangelical Revival. From a similar spiritual base there developed other forms of voluntary organization, concerned with mission, both at home and abroad; for example, the Society for Promoting Christian Knowledge (SPCK) and the Society for Propagating the Gospel (SPG) were founded in 1699 and 1701 respectively, and were to be a considerable force in the century that followed. At its best this same

---

[21] Quoted in E. G. Rupp, *Religion in England, 1688–1791* (Oxford, 1986), 219. John Wesley took the notion of a disciplined rule of life from Taylor. Law convinced him of 'the absolute impossibility of being *half a Christian*' (Bebbington, *Evangelicalism*, 37–8).

tradition issued in a series of humanitarian initiatives that continued through the eighteenth century, contributing to the founding of hospitals and charity schools, to the prison reform movement, and eventually to anti-slavery. At its less attractive, in the late seventeenth and early eighteenth centuries, it triggered a phase of social Puritanism, with societies for the reformation of manners set up to press for the enforcement of the morality laws, using informers to stimulate prosecutions.

There were thus two discernible themes in the Church of England in the eighteenth century: on the one hand, a spirit of moderation and mistrust of mystery; on the other, traditions of religious discipline and service. It would, however, be misleading to imply a sharp polarization between these positions. The labels in question are helpful only as broad descriptions of attitudes: despite the deep antagonisms that were occasionally unleashed when variations in religious outlook became superimposed on political differences, one cannot speak of *parties* in the early eighteenth-century Church in the same way as in the nineteenth century. It was, nevertheless, against the backdrop of these two strands in contemporary religious life that the Evangelical Revival should be seen. With latitudinarianism it took most immediate issue. In the face of the Church's apparent organizational and spiritual failures the Revival called men to take religion seriously again, to wake up to the fact of sin, and to be on guard against overconfidence that all would be well with an easygoing and tolerant God. Thus far the Revival endorsed the High Church programme, and it was indeed the disciplines and spirituality of the High Church tradition that nurtured some of the leaders of the coming Revival. It was, however, the rather joyless rigour of that tradition, and the implication that salvation had to be earned through self-discipline and individual effort, that the leaders of the Revival rejected also. They saw it as only offering impossible goals and inevitable failure, and an essentially miserable view of man's relationship to God.[22] In its place they set the

---

[22] As early as 1725, John Wesley had baulked at the gloom of Jeremy Taylor (Rack, *Wesley*, 401).

redemptive work of Christ and the offer of a free and unmerited salvation. For evangelicals Christianity was not the comfortable proposition the latitudinarians believed: sinful men were heading inexorably to the torments of hell, and only the saving work of Christ could drag them back. Converted sinners were, in one of Revival's abiding images, 'brands plucked from the burning', rescued dramatically from terrible punishments. Thus evangelicals were urgent in their call to others to flee from wrath and be reborn. They did not admit that there was anything novel about such propositions; they were a revival and not an innovation. Their critics feared the impact that such teachings (and evangelicals' asserted right to proclaim them) would have upon the health and sanity of individuals and society. To this, the response of the Revival was that their doctrines were those of the Bible and the Reformation, and were enshrined in the Articles, Prayer Book, and Homilies of the Church of England.

It would be wrong, however, to see the Revival as something uniquely British. Movements with similar characteristics, both in terms of theology and missionary zeal, occurred in continental Europe and America. These phenomena, in other words, cannot be explained solely as a reaction to a single set of external stimuli. Yet they did not develop in complete isolation from one another. Many of those involved took a close interest in developments elsewhere: they exchanged information about what was happening, both for mutual encouragement and advice, and to support their shared view of God's working in human history. The Revival's Puritan and High Church inheritance gave it, moreover, a natural affinity with that emphasis upon acceptance of forgiveness, and devotion to the crucified Christ, which were hallmarks of a group of European Protestants with English links, the Moravian Brethren.[23]

---

[23] W. R. Ward, *The Protestant Evangelical Awakening* (Cambridge, 1992), 1–4; Bebbington, *Evangelicalism*, 20, 37–40. Huguenot refugees in England provided another potential link between Continental Protestantism and the Revival: for example, Wesley occasionally served Huguenot congregations in England, and made use of Huguenot premises (Ward, *Evangelical Awakening*, 298).

Within England and Wales,[24] the term 'Evangelical Revival', though a useful generic description, embraced a series of distinct elements. Some of these strands were related, in the sense that they sprang from the influence of other individuals already touched by the Revival; others appear to have come into spontaneous existence. An early sign of the new movement occurred in South Wales in the first decade of the eighteenth century, when Griffith Jones, rector of Llanddowror, who had been influenced by the missionary initiatives at Halle, the centre of German Pietism, commenced itinerant preaching and established a system of circulating charity schools. In the 1730s Jones was instrumental in the conversion of two clergymen, Daniel Rowlands and Howel Davies. With the layman Howel Harris,[25] who had been independently converted around the same time, Rowlands and Davies were to be pillars of the Revival in Wales over the coming decades. By the early 1740s the Welsh Revival had formed its converts into local societies, within a structure of regular district meetings, and subject to an overall Association. By 1750 there were over 400 such societies.[26] Theologically they were Calvinists, and this set them apart from Wesleyan Methodism, which made few inroads into Wales until the following century. The Welsh Calvinistic Methodists were to remain a distinct force within the Evangelical Revival, although they had occasional links with their counterparts in England, and their leaders participated frequently in work across the border.

---

[24] Scotland had her own experience of revival, including a seventeenth-century instance of what would later have been interpreted as signs of a religious awakening (ibid. 17). The most notable Scottish revival occurred in and around Cambuslang, near Glasgow, from 1742. The Cambuslang revival followed twelve months of preaching on regeneration, and there is evidence that the ministers most involved knew of the work of the American revivalist Jonathan Edwards (J. Gillies, *Historical Collections relating to remarkable periods in the success of the Gospel* (Glasgow, 1754), 339). A significant proportion of the Established Church in Scotland was sympathetic to the doctrines of the Revival (Bebbington, *Evangelicalism*, 20, 33).

[25] There was a specifically Welsh dimension to Jones's work, since it aimed, in part, at resisting what he saw as the corrupting influence of English culture (Ward, *Evangelical Awakening*, 317; on Harris, see below).

[26] Rack, *Wesley*, 282–3; Ward, *Evangelical Awakening*, 323.

A second element within the Revival stemmed from the group of serious young men at Oxford who formed round John and Charles Wesley (1703–91, and 1707–88) in the late 1720s. The Oxford Holy Club, as the group came to be called, was committed to prayer and spiritual improvement, to charitable work and to regular sacramental worship. The group stood in the traditions of the earlier religious societies and thus graphically illustrated the roots of many of the Revival's future leaders in High Church piety and practice.[27] From its members three distinct groups were to develop. The first in order of time derived from one of the younger and later members of the Club, George Whitefield (1714–70) son of a Gloucester innkeeper, who went up to Oxford in 1732. After first immersing himself in the austerities of High Church discipline, Whitefield passed in 1735 through a conversion experience that convinced him of his place in God's favour and set him on the course of his life's work. After ordination in the following year he began a preaching career—in churches first, and then in the open air and in his own chapels—whose power and appeal to all levels in society marked him out as one of the outstanding popular orators of his own or any age. In contemporary perception he was often seen as the founder of the Methodist Revival, and his seven visits to America (he died during the last) ensured him an equal place in the hagiography of British and American revivalism. Whitefield's adherents, Calvinists like the Welsh, were formed like the latter into a loose association of societies and congregations: by 1747 there were thirty-one such societies.[28] But his frequent absences abroad limited the extent to which he could wield a cohesive influence over them.

It was not until 1738 that the Wesleys, independently but within a short period of each other, passed through their own conversion experience. They too were brought to a sense of personal acceptance by God that was not conditional on

---

[27] There were also Puritan influences on the Wesleys, particularly through their mother. There were more Puritan writers in John Wesley's *Christian Library* than any other genre, although mostly they were former Anglicans (Rack, *Wesley*, 307).

[28] Bebbington, *Evangelicalism*, 30.

merit or achievement—even though they never lost the concern with holiness that the Holy Club had symbolized. It was Whitefield who first induced John to preach out of doors, and from this developed the career of peripatetic preaching that continued to the end of John's long life. Wesley may not have rivalled the dramatic power of Whitefield's oratory, though the evidence of his impact on congregations is substantial. But he had, what Whitefield lacked, the capacity to weld the growing multitude of his followers into a disciplined, hierarchical, and nationwide organization, devoted to the growth of its members in spirituality and holiness. Over that organization he exercised the most minute control, travelling incessantly to oversee and encourage his societies, and attending, through his writings, to their health and literary needs as well as to their souls. Even Wesley's organizational skills, however, were unable to preserve the impression—which looked increasingly like a fiction by the time of his death—that the mass movement he had created from a mix of Anglicans, Dissenters, and the unchurched was merely a distinct but loyal grouping within the folds of the Established Church.

The third of the Holy Club members to establish a grouping of his own—albeit on a much lesser scale than Whitefield or Wesley—was Benjamin Ingham, whose own conversion experience occurred in 1737. Ingham, who later became linked by marriage with Lady Huntingdon, began preaching in Yorkshire in the late 1730s, and this ministry led to the establishment of his own connexion of separate congregations.[29] Like Whitefield's followers, the Inghamites were Calvinist in theology, and there were to be other such groupings of Calvinistic evangelicals in England. Thirty years or so after the start of Ingham's ministry, for example, Rowland Hill, a young Cambridge-educated clergyman, began an itinerant ministry that similarly led to the establishment of a group of his own congregations.[30] It is in this general setting, as an association of Calvinistic evangelicals, eventually distinct from the Church of England, although closer to it in some

---

[29] See below, Ch. 3.   [30] Ibid.

respects than any other such grouping, that the Countess of Huntingdon's Connexion has to be seen.

All of the initiatives so far described resulted in groupings that operated to a greater or lesser extent outside either the Established Church or established Dissent. But evangelical theology presupposed no particular type of Church government, and for a significant group of Anglicans there seemed nothing inconsistent in preaching such doctrines while remaining within the parochial structures of the Church of England. Some of these men owed their conversion, directly or indirectly, to the work of Wesley or Whitefield. More often they made an independent way to conversion, finding like Wesley that a faith which focused too exclusively on austerity and discipline could not bring them the release they sought. The point to note is that the Evangelical party in the Church of England was no mere reflection of Wesleyan Methodism— nor even of Whitefield's Calvinistic Methodism, with which it had more in common theologically—but was to a considerable extent an independent and coincidental development, even though some of its clergy were converted by Methodist preaching or influence. This explains the haphazard distribution of Evangelical clergy in the early years. Some of these men showed scant regard for the niceties of parochial boundaries, preaching outside their parishes when need arose, and ready to give occasional assistance elsewhere in the Revival, even if this meant ministering in unconsecrated buildings. Others, particularly as the century wore on (and especially when the French Revolution triggered fears for the very fabric of British society) were more cautious about anything that might threaten the structures and stability of the Church.[31]

By remaining within the folds of the Church of England, these men ensured that the doctrines of the Revival maintained their place within the gamut of Anglican catholicity. The same effect was to be achieved within the body of Dissent. Undoubtedly some Dissenters feared the Revival, and with good reason, as they lost members to Wesleyan

---

[31] Also, as their numbers grew, there was less need to work outside their own parishes (Bebbington, *Evangelicalism*, 31; Rack, *Wesley*, 287).

Methodism and to the various groupings of Calvinistic evangelicals.[32] The motives of such converts may have been doctrinal, in reaction against heterodox opinions within their own congregations, or they may simply have been drawn by the liveliness of Methodist preaching and the assurance of salvation which it seemed to hold out. But the impact of the Revival was not all one way. There were, for example, some evangelical Dissenting ministers active before the Revival itself got under way.[33] And orthodox Dissent underwent a resurgence in the later years of the century, inspired by both the teachings and the methods of the Revival—in particular by itinerant preaching and by the model of ministerial training that came from the Countess of Huntingdon herself. Nor was the influence only one of example, for there were many instances of Dissenting congregations that drew directly upon the Revival's ministerial resources, or owed their origins to its preachers.

The Evangelical Revival was therefore a many-faceted development, embracing in England Anglican (mainly Calvinistic) Evangelicals, Wesley's Arminian Methodists, revivified Dissenters, and groups of Calvinistic evangelicals outside the Church of England. It is against this diverse background of religious experimentation and renewal, as well as the broader canvas of eighteenth-century religion, that the Countess of Huntingdon's Connexion has to be seen.

---

[32] Isaac Watts was initially suspicious of the Revival as an Anglican-led movement; his views were changed by what he learned of the Revival in New England (Ward, *Evangelical Awakening*, 245, 247).

[33] Ibid. 34. Doddridge, who called in 1730 for Dissenting ministers to be 'evangelical and experimental', was representative of a significant minority among his peers (ibid. 347).

3

Selina, Countess of Huntingdon: Early Life and the Start of the Connexion

BIRTH TO 1750

The future Countess of Huntingdon was born Selina Shirley, second daughter of the 2nd Earl Ferrers, on 24 August 1707. The Shirleys were a Leicestershire family, ennobled since 1677. Amongst Selina's ancestors was Sir Robert Shirley, whose attachment to the Royalist cause and the Church of England found expression during the Commonwealth period in the building of an Anglican church on his estates at Staunton Harold. It was a bold act for which Sir Robert paid the penalty of imprisonment and early death: a tablet over the entrance to his church commemorates the fact that he had 'done the best things in the worst season and hoped them in the most calamitous'.

Selina's home life was difficult, and family relations were troubled. Her father was at odds with his own father; Selina and her sisters were to be involved in protracted law suits with the children of her grandfather's second marriage; and they were to fall out with each other. Selina's own parents were separated, and for much of her life she was estranged from her mother. And financial circumstances were constrained.[1] She was married in 1728 to a near neighbour at Donnington Park, Theophilus Hastings, 9th Earl of Huntingdon, then in his early thirties. The Hastings family had shown its zeal for the Puritan cause in the time of Elizabeth, but like the Shirleys, supported the Crown in the seventeenth century.[2] Theophilus himself included in his immediate

---

[1] Welch, 1, 9, 12–13, 29, 30, 33; Schlenther, 5.
[2] A. G. Dickens, *The English Reformation* (London 1970), 430; Welch, 15.

family circle a number (in particular, his sisters Margaret and Frances, his half-sister Lady Betty Hastings, and his kinsman Henry Hastings) who were to show themselves over the coming years not only zealous in their religious observance after the fashion of the age, but possessed of a spirituality that focused upon man's sin and dependence on God's grace. These were aspects of the Gospel to which the Evangelical Revival was shortly to give prominence.[3]

Selina's marriage, which lasted only eighteen years until the Earl's early death in 1746, was clearly a love match. She was his 'Lady Leney' and his 'old goody';[4] she loved him 'to an excess of passion';[5] and when they were parted, she longed to be back 'in the arms of my dear love'.[6] She was to survive him by some forty-five years but it was said that to the end she still wept at the mention of his name.[7] To her children, her 'little Jewells', she was similarly committed.[8] She bore four sons and three daughters, three of whom (two sons and a daughter) failed to outlive their father. She herself was survived only by one daughter, the then Countess of Moira, through whose descendants the Huntingdon title was eventually to descend, since none of her sons had legitimate issue.

A couple in the Huntingdon's position could not be uninvolved in society, and the accounts of society gossip, both in the letters she received from friends and in her own, are evidence of a degree of interest on Lady Huntingdon's part.[9]

---

[3] Lady Margaret Hastings to 'My Dr Br', 12 Apr. n.y. and n.d., DE23/1/1443,1448, LRO; Lady Frances Hastings to Lord H, 7 Jan. 1739/40, HA 4993; Lady Betty to Lord H and LH, 6 Dec. 1739, 14D32/231, LRO; Henry Hastings to LH, 1 Oct. and 24 Dec.1739, HA 5656, 5669. Amongst the charitable objects to which Lady Betty (1682–1739) devoted herself were charity schools in the vicinity of her Yorkshire estates, the support of undergraduates at Oxford, and the maintenance of some of Whitefield's early converts (T. Gibbons, G. Jerment, and S. Burder, *Memoirs of Eminently Pious Women* (London, 1815), i. 263–79; Lady Betty to LH, 24 Apr. n.y., 26 July n.y., 10 Apr.1738 14D32/212, 218,226, LRO; Tyerman, *Whitefield*, i. ch. 4).

[4] Lord H to Lady Selina Shirley, 22 May 1727, E1/1(1),CF. LH to Lord H, 13 Mar. 1731, 14D32/68, LRO.

[5] LH to Lord H, 19 Feb. 1731/2, HMC, iii. 10.

[6] LH to Lord H, 6 Mar. 1731/2, 14D32/67, LRO.   [7] Seymour, i. 9.

[8] LH to Lord H, 17 May 1743, 14D32/72, LRO.

[9] e.g. Countess of Strafford to LH, 26 Aug. 1733, H.A. 13210; LH to Lord H, 14 and 19 Feb. 1731/2, HMC, iii. 10.

But she was not an uncritical observer. Lotteries she evidently enjoyed, but operas attracted less, sexual impropriety shocked, and the grand ball in Bath in 1732 was she said 'in my way of thinking…very stupid'.[10] Politics interested her, judging from the accounts of political events which she transmitted to her husband while he was out of London, and she was one of the group of peeresses who gained access by physical force to the gallery of the House of Lords in a celebrated incident in 1738.[11] The eulogy of her by her friend the Countess of Strafford in 1731 suggests a woman who was an agreeable and lively companion, but also an individual of firmly independent spirit, who would not easily be conformed to the spirit and mores of the age.[12] In fact, although she participated in the social life of Bath, where she spent considerable periods in the 1730s, the impression given by her letters is that she was there for her health rather than for any pleasure in the fashionable activities that were on offer.[13] To the godly and philanthropic Lady Betty Hastings, who was a surrogate mother to Lady Huntingdon, it was a source of satisfaction that the Huntingdons preferred home life in the country to the delights of fashionable society.[14]

From the early years of her marriage Lady Huntingdon was involved in religious and philanthropic schemes of various kinds. A purchase of over £10 worth of Bibles and Prayer Books in 1729, book purchases from the SPCK in 1730, and enquiries into the price of Communion plate in 1732, all suggest support for religious initiatives of some kind.[15] She contributed to the SPCK which sought her interest in work in

---

[10] LH to Lord H, 12 Apr. 1732, HMC, iii. 14. Nor was she much enamoured of opera (Lady Wentworth to LH, 27 May 1731, 14D32/612, LRO).

[11] LH to Lord H, 8 Dec. 1744 and Aug. 1746, HMC, iii. 48, 61; Welch, 27.

[12] She did, however, feel it necessary to warn her friend not to 'coquete it with Lord Harborough, for I shall keep him for myself' (Countess of Strafford to LH, 25 Oct. 1731, HA 13203).

[13] LH was a patient of Dr Cheyne, who specialized in the treatment of melancholia in fashionable society; he promised to make her as 'healthy and cheerful' as any lady in England (Dr Cheyne to Lord H, 29 Aug. 1734, 14D32/366, LRO; Welch, 23–4).

[14] Lady Betty to LH, 18 Dec. n.y. and n.d. (marked 1732), H.A. 4727; 4745; Welch, 33.

[15] Receipts dated 5 Mar. 1728/9 and 15 Dec. 1730; D. Williams to LH, 18 Jan. 1731/2, 14D32/473, 476, 534, LRO.

Europe and India,[16] and she was an early supporter of Thomas Coram's scheme to start a Foundling Hospital in London.[17] But her interest extended to the practice of religion, as well as to great schemes for its propagation; in 1735, for example, there is an interesting (and perhaps prophetic) reference to a woman preacher whom Lady Huntingdon was intending to hear.[18]

Lady Huntingdon's personality, passionate but serious-minded, was fertile ground for the evangelical conversion through which she was to pass in July 1739. The instrument of that conversion appears to have been her sister-in-law, Margaret Hastings, whose own introduction to evangelical faith had come through the influence of the Revd Benjamin Ingham (1712–72) who had been with the Wesleys in the Oxford Holy Club and in Georgia, and who had undergone an evangelical conversion early in 1737.[19] Margaret, who was later to marry Ingham, first came in contact with him when he was preaching in Yorkshire, and while she was staying with Lady Betty Hastings at the latter's Yorkshire seat at Ledstone. Lady Huntingdon was evidently much affected by her sister-in-law's happy spiritual state, compared to her own uncertainty about her standing with God;[20] it appears to have been from discussions with her, and after a period of serious

---

[16] Henry Newman to LH, 17 Dec. 1730, HA 9593.

[17] Coram to LH, 15 Sept. 1739, HA 1624. On Coram's project, see E. G. Rupp, *Religion in England, 1688–1791* (Oxford, 1986), 314–16.

[18] Elizabeth Cart to LH, 8 Jan. 1735, HA 1238. The meeting house where she was to speak was also kept by a woman. Most probably she was a Quaker (M. R. Watts, *The Dissenters, from the Reformation to the French Revolution* (Oxford, 1978), 316; on Mrs Cart, see Welch, 52–3).

[19] J. D. Walsh 'The Cambridge Methodists' in P. Brooks (ed.), *Essays in Christian Spirituality, Essays in honour of Gordon Rupp* (London, 1975). In June 1739 Ingham was banned from preaching in churches in the York diocese, a fact that makes the more striking the friendship and respect that the various members of the Hastings family were prepared to extend to him. Ingham's activities in Yorkshire led to the establishment of a connexion of congregations (at one stage around 80 in number) that for a period from 1747 adopted Moravian disciplines. Ingham seceded from the Church of England, which ruled out the chance of reconciliation with the Methodists when he broke with the Moravians in 1753. He began ordaining his preachers in 1756. At the end of the 1750s his societies were disrupted by doctrinal disputes that severely reduced their number (L. Tyerman, *The Oxford Methodists* (London, 1873), *passim*; Colin Podmore, *The Moravian Church in England, 1728–1760* (Oxford, 1998), 107, 115–17). [20] Seymour i. 14.

illness, that Lady Huntingdon came eventually to the point of conversion. Margaret, it seems, was not with her when the moment of dawning came, for at the end of July she wrote to express her and Ingham's pleasure at the news.[21] It was subsequently arranged that Ingham should visit Donnington[22] but the man from whom she received the most immediate advice was the Revd Thomas Barnard of Leeds, who had recently taken on the tutorship of her son, George, and whom Lady Huntingdon had previously met at Ledstone.[23] Barnard, Master of the Leeds Grammar School,[24] had been a religious confidant of Lady Betty Hastings. He had already formed the view that the Countess was close to the Kingdom of God and had told her so. He was thus a natural person for her to include among those she told of the experience through which she had passed. She was fortunate in this decision, for Barnard's letters to her in the critical early days of her new-found faith display a maturity of spiritual perception, gentleness in giving advice and encouragement, and a sound practical appreciation of the problems a person in her situation would have to face.[25]

It is difficult to determine how far Lady Huntingdon's conversion, like Wesley's, represented a personal appropriation of God's salvation and assurance that she was forgiven— or whether, at this stage, it was more an act of sorrow over past sins and commitment for the future. What particularly struck Barnard in her description of her conversion was the

[21] Lady Margaret to LH, 28 July [1739], 14D28/252, LRO.
[22] Lady Margaret to LH, 8 Aug. [1739], 14D28/255, LRO.
[23] Lady Betty Hastings to LH (n.d. but marked '1738'), HA 4760; Welch, 28.
[24] Barnard (1685–1750) was educated at St John's College, Cambridge; author of *An Historical Character... of the Right Honourable Lady Elizabeth Hastings* (Leeds, 1742) and of the Latin epitaph to her in Ledsham Church. By the time of his account of Lady Betty, he had turned against the 'Methodists'. Among Barnard's pupils in Leeds was Theophilus Lindsey, godson of Lord Huntingdon, and subsequently founder of the Unitarian Chapel in Essex Street, London (R. V. Taylor, *Biographia Leodiensis* (London, 1865), 584–7).
[25] Barnard's links with LH do not appear to have continued long after the death of Lady Betty Hastings at Christmas 1739. This may have been due to his opposition to the irregularity that was becoming associated with the Revival, and possibly also because he was seen by the Huntingdons as having been close to (and influential upon) Lady Betty, whose failure to leave them any significant share in her estate came as a bitter blow (Schlenther, 17–18).

statement that she 'would undergoe every Thing to come to the true knowledge of my only Saviour', which may suggest that she was still seeking. Barnard's response, presumably intended as encouragement, referred to her having given herself to the life of religion.[26] In Margaret Hastings, Lady Huntingdon's most immediate link with the Revival, there appears to have been no sharp break between the old High Church spirituality of the sort in which the Wesleys had been brought up—with its emphasis on the need for holiness, dedication, and effort—and what the Revival proclaimed as the offer of immediate acceptability to God by the operation of grace. Margaret, after her own conversion and in appeals to her brother, recommended him the interesting mixture of Whitefield's sermons and what seems likely to have been Jeremy Taylor's *Holy Living*.[27] In a similar vein, immediately after Lady Huntingdon's conversion, Margaret expressed pleasure at the prospect of a visit to Donnington by William Law, since she supposed from his writings that her sister-in-law would be delighted by his company.[28] But whether or not at this early stage Lady Huntingdon experienced a warming of the heart like Wesley's, it cannot be doubted that the sense of being rescued by God's grace, of having personally been plucked as a brand from the burning, sinner though she was, was to be a developing and living element in her faith over the half-century that was to come.

It is not clear how far Lord Huntingdon followed his wife in her new profession, but it seems unlikely that he was actively hostile. It is difficult, indeed, to believe that Lady Huntingdon could have engaged to the extent she did

---

[26] Barnard to LH, 28 July 1739, DE23/1/1428, LRO.
[27] Lady Margaret to Lord H, 12 Apr. n.y. and n.d., DE23/1/1443, 1448, LRO.
[28] Lady Margaret to LH, 9 Sept. (1739), 14D28/257, LRO. This is not to suggest that the notion of being 'born again in the Holy Spirit' is absent from Law's thinking, indeed it is a phrase that recurs in *A Serious Call* (1728). But it is set in the context of the Christian's renunciation of the ways of the world, and the living of life 'in such wisdom, and purity, and holiness *as might fit them* to be glorious in the enjoyment of God' (italics added) (*A Serious Call* (Fontana edn., 1965), 95). Whatever LH's reaction to the Law of *A Serious Call*, she plainly responded warmly to the mystical vein of his later writings. In 1749, the year of its publication, she bought one hundred copies of Law's *The Spirit of Prayer*, to give to acquaintances (R. Parkinson (ed.), *The Private Journals and Literary Remains of John Byrom* (Chetham Society, Manchester, 1854–7), ii (Chetham Society, vol. 44), 491–2).

over the following years, both in evangelistic work and in extensive contact with the leaders of the Revival, had not Lord Huntingdon been broadly supportive.[29] The family, moreover, clearly believed that he had undergone some change in his religious principles at the same time as his wife. Margaret's letter in response to the news of her sister-in-law's conversion was evidently intended for both Earl and Countess. Another sister rejoiced that God had manifested himself to her 'dear Brother and Sister'. Lady Frances, a few months later, wrote of the example of 'Gospel Holiness' given by her 'Brother and Sister Huntingdon'.[30]

The precise timing of Lady Huntingdon's introduction to the other leaders of the Revival is difficult to determine. Ingham, who was her immediate point of contact, was a member of a society (not formally Moravian, but Moravian in foundation and character) which had been established in London in May of the previous year, and was now meeting in a room in Fetter Lane. Very soon after Lady Huntingdon's conversion experience, he sought her support for the Brethren's proposed orphanage at Herrenhaag in Wettaravia.[31] At this early stage Lady Huntingdon may have perceived no distinction between the Revival as it was developing at large in England, and the work of the Moravians which had been so significant an influence on many of the early Methodists.[32] In May 1740, Ingham informed the Moravians' aristocratic leader, Count Zinzendorf, that the Huntingdons ('Comitis & Comitissee de Huntingdon') had subscribed twenty and a half guineas to the orphanage project, and that they

---

[29] A later Countess of Huntingdon concluded that laziness may have played a part in his relaxed attitude (Margaret Lane, 'The Queen of the Methodists', in *Purely for Pleasure* (London, 1966)).

[30] Lady Margaret to LH, 28 July (1739); ? to LH, 29 July (1739); Lady Frances to LH, 10 Mar. 1739/40, 14D32/253, 220, 244, LRO. Against this, there is Seymour's claim that Lord Huntingdon admitted to being unable to comprehend the doctrine of Atonement—a statement consistent with James Hutton's comment in Nov. 1740 that Lord Huntingdon 'could not distinguish between the preaching of the clergy and that of ourselves' (Seymour, i. 50; D. Benham, *Memoirs of James Hutton* (London, 1856), 67–8).

[31] Podmore, *Moravian Church*, 39–40; Ingham to LH, 23 Oct. 1739, DE23/1/1431, LRO.

[32] Professor Rupp commented that at this period 'it was as though inside every Methodist there was a Moravian trying to get out' (*Religion in England*, 337).

sought the prayers of his congregation that they might be truly turned to the Lord. The same letter gives an insight into Lady Huntingdon's early working out of the implications of her conversion; she wanted, he reported, a doctor of Moravian persuasion who would live with her family and work among the sick and the poor. There is about the Huntingdons something of the sense of a whole household having been converted. Another half-guinea was contributed to Herrenhaag by the Countess's servant Martha Mott, who was seeking the Lord ('excitata est Dominum Jesum desiderare et insequi') while one of Lord Huntingdon's servants, David Taylor, was to become a noted, if erratic, field preacher.[33] The change in Lady Huntingdon was also accompanied by more immediate effects within the household. In 1740 an observer commented on Lady Huntingdon's reputed 'very violent temper', but recorded the testimony of her lady's maid that 'she has not been in a passion for more than twelve months'.[34]

Lady Huntingdon's first meetings with the Wesleys and Whitefield cannot be dated for certain. Seymour suggests that her conversion was followed by an immediate invitation to the Wesleys to visit her at Donnington,[35] though such a visit is not compatible with Wesley's known movements at this time.[36] Whitefield was in America until March 1741, but it is notable that although Margaret Hastings and her sister-in-law had apparently not yet met him, they regarded their shared conversion experience as giving them an interest in defending him against detractors.[37] By 1741 John Wesley

[33] Ingham to Zinzendorf, 26 May 1740, Meth. Arch. (Ingham) (Rupp, *Religion in England*, 486). Taylor apparently started by reading Bishop Ken's works at open-air meetings. (LH to 'Reverend Sir', n.d., 14D32/571, LRO). For examples of LH's subsequent despair over Taylor's independent spirit, see LH to JW, 29 Apr. 1742, Meth. Arch. (LH), 107, and Curnock, iii. 112 n. Taylor's work led to the formation of societies in Cheshire that subsequently became Moravian. Taylor himself was received into the Moravian Church in 1750 and expelled in 1765 (Podmore, *Moravian Church*, 97, 118).   [34] Benham, *Memoirs of Hutton*, 67.
[35] Seymour, i. 17.   [36] Curnock, ii. 462 n.
[37] Of Whitefield's *Journal*, published late the previous year, and which had occasioned controversy over his remarks on the clergy, Margaret wrote, 'provided there were any little things in [them] that were unguarded, if they are not sinful we need not lessen or take our love from him' (Lady Margaret to LH, n.d., 14D32/273, LRO; Tyerman, *Whitefield*, i. ch. 4).

had become a regular confidant of the Countess. The Huntingdons stayed at Enfield Chace in the first half of that year, and this made access from London relatively easy. In April, John Wesley spent a day there, and visits are recorded again in June, July, and August—on one occasion including discussions with Lady Huntingdon from 10 p.m. until 2 a.m. in the morning.[38] At this stage Wesley seems to have been seeking and following her advice, as well as giving it. She may have influenced the subject matter of the University sermon he preached in July 1741,[39] and it was possibly at her instigation that he had made a tour of the Midlands in June that year.[40]

By 1741 a series of divisions had shaken the harmony of the new movement. The first had ended the co-operation with the Moravians symbolized by the Wesleys' participation with them in the Fetter Lane society.[41] From the start of 1739, Fetter Lane had, through its network of contacts, become the effective headquarters of the Revival nationwide. During the latter part of 1738, however, the society had taken on a number of distinctly Moravian characteristics (despite the opposition of John Wesley on several issues) and this process accelerated in 1739, during long periods of which Wesley was away from London. Opposition to the Church of England hardened within the society during 1739, and increasing emphasis came to be placed on the doctrine known as 'stillness': the belief, in essence, that incomplete faith was no faith at all, and that those not yet possessed of full faith should abstain from all the outward forms of religious profession (the 'means of grace': prayer, worship, sacraments, etc.) until they did. Wesley opposed both the spread of these views and the challenge to his authority that went with them. In July 1740 he led a walkout from Fetter Lane, the seceders joining forces with the Methodist Society which he had already established at the

---

[38] Wesley's Diary for 15 Apr., 7, 16 and 28 June, 11 July and 4 Aug. 1741, *Works*, xix. 58, 463, 464, 466, 467, Curnock, ii. 471 n.   [39] Curnock, ii. 478 n.
[40] Ibid. 462 n.
[41] C. J. Podmore, 'The Fetter Lane Society, 1739–40', *Proceedings of the Wesley Historical Society*, 47/5 (May 1990). This was effectively the first Methodist society until the withdrawal of Wesley and his supporters.

Foundry in Moorfields.[42] There is no evidence that Lady Huntingdon was directly involved in these events,[43] but she could not escape the stillness issue altogether. In the course of 1741 Charles Wesley was drawn back to the Moravians, a position from which Lady Huntingdon played a major part in rescuing him—becoming in the process the subject of attack from the 'still ones'.[44]

The second of the controversies in this early period was between Wesley and Whitefield over the doctrine of predestination. Whitefield followed the Calvinist tradition of mainstream English Puritanism, believing that God's grace called forth an irresistible response in those he had chosen, and that those who were thus of the elect could be confident that God would never let them go. Against this Wesley held that the possibility of salvation was open to all, combined with a belief that some Christians might, even in this life, reach a state of total victory over all conscious sin.[45] These differences

---

[42] Podmore, *Moravian Church*, ch. 2, *passim*. Podmore argues that, despite the impression conveyed by JW's *Journal*, JW had not been the prime mover in establishing the society; that there had been traces of the stillness doctrine in the society from early 1738 (i.e. it was not a novelty introduced by the Moravian leaders who arrived in England in the autumn of 1739); and that JW's acquisition of the Foundry from early 1740 showed that his secession from Fetter Lane had been planned for some time. Podmore concludes that the main responsibility for the rift lay not with Moravians *per se*, but with an extreme and volatile group within the English section of the society (Rupp, *Religion in England*, 363–7; Tyerman, *Wesley*, i. 301–10). Seymour i. 35–6 claims that LH joined in the Fetter Lane secession, but quotes no documents to this effect.

[43] Welch, 45 n. 42 doubts that LH knew Wesley by then, or that she belonged to the Fetter Lane society at all.

[44] LH to CW, 24 Oct. 1741, Meth. Arch (LH), 1. The marriage of Lady Margaret Hastings to Ingham at the end of 1741, in the face of sustained opposition from the Huntingdons to such a socially unacceptable match, appears to have contributed to LH's subsequent long-term alienation from the Moravians. There was a rapprochement of sorts between the Countess and the Moravians around 1760—including two visits by her to the Moravian congregation at Bedford—but these links soon broke. Relations between JW and the Moravians were chequered, not least because the Moravians were anxious to negotiate a special relationship with the Church of England, and they feared that too close an association with JW might hinder their ambitions. Whitefield lost a significant number of his own followers to the Moravians in the course of the 1740s, and he became concerned at both their doctrines and their finances (Welch, 47, 85–8; Schlenther, 21, 49–50; Podmore, *Moravian Church*, 78–80, 80–96; W. R. Ward, *The Protestant Evangelical Awakening* (Cambridge, 1992), 313, 316).

[45] J. Lawson, 'The People called Methodists: Our Discipline', in R. Davies and G. Rupp (eds.), *A History of the Methodist Church in Great Britain* (London, 1965), i. 186.

were largely contained, prior to Whitefield's departure to America in 1739, but they were brought into the open by a robust exchange of transatlantic correspondence between the two men in the course of 1740—an exchange that spilled over into a pamphlet controversy in England and a division within the Methodist Society in Bristol.[46] The breach between Wesley and Whitefield was confirmed on the latter's return to England in March 1741.

It is unlikely that Lady Huntingdon played an overt part in these events, but it is notable (in view of her later leadership of the Calvinist cause[47]) that at this stage her loyalties were firmly with the Wesleys. When Lady Huntingdon met Whitefield by chance in February 1742 she was staunch in her defence of the Wesleys, declining to be swayed by Whitefield's belief that she was herself one of the elect; in her view, *not* believing in election meant that she was the more totally dependent on Christ to deliver her from sin.[48] At this stage her confidence in the Wesleys' view of salvation was complete. In April 1742, for example, she told John that 'you are the only one with your Brother that has ever showed the riches of the Gospel'.[49]

There was a reconciliation of sorts between Wesley and Whitefield in the latter part of 1742,[50] a fact which may explain Lady Huntingdon's reported attendance at Whitefield's Tabernacle that winter.[51] But there is evidence in 1743 that she was still firmly on guard against predestination,[52] and though Whitefield was in the circle of her correspondents,[53] Wesley's West Street chapel apparently remained for some time her regular place of worship in London.[54]

---

[46] Tyerman, *Wesley*, i. 311–25.   [47] See below, Ch. 6.
[48] LH to (?) JW, 19 Feb. 1742, Meth. Arch. (LH), 3. Whitefield's evident uncertainty about her views shows that she had not been prominent in the controversy. This early attachment to the Wesleys suggests that some modification is needed of Tyerman's claim that it was Whitefield's Calvinism that won him LH's support; more accurately, it seems, *she* needed to modify her position before the close bond with Whitefield could be forged. (cf. Tyerman, *Whitefield*, i. ch. 6).
[49] Ibid. 107.   [50] Ibid. ii. ch. 1.   [51] Ibid. ch. 2.
[52] LH to CW, 4 June 1743, Meth. Arch.(LH), 12.   [53] Cf. Seymour, i. 65.
[54] JW to Mrs Hutton, 22 Aug. 1744, *Works*, xxvi. 113–14.

On John she pinned her hopes for the renewal of the Church[55] and to both brothers she looked for leadership and support. Charles's hymns were a comfort to her,[56] and it appears that it was to him that she unburdened in times of spiritual distress.[57] She was, however, no passive devotee of a pair of winsome religious leaders, and there are signs already of the confidence in her own judgement and authority that was to mark her later years. Though she had nothing but praise when John consulted her about his Journal, prior to publication in 1742,[58] she offered Charles firm (and evidently unsolicited) advice against the publication of a funeral elegy in the same year.[59] John, as noted, appears to have been influenced by her to make his Midlands tour in 1741, and, in 1743, according to his own account, it was Lady Huntingdon who first directed him to the needs of the Newcastle colliers.[60] She it was who encouraged Wesley in the publication of the 'chaste collection of English poems' which he had brought out in 1744.[61] In the same year she played host at her London house to those attending the first Methodist conference.[62] Nor were the Wesleys alone as a source of potential influence. By early 1744 she was in regular correspondence with George Whitefield, a development that may signal the start of her move towards Calvinism.[63] Howel Harris[64] was introduced to her in August 1743 and

---

[55] 'Nothing less do I look for from you, than making our sinful apostate Church the footstool of Christ' (Curnock, ii. 48 n).

[56] LH to CW, Apr. 1742, Meth. Arch. (LH), 4.

[57] LH to (?) CW, n.d. 1743, Meth. Arch. (LH) 13. There are signs that she found John a colder individual than his brother, and there may lie the seeds of their later estrangement. She was to tell Charles, 'I could not help telling him (John) I was sure *you lov'd me* better *than he did*'—to which John's response had been that it was only that Charles showed it more (LH to Charles Wesley (? late May 1743), Meth. Arch. (LH), 97).   [58] Seymour, i. 46, 51.

[59] LH to JW, 4 Aug. 1742, Meth. Arch. (LH), 117.

[60] JW to the mayor of Newcastle upon Tyne, 12 July 1743, *Works*, xxvi. 100–2.

[61] JW to LH, Aug. 1744, *Works*, xxvi. 114–16. The poems are dedicated to her, but at her request the dedication contained no personal information about her (LH to CW (stamped 5 Sept. 1744), Meth. Arch. (LH), 16).   [62] Curnock, iii. 143 n.

[63] Schlenther, 26.

[64] Harris (1714–73) was a major force in the development of Calvinistic Methodism in Wales. He was converted in 1735, and went to Oxford that year, intended for Anglican ordination, but left almost immediately to embark on a career of lay evangelism. His home village of Trevecca (Trevecka) in Breconshire was the location of the religious settlement, which he founded in the 1750s, as well

was to become a regular confidant.⁶⁵ Lady Huntingdon's early contact with William Law has already been noted; those links were evidently to lead to a sufficient bond between them for Law to address to her a series of subsequently published letters.⁶⁶ In 1744 Lady Huntingdon received a visit at Donnington from Law's admirer and supporter, John Byrom;⁶⁷ by this stage also she was in correspondence and direct contact with Philip Doddridge.⁶⁸

Already she was exercising a measure of spiritual authority and influence within the movement. Thomas Maxfield, for example, Wesley's lay assistant of whose preaching Wesley had initially disapproved—was encouraged by her in the exercise of his ministerial gifts.⁶⁹ There was also the influence that she could muster in the wider world. In 1742, probably for the first time, but certainly not the last, she was involved in efforts to secure ordination for a man described as lacking formal education, but patently called by the Holy Spirit.⁷⁰ In 1774 she was consulted by a congregation in

---

as the training college that LH founded in the following decade. On the influence on Harris of revival movements on the Continent and in America, see Ward, *Evangelical Awakening*, 322.

⁶⁵ G. F. Nuttall, 'Howel Harris and "The Grand Table": a Note on Religion and Politics, 1744–50', *Journal of Ecclesiastical History*, 39/4 (Oct. 1988), traces the substantial contact which Harris was to have with LH and her circle over the years to 1750. ⁶⁶ Parkinson (ed.), *Byrom*, ii. 629.

⁶⁷ Ibid. 382–4. Byrom (1692–1761) was a Manchester layman who had decided against both ordination and the practice of medicine in favour of a career as a Christian apologist and man of letters (including hymn-writing and the development of a system of shorthand). He was a staunch Jacobite sympathizer. With Law he developed an interest in mystical writings.

⁶⁸ LH to Doddridge, 27 Feb. 1743/4 and 10 May 1744, G. F. Nuttall, *Calendar of the Correspondence of Philip Doddridge, D.D.* (Historical Manuscripts Commission, HMSO, London, 1979), Letters 953 and 968; Seymour, i. 64–5. Doddridge (1702–51) was a Dissenting divine and hymn-writer who from 1730 had been in charge of the Dissenting Academy in Northampton. Catholicity of approach (within Dissent and between Dissenters and the Established Church) was his hallmark; some of his fellow Dissenters were as suspicious of his friendship towards Whitefield as some Anglican clergy were of such contacts among their colleagues (Tyerman, *Whitefield*, ii. ch. 2).

⁶⁹ LH to JW, 31 Jan. 1741/2, Meth. Arch. (LH), 111.

⁷⁰ W. Chapman to LH, 22 Apr. and 12 June 1742; M. Cocks to LH, n.d., 14D32/536, 556; DE23/1/1435, LRO. In 1746 there was an attempt, apparently unsuccessful, to persuade her to use her influence with the Archbishop of Canterbury in another ordination case. (G. M. Roberts, *Selected Trevecka Letters* (Caernarvon 1956 and 1962), i. 190, 209).

Nottingham on the response they should make to a magistrate who was seeking to restrict their times of meeting; her advice, apparently to their surprise, was in favour of submission.[71] The stakes were higher the following year however, when Lady Huntingdon, like the Wesleys, was caught up in the accusations of Jacobite sympathies laid against the Methodists during the Forty-five. Such allegations were not without some substance, for both she and her husband came from families with Jacobite leanings, and they had contacts with a number of leading Jacobite sympathizers. Lady Huntingdon, through her contacts with Lord Carteret as Secretary of State, secured the King's acknowledgement of her loyalty and a royal instruction to the magistracy to uphold the principles of religious liberty.[72]

Much of the early working out of her faith, in the years while Lord Huntingdon was still alive, was done on two levels: through contacts and influence in fashionable society, and by charitable and evangelical work among the humble. Serious-minded though she had been before her conversion, the change in her was clearly noticeable in the circles in which she moved, and she was not a person to conceal her faith or to pass over the opportunities for sharing it. The Duchesses of Marlborough and Buckingham were among the fashionable friends that she attempted to influence, and the Prince of Wales appears to have been impressed by her faith and commitment. Indeed, as Dr Nuttall has shown, there was to be a striking congruity between those who attended preaching organized by Lady Huntingdon in the later 1740s, and the political opposition to Walpole which centred on Leicester House and the Prince of Wales.[73]

---

[71] LH to CW (stamped 5 Sept.) 1744, Meth. Arch. (LH), 16. She disapproved, she told Charles, of those who thought that serving God gave them an entitlement to be the master of others, rather than their servants.

[72] Schlenther, 27–30; Seymour, i. 67–8.

[73] Nuttall, 'Howel Harris and "The Grand Table"', 540–1. According to Seymour, the reaction of the two Duchesses to Lady Huntingdon was very different, Marlborough hoping that 'my wicked heart may gain some good from you in the end', but Buckingham finding it 'monstrous' for the Methodists to suggest that she had 'a heart as sinful as the common wretches that crawl on the earth'. (Seymour, i. 24–7); Welch, p. 212, however, claims that the Marlborough letters quoted by Seymour were forgeries. There is apparently no known source for the Prince of

In Bath, which she continued to visit for her health, and where she was part of a small Methodist society, it was rumoured that she had made a Methodist of the celebrated physician Dr Cheyne.[74] Doubtless she was an object of puzzlement to many of her circle, and their reaction to her may not always have been easy to gauge. When one of the Huntingdons' dinner guests observed at the relevant stage in the meal that he would have made a bad Romanist because of his inability to eat fish or pray ten times a day, Lady Huntingdon was unsure whether this was a veiled attack upon her.[75]

Alongside her role in society, Lady Huntingdon maintained her support for foreign missions (through SPCK) and her acts of practical charity.[76] For a period she supported a school at Markfield, near Leicester, but gave this up in 1742, having decided to confine her efforts to the children of those already converted.[77] Soon afterwards, she was describing more overtly evangelical plans for a further school at nearby Ratby, that the master would combine with a shop selling Wesley's publications.[78] Personal evangelism became an increasing part of her ministry. Her own servants were an immediate object of attention, and there is evidence of her praying and reading with them.[79] In 1742 she determined to take some of the very poor into her care, and to get them to attend her twice a week; she sought John Wesley's advice whether to expound the Scriptures to them and whether it would be appropriate for her to form them into a band.[80] Her policy, she said in 1744, was to speak of the

---

Wales's supposed expression of regard for Lady Huntingdon ('when I am dying, I think I shall be happy to seize the skirt of Lady Huntingdon's mantle, to lift me up with her to heaven') other than Seymour, i. 174 n., but the Prince's sympathetic attitude towards Lady Huntingdon's circle is beyond doubt.

[74] LH to Lord H, 2 Jan. 1741/2, (HMC, iii. 32); LH to CW, Jan. 1743, Meth. Arch. (LH), 5. The doctor, in turn, lent her books of mystical theology (Parkinson (ed.), *Byrom*, ii. 330–2).
[75] LH to CW, n.d.(stamped 16 Aug.) ?1744, Meth. Arch. (LH), 84.
[76] Extract from SPCK minutes of 13 Aug. 1745 (sent to LH); Henry Hastings to LH, 13 Sept. 1746, 14D32/572, 196, LRO.   [77] Seymour, i. 51; Schlenther, 23.
[78] LH to JW, 29 Apr. 1742, Meth. Arch. (LH), 107. LH envisaged a church being raised there also.
[79] LH to CW n.d. (stamped 16 July), Meth. Arch. (LH), 85.
[80] LH to JW, 29 Apr. 1742, Meth. Arch. (LH), 107.

Gospel to whoever she met, of whatever rank, and she described how the work she did for people's bodily health brought many to her from many miles around—whereupon she read, sang, and talked to them.[81] In 1746 she had plans for her family chaplain to serve a group of churches and hold meetings in her own home.[82]

For Lady Huntingdon in these years there were only two things that mattered, her faith and her family. Her conversion did not lessen her expression of love for her husband, who was the centre, she said, of all earthly happiness.[83] She feared 'outliving what I so passionately love' and welcomed sickness 'with the view of going first'.[84] Reading her letters to her husband in parallel with those to the Wesleys, however, conveys the impression of someone living in two worlds; between, for example, the anxious mother who watched the progress (in one case fatal) of smallpox through her children in 1743,[85] and the austere Christian who felt herself sinful to have taken pleasure in Charles Wesley's concern for her in her bereavement.[86] Despite her indifference to the world, for example, she was flattered by Lord Chesterfield's praise for her son Francis and told her husband that he 'did say so much about him that I really believe he never said of any boy before'.[87] There is, nevertheless, an underlying

---

[81] LH to CW, n.d. (stamped 16 Aug.), Meth. Arch. (LH), 84.

[82] LH to Doddridge, (? 17) June 1746 (Nuttall, *Doddridge*, Letter 1164).

[83] LH to Lord H, 20 May 1743, 14D32/73, LRO. Dr Schlenther does, however, detect some evidence of a cooling in their relationship after 1739, and points out that thereafter she bore no further children (Schlenther, 31).

[84] LH to Lord H, 17 May 1743, 14D32/72, LRO.

[85] LH to CW, n.d. 1743; LH to Lord H, 4, 11, and 17 May 1743, n.d. (stamped 20 May), 26 and 17 May 1743 14D32/69, 71, 74, 76, 70, LRO.

[86] LH to CW, n.d. 1743, Meth. Arch. (LH), 8. This is not to imply that religious sentiments were absent altogether from her letters to her husband. For example after the death of her son, and while others of her children were still ill, she wrote to him of her total dependence on God in her troubles: 'let us my dear dear life submit all to the Divine will' (LH to Lord H, 17 May 1743 14D32/72, LRO).

[87] LH to Lord H, 8 Aug. 1746, HMC, iii. 61. Lord Chesterfield (the object of Dr Johnson's waspish comment, 'This man I thought had been a Lord among wits but, I find, he is only a wit among Lords'), was to assume the role of mentor and friend to Francis after his father's death. See A. Francis Stuart (ed.), *Letters of Lord Chesterfield to Lord Huntingdon* (London 1923). He was on friendly terms with LH, but it was an extraordinary decision on her part to place her son in the care of a man whose views on religion and morality were so contrary to her own (Schlenther, 57).

sense in these years of weariness with her earthly existence and a desire to escape from it. At one stage she even outlined to Charles Wesley her vision of building a town in which God's people could live as a separate community, safe from the world and its troubles.[88]

The early death of Lord Huntingdon in October 1746 left Lady Huntingdon with sole responsibility for her children and their fortunes, since Francis was not to come of age for another four years.[89] Doubtless, amidst the business demands which this placed upon her, and the strains of assimilating her grief, she speculated about the implications of her bereavement for the future working out of her Christian calling. In February 1747, she told Doddridge she dreaded 'slack hands in the vineyard'; but in April she debated with Harris whether she should retire from the world.[90] There was clearly a chance that she would take this course. Given her instinct to retreat from the world, even in Lord Huntingdon's lifetime, and the common interest in mystical religion which she shared with Law and Byrom, there must have been a strong pull towards the inner consolation of religion, and specifically to the experience of spiritual prayer which was to be the theme of Law's next work. The argument which Law developed in *The Spirit of Prayer* of 1749–50 (a book, as noted, which Lady Huntingdon bought in bulk to give to friends) was that 'there is but one good prayer... and that is a prayer in and from the Spirit, or as the Spirit of God moves you in it or to it.'[91] It was a theme which chimed with the Quaker emphasis on 'inner light', and Harris became anxious later in 1747

---

[88] LH to CW, n.d. (stamped 16 July), Meth. Arch. (LH), 85.
[89] LH's management of her husband's estate was to be a source of disagreement with Francis for decades to come. LH to 10th Earl of Huntingdon, 29 Aug. (? 1775), 20 Nov. 1781, HA 5859, 5861.
[90] LH to Doddridge, 23 Feb. 174(?6/)7, Nuttall, *Doddridge*, Letter, 1222; Harris's Diary for 9 Apr. 1747.
[91] *The Spirit of Prayer*, part II, quoted in Stephen Hobhouse, *William Law and Eighteenth Century Quakerism* (London 1927), 291. Law's book was to become a major Quaker text in the 19th century (Hobhouse, *Law*, 295 n). Seymour disapproved of the work, and he would have been surprised at the evidence of LH using it as an evangelical tract, as she was still doing in the mid-1750s (Seymour, i. 223; LH to CW, 27 July 1756, Meth. Arch. (LH), 59).

that Lady Huntingdon and 'Mr. Hutchins', who was by then her chaplain, were putting the testimony of the Spirit above the authority of Scripture and 'Warp[ing] tow[ar]ds Quaker[is]m and Mr. Law'.[92] Despite this apparent inclination to withdrawal from the world, however, Lady Huntingdon's public profile was sufficiently prominent to arouse opposition, even at this stage. On 21 May 1747, she wrote to Doddridge; 'They called out in the open streets for me, saying, if they had me they would tear me to pieces.'[93]

The year 1748 was marked both by Whitefield's return from America, where he had been since 1744, and by his entry into Lady Huntingdon's confidence. Harris appears to have been the means of bringing them together, at the stage, Tyerman suggests, when Lady Huntingdon was ready to move out of mourning and into a new phase of her life. Whitefield was persuaded to preach to aristocratic gatherings at her house on a number of occasions, and in September became one of her chaplains.[94] Lady Huntingdon had by this step forged a link with the foremost popular evangelist of the day. She had also signalled more clearly her transition to the Calvinist wing of the Revival that was to be her permanent home. This did not mean a total break with Wesley, who preached at her house early in

---

[92] Harris's Diary for 3 July 1747; Roberts, *Trevecka Letters*, ii. 11. Roberts follows Tyerman in identifying Hutchins as Richard Hutchins, a colleague of Wesley's, who subsequently became rector of Lincoln College, Oxford, but who was not an Oxford Methodist (see V. H. H. Green, *The Young Mr. Wesley* (London, 1961), 124 n.). It is more probable that it was John Hutchings of Pembroke College, who had been in the Holy Club, joined the Moravians, and eventually came to a sorry end (Curnock, ii. 94 n; Podmore, *Moravian Church*, 117–18). Harris had threatened to break with LH over the authority of Scripture, so his continued friendship can be taken as a sign that he was persuaded that her orthodoxy was not in question. The Wesleys appear to have been anxious, back in the early 1740s, that she might have been drawn into Moravian stillness and what she herself called 'misty sesam' (mysticism). That she was able to analyse this as one of her own fears is probably a sign that there was little chance of it happening (LH to ?, n.d., Meth. Arch. (LH), 91).

[93] Nuttall, *Doddridge*, Letter 1241. Dr Schlenther links this to her political rather than religious reputation (Schlenther, 30).

[94] Tyerman, *Whitefield*, ii. 21–2; Seymour, i. 88–93; LH to Doddridge (? 30 Aug. 1748); Nuttall, *Doddridge*, Letter 1392. Dr Schlenther suggests that it was only the prospect of her patronage which persuaded him to return from America when he did (Schlenther, 39).

1749,[95] but it did mean that she was with the principal Calvinists, Harris and Whitefield, when schemes for closer harmony between their various societies and Wesley's were discussed in April 1749.[96] Lady Huntingdon was involved in the subsequent discussions with the Wesleys, which focused both on doctrinal issues and on the extent of Wesley's dominance over the new movement: Whitefield, for example, objected to him monopolizing the name Methodist.[97] Some points of agreement were reached in August, particularly in regard to discipline within the movement, and a more wide-ranging entente was symbolized in January 1750 (apparently as a result of Lady Huntingdon's efforts) with an exchange of pulpits between Wesley on the one hand and Whitefield and Harris on the other.[98] Cutting across the theological divisions, however, was personal animosity between Harris and Whitefield (triggered by Harris's jealousy at Whitefield having supplanted him in Lady Huntingdon's favour) which led to Whitefield barring Harris from preaching at the Tabernacle in late 1749.[99]

By the end of the 1740s Lady Huntingdon was assuming a pivotal role within the Revival. Already the main themes of her work over the coming decade are apparent. One element in this was her readiness to use her position in society (as she had already done during the Forty-five) in defence of Methodists under attack. Seymour describes, for example, how in 1748 she intervened to secure financial restitution to the North Wales Methodists who had been fined as a result of the hostility of Sir Watkin Williams Wynn;[100] the following year she used her political contacts on behalf of the persecuted Methodists of Cork.[101] A variant on this was

---

[95] Tyerman, *Whitefield*, ii. ch. 4. Wesley was, however, deeply offended by LH's show of support for Whitefield, whom he felt she had poached from him (Schlenther, 39). [96] Harris's Diary, 29 Apr. 1749.
[97] Ibid. 2 Aug. 1749. In Harris's *Autobiography* he presents himself as having been summoned by Lady Huntingdon to assist in uniting Wesley and Whitefield (Trevecca Letter no. 3222).
[98] Harris's Diary for 3 and 4 Aug. 1749 and 21 Jan. 1750. JW's Journal for 19 and 21 Jan. 1750, *Works*, xx. 318–19; Seymour, i. 117–19. CW thought the meeting in Aug. 1749 had achieved nothing (CW's *Journal* for 3 Aug. 1749, ii. 63; Schlenther, 45).
[99] Schlenther, 42.   [100] Seymour, i. 110.
[101] Ibid. ii. 150–1. JW's Journal for 20 July 1749 describes the nature of the persecutions (*Works*, xx. 285–90).

the defence of the reputation of the Methodist leaders as when, also in 1749, she extracted (and published) a grovelling apology from the bishop of Exeter for having wrongly accused Wesley and Whitefield of publishing a forged version of his diocesan charge.[102] Drawing-room gatherings, addressed by the leaders of the Revival,[103] constitute another theme. Acts of charity, patronage, and ministry to the poor, constitute a third.[104] A fourth element, and one that looks forward to her own later efforts to provide training for the ministry, was support for would-be ministers.[105] What was perhaps most distinctive about the period was the strategic role which Lady Huntingdon was prepared to play in influencing the course of the Revival. This was shown not only in the attempted union of 1750 but when she had persuaded Whitefield the previous year to give up his leadership role of the Calvinistic wing of the Revival—possibly because she wanted him as a reforming influence within the Church of England, and not as the leader of a sect.[106]

THE 1750S

A significant aspect of Lady Huntingdon's broader role during the 1750s was her concern to preserve harmony within the movement. That meant discouraging anything that might make for controversy, regardless of the quarter from which it came. She was pleased in 1753 (she told Charles Wesley) that Whitefield had not had time to copy out a letter he had thought of printing, and which she clearly thought would stir up trouble.[107] The following year, when she thought trouble was brewing again, she threatened (with

---

[102] Seymour, i. 95–6.

[103] e.g. Harris's Diary for 18 Apr. 1749. For evidence of Doddridge preaching at her house, see Seymour, i. 86.

[104] Doddridge wrote: 'Lady Huntingdon is quite a mother to the poor; she visits them and prays with them in their sicknesses; and they leave their children to her for a legacy when they die, and she takes care of them' (Seymour, i. 86). See also Welch, 93–4 for examples of acts of charity to individuals.

[105] Doddridge to Benjamin Fawcett, 26 June 1750 (Nuttall, *Doddridge*, Letter 1630; Seymour, i. 154). [106] Tyerman, *Whitefield*, ii. ch. 4.

[107] LH to CW, n.d. 1753, Meth. Arch. (LH), 23.

disarming frankness) to send her thoughts on the issue by every post;[108] a year later she sought to persuade the Wesleys that Whitefield had no ambition to gain influence over their societies, 'but what preaching and sermon may gain him'.[109] In 1759, at a time of national anxiety at the threat of a French invasion, Lady Huntingdon instituted a series of prayer meetings at her London home in which the Wesleys and Whitefield participated, along with a number of prominent clergy from the two sides of the Revival. It was a uniting experience not just across the theological divide but between the two Wesleys, Charles recording that he had not felt so close to his brother for many years.[110]

Of the two brothers, it was Charles to whom Lady Huntingdon related more easily. Reconciled in 1751, after a short break,[111] their relationship became so warm that by 1752 John felt threatened by their closeness.[112] In 1753 that friendship was further cemented when Lady Huntingdon nursed Charles's wife through smallpox, writing to Charles (attending his brother who was also seriously ill) letters that breathe both good sense and compassion.[113] The Countess's own experience well equipped her to sympathize when Charles's infant son died of the disease: 'the Chance against us parants [*sic*]' she told him, 'is for happiness a hundred to one.'[114] The following years saw more signs of the different relationship she had with the two brothers. On the one hand there were friendly letters to Charles, a visit to his wife, and even a gift of an embroidered handkerchief.[115] On the other

[108] LH to CW, 17 Dec. 1754, Meth. Arch. (LH), 38.
[109] LH to CW, 23 Dec. 1755, Meth. Arch. (LH), 52. Towards the Moravians LH found it less easy to be charitable; in 1757 Harris 'had a strong battle to moderate' her attitude to Zinzendorf (Harris's Diary for 7 (o.s.)/18 (n.s.) Aug. 1757).
[110] Seymour, i. 396–7; Tyerman, *Wesley*, ii. 323; JW's Journal for 27 Feb. 1759, *Works*, xxi. 178; CW to his wife, 27 Feb. n.y., *Journal*, ii. 219.
[111] CW's *Journal*, for 1 and 3 June 1751, ii. 81–2.
[112] Tyerman, *Whitefield*, ii. 289.
[113] She told Charles at the start of the illness that she would be frank in telling him everything, so that he need not worry that anything was being hidden (LH to CW, 1, 3, 6, 10, 26 Dec. 1753, Meth. Arch. (LH), 25, 30, 26, 27, 28; Seymour, ii. 381; CW's *Journal* for 6 Dec. 1753, ii. 100).
[114] LH to CW, 8 Jan. 1754, Meth. Arch.(LH), 33.
[115] LH to CW, 4 May and 22 Sept. 1755; LH to Mrs Wesley, 5 (or 6) Oct. 1755; LH to CW, 17 Apr. 1756; LH to Mrs Wesley, 30 June 1757, Meth. Arch. (LH), 40, 48, 50, 54, 63.

there was suspicion that John had been avoiding her[116] and concern that the financial support which, if necessary, she was prepared to give Charles, should benefit him and not his brother.[117]

The 1750s saw the development of Lady Huntingdon's contacts with other evangelical leaders. The majority of these were Anglican clergy on the Calvinist wing of the Revival. One such was William Romaine[118] who, having been turned out of his lectureship at St George's, Hanover Square in the early 1750s, was brought to Lady Huntingdon's attention by one of his supporters at St George's, a kinsman of the Countess, the Earl of Northampton. Romaine became another of her chaplains and undertook itinerant preaching on her behalf (almost always in churches as he was opposed to field preaching) during periods when his other pulpit at St Dunstan's was closed to him.[119] His ministry with Lady Huntingdon was to include preaching at her house and, in the next phase of her work, at the principal chapels of the Connexion during 1760s and 1770s. Another Calvinistic Anglican to come into Lady Huntingdon's circle in this period was Martin Madan.[120] Lady Huntingdon was one of those who encouraged Madan to think of ordination, and helped him to achieve it in the face of some opposition.[121] Madan spent some time with Lady Huntingdon in the summer of 1756, an experience which convinced her of

---

[116] LH to CW, 4 Aug. and 15 Sept. 1755, Meth. Arch. (LH), 44, 47.
[117] LH to CW, 27 Nov. 1756, Meth. Arch. (LH), 62.
[118] 1714–95. Noted Oxford Hebraist, subsequently lecturer at St Dunstan's-in-the-East and briefly (until turned out) at St George's, Hanover Square; from 1766 rector of St Anne's, Blackfriars. Popular preacher and author of influential devotional works on *The Life*, *The Walk*, and *The Triumph of Faith* (respectively 1763, 1771, and 1795). On his ultimate withdrawal from LH, see below.
[119] Seymour, i. 130, 273–4; Schlenther, 50–1, 69.
[120] 1726–90. Madan was a barrister, converted through a chance hearing of Wesley's preaching, and subsequently ordained; one of LH's chaplains from 1761; chaplain of the Lock Hospital, London, an institution for fallen women. Madan's experience at the Lock convinced him that a major incentive to prostitution would be removed if seducers were compelled to marry their victims, even if they were themselves married already. Publication of these views (in *Thelyphthora* in 1780), despite requests from LH and others that he suppress the work, led to a storm in the evangelical world and effectively ended his career (Seymour, ii. 464; Welch, 105 n.).
[121] Seymour, i. 165–6.

The Start of the Countess's Connexion 43

the valuable contribution he would make in future,[122] and the following year, according to Seymour, she engaged him to undertake a preaching tour with Romaine.[123] Like Romaine his contribution to the Countess's work was to involve some domestic preaching and preaching tours, and later service at her chapels—although (possibly even more so than Romaine) he was firm in his opposition to field preaching.[124]

Henry Venn[125] was another clergyman who entered Lady Huntingdon's circle around the same time as Madan. The final stages in Venn's conversion occurred through the influence of Lady Huntingdon.[126] Like Romaine and Madan he joined the group of clergy on whose services Lady Huntingdon was to call in due course for the supply of her chapels—when the demands of his own parish (and of his children's holidays) permitted.[127] A new ally of a rather different sort was the eccentric John Berridge,[128] who passed through a conversion experience following his appointment to the living of Everton in 1755. His changed sentiments had an impact on his preaching (inside and outside his church) which led to a local revival that came to the ears of

---

[122] LH to CW, 27 July 1756, and two letters marked Aug. 1756, Meth. Arch. (LH), 59, 60, 61; LH to Mrs. Barlow, 31 July 1756, MS letter in the Central Library, Bath.   [123] Seymour, i. 428 n.
[124] Seymour, i. 396, 291, 323, Roberts, *Trevecka Letters*, ii. 91; Shirley to LH, 21 Oct. 1771, F1/1570,CF.
[125] 1725–97. Fellow of Queens' College, Cambridge; curate of Clapham; following his conversion became vicar of Huddersfield (1759–71) and then of Yelling, Huntingdonshire. He published an influential work of evangelical ethics, *The Complete Duty of Man* (1763). Venn was a moderate Calvinist who opposed the tendency of extreme predestinarianism to undermine morality (Walter Sellon to LH. 20 Nov. 1771; Shirley to LH, n.d., E4/4(6), F1/1567,CF). He was the father of John Venn, prominent in Anglican Evangelical circles at the turn of the century, as rector of Clapham and a founder of the Church Missionary Society.
[126] Seymour, i. 224–5.
[127] Ibid. ii. 23; Venn to LH, 20 May 1770; Glascott to LH, Apr. 1768; Wills to LH, 30 July 1770, F1/93, 1418, 1770, CF. Seymour disputes John Venn's claim that his father later rejected preaching in unconsecrated places, quoting instances of him doing so as late as 1790, until infirmity prevented him from continuing (Seymour, i. 291–2). Wesley implied that Venn was more irregular than himself (JW to Thomas Adam, 19 July 1768, *Letters*, v. 98).
[128] 1716–93. Former Fellow of Clare College, Cambridge; vicar of Everton in Bedfordshire from 1755.

Lady Huntingdon. According to Seymour's account, Romaine and Madan were sent to investigate the convulsions and other physical manifestations which were reported amongst those who heard his preaching; satisfied of the genuine nature of the work, Lady Huntingdon herself travelled to Everton to support Berridge, and thereafter took him back with her to London to introduce him to her own religious circle and Whitefield's chapels.[129] Berridge, like the others mentioned, was subsequently to preach at Lady Huntingdon's chapels when his other commitments permitted.[130]

A contact initiated from the beginning of the 1750s, apparently at Lady Huntingdon's behest, was with James Hervey.[131] Hervey had by then published the first of the markedly Calvinistic works by which, despite his poor health and early death, he was to have a substantial influence upon the Revival. Through Lady Huntingdon, Hervey was brought to London for his health, and in consequence joined the ranks of the evangelicals engaged in drawing-room ministry to the upper classes.[132] Hervey joined her circle not long before Doddridge left it. The latter part of 1751 saw Lady Huntingdon caring for Doddridge in Bath, prior to his departure for Lisbon, a trip which she had played a major part in funding as a final (and unsuccessful) attempt to reverse the consumption from which he was suffering.[133]

One other newcomer deserves mention in the 1750s: John Fletcher,[134] whose reputation had reached Lady Huntingdon's

---

[129] Seymour, i. 397–400.

[130] Their priorities did not always agree. It was a disagreement over dates that led to Berridge's celebrated observation that his instructions 'must come from the Lamb, not from the Lamb's wife'—one instance of the caustic wit for which he was known (not always favourably) within the Revival (Seymour, ii. 20).

[131] 1714–58. A former pupil of John Wesley and member of the Oxford Holy Club; subsequently incumbent of Weston Favell and Collingtree, near Northampton (Seymour, i. 123; Green, *The Young Mr. Wesley*, 188; LH to Doddridge (*c*.12 Jan. 1749/50), Nuttall *Dodderidge*, Letter 1569).

[132] Seymour, i. 160–2.

[133] Doddridge died in Lisbon (ibid. 448–52; T. Belsham, *Memoirs of the Late Reverend Theophilus Lindsey, MA* (London, 1873), 319).

[134] 1729–85. French-speaking Swiss; came to England in 1750; converted 1754; ordained deacon and priest in 1757, following contact with the Methodist societies, and thereafter offered his services to Wesley; vicar of Madeley from 1760; designated as Wesley's successor in 1773, but died before him (see Patrick Streiff,

ears through the Wesleys and Whitefield. In 1759 he found himself introduced to 'une prodige moderne, une Comtesse humble et pieuse',[135] who pressed him to participate in her drawing-room ministry. This he undertook to do, having weighed the possibility of it conflicting with his commitments to the Wesleys. Wesley was worried about the more significant constraints on Fletcher's time implicit in his acceptance of the living of Madeley in Shropshire in 1760.[136] Parish life was not, however, to prevent him from occasional preaching for Lady Huntingdon nor from accepting the presidency of her college in 1768.[137]

As these various contacts show, the 1750s was a decade in which Lady Huntingdon was extending her activities and the team of helpers and advisers on which she could draw. There were other highlights also, such as the rebuilding of Whitefield's Moorfields Tabernacle in 1753 (an initiative in which Lady Huntingdon appears to have taken a close interest[138]) and the opening of a new chapel for him in Tottenham Court Road in 1756. Whitefield considered placing his new chapel under Lady Huntingdon's patronage as a peeress as an alternative to licensing it as a Dissenting meeting house under the Act of Toleration. The decision not to follow the patronage route (significantly, given that Lady Huntingdon tried the device subsequently with her own major chapels) was taken in the light of legal advice that the privilege was applicable only in strictly limited circumstances.[139]

There were also family matters to occupy her attention. Her eldest son, Francis, had been away from England on the

---

Reluctant Saint? A Theological Biography of Fletcher of Madeley (Epworth Press, Peterborough, 2001)).

[135] Fletcher to CW, 15 Nov. 1759, Meth. Arch. (JF), 61.

[136] One of Madeley's attractions for Fletcher was that it offered more work and less money than the living he had previously been offered and declined. Wesley never properly understood Fletcher's preference for the parochial ministry over itinerancy, or accepted that God had really called Fletcher to Madeley (P. S. Forsaith, 'Wesley's Designated Successor', *Proceedings of the Wesley Historical Society*, 42/3; Streiff, *Fletcher*, 60–1, 64–5).

[137] For Fletcher's involvement with Trevecca College and his role in the doctrinal controversies of the 1770s, see Chs. 5 and 6. [138] Seymour, i. 202–3.

[139] Ibid. 205–7.

Grand Tour since 1749, and in 1755 and 1756, in anticipation of his return, Lady Huntingdon found herself back at Donnington Park, supervising building work on his behalf.[140] The demands on her were clearly considerable: in 1756 she described herself as a 'pack-horse', taken up with business, workmen, and sickness, night and day. But there is no sense of complaint in her letters; possibly she was glad to do anything to sustain the affection of her son and keep open the possibility that he would one day follow her religious sentiments.[141] It was a battle she lost with him, and lost also in the case of her elder daughter Elizabeth, who in 1752 moved out of her influence by marrying an Irish peer, Lord Rawdon, subsequently Earl of Moira. Lady Huntingdon rejoiced that her new son-in-law was a man in whom great fortune was combined with great seriousness, but it is clear that a principal motive for Elizabeth marrying was to escape her mother's religious dominance.[142]

The decade was one of loss in other ways. Two of the Countess's sisters-in-law, Frances and Anne, died in 1751 and 1755 respectively. In 1758, occurred the death of Lady Huntingdon's youngest child, Henry, then aged eighteen.[143] Finally, 1760 saw the execution for murder of her cousin, the 4th Earl Ferrers. Parts of the Earl's estates were escheated to the Crown, following his conviction, and this exacerbated the complexities of the Countess's own financial position.[144]

---

[140] Welch (p. 75) quotes various contemporary criticisms of the taste displayed by Lady Huntingdon in the work, though one of these was by John Byng, who rarely had a good word to say of any house he encountered in his extensive travels (*Byng's Tours*, ed. D. Sugden (London, 1991)). More significantly, Francis himself was appalled, and spent nearly a decade altering the alterations (Schlenther, 59 and n).

[141] LH to CW, 4 May 1755, Meth. Arch. (LH), 40; LH to Francis, 21 July 1755; Theophilus Lindsey to Francis, HMC, iii. 100, 111; LH to CW, 29 June 1756, 5 and 27 July 1756, 3 Feb. 1758. Meth. Arch. (LH), 57, 58, 59, 64. One letter of hers to Francis avoids directly evangelical preaching, but sets her sense of an eternal order against his 'real truly earthly' pleasures; it speaks as much of a generational as a religious gap between them (LH to Francis, 20 Jan. 1758, HMC, iii. 134).

[142] Mother and daughter were never to meet again, and there was apparently no contact at all between them during the last twenty years of LH's life (LH to CW, 4 May 1755, Meth. Arch. (LH), 40; Belsham, *Lindsey*, 321; Seymour, i. 460; Schlenther, 60, 62).

[143] LH to CW, 10 Oct. and 5 Dec. 1758, Meth. Arch. (LH), 66, 67.

[144] Welch, 78.

The Start of the Countess's Connexion

Lady Anne's death had not been without its attendant consolations, however. Lady Huntingdon was delighted when Ingham appeared in the midst of the funeral preparations, a contact which she believed would help reconcile him to the family.[145] Lady Huntingdon followed Ingham back to Yorkshire to see Margaret who was 'in vast affliction' (from some unspecified cause); Lady Huntingdon told Charles Wesley that she had found the Inghams 'very simple of heart' and it may have been on this occasion that she attempted (unsuccessfully) to effect a reconciliation between Ingham, whose societies were now cut off from the rest of the Revival, and Whitefield and the Wesleys.[146] Despite the fact of Ingham's continued isolation, however, Lady Huntingdon maintained contact with him over the following years,[147] though it seems likely that those links became more tenuous later, particularly after Margaret's death in 1768.[148]

Despite the evidence of activity during the 1750s, there are periodic signs that Lady Huntingdon was still unsure whether she had yet found her true role. In 1752 she wrote that she had been in darkness for two years, seeking God's will for her.[149] In 1756—by which time she had established herself in a small religious colony with a group of similarly minded ladies at Clifton, near Bristol—she confessed to a fear of settling down to what she most dreaded, 'to live for myself'.[150] In 1758 she was waiting for guidance on what she was being called to next.[151] Equally uncertain was her impact

---

[145] LH to CW, n.d. (but stamped 7 July), Meth. Arch. (LH), 42. LH had renewed contacts with Margaret, quite soon after the latter's marriage, but the estrangement between Ingham and his wife's family appears to have continued (Welch, 47. Schlenther, 45).

[146] LH to CW, n.d. (marked 24 July 1755), 27 Aug. 1755, Meth. Arch. (LH), 43, 46; Seymour, i. 268–9.

[147] She is said to have stayed with the Inghams in 1760, for example, and to have taken either Venn or Romaine there with her (Seymour, i. 233, 273).

[148] The last reference to him in the Cheshunt archives is an enquiry on his behalf about the size of LH's finger for a mourning ring for Margaret (Jane Mott to LH, 28 May 1768, F1/1432,CF).

[149] LH to (?) CW, 7 Oct. 1752, Meth. Arch. (LH), 24.

[150] LH to CW, n.d. (marked Aug. 1756), Meth. Arch. (LH), 61. The community was comparatively short-lived, mainly owing to the rival attraction of the Moravian congregation in Bristol, which was joined by several of the women (Welch, 84–5; Schlenther, 49).   [151] LH to CW, 2 Feb. 1758, Meth. Arch. (LH), 64.

upon others. One correspondent, not himself sympathetic to Methodist enthusiasm, described her to Doddridge in 1750 as a 'gentle angel', while Wesley in 1761 found her a 'more charming woman than ever'.[152] But to a correspondent of Charles Wesley in 1755 she came over as self-important and confused, presenting 'a hotch-potch of opinions gleaned from everywhere without discretion, which, as she delivers them, encounter each other with repugnancies, to the amazement surely of the shrinking, to the admiration of the simple and the confusion of her own heart'.[153]

THE 1760S

A new phase in the Countess's work began in 1761 with the opening of the first of her own chapels, at Brighton. It may have been her son Henry's final illness that brought her to Brighton initially, but the precise impetus for the decision to build a chapel is unclear. Seymour suggests that her ministry arose from the gathering of poor women who came together spontaneously to be instructed by her, after she had been overheard ministering to the physical and spiritual needs of a soldier's wife.[154] It may alternatively have been a perceptive appreciation on Lady Huntingdon's part of the way Brighton (at that time meagrely supplied with places of worship) would develop as a fashionable resort. Or it may have stemmed from the curious incident of a local inhabitant (previously unknown to Lady Huntingdon) who met the Countess by chance and informed her that she had dreamed, years before, of a person answering her description coming to Brighton and 'doing much good'.[155] Possibly all three factors played a part, together with a recognition that Wesley had as yet made few inroads into Sussex, and that Brighton would provide a convenient base for the

---

[152] Robert Phillimore, *Memoirs and Correspondence of George, Lord Lyttleton*, (London, 1845), i. 420–3; Parkinson (ed.) *Byrom*, 629.
[153] George Stonehouse to CW, 2 Apr. 1755, Meth. Arch. (Letters to CW), vol. 6.
[154] Seymour, i. 312.
[155] The story is told by Augustus Toplady, *Works* (London, 1794), 183.

development of a ministry in the county.[156] In 1759 Whitefield was brought down to preach in the open air, possibly to test the scope for a permanent ministry; in 1761 a small chapel was opened (by Madan) adjoining the house which Lady Huntingdon had acquired in North Street, Brighton.[157] To finance the undertaking she borrowed £500 (with interest) from her friend, Lady Gertrude Hotham, and she may also have sold some of her jewels.[158]

The usefulness of Brighton as a bridgehead for work in Sussex was confirmed soon after its opening when Lady Huntingdon was approached by the owner of a house called Ote Hall (or Oathall) some eight miles north of Brighton, near Wivelsfield. The suggestion, which Lady Huntingdon accepted, was that she should rent the house, converting the great hall into a place of worship, and using the upper rooms for herself or visiting ministers.[159] Ote Hall became a Connexional chapel in its own right,[160] although its nearness to Brighton meant, in the early years at least, that the two chapels were treated together for the purpose of arranging

---

[156] N. Caplan, 'Outline of the Origins and Early Development of Nonconformity in Sussex, 1603-1803' (1961), iv, MS in Dr Williams's Library, London; J. D. Walsh, 'The Origins of the Evangelical Revival' in G. V. Bennett and J. D. Walsh (eds.), *Essays in Modern English Church History in Memory of Norman Sykes* (London, 1966).

[157] Seymour, i. 314.

[158] Legal agreement between LH and Lady Gertrude Hotham, 16 Feb. 1762, F1/6 and 7,CF. Lady Gertrude was the sister of the Earl of Chesterfield. She had been an intimate of LH from the early 1750s, supporting her in her mission to fashionable society, and occasionally making her house available for preaching by the leaders of the Revival (see Seymour, i. 121, 210; ii. 1). Her son, Sir Charles Hotham, became a committed member of the same circle after the early death of his wife in 1759 (ibid. 456-7). There is evidence that LH's friend Miss Orton sold jewels to finance the rebuilding of the Brighton chapel in 1774, and this may be the source of the story of LH selling jewels to finance the original chapel (see Mrs Haweis's footnote on LH to Mrs Haweis, 1 May 1774, Bridwell Library MS, 82).

[159] Seymour, i. 316-17.

[160] The precise date of its foundation is not clear. It was registered in the Lewes archdeaconry as a 'presbyterian' meeting in Mar. 1762, but unregistered at LH's request in May 1763 (Caplan, 'Nonconformity in Sussex'). The Ote Hall chapel in Wivesfield Green celebrated its bicentenary in May 1978, commemorating thereby the move of the congregation out of the house to their current place of worship in the village—information for which I am indebted to the then minister, Mr A. L. Spencer. LH was, however, to retain the use of some rooms in the house after 1778 (LH to Mrs Wills, 11 May 1779, Rylands MS (LH); H. Killey to LH, Jan. 1789; T. Jones to LH, 21 June 1790, F1/807, 923,CF).

preaching supplies.[161] Lady Huntingdon stayed in the house on occasions.[162] Sometimes the place was used for what appear to have been religious house parties: when Howel Harris was staying there in 1765, he described how he discoursed daily 'in the family' to a company that included 'Sir Charles Hotham & 2 Elderly Ladies'.[163]

During the 1760s the presence thus established in Sussex for the Countess's Connexion[164] was to spread more widely. Possibly her initiative coincided with a general development of new independent congregations in the county; 1764 and 1765, for example, witnessed the registration of no less than seven new congregations of Protestant Dissenters in Sussex (at Henfield, Bolney, Rottingdean, Hurstpierpoint, Lindfield, Rigmer, and Ditchling).[165] It is not possible to say how far these may be attributed to the efforts of the Connexion, although it may be significant that the registrations of the first three were in the name of Richard Harman, a layman who was to take a prominent part in the administrative affairs of the Brighton and Ote Hall chapels, and more generally in the Connexion's work in the county.[166] Of the seven places listed, four—Hurstpierpoint, Ringmer, Ditchling, and Rottingdean—are known to have been the scene, before the decade was out, of preaching by men connected with Lady Huntingdon and based at Brighton.[167] Other places in Sussex visited by preachers operating from

---

[161] For evidence of interchange between the two chapels, see Maxfield to LH, 19 Sept. 1766; Glascott to LH, 29 July 1767; Scott to Shirley, 13 Dec. 1777, F1/1395, 1403; E4/1 (23),CF.

[162] Lady G. Hotham and Mrs Carteret to LH, 7 June 1768; Lady Manners to LH, 20 July 1772; Maxfield to LH, 19 Sept. 1766; Glascott to LH, 6 Oct. 1766, F1/32, 187, 1395–6,CF.

[163] Harris to Mrs Harris, 1 June 1765 (Trevecca Letters, no. 2603).

[164] It is not certain when the term 'Connexion' was first used of those associated with LH. But as the 1760s progressed and the task for her loose band of occasional helpers became more defined, it is increasingly meaningful to talk of them in more formal, organizational terms.   [165] Caplan, 'Nonconformity in Sussex'.

[166] Harman to LH, 19 Apr. 1769; 5 July 1769; 16 Mar. 1772; 8 Jan. 1774; Peckwell to LH, 6 Apr. n.y., F1/60, 72, 175, 320, 1244, CF. He also registered a congregation in Brighton at this time.

[167] Seymour, i. 382–3; De Courcy to LH, 8 July 1769; Sheppard to LH, 19 Jan. 1769; Peckham to LH, 14 June 1768, F1/73, 46, 34,CF.

The Start of the Countess's Connexion 51

Brighton in the 1760s included Ferring and Arundel in 1767,[168] Angmering in 1768,[169] and Laughton in 1769.[170] In 1765 Lady Huntingdon established a new centre of Connexional activity with the opening of the third of her chapels, at Bath. In the next phase of her life, Bath and Trevecca College (founded three years later) became Lady Huntingdon's main places of residence, and thus the focal points for her work. As has been seen, she was no stranger to Bath, nor to the problems of ministering in so fashionable a resort, and it appears that she was already attempting an informal ministry in the city. She could reasonably have argued, indeed, that in opening a new chapel she was responding to a practical need, since the existing Wesleyan society in Bath was small, and there were insufficient Anglican churches for the population.[171] But the decision to build a chapel implied a particular challenge to polite society. Lady Huntingdon clearly felt the isolation of her position; in 1764 she wrote that 'My Chapel is above Ground & I find I am heartily *wished to die* before it is finished.'[172] The chapel plainly met its object of reaching out to the aristocracy, even if curiosity (perhaps even a sense, as Horace Walpole suggested, of attendance at Lady Huntingdon's chapel becoming one of the events of a fashionable season)[173] played a part in attracting congregations. According to Seymour, Whitefield's dedication of the chapel in October 1765 was attended by 'great numbers of the nobility' specially invited by Lady Huntingdon,[174] and there is

---

[168] Glascott to LH, 31 Aug. 1767, F1/1404,CF; Cyril H. Valentine, *The Story of the Beginnings of Nonconformity in Arundel* (Harpenden, c.1925), 16–17.
[169] Shipman to LH, 23 June 1768, E4/5(4),CF.
[170] De Courcy to LH, 8 July 1769, F1/73,CF.
[171] In 1764 the Revd Walter Shirley (see below) was in correspondence with her about a possible 'return' to Bath (Shirley to LH, 24 Apr. 1764, F1/1392,CF; Ian Crowe, 'Methodism and its Critics in Eighteenth Century Bath', M. Litt. thesis (Bristol, 1991), 9, 23).
[172] LH to CW, 9 June 1764, Meth. Arch. (LH), 75. Two years later the talk of LH in Bath was 'that her son has taken out a Statute of Lunacy against her: that Madness is incident to the family: and that she is sister to that Lord Ferrers, who was hanged at Tyburn'. *Letters from Bath, 1766–1767, by the Rev. John Penrose*, eds. Brigitte Mitchell and Hubert Penrose (Gloucester, 1983), 60.
[173] Seymour, i. 477. Walpole's description of the chapel—'very neat, with *true* Gothic windows'—gives the sense that the building's physical appearance was also designed to appeal to fashionable sensitivities.   [174] Ibid. 468.

evidence of fashionable attendance continuing over the coming years.[175] At a more mundane level, however, the chapel was to expose Lady Huntingdon to some of the conflicting priorities involved in maintaining preaching supplies at more than one major location. At the time of the opening she was involved in an argument with Romaine over whether his attendance in Bath was more important than his continued preaching at Brighton and Ote Hall.[176] Her correspondence over the following years shows periodic evidence of confused dates and muddled plans.[177] Nor were the financial needs of the chapel allowed to be very far from her mind.[178]

Seymour claims that around the time of the opening of the Bath chapel Lord Chesterfield provided an opening for her in the Midlands, by making available his house and chapel at Bretby, near Burton-upon-Trent. According to this account, Lady Huntingdon established a preaching presence there for a period, to congregations both in the chapel and in the open air in the park. But though Seymour speaks of Bretby as one of her 'chapels', there are no subsequent references to work there.[179]

There was to be one more new chapel opened in the 1760s, at Tunbridge Wells in 1769. The town had been in her eye for some time. In 1763, according to Seymour, she made an expedition there with Madan and Venn, who preached both in a Presbyterian meeting house (which Wesley had previously used) and in the open air.[180] Subsequently she acquired a house in the Mount Ephraim area of the town, and had by 1768 established a regular preaching presence (possibly in her house) before finding a suitable nearby spot to build what she termed an 'altar'.[181]

---

[175] e.g. Lloyd to LH, 21 Mar. 1768; Sheppard to LH, 19 Jan. 1769, F1/25, 46,CF.
[176] Seymour, i. 467.
[177] e.g. Glascott to LH, 3 July 1767; Lloyd to LH, 6 Mar. and 13 Oct. 1768; F1/1402, 1415, 41,CF; LH to Whitefield, 17 Apr. 1768, Meth. Arch. (LH), 115.
[178] Lloyd to LH, 23 Apr. 1768, F1/1421,CF.
[179] Seymour, i. 466, 133, 290, 366.
[180] Ibid. ii. 124–5, which quotes her account of Venn's and Madan's preaching.
[181] LH to Whitefield, 17 Apr. 1768, Meth. Arch. (LH), 115; Maxfield to LH, 16 Apr., 5 and 14 May 1768; Glascott to LH, 30 May 1768, F1/1419, 1425, 1429, 1433,CF.

The Start of the Countess's Connexion

As with Brighton, it is likely that Lady Huntingdon wanted to establish a centre for the development of work in the county, as well as catering for those drawn to the town as a fashionable watering place. There was evidence, even before the establishment of the chapel, of a preaching opportunity opening up in the vicinity,[182] and the chapel, like that at Bath, was built to appeal to the refined sensitivities of visitors to the Wells 'after the Gothic taste, in a plain but very elegant manner'.[183] Whitefield performed the opening ceremony, one of his last public acts before leaving England for the last time.[184]

By the time Tunbridge Wells was opened, Lady Huntingdon had secured for herself an alternative source of preaching manpower in the students of the training college which she had opened in South Wales the year before.[185] During the 1760s she had also been expanding the circle of clerical helpers on whose services she could draw. One such was her cousin, Walter Shirley,[186] who had become rector of Loughrea in the Irish diocese of Tuam in the late 1750s, and who owed his conversion principally to the influence of Henry Venn.[187] His references to his parish do not suggest that he had the fulfilled parochial ministry of a Berridge or a Fletcher,[188] and the possibility of his exchanging his Irish living for one in England, together with the impediments which his Irish commitments placed on his ability to serve Lady Huntingdon, form a recurring theme of his letters.[189] From around 1760, however, his involvement with the Countess's work was to increase. He was ministering in Bath in the early 1760s, and although he declined her invitation to become more regularly involved after the opening of the

---

[182] Lloyd to LH, 5 May 1768, F1/1424,CF. A correspondent at the end of the century commented on how Tunbridge Wells had once been a mother church to the area. (S. Dickenson to Lady AE, 23 Oct. 1795, F1/1030,CF).

[183] *Lloyds Evening Post*, Monday 31 July 1769, 102.

[184] Tyerman, *Whitefield*, ii. 560   [185] Ch. 5 below.

[186] The Hon. and Revd Walter Shirley (1725–86) was the fourth son of the 1st Earl Ferrers, and brother of the 4th Earl (who was hanged) and of the 5th and 6th Earls.

[187] Seymour, ii. 155 n.   [188] e.g. Shirley to LH, 6 Sept. 1760, E4/1(2),CF.

[189] Shirley to LH, 18 July 1767, 12 May (? 1772), 17 Sept. 1782, 14 Sept. 1779, E4/1(5) (7) (24), F1/448,CF.

Bath chapel,[190] there are signs of growing participation in her activities, as well as preaching for Whitefield.[191] In 1770 he joined the ranks of Lady Huntingdon's official chaplains, in succession to Whitefield,[192] and over the following decade was to play a significant part in the work of her major chapels.

Another clergyman whose contacts with Lady Huntingdon developed in the 1760s and who was to play a major part in the later history of the Connexion, was Thomas Haweis.[193] Haweis had been educated at Truro Grammar School under a celebrated evangelical schoolmaster, George Conon, and converted through the ministry of one of Conon's earlier pupils, Samuel Walker, curate of Truro. Haweis went up to Oxford in 1755 with the promise of financial support from Joseph Jane, the evangelical vicar of St Mary Magdalen, Oxford, whose curate he subsequently became. While at Oxford Haweis was responsible for the formation of a circle of evangelical young men who constituted what was in a sense a second Holy Club. Haweis had come to Whitefield's attention in the 1750s,[194] and may have become acquainted with Lady Huntingdon then also; by his own account she showed him kindness when episcopal and other hostility effectively drove him from his Oxford curacy in 1762.[195] On moving to London to assist Madan at the Lock, Haweis joined briefly the circle of clergy on whom Lady Huntingdon could call for service at her chapels.[196] Haweis's decision to

---

[190] LH to CW, 9 June 1764, Meth. Arch. (LH), 75. Shirley to LH, 24 Apr. 1764, F1/1392,CF.
[191] Seymour, ii. 156, 13, 99. Shirley to LH, 18 July 1767, E4/1(5),CF.
[192] Shirley to LH, 19 Nov. 1770, F1/1568,CF.
[193] 1735–1820. Matriculated at Christ Church, Oxford, 1755; deacon 1757; priest 1758; curate of St Mary Magdalen, Oxford, 1757–62; assistant curate of the Lock Hospital, 1762–4; rector of Aldwincle, Northamptonshire, 1764–1820. Author of hymns and hymn tunes, devotional works, biblical commentaries and translations, and historical works including a Church history from the time of Christ to the Evangelical Revival. One of the initiators of the London Missionary Society in 1795 (A. S. Wood, *Thomas Haweis* (London, 1957)). [194] Seymour, i. 226.
[195] Thomas Haweis, *An Impartial and Succinct History of the Rise, Declension and Revival of the Church of Christ, from the Birth of our Saviour to the Present Time* (London, 1800), iii. 247; *Evangelical Magazine* (1800), 287; Wood, *Haweis*, 89.
[196] Ibid. 89–90 n. 5.

accept the living of Aldwincle in 1764 brought that first period of association with Lady Huntingdon to an end, as well as involving him in an episode of public controversy over allegations that he had acquired his living by simony, that was to last most of the decade—a row into which Lady Huntingdon intervened in 1768 on his behalf, but on her volition and with not the happiest of effects.[197] Haweis retained the Aldwincle living for the remainder of his life, but in 1774 was to return to active service in the Connexion when he joined the ranks of Lady Huntingdon's chaplains.[198] He remained near the centre of the Connexion's affairs for the rest of that decade and then again, after a gap of some years, during the final years of Lady Huntingdon's life; at her death he found himself one of the four trustees to whom Lady Huntingdon entrusted the future management of the Connexion.

A younger but equally significant recruit during the 1760s was Cradock Glascott[199] who may well have been part of Haweis's latter day Holy Club.[200] He was a curate in 1766 when Lady Huntingdon invited him to join her as full-time member of her developing Connexion; he did so in May 1767, once he was free of his curacy.[201] Glascott had thought himself fit only for a country congregation, but he was very quickly engaged across the range of Connexional work, preaching at the major chapels and undertaking preaching tours,[202] as well as doing temporary duty for some of the

---

[197] Haweis's patron, by then imprisoned for debt, claimed that Haweis had agreed, before accepting the living, that he would subsequently resign or purchase the advowson, an action which, if Haweis had so agreed, would have constituted the offence of simony. The patron was represented as the injured party in the pamphlet campaign that developed against Haweis; LH's remedy of herself buying the advowson (in order to end what she saw as a damaging scandal) was represented as the payment of hush money, and for a time, made matters worse (Ibid. 105–9, 127–41).

[198] Ibid. 149; LH to Hawksworth, 2 Apr. 1774; Peckwell to LH, 28 Mar. 1774, G2/1(10); F1/283,CF. Apparently, the appointment was not officially registered with the ecclesiastical authorities until 1779.

[199] c.1743–1831. Jesus College, Oxford, 1760; BA, 1763; ordained deacon, 1765; curate of Cleveley, Berkshire, 1765–7; MA, 1767; vicar of Hatherleigh, Devon, 1781–1831.   [200] Wood, *Haweis*, 74.

[201] Glascott to LH, 6 Oct. 1766; 15 May 1767, F1/1396, 1401,CF.

[202] Roberts, *Trevecka Letters*, ii. 114. Glascott may have been preaching at Brighton as early as 1765 (LH to (?) n.d. (but marked 1765), Bridwell Library MS, 59).

principal leaders of the Revival to free them for service in the Connexion.[203] Glascott's association with Lady Huntingdon nearly came to an end in 1769, after reports that he had offered his permanent services to Madan at the Lock,[204] and for a time, he wondered whether to accept another curacy. But he was restored to favour, something which was to happen again in 1776 after he had been bold enough to mention his thoughts of marriage and a more settled ministry,[205] and in 1781 when he did actually accept a living.[206] Rarely did relations with Lady Huntingdon survive her suspicions that followers were less than totally loyal, and this repeated restoration to favour may be a testimony to the winsomeness of Glascott's personality. Certainly he emerges as one of the most appealing of all Lady Huntingdon's circle. In the midst of the doctrinal arguments in which the Connexion became embroiled in the early 1770s, for example, Glascott wrote that though he himself favoured the system 'commonly called *calvinistic*', he knew that 'many good and eminent persons have disagreed', so that he favoured moderation and tenderness.[207]

A near contemporary of Glascott, but from Cambridge, was Rowland Hill.[208] Rowland was the younger brother of Richard Hill, who succeeded to the baronetcy of Hawkstone in 1783, and was a prominent evangelical layman and an MP.[209] Rowland had been converted through his brother's

---

[203] There were plans for him to do this for Romaine in 1767 (Glascott to LH, 8 Oct. 1767, F1/1406,CF); for Fletcher and Maxfield in 1768 (Lloyd to LH, 13 Oct., 20 June 1768, F1/41, 35,CF); and for Berridge in 1769 (Seymour, ii. 28).

[204] Lloyd to LH, 1 July 1769; Glascott to LH, 29 May, 13 June 1769; de Courcy to LH, 8 July 1769, F1/71, 1468, 1470, 1474, 73,CF. There was a romantic entanglement also, though the girl's mother praised the role Glascott had played in the incident (Mrs Leighton to LH, 6 Mar., n.y., F1/1211,CF).

[205] Glascott to LH, 18 Dec. 1776, F1/371,CF.

[206] If it were true, as P. E. Sangster suggested in 'The Life of the Rev. Rowland Hill and his Position in the Evangelical Revival', D. Phil. thesis (Oxford, 1964), 140, that Glascott promised his bishop that he would never preach outside his parish, he did not keep his word; he remained an active member of the Connexion to the end of LH's life and beyond (e.g. Glascott to LH, 27 Apr. 1791; Glascott to Mr Kingston, 26 Mar. 1801, F1/2176, 2390,CF).

[207] Glascott to LH, 3 June 1771, F1/125,CF.

[208] 1744–1833. St John's College, Cambridge, 1764; BA, 1769; MA, 1772; ordained deacon 1773.

[209] Richard had done some early field preaching and was to play a significant part in the St Edmund Hall affair in the late 1760s (see Ch. 5), but his

influence, and he was to attract opposition at Cambridge on account of the religious group which formed around him and the irregular preaching on which he embarked. Whitefield and Berridge both became supporters of the young evangelist,[210] and at some stage in the later 1760s he was brought to the attention of Lady Huntingdon. Rowland stayed with her in Bath in 1767, when she treated him 'as my own son—received into my house and preached in my pulpits'.[211] She attempted to reconcile his parents to their son's religious views, without apparent success at the time, though with some later beneficial effects.[212] Rowland was to continue occasional preaching for her in the late 1760s, and early 1770s, as well as in Whitefield's and other pulpits,[213] although it was not until 1773 that he finally secured ordination to the diaconate. He was never priested. Later in the 1770s he was to fall out with Lady Huntingdon, however, and deep hostility replaced the warmth with which she had previously regarded him.[214]

Three others of Lady Huntingdon's clerical helpers in the 1760s deserve mention. One was Joseph Townsend,[215] who was converted through his sister Judith, subsequently the wife of Thomas Haweis. Townsend's father, Alderman Townsend, was the MP for Lord Shelburne's borough of Calne, a link which, despite parental opposition to Methodist doctrines, was to prove a valuable asset in Townsend's ministry, especially when he was preaching in Ireland in 1770.[216] Townsend's living of Pewsey was sufficiently close to Bath for

---

contribution to the wider evangelical cause was to prove limited (F. K. Brown, *The Fathers of the Victorians* (Cambridge, 1961), 68; Sangster, 'Rowland Hill', 151–3).

[210] Rupp, *Religion in England*, 479.   [211] Seymour, ii. 10.
[212] Rowland Hill to LH, 7 Jan. 1772, F1/164,CF.
[213] Peckham to LH, 14 June 1768, F1/34,CF. Peckham was not enamoured of Hill's theatrical airs and unguarded expressions (see also Seymour, ii. 49–50; Sangster, 'Rowland Hill', ch. 2).   [214] Seymour, ii. 318.
[215] 1739–1816; son of an alderman who was later an MP. Clare Hall, Cambridge; BA, 1762; MA, 1765; subsequently fellow. Rector of Pewsey, Wiltshire from 1764. Publications included a travel journal, works on medicine and the Poor Laws, and a major study of the life of Moses (Wood, *Haweis*, 90–1; *DNB*; *Blackwell*).
[216] Seymour, ii. 159 n. Mrs Phillips to LH, 23 July 1770; Mrs Shirley to LH, 4 Aug. n.y., F1/1505, 1506,CF. There was recurring speculation, which came to nothing, that Shelburne might make Townsend a bishop (Mrs Shirley to LH, 10 Sept. n.y.; Lloyd to LH, 13 Sept. 1782. F1/1262, 1863,CF).

him to be able to provide regular assistance from there.[217] Despite his involvement in the 1760s, however, there is little evidence of his serving the Connexion in the following decade. Much the same goes for William Jesse,[218] who may have been another of Haweis's Oxford group in the late 1750s.[219] Jesse became associated with Lady Huntingdon about the same time as Haweis. He was one of those to whom Lady Huntingdon looked regularly for assistance during the 1760s,[220] but again there is little evidence of active involvement thereafter.[221]

The pattern repeats itself with Richard de Courcy,[222] the descendant of an ancient Irish family, who was Shirley's curate in Ireland for a spell, before coming to England in the late 1760s. He had not been able to secure priest's orders in Ireland, and his journey to England, apparently at Lady Huntingdon's invitation, seems to have been designed to facilitate his chances.[223] His services for Lady Huntingdon included an extensive preaching campaign in Sussex in the summer of 1769, and Seymour claims that he participated in the opening ceremonies at Tunbridge Wells.[224] In 1770 he

---

[217] Roberts, *Trevecka Letters*, ii. 92; Glascott to LH, 23 Dec. 1766 and 15 May 1767; Lloyd to LH, 6 Mar. 1768, F1/1397, 1401, 1415,CF. In 1765, LH hoped he would come to Brighton, and also join Romaine and Venn in accompanying her on a trip to Derbyshire (LH to Mrs Wadsworth, 7 Mar. 1765; LH to Townsend, 4 June 1765, Bridwell Library MSS, 2, 51).

[218] c.1739–1815. Trinity College, Oxford, 1757; BA, 1761. Vicar of Hutton Granswick, Yorkshire, 1767; vicar of West Bromwich, 1790. Published works on Christian evidences and *Parochialia* (letters to a cleric on the discharge of parish duties) (*Blackwell*). [219] Wood, *Haweis*, 74.

[220] LH to Townsend, 4 June 1765, Bridwell Library MS, 51; LH to CW, 4 Feb. 1767, Meth. Arch. (LH), 76; Glascott to LH, 5 June 1768, F1/1434,CF.

[221] By 1781 he was regarded formally as having left her, although this did not prevent her, two years later, recommending him to the patronage of the evangelical layman John Thornton (Seymour, ii. 460; Thornton to LH, 7 Oct. 1783, F1/554,CF).

[222] Trinity College, Dublin. Later curate of Shawbury and then vicar of St Alkmond's, Shrewsbury (J. W. Middelton, *The Ecclesiastical History of the First Four Decades of the Reign of George III* (London, 1822), 62–4).

[223] Seymour, ii. 156–8; Tyerman, *Whitefield*, ii. 516. There is some disagreement over the date of De Courcy's arrival in England, though 1769 seems the most likely (Fletcher to LH, 12 Apr. 1769, F1/1464,CF).

[224] Mrs Carteret to LH, n.d., F1/1144,CF; Seymour, i. 382–5; ii. 128–9. Seymour must be wrong in saying that he gave the sacrament at Tunbridge Wells, since at this stage he was still only a deacon.

preached for Whitefield and Wesley in London, before going to Scotland the following year[225] to join forces with Lady Glenorchy.[226] De Courcy was one of those whom Lady Huntingdon later described as having left her.[227] Despite the signs that he remained on good terms with her during the 1770s—for example, by assisting one of her students to ordination by providing a curacy at his parish in Shrewsbury, offering his pulpit to her ministers, and recommending a student to her college—there is no evidence that he himself preached for her again.[228]

The building of chapels and the development of a corps of clerical assistants,[229] which were the leading features of Lady Huntingdon's work during the 1760s, meant that her contribution to the Revival had entered a new phase. From a very early stage, as seen, she had provided the leaders of the Revival with counsel and support, and the 1760s witnessed a continued contribution by her to the strategic development of its disparate factions. Likewise, she continued to bring aristocratic support to the movement, and used her position in society to expose to evangelical doctrines many who would not otherwise have come in contact with them. But it was the first tentative steps she had taken towards the establishment of a distinct organization that mark out the 1760s as a watershed in her life. Cautiously—and late in the day compared with Wesleyan and other groups who had

---

[225] Maxfield to LH, 21 Feb. 1771, F1/1528,CF.

[226] 1741–86. A Scottish friend and counterpart of LH, converted in part through the efforts of Rowland Hill's sister; established a small group of chapels, principally in Scotland, but also at Exeter, Matlock, and Bristol. She had initially attempted to maintain a balance between Wesley's preachers and those sympathetic to Calvinism; despite de Courcy's early catholicity, his coming to Edinburgh marked for both of them a clear alignment with the latter camp. [227] Seymour, ii. 460.

[228] De Courcy to LH, 27 Nov. 1776; R. Leggett to Mr Barry, 28 Feb. 1777; J. Williams to LH, 13 Oct. 1787, F1/1737, 1745, 1964,CF.

[229] Including those mentioned, plus the Wesleys and Whitefield, LH could call on around twenty. Other names which occur in the late 1760s, either as willing to help her directly, or as prepared to supply other churches to free them for service to the Countess, were Edward Davies, Howel Davies, Thomas Davies, Richard Hart, Hatton, Moor (the ordinary of Newgate), Matthew Powley, James Rouquet, Edward Sheppard, and Edward Spencer. Some of these occur on the list of thirty or more 'Labourers who are ministers of the Church of England' which JW compiled in 1764 (JW's Journal for 19 Apr. 1764, *Works*, xxi. 454–61).

already established the pattern of a popular religious movement—she had begun to create an entity which was recognizably the Countess of Huntingdon's Connexion. The scale of her work at this stage, however, should not be exaggerated. In 1767 Wesley quoted an estimate of some 24,000 members of Wesleyan societies in Great Britain and Ireland;[230] it is doubtful whether even those who regularly attended Lady Huntingdon's preachers at the end of the decade had yet reached a tenth of that number. Nor is it clear how far she had intended to form a distinct grouping of her own. Her work up to this point can be seen as a continuation of her role as helper and sustainer. It is even possible to regard her as part of the tradition of voluntary religious organizations characteristic of the eighteenth-century Church of England, such as missionary societies or the Elland Society, formed to support the education of ordinands.[231] She organized clergymen to make their proclamation more effective; she built chapels (capable of being regarded as chapels of ease within the parochial structure) to ensure that the Gospel was preached where otherwise it would not be heard; she founded a training college in order (initially) to provide an additional source of Church of England personnel. Yet the steps that she had taken during the 1760s, coupled with the fresh source of preaching manpower that her college provided, meant that the close of the decade saw her Connexion poised on the brink of a significant expansion. Very soon the pattern that was started in Sussex, of itinerant preaching leading to the establishment of new congregations, was to become a feature of the Connexion's work over large parts of the country. Nor were the opportunities open to her constrained by the fact that she was so much behind the other leaders of the Revival in establishing her own network of societies. Rivalries there certainly were in individual localities. But over the country at large there was still a rich

---

[230] JW to R. Costerdine, 24 Nov. 1767, *Letters*, v. 66.
[231] It has been suggested that Wesley's societies are best understood, in the first instance, as some kind of religious order within the Church of England (J. Lawson, 'Our Discipline' in Davies and Rupp (eds.), *History of the Methodist Church*, i. 209).

harvest to be brought in. In 1772, John Newton[232] wrote that 'if I am not much mistaken it is possible to travel more than a hundred miles upon a line in several parts of this kingdom and not come within ten or perhaps twenty miles of a parish on either hand, that has the blessings of a stated parochial Gospel ministry...perhaps (there are) not three in a county upon an average.'[233]

It was this fertile territory that the Countess's Connexion was now poised to enter.

---

[232] 1725–1807. Hymn-writer and author of prose works; after an adventurous seafaring career was ordained as curate of Olney in 1764; rector of St Mary, Woolnoth from 1780; friend of the poet William Cowper; collaborated with almost all who were sympathetic to the Revival, inside and outside the Church, and within Dissent (see Bruce Hindmarsh, *John Newton and the English Evangelical Tradition* (Oxford, 1996)).

[233] Newton to Lord Dartmouth, 11 Nov. 1772, HMC (Dartmouth), iii. 200. In Newton's view the progress which the Revival had made in the established Church did not yet make up for defections from the Gospel among Dissenters over the previous fifty years; the Presbyterians had suffered worst, and he feared that some of the Independents 'are upon tiptoes to follow them'.

4

The Life of the Countess of Huntingdon's Connexion

ITINERANT PREACHING AND THE ESTABLISHMENT OF CONNEXIONAL CAUSES

The initiation of Connexional work

The founding of Trevecca College in 1768 marked a turning point in the life of the Countess of Huntingdon's Connexion.[1] It is not clear whether Lady Huntingdon realized in advance that she was establishing a cadre of immediately available itinerant evangelists. But it was not long before the students were testing their ministerial gifts, first in the vicinity of the college, but then much further afield.[2] By the end of the decade, Lady Huntingdon had a team of young men—perhaps a dozen or more in the course of each year[3]—available for use as itinerant preachers anywhere in the country.

There was nothing unique to the Evangelical Revival about itinerant preaching. Its roots run back into Apostolic times, while the friars of the later Middle Ages showed its value as a stimulus to established church life, as well as being a tool for evangelism. In England, after the Reformation, it is possible to trace a diverse tradition that embraces the Jesuit mission of the sixteenth century, Baptist itinerants before the Commonwealth, the peripatetic ministry of some

---

[1] Ch. 5, below.
[2] On the students' involvement in itinerant preaching, see below.
[3] Below, p. 188.

of those ejected at the Restoration, and the 'public travelling friends' (Quakers) of the end of the seventeenth century.[4] In Wales, the origins of the Evangelical Revival are bound up with the circulating charity schools, the system of itinerant teachers moving from village to village, which was established by Griffith Jones, the rector of Llanddowror, in the 1730s.[5] For Whitefield, Wesley, and other leaders of the Revival, itinerancy was a major instrument in proclaiming the message and winning converts; for Wesley, in particular, itinerancy (his own or that of his principal helpers) was the means of preserving the cohesion of the organization and maintaining standards.[6] When she opened Trevecca, Lady Huntingdon had had three decades in which to observe the impact of itinerancy, both by well-known preachers and by their humbler lay brethren, and she had seen its role in establishing and sustaining a network of congregations. It is little surprise, therefore, that itinerant preaching became a major feature of the life of the college.

The reception that preachers could expect varied considerably. Dissent was more firmly established in certain areas than others—notably in parts of the country characterized by large parishes where manorial and clerical control was consequently loosest. Methodism encountered a similar effect. Poorer upland, heath and woodland areas, areas where land was less in demand and more open to new settlements and chapel-building, and areas less subject to the oversight of parson and squire (and the deference associated with it), were particularly receptive to new religious movements. By contrast, tightly controlled 'estate' parishes could be the most difficult.[7] The pattern of opposition which the

---

[4] D. W. Lovegrove, *Established Church, Sectarian People, Itinerancy and the Transformation of English Dissent, 1780–1830* (Cambridge, 1988), 17, 22; M. R. Watts, *The Dissenters, from the Reformation to the French Revolution* (Oxford, 1978), 308.

[5] Ibid. 424, 425.

[6] F. Baker, 'The People Called Methodists: Polity' in R. Davies and G. Rupp (eds.), *A History of the Methodist Church in Great Britain* (London, 1965) i. 230.

[7] Alan Everitt, 'Nonconformity in Country Parishes', *Agricultural History Review*, 18 (1970), supplement; J. D. Walsh, 'Methodism and the Local Community in the Eighteenth Century', *Vie Ecclesiale, Communauté et Communautés* (Paris, 1989), 141; Bebbington, *Evangelism in Modern Britain* (London, 1989), 26–7.

Connexion encountered showed how significant this sort of local influence could be.[8]

In addition to these underlying social factors, it was also the case that when the students left the College on preaching tours, they did not go—despite the imagery they sometimes used—into a totally pagan wilderness. Though they might be entering areas not previously penetrated by their brethren, it was unlikely that there would not be some people there who would be actively sympathetic towards them, and who would in due course play a vital part in the establishment of the work. The religious background of such people varied greatly: sometimes orthodox Dissenters dissatisfied with Unitarian doctrines in their own chapels; sometimes converts to evangelical doctrines (through Wesleyan or other itinerant preachers) who were now unsupplied; sometimes Churchmen disillusioned by the coldness or sterility of preaching in their parish churches. From such people, very frequently, came the initiative in bringing students into an area; upon them it fell to publicize the students' coming, and where appropriate to find places in which they could preach; they too, if they remained of the same mind when the students had gone on, were likely to form the nucleus of the new congregations. Such people could have a decisive influence upon the pattern of work within their area. For example, the two students preaching at Longtown in Herefordshire early in 1770 were invited on to Ross by a mercer of that town who, though a Dissenter, was evidently not sufficiently in harmony with his brethren to be granted the use of the meeting house. There were prospects, nevertheless, that a congregation might be established.[9]

Once students were known to be active in an area, invitations, whether from individuals or from groups of worshippers already in existence, were regularly received: that was one reason why the Connexion soon developed an impetus of its own. A typical early instance was in Worcestershire in 1771, when the student John Harris reported calls to two or three new places.[10] As the 1770s advanced, and the pace and

[8] Below, pp. 112–15.
[9] Mead and Glazebrook to LH, 15 Feb. 1770, F1/87,CF.
[10] J. Harris to LH, 8 (? Nov.) 1771, F1/1187,CF.

range of the work increased, such invitations became commonplace. 1774, for example, saw invitations from the West Country;[11] from Singleton, Petworth, and other places in Sussex;[12] a second invitation from Nottingham;[13] and many calls from the Chelmsford area.[14] Such invitations continued in the 1780s. In 1783, for example, Samuel Beaufoy was called to Childham in Sussex by a farmer of that town;[15] in the same year, also in Sussex, John Lloyd was unable to answer all the calls he was receiving[16]—and this despite the fact that Sussex had been a centre of Connexional activity since the 1760s. Sometimes invitations might result in only a single visit, or visits for so long as the individual student to whom they were addressed remained in the area. In other cases, the contact thus established with the Connexion proved more permanent—at least to the extent of establishing a nucleus of potential adherents ready to respond to Connexional preachers on a later occasion.

It would be wrong, however, to imply that the development of the Connexion's work was purely reactive, depending upon the presence in any area of a fifth column ready to invite them in. The existence of sympathizers was invaluable, providing as it did not only the prospect of food and shelter for the preacher, but a building (or a field) in which to preach, and some degree of advance publicity. But the absence of such help did not mean that entry to the town or village in question would not be sought. There was obviously a considerable element of personal initiative on Lady Huntingdon's part in the events leading to the establishment of her major chapels like Brighton, Bath, or in the later period, Spa Fields,[17] but even outside these major centres there were instances of what appeared to have been deliberate decisions to attempt to establish a Connexional presence. In 1773 she wrote that she intended sticking to what she called

---

[11] Samuel Clark to LH, 21 May 1774, F1/297,CF.
[12] Peckwell to LH, 25 Feb. 1774, F1/1677,CF.
[13] Glascott to LH, 11 June 1774, F1/1698,CF.
[14] E. Bryant to LH, 12 Dec. 1774, F1/1711,CF.
[15] Samuel Beaufoy to LH, 7 July 1783, F1/2025,CF.
[16] Lloyd to LH, 21 Apr. 1783, F1/514,CF.   [17] See below, Ch. 6.

her old rule of only going where called. Yet only a few months later, she spoke of her plan 'to sound a General & Universal claim over England, in the fields & Citys [*sic*] where the Gospel has not yet been sounded. I see daily our work is more & more universal, both from the leadings of God and also the lively & intrepid spirit of many...in the College.'[18]

Though Lady Huntingdon never attained coverage of the whole country in this way, there are examples, over the following years, of her taking the initiative in particular areas. In 1775, for example, while staying with the Revd Thomas Wills,[19] at St Agnes in Cornwall, Lady Huntingdon found herself drawn to the tin-miners of the area, and wrote of her desire to make two or three new establishments in the heart of the mining country—the premises for the first of which she had already acquired.[20] Contemplating her convalescence in Teignmouth, Devon, three years later, she expressed her sense of having been called to the area and speculated about the prospect, if she could round up sufficient ministerial support, of a 'Romp' in the district.[21] Previous student contacts in the area appear to have been limited, and on arrival she resolved on a scheme to spy out the prospects in Torbay by taking lodgings for a few nights each at several places around the coast. The special significance of Torbay (the place of William of Orange's disembarkation in 1688) was not lost on Lady Huntingdon—'our great temporal deliverer and protector of our Christian liberty having landed there'.[22]

---

[18] LH to Hawkesworth, 13 Oct. 1773, G2/1(8),CF; LH to Mrs Haweis, 17 May 1774, Bridwell Library MS, 82.
[19] 1740–1802. Like Haweis, Wills was a pupil of Conon at Truro Grammar School, and subsequently met Haweis at Oxford. Deacon, 1762; priest, 1764; curate of St Agnes, Cornwall, until he resigned to work full-time in the Connexion in 1778. Married a niece of LH, and was a major figure in the Connexion during the events surrounding its secession from the Church of England in the early 1780s, performed the first Connexional ordination in 1783. Subsequently incurred LH's displeasure and was dismissed from the Connexion in 1788 (J. White Middleton, *An Ecclesiastical Memoir of the First Four Decades of the Reign of George III* (London, 1822), 403–4; Seymour, ii. 54–5; *Memoirs of the life of the Reverend Thomas Wills...by a Friend* (London, 1804)).
[20] LH to Hawkesworth, 23 Sept. 1775, G2/1(15),CF.
[21] LH to Wills, 7 Aug. 1778, Rylands MS, 346/185A, no. 6.
[22] LH to Wills, and to Wills and Mrs Wills, 7 and 20 Aug. 1778, Rylands MS, 346/185A, nos. 6 and 7.

Coincidentally, both these examples come from the West Country, but there is no evident link between them. There were also occasions when individual preachers sought to initiate new areas of work. One early example was the Revd Henry Peckwell,[23] who in 1774 reported that he had been successful at last in his attempt to secure an opening in his home town of Chichester. In this instances the exercise was made easier by the fact that Peckwell already possessed property in Chichester, which was capable of conversion into a chapel.[24] A decade or so later, Wills, on a tour of the Midlands and the North, appears to have made deliberate attempts to initiate work at Stourbridge, Dudley, and Manchester, starting in each place with open-air preaching but attempting to secure the use of premises before moving on.[25] Such efforts were not confined to the more eminent of the Connexion's preachers; in 1787, a former student, David Phillips, received 5 guineas in expenses from the central 'Travelling Fund'[26] on account of his trip to the Isle of Wight to arrange a new call for the Gospel.[27]

Open-air preaching was generally a necessity in places where there were no existing contacts to arrange preaching places—and might still be deemed desirable even where there were sympathizers already present. In 1766 John Wesley commented that it was 'a shame to preach in a house before October',[28] a maxim with which, in the following decade, the Connexion's preachers appear to have had some sympathy. The early 1770s, in particular, provide many examples of the sort of field and street preaching traditionally associated with the origins of Methodism. Ministers and

---

[23] 1747–87. Peckwell was originally intended for a career in the Italian silk trade; influenced in his late teens by attendance at Whitefield's Tabernacle. Matriculated at St Edmund Hall, Oxford, in 1770, then came to the attention of LH, whose chaplain he became in 1773. In 1774 a chapel in Princes Street, Westminster, was repaired and opened for him; subsequently presented to the living of Bloxham-cum-Digby, Lincolnshire. Peckwell became involved in medical and charitable work, and died from infection contracted while performing an operation. His daughter Selina was a goddaughter of Lady Huntingdon (*DNB*; Seymour, ii. 199–200 n.).
[24] Peckwell to LH, 12 Jan. and 19 Feb. 1774, F1/1669, 1675,CF.
[25] *Life of Wills*, 156, 157, 167.   [26] Below, pp. 168–71.
[27] Receipt, 28 Dec. 1787, E4/15(8),CF.
[28] JW to James Rea, 21 July 1766, Wesley, *Letters*, v. 23.

students found themselves preaching in fields, at crossroads, in the dark, in the rain, and on the beach.[29] Ministers and students alike faced opposition, sometimes of an organized kind and often very violent.[30]

Open-air preaching, however, was most obviously a function of the early life of a new connexion. The stage was inevitably reached when the need to consolidate what had been achieved, and to minister to the congregations that had been formed, placed conflicting demands upon the resources of the Connexion. Peckwell recognized this in 1774, although he appeared reluctant to accept that they had yet passed into the more settled phase of the Connexion's development; it would be better to preach than to build that summer, he told Lady Huntingdon, because with the former they would not be committed to the maintenance of supplies.[31] Field preaching certainly seems to have become less frequent in the later 1770s and the 1780s—to the regret of some preachers[32]—but sufficient instances are recorded to show that the practice had by no means died out. Notable examples from the 1780s, of which extensive details have been preserved, were the individual preaching tours of Glascott, Piercy, and Wills in 1781, and the latter's further tours in 1784 and 1785.[33] Glascott's reports to Lady Huntingdon during his journey, which he began at Bristol in July 1781, and which took him through Lincolnshire, Derbyshire, and Yorkshire before his return there in September, provide a classic account of an eighteenth-century preaching tour. The open fields ('the heavens my sounding board' as they had been for Whitefield) combined with churches, meeting houses, and chapels (Wesleyan as

---

[29] Glascott to LH, 25 Sept. 1769 and 24 May 1774; Glazebrook to LH, 13 Dec. 1770; Holmes to LH, 11 July 1774, F1/1476, 1696, 114, 309,CF.
[30] Among typical examples of opposition by the mob to itinerant preachers are Maxfield to LH, Dec. 1768; Peckwell to LH, 1 Mar. 1774; and Glascott to LH, 24 May 1774, F1/1450, 275(b), 1696,CF. On the Connexion's response to attempts to disrupt its formal services, see below, pp. 115–17.
[31] Peckwell to LH, 5 May 1774, F1/288(a),CF.   [32] *Life of Wills*, 71.
[33] Ibid.; *Extracts of the Journals of several ministers of the Gospel, in a series of letters to the Countess of Huntingdon* (London, 1782).

well as Connexional) to provide preaching places; forthcoming sermons were announced in advance by individuals or through newspaper advertisements; and open-air congregations in the order of thousands were reported. Glascott found time, like a man of his age, to reflect as he rode how the beauties of nature mirrored the glories of God; and he concluded from his experience, doubtless recalling the opposition he had faced in earlier years, that prejudices against open-air preaching were declining.[34] Far less is known about the Welsh tour which David Jones of Llangan undertook in 1789, but his comment afterwards that he had been out nearly six weeks, covered nearly 700 miles and preached twice every day, frequently in the open, suggests that the basic pattern remained unchanged.[35]

Among those who responded to the Connexion's preachers there would inevitably have been a proportion whose previous Christian adherence was either nominal or non-existent, and who began thereafter to participate regularly in worship. In the nature of things it is difficult to estimate how significant an element these represented—although much was naturally made in writing to Lady Huntingdon of the presence, at initial sermons or in the newly formed congregations, of those who had not previously been touched by the Revival. It was reported at Ashby in 1772, for example, that many were attending preaching who had not previously been seen elsewhere;[36] in the following year, John Clayton wrote of the opening in Cornwall of two new places that had never previously heard a Gospel sermon.[37] In the same county in 1777, indeed, Wills commented that he had more hopes in 'new' places than where there was an established Dissenting presence.[38] But what is also clear is the part often played in new causes by those who were either already sympathetic to evangelical teachings or were members of a denomination.

---

[34] Glascott to LH, 16 July 1781, 27 July, 4 and 20 Aug. 1781, E4/11, (1,2,4,5),CF. [35] Jones to LH, 8 Oct. 1789, F1/864,CF.
[36] J. Adams to LH, 22 Jan. 1772, F1/1579,CF. Rack, *Wesley*, 441 doubts whether many Wesleyan converts had previously been wholly unchurched.
[37] John Clayton to LH, 23 Jan. 1773, F1/1632,CF.
[38] Wills to LH, 28 Aug. 1777, F1/1783,CF.

A striking example of the former was Putsham in Somerset where students found, when they arrived in 1770, that a society was already in existence, as a result of two of the inhabitants having been stirred by reading Whitefield's sermons.[39] Another instance of work initiated by someone already on the road to faith was shown in a letter from an inhabitant of Sydling near Dorchester who in 1787 described how, already possessed of some light, he had invited over the student Mills, then preaching at Dorchester. Mills's first sermon, in the house of a poor woman, attracted some 150 people, a number which had risen to 200 when he returned a fortnight later; thereafter a fortnightly sermon was instituted and a society formed for study and prayer.[40] Just occasionally, too, it is apparent that areas that were supposedly 'new', so far as the Connexion was concerned, must have been in contact with branches of the Revival well before there is evidence of the Connexion's preachers having arrived. This was the case at Partney in Gloucestershire, where it was remarked in 1789 that its people had sat under the Gospel for the past twenty years.[41]

The outward success of such activities is most obviously measured in terms of the founding of new congregations, and in their ability to sustain permanent premises of their own. But the Connexion's preachers did not lose sight of the fact that their message was addressed primarily to the hearts and consciousness of individuals. Their Master had taught of joy in Heaven over each single repenting sinner, and their correspondence reflected as much concern with evidence of actual 'saving conversions', as with the overall numbers of those who attended. The numbers of the former were often quite small. One student wrote, for example, that seven or eight had been awakened under him;[42] another that there

---

[39] Hawkesworth to Howel Harris, 9 Oct. 1771, Trevecca Letters, no. 2700. Putsham had a somewhat chequered history subsequently, but was still being regularly supplied by the Connexion at the time of LH's death (see especially Glazebrook to LH, 15 Apr. 1772; Spurrier to LH, 26 Jan. 1778; McKain to Lady AE, 26 Sept. 1791, F1/177, E4/2(38), F1/977,CF).
[40] John Hopkins Jnr. to LH, 3 Oct. 1787, F1/1962,CF.
[41] John Lewis to LH, 22 Jan. 1789, F1/808,CF.
[42] Mead to LH, 15 Nov. 1771, F1/139,CF.

had been 'several' awakenings;[43] and a third that six ascribed their awakening to him.[44] Occasionally the numbers quoted reached double figures, as with the ten reported at Wolverhampton in 1783,[45] and the twenty to thirty in two or three adjacent parishes, following the summer labours of another preacher in 1776.[46] More normal was the case of Pentycross, however, for whom Revival in his parish consisted of two or three individuals awakened each week.[47] Another writer reported engagingly that three had been called at Ote Hall, plus a further three they were not sure of.[48] The assumption of each of these correspondents appeared to be that Lady Huntingdon would be as enthusiastic about such results as the preachers were themselves. Their concern with the value and significance of each individual soul was an important element in the life and development of the Countess's Connexion.

There is evidence that all the main reformed denominations—including the Church of England—were represented in the new Connexional congregations. The initial Dover congregation, for example, was formed from a group of former Wesleyans;[49] the Worcester congregation in 1775 included Baptists, Wesleyans, and Presbyterians;[50] while the group at Basingstoke, which sought entry to the Connexion in 1783, was said to be a mix of Churchmen and Dissenters.[51] Basingstoke, indeed, was typical of a not infrequent situation: an existing congregation, in some cases already possessed of an appropriate building, turning to the Connexion as a source of preaching supplies. Other examples of established congregations seeking the Connexion's help were the

---

[43] A. Crole to LH, 3 Apr. 1775, F1/322,CF.
[44] T. French to LH, 3 Dec. 1777, F1/418,CF.
[45] T. Hasker to LH, 31 Jan. 1783, F1/1880,CF.
[46] Molland to LH, 14 Jan. 1777, F1/377,CF.
[47] Pentycross to LH, 19 Feb. 1783, F1/509,CF. Pentycross's experience seems on a par with John Newton's, who estimated after ten years at Olney that around 100 had been awakened under his ministry (Bruce Hindmarsh, *John Newton and the English Evangelical Tradition* (Oxford, 1996), 188).
[48] Lloyd to LH, 21 Apr. 1783, F1/514,CF.
[49] William Atwood to Robert Keen, 12 Mar. 1776, F1/1728,CF.
[50] Crole to LH, 3 Apr. 1775, F1/322,CF.
[51] B. Loader to LH, 10 May 1783, F1/522,CF.

'Society of Dissenters called Independants [*sic*]' at Warwick in 1771;[52] Rotherhithe in 1783;[53] and Rickmansworth in 1789.[54] Two further examples of such moves illustrate, in addition, the breadth of the religious heritage upon which the Connexion drew. In 1788 the Connexion received a plea for help from an existing but still struggling congregation at Huntingdon—a cause which owed its origins to the combined efforts of a former student of the Dissenting academy run by Dr Addington, and a lay preacher from a Dissenting society at Bedford.[55] More idiosyncratic still was that at Bradford-upon-Avon which originated from the conversion to the doctrinal position of the Connexion of a former Wesleyan lay preacher who then returned to his home village to raise a congregation of his own; he and his people sought full communion with Lady Huntingdon in 1790.[56]

Admission to the Connexion was not automatic, however, either for established congregations or new ones. Lengthy negotiations ensued with Rotherhithe in 1783 over the financial basis upon which they would be allowed to join;[57] while Samuel Beaufoy in the following year thought it necessary to check in advance whether Lady Huntingdon would be prepared to admit 'into her line' any new causes he succeeded in establishing during the coming season.[58] Although there is no evidence that Lady Huntingdon adopted any equivalent of the rule to which Wesley was forced in the late 1760s, that two-thirds of the cost of a building should be subscribed in advance of the construction starting,[59] she (or her advisers) clearly needed to anticipate the likely financial demands of any new congregation, especially if building operations were in prospect: in 1774, for example, Peckwell drew to her attention the doubtful

---

[52] Petition to LH dated 26 Nov. 1771, F1/148(a),CF.
[53] Wills to LH, 9 Sept. 1783, F1/1901,CF.
[54] Readshaw to LH, 30 Mar. 1789, F1/2067,CF.
[55] John Nicholls to LH, 20 Nov. 1788, F1/787,CF.
[56] Glascott to LH, 8 Aug. 1790, F1/2127,CF.
[57] Wills to LH, 20 Sept. and 2 Oct. 1783, F1/1905, 1907,CF.
[58] Beaufoy to LH, 12 Feb. 1784, F1/597,CF.
[59] JW to R. Costerdine, 6 Feb. 1769, Wesley, *Letters*, v. 126. For the growing problems of building debts for the Wesleyans in the 1760s, see Baker, 'Polity', 252–3.

ability of the embryo congregation at Lewes to meet the financial commitment they were undertaking.[60] If a congregation became unable to meet its commitments, the onus (moral if not legal) might be on Lady Huntingdon to lend support. So extensive were the monetary demands upon her, as will be seen later in considering the general financial basis upon which the Connexion operated, that she could ill afford to allow any further expectations to develop.

Financing and building new chapels

Some congregations—like the one at Spitalfields in 1773 whose elders sought help in the repayment of the chapel debt in order (in part, at least) to escape the persecution of their wives for having engaged in the work in the first place[61]— clearly assumed that a personage of Lady Huntingdon's standing would have money to spare for building enterprises. Sometimes she was prepared to share in the financial burden involved in starting a new cause. At Ashby in 1771–2 Lady Huntingdon appears to have shouldered the whole cost of converting premises into a place of worship.[62] The more normal pattern, however (where she was prepared to be financially involved at all) was by a contribution to a locally funded initiative. In 1773 she signified her willingness to contribute £100 towards the establishment of a chapel in Dublin, provided certain strict conditions were satisfied— principally that the whole scheme was properly costed and the money raised before any financial commitments were entered into.[63] The following year Peckwell sought a similar contribution from her for the building of the Chichester chapel (plus another £50 if she could afford it), as well as gifts from two other aristocratic friends.[64] Around

---

[60] Peckwell to LH, 16 Mar. 1774, F1/281,CF.
[61] Petition to LH, 11 Dec. 1773, F1/260,CF.
[62] T. Adams to LH, 25 Dec. 1771 and 5 May 1772, F1/1558, 1602,CF.
[63] LH to Hawkesworth, 10 Feb. 1773, Congregational Library, IIa, 17, no. 25. Her letter to him the previous day made clear her anxiety about becoming involved in the building debt, hence the strict terms of this formal letter (LH to Hawkesworth, 9 Feb. 1773, G2/1(5),CF).
[64] Peckwell to LH, 28 Mar., 6 Apr., and 16 Mar. 1774, MSS, F1/283, 1244, 281,CF.

the same time, Lady Huntingdon advanced another £100 without security for building the Gainsborough chapel.[65] It was important that any contribution she might make should be matched by the congregation's ability to play its own part; in the Lewes example already quoted, Peckwell encouraged her to seek evidence of the congregation's ability to raise substantial sums itself before she made any contribution of her own—otherwise the whole burden might fall on her.

On other occasions Lady Huntingdon might contribute on a scale far more modest than the examples quoted, but no less vital to the establishment of a cause. The rents of the premises to be used at Grantham and Stamford in 1774, for example, were respectively £7 and £8 per year, and in each case Glascott looked confidently to her to see the congregations over this aspect of their initial burdens, until they had become established.[66]

It may not be without significance that the above examples should be concentrated in the early 1770s, when the period of Connexional expansion had still some way to run. The impression from the Peckwell correspondence just quoted is that taking a new place into the Connexion would be attended by some sort of demand on her resources. Her ability to meet such demands was inevitably reduced as the range of them increased. The message to new causes was generally that congregations must look elsewhere for the funds to provide premises.[67] This message was not always properly understood. The Birmingham committee in the later 1780s, for example, failed to realize that they were expected to bear the purchase price of their chapel and there were bitter recriminations when the truth dawned.[68] Occasionally congregations might seek help from established

---

[65] 'A Brief Historick Record'.
[66] Glascott to LH, 11 June and 18 Apr. 1774, F1/1698, 285,CF.
[67] This is not to imply that significant financial requests were not made later. In 1788, for example, application was made to her for £100 of the £165 it would cost to build a meeting house at Framfield (Burgwain to LH, 23 Oct. 1788, F1/777,CF).
[68] S. Seager to Mr Best, 12 Nov. 1788, F1/782,CF. LH had initially purchased the former playhouse that they were to use (*Life of Wills*, 164–5).

Dissenting charities, such as the application by the Dorchester congregation in 1776 to the secretary of a society linked to the Dissenting church in the Old Jewry.[69] It is not recorded whether they were any more successful in this approach than the Chatteris congregation who failed the following year in their application to the Societas Evangelica, which had been recently founded to support lay preachers in the London suburbs.[70]

Where neither Lady Huntingdon nor one of the religious charities was prepared to help, congregations were forced back on their own resources. Occasionally their membership might include someone wealthy enough to bear a substantial part of the costs involved. This happened with the chapel at Woodbridge in Suffolk, which appears to have been founded and financed very largely through the efforts of one local man, Jonathon Beaumont.[71] More often congregations were forced to have recourse to local collections, and where these failed to raise sufficient funds for the costs involved, they had to look to the wider religious world, particularly London. Stamford in 1774, Chatteris in 1777, and Wigan in 1785 were examples of causes which looked to collections amongst religious sympathizers in the capital as the solution to their financial difficulties.[72]

How much it might cost to build and fit out a chapel naturally varied considerably, depending on its size and the area of the country. Dorchester's figure in 1775 of 45 guineas for land and materials, plus £200 for the actual building, appears pretty representative of what a small town congregation might have to pay to meet their needs.[73]

---

[69] Molland to Dr Ford, 26 Mar. 1776, F1/351,CF. On the Old Jewry congregation, see H. McLachlan, *Letters of Theophilus Lindsey* (Manchester, 1920), 31, 116.

[70] Lovegrove, *Established Church, Sectarian People*, 79; Glascott to LH 24 Dec. 1777, F1/1808,CF. Shipston was similarly unsuccessful with Societas Evangelica in 1777 (Jacobus Newbon to LH, 31 [*sic*] June 1777, F1/396,CF).

[71] Beaumont to LH, 18 June 1787 and 26 Jan. 1789, and to Lady AE, 26 July 1792, F1/1947, 2059, 2225,CF.

[72] Glascott to LH, 18 Apr. 1774 and 24 Dec. 1777; Spa Fields minute book for 21 Jan. 1785, F1/285, 1808; D1/1, p. 28, CF. In this area, as in others, the Connexion was less centrally directed than Wesleyan Methodism. In 1767, for example, Wesley took steps to pay off accumulating building debts by a series of appeals among wealthier Methodists; he was himself prepared to head subscription lists for local appeals (Baker, 'Polity', 230).

[73] Molland to LH, 11 Dec. 1775, F1/342,CF.

Taunton's estimate in 1770 was about the same, and so was that at Lewes in 1774—although Lady Huntingdon was warned that the fitting out of the latter might push the figure substantially higher.[74] Since the fitting out of the Stamford chapel in the same year had cost £80, there was some justification for caution.[75] Costs do not appear to have risen significantly over time; more than a decade after these examples, West Bromwich was able to plan on the basis of £250 for their new place of worship.[76] But the location and prospective popularity of the chapel (and thus its size) did make a big difference. Norwich in 1777 was said to have cost between £1,300 and £1,400, although these figures were clearly regarded as excessive by the correspondent who reported them.[77] The rebuilt Argyle chapel in Bath, opened in 1790 for the congregation which had seceded from Lady Huntingdon's chapel a decade before, cost nearly £2,000.[78] A chapel described as well placed for the Oxford Street area, in which Lady Huntingdon expressed interest in 1783, was said to have cost its then owner more than £3,000.[79]

Given the cost and effort involved in building new premises, it is surprising that more use does not appear to have been made of the redundant chapels of other denominations. This did occasionally happen, as shown at Harwich in the mid-1770s, where a base for the work was provided by a former meeting house in which there had been no regular preaching for some years.[80] The breakaway group at Dover in 1789 acted similarly, by setting up their new cause in a former Quaker meeting house.[81] Such practices were not limited to the Connexion and its former associates: the rector of Halburton in Devon recorded in 1764, in response to a visitation query, that 'There is indeed a Meeting House,

---

[74] T. Parson to LH, 18 Aug. 1770; Peckwell to LH, 16 Mar. 1774, F1/1508, 281,CF.   [75] Glascott to LH, 18 Apr. 1774, F1/285,CF.
[76] Petition to LH, Nov. 1787, F1/687,CF.
[77] Lawrence Coughlan to LH, 29 Mar. 1777, F1/386,CF.
[78] W. Tuck, *Notes on the History of the Argyle Chapel, Bath* (Bath, 1906).
[79] William Taylor to LH, n.d. MS, F1/1370,CF.
[80] E. Bryant to LH, 5 Oct. 1775; Dunn to LH, 8 July 1776, F1/1720, 366,CF.
[81] Watkins to LH, 16 July 1789, F1/845,CF.

formerly occupied by the Presbyterians, but of late it is frequented by the new Sect of the Methodists.'[82]

Social origins of congregations

The social roots of Lady Huntingdon's congregations were in general less diverse than their religious origins. Although the first thrust of her activities had been directed towards more fashionable centres of population, the broad picture is of work among labourers and small tradesmen.[83] The Connexion made no secret of the fact that it was with the lower strata of society that its appeal most generally lay. There was no note of regret or surprise in the report from Lady Huntingdon's friend, Lady Manners, in 1773, that it was generally the poorest that attended at Gainsborough.[84] Of Worcester in 1784 it was said that the congregation numbered no gentlemen, and only one gentlewoman.[85] Preston described themselves in 1788 as mostly labourers,[86] while at Banbury in the same year, there were only three people capable of making any contribution towards the support of the work, since the rest were merely common tradespeople.[87] Despite this, however, standards of literacy, at least among members of societies (if not the broader membership of congregations) appear to have been quite high; it was not uncommon for the members of a society jointly to sign letters to Lady Huntingdon, but it was only ever a very small proportion who were unable to write their names. However humble their origins might be, moreover, congregations did not hesitate to address their message to all levels

---

[82] Quoted in Arthur Warne, *Church and Society in Eighteenth Century Devon* (Newton Abbot, 1969), 100. Sometimes chapels were built as speculative ventures, available to the highest bidder (Welch, 193).

[83] The Connexion was not unusual in this: artisans and small tradesmen were proportionately twice as numerous in Methodists ranks as in society at large (Bebbington, *Evangelicalism*, 25). Unskilled workers were heavily outnumbered by artisans (Rack, *Wesley*, 440).

[84] Lady Manners to LH, 7 Jan. 1773, F1/209,CF.
[85] Mrs E. Paul to LH, 19 Feb. 1784, F1/598,CF.
[86] Preston to LH, 2 Aug. 1788, F1/749,CF.
[87] R. Lambert to LH, 19 Sept. 1788, F1/768,CF.

of society. James Stevenson, of the Newark chapel, was a fishmonger, but he could still ask in 1788 for the removal of an insufficiently refined preacher on the basis that 'Newark is a very polite Town, so that nothing but politeness will go down with them.'[88] And even Bath, possibly the Connexional chapel directed most to the highest reaches of society, was, for a time at least, in the hands of tradesmen: the 'Chapel organizers' to whom Lady Huntingdon granted power of attorney in 1783 comprised a builder, a currier, a tallow chandler, and a haberdasher.[89] John Wesley, it is true, could comment as late as 1789 on the 'marvellous condescension' of God in providing 'such places as...Lady H's chapels, for those delicate hearers, who could not bear sound doctrine if it were not set off with...pretty trifles'.[90] But the fact was that the proportion of such people to the totality of the Connexion's membership was small indeed, as was the number of chapels of the standard of elegance which Wesley plainly had in mind. And when the aristocracy or the gentry did appear at services, even at the grander chapels, it was a matter sufficiently unusual to be worthy of comment.[91]

THE PREACHERS OF THE COUNTESS OF HUNTINGDON'S CONNEXION

By the early 1770s, and for the rest of Lady Huntingdon's life, those supplying her congregations can be categorized into three main groups. By far the largest of these were present or former students of Trevecca College. But these men worked alongside a small but influential group of Church of England clergymen, a good deal of whose time in the Connexion would be spent supplying the major chapels, but who participated also on occasions in itinerant preaching. And there was a third group of men who were already active as preachers outside the Connexion, independently or in

---

[88] Letters to LH of 19 Apr. and 4 May 1788, F1/2007, 2011,CF.
[89] Power of attorney dated 12 July 1783, F1/533,CF.
[90] JW's Journal for 10 Apr. 1789, Curnock, vii. 485.
[91] For example, De Courcy to LH, 8 July 1769, and Shirley to LH, 24 Oct. 1770, F1/73, 1566, CF.

association with others, who became absorbed into the Connexion without passing through the preliminary stage of admission to the college. We shall consider these last two categories, and the routes by which they became associated with Lady Huntingdon, before turning to the function of student preachers within the Connexion.

Clergymen in the Connexion

Some of the clergy who assisted Lady Huntigdon in the period after 1770 had been associated with her previously, when the style of the Connexion's work had been very different, but their number is not large—and by choice or by death they were, with a few exceptions, to leave the ranks of her preachers as the decade progressed. The one outstanding exception to this was Cradock Glascott, who had joined Lady Huntingdon in 1765, remained in her full-time service until he accepted a living in 1781, and continued to serve on a part-time basis for the rest of her life.[92] Of less significance in the overall life of the Connexion, but providing similar continuity, was the Revd Edward Shepherd of Bath, who is recorded at the chapel from December 1765[93] and at some of the other major chapels over the next seven or eight years. Thereafter he figures less in the Connexional records, though the impression given is that he was engaged from time to time as some sort of reserve supply for the Bath chapel; he was certainly still there in 1789.[94] Continuity of a sort was provided also by Thomas Haweis, whose links with Lady Huntingdon, as seen, dated from the early 1760s, although he did not formally join the Connexion until 1774. He combined rectorship of Aldwincle with an active role in the affairs of the Connexion until its secession from the Church of England, and then became involved again in its activities in the final years of Lady Huntingdon's life.[95]

---

[92] The Cheshunt archive contains over 80 letters from Glascott to LH.
[93] LH to Mrs Wadsworth, 16 Dec. 1765, Bridwell Library MS, 56. On his first occasion, LH 'did nothing but sweat and pray', but he acquitted himself well.
[94] Miss Scutt to LH, 13 Dec. 1777; Godde to LH, 16 Aug. 1769; Shirley to LH, 28 Nov. 1776; Taylor to LH, 16 Aug. 1789, E4/2(1), F1/75, 1738, 2094,CF.
[95] A. S. Wood, *Thomas Haweis* (London, 1957), 158, 168.

Apart from these three, there appear to have been no clergymen still actively engaged with Lady Huntingdon in the final years of her life who had been similarly employed prior to 1770. But a number did continue over from the 1760s to the 1770s, and they illustrate the diversity of origins of those responsible for the direction of the Connexion in this crucial transition period. One such was Walter Shirley, who played a leading role (by writing as well as preaching) in the 1770s, but faded from active involvement by the end of the decade; he served a period at the Countess's Spa Fields chapel in 1781, but there is no evidence that he preached for her again before his death in 1786.[96] Very different in background was Thomas Maxfield, who combined running his own chapel in the City of London with service at Lady Huntingdon's chapels from the middle 1760s; he was similarly involved in the early 1770s, but by the end of the decade was seeking a reconciliation with the Wesleys.[97] The degree of continuing support which Lady Huntingdon received in the 1770s from some of the other clergymen who had served her chapels in the previous period was to vary considerably. Joseph Townsend, for example, fades substantially from the picture as the 1770s advanced. He itinerated in Cornwall in 1776, and in the following year offered to supply for Wills at St Agnes, to release the latter for service at the Bath chapel. But by 1781 his links with the Connexion had ended, and he was eventually to abandon the Revival altogether.[98] Henry Venn appears by contrast to have continued helping at the Countess's chapels during most of the 1770s.[99] But John Berridge, although he maintained his earlier idiosyncratic role as friend and adviser to Lady Huntingdon, does not appear to have preached for her

---

[96] e.g. Shirley to LH, 24 Apr. 1764; Glascott to LH, 9 Oct. 1781, F1/1392; E4/11(8),CF.

[97] Maxfield to LH, 29 Aug. 1766, F1/1394,CF; Tyerman, *Wesley*, iii. 296.

[98] Mrs Wills to LH, 3 Feb. 1776; Haweis to LH, 10 Aug. 1777, F1/1723, 1757,CF; Seymour, ii. 460.

[99] Ibid. 106–7. Venn to LH, 20 May 1770; Shirley to LH, 12 May 1774; Wills to LH, 3 July 1777; Godde to Wills, 31 July 1777, F1/93, 1692, 1770, 398,CF; T. W. Aveling, *Memorials of the Clayton Family* (London, 1867),165.

in the later period, although he did occasionally do so at some other Calvinistic Methodist chapels.[100]

If some of Lady Huntingdon's earlier clerical supporters played a lesser part as time went on, there were new recruits to take their place. Henry Peckwell has already been noted. Lady Huntingdon regarded his formal association with the Connexion in 1773 as a substantial prize, and he was a major force in the Connexion during the middle years of the decade, both at established chapels and in new areas. He too was to fade out later, however, although there is not evidence of a breach as such: there is no record of his having preached for Lady Huntingdon for some time prior to 1780, or of his doing so again before his death in 1787.[101] In contrast to Peckwell stands Rowland Hill, whose early contacts with Lady Huntingdon have already been noted.[102] Marginally older than Peckwell (although ordained a year later) he proved too unrestrained a spirit to be confined within the structures of the Connexion, comparatively informal though they might still be, and he did not have the impact on its life of some of the other clergy involved with Lady Huntingdon in the 1770s. When he eventually lost Lady Huntingdon's good opinion,[103] the rift continued to the end of her life. His Cambridge contemporary, Thomas Pentycross,[104] on the other hand, came to play an active part in the Connexion as the decade progressed. He would possibly have continued that role throughout the 1780s had he not incurred Lady Huntingdon's displeasure by his decision

---

[100] e.g. Taylor to LH, 24 Mar. 1784, F1/1936,CF; R. Whittingham (ed.), *The Works of John Berridge, with an Enlarged Memoir of His Life* (London, 1838).

[101] e.g. Lloyd to LH, 16 Apr. 1770 and 30 May 1772; LH to Hawkesworth, 15 June 1773; Peckwell to LH, 13 July 1780, F1/1491, 1603; G2/1(7); F1/469,CF.

[102] See above, pp 56–7.

[103] E. Sidney, *Life of the Rev. Rowland Hill* (5th edn., London, 1861), 140, 171–2.

[104] 1748–1808. Educated at Christ's Hospital and Pembroke College, Cambridge. Curate of Horley, Surrey 1771, from which he was dismissed in 1774 after preaching for LH in Brighton, and became rector of Wallingford the same year (F1/320,CF; J. W. Middelton, *Ecclesiastical History*, 60, 165; *Gentleman's Magazine* (1808), i. 271). As an undergraduate he had entertained serious doubts about the liturgy and doctrines of the Church of England; at one stage he talked of leaving Cambridge for LH's college at Trevecca, and of founding his own independent congregation (Sidney, *Rowland Hill*, 86–7).

against secession from the Church of England in 1784, despite strong prior indications that he would secede.[105] Two clergymen who associated themselves full-time with Lady Huntingdon during the 1770s, and who did subsequently secede from the Church in favour of the Connexion, were William Taylor and Thomas Wills. Taylor became prominent in Connexional affairs following his involvement in 1776 in the decision to open as a place of worship the London amusement palace which was subsequently to become Lady Huntingdon's Spa Fields chapel—the start of the chain of events which culminated in the Connexion's secession from the Church of England.[106] The implication, from the absence of any earlier reference that can with certainty be linked with Taylor, is that it was this event which brought him to Lady Huntingdon's attention; thereafter he was actively involved in the preaching and policy-making of the Connexion. He himself seceded from the Church in 1783, and continued to play a leading role until his decisive rift with Lady Huntingdon in 1790.[107] Thomas Wills's early links with Lady Huntingdon have already been mentioned. He was providing occasional service for the Connexion by at least as early as 1773 and this he continued to do alongside his commitments at his Cornish curacy. There was at least one abortive attempt to find a basis on which he could become a full-time member of the Connexion, before the step was finally taken. But once it was, he held a leading place among the small coterie of Lady Huntingdon's friends,

---

[105] Sidney, *Rowland Hill*, 44; Pentycross to LH, n.d; Taylor to LH, 26 Sept. 1782; 30 letters to LH from Pentycross, Mrs Pentycross, Lloyd, and Thomas Perry, dated 1782–4, F1/1254, 1864, E4/13,CF. [106] Below, Ch. 6.
[107] Seymour, ii. 304–5. The implication of the letter from Toplady which Seymour prints, is that she had not previously known him, but there is a request for Taylor to be sent to Brighton as early as 1777 (Miss Scutt to LH, 20 Feb. 1777, E4/2(11),CF). For his subsequent career in the Connexion, see, *inter alia*, Taylor to LH, 22 July 1779, 16 Aug. 1780, 10 Feb. 1782; Lloyd to LH, 16 Jan. 1783; Taylor to LH, 31 May 1783, n.y., n.d. (but stamped 3 Apr.); Lloyd to Taylor, 30 Jan. 1788; Lloyd to LH, 14 May 1788; Taylor to LH, 27 Apr. 1789, 3 Aug. 1789, 20 Nov. 1789; Haweis to LH, 6 Jan. 1790; N. Rowland to LH, 20 Feb. 1790; Taylor to Best, 5 Apr. and 16 Nov. 1790, 25 Jan. 1791, F1/1831, 1855, 1868, 1879, 1890, 1370, 1374, 1990, 2014, 2073, 2092, 2113, 2115, 886, 2126, 2157, 2167,CF. For the rift with Lady Huntingdon, see also Ch. 7.

preachers, and advisers, until he too fell foul of her and was dismissed a decade later.[108]

These, then, were some of the clergy who served the Countess's Connexion, full-time or in conjunction with the tenure of office in the Church, during its crucial transition from a personal grouping into a national denomination. Though there are some similarities between individuals, as noted, it is not easy to detect any common theme between the group as a whole—and still less between them and some of the other clergy who participated in the Connexion's work, most notably the beneficed Welsh clergy who made a major contribution in the 1780s. Certainly the Countess's clergy differed considerably in the expectations they might reasonably have held as to their chances of Church preferment, had they not become associated with her. Perhaps all they had in common was a preparedness to accept the likely adverse consequences of involvement with the Connexion. Because, on balance, they had more to lose from their involvement in the Connexion than those preachers for whom the Connexion offered the prospect of upward social movement, they were always likely to be, if not an outright conservative influence, at least a restraining force on what might otherwise have become a substantially less organized and disciplined movement than the one which actually emerged. Without her clergy, Lady Huntingdon would not have been able to resist the influence of the wilder forces in her Connexion. The story of the Connexion during these years is in part that of the interaction between the representatives of Anglican order and regularity, and the other elements that attached themselves to the Connexion or were recruited to it from Trevecca College.

Other established preachers recruited to the Connexion

It is even less easy to generalize about the small group of men, already established as lay preachers, who were drawn

---

[108] See, *inter alia*, Wills to LH, 14 and 18 Nov. 1776 and 3 July 1777; Spa Fields minute book, *passim*; Records of the Apostolic Society, *passim*; LH to Wills, 12 Oct. 1774; E. Jones to LH, 9 Jan. 1788, F1/1733, 1735, 1770; D1/1; C5/2,CF; Rylands, ENG. MS, 346/338; Gloucester Record Office, D. 2538–8/1/2; also below, Ch. 7.

into association with the Connexion. They were certainly fewer than the clergy, and left much less of a mark either upon the main chapels or the general development of the Connexion. No outstanding lay figure of the status of Howel Harris, for example, lent his services to the Connexion in this later period. Nor is it always certain, in the case of applications to join the Connexion by men already active in preaching, whether what they envisaged was immediate service, or a preparatory period at the college first. William Wren, for example, who asked to come under Lady Huntingdon's 'wing' in 1777, and who had already been preaching in several towns and villages in Hampshire and Sussex, was certainly sent to college in the first instance.[109] A rather similar case was that of John Bartholomew, who applied to Lady Huntingdon in 1782 when he had already been preaching for some time, including to some Connexional societies, but who clearly associated formal admission to the Connexion with a preliminary period at college.[110] It is not clear on what basis the Mr Allen, then in receipt of half a guinea a week for preaching at a town in Devon, who sought admission in 1774, expected to serve. Shirley's discussion of the proposal with Lady Huntingdon turned wholly on the question of the man's usefulness, set against the cost of maintaining his six children; cost was held to rule him out.[111] But David Gold, described as a young preacher at Gravesend, who applied in the same year, was successful (perhaps because he had only two children), and there is no evidence of his going to Trevecca College before he began work.[112]

A group of applications from existing preachers came around 1790; they indicate the variety of background and experience upon which the Connexion was able to draw, and stand in sharp contrast to the clergy who served in its ranks at the same time. Two were from former Wesleyans: Nathaniel Ward, an ex-lay preacher who had left the

---

[109] Wren to LH, 10 Nov. 1777, F1/1798,CF; Seymour, ii. 113.
[110] Bartholomew to LH, 23 Dec. 1782, F1/1878,CF.
[111] Shirley to LH, 12 May 1774; Lloyd to LH, 16 June 1774, F1/1692, 300,CF.
[112] Peckwell to LH, 5 May and 1 Aug. 1774; F1/288, 1708,CF.

Wesleyans and operated independently in Nottinghamshire and Derbyshire for some time before applying to the Connexion in 1790; and John Burge, a former exhorter, in 1791.[113] In April 1791 application was made to Lady Huntingdon by a Joseph Priestley, who dated his conversion nearly forty years earlier, and detailed for her his career of field, market-place, and chapel preaching over the intervening years.[114] Another variant occurred the following year when the Connexion received a joint application from two men who had been labouring for several months in what they described as a respectable connexion near the Metropolis.[115]

It is striking that in comparison with the regular service of the Connexion by clergymen already described, there should have been no equivalent assistance from Dissenting ministers. This may in part be testimony to the Church loyalties which the Connexion professed, but it is particularly notable given the impact which the Connexion was to have upon so many Dissenting congregations.[116] References to Dissenting ministers in Connexional pulpits are rare, though there were odd instances, like the 'Barlow of Bath' who helped at Frome in 1777, during a period when that chapel was unsupplied.[117] In a special category were those former Trevecca students who had been ordained as Dissenters, but who subsequently provided the Connexion with occasional help. One such was Richard Leggett, at college in the later 1770s, and for a period assistant to the Dissenting minister, John Edwards of Leeds, who on the eve of his own Dissenting ordination in 1783 offered Lady Huntingdon his occasional services.[118] Similarly, John Clayton, a student from earlier in

---

[113] T. Young to LH, n.d.; J. Ford to LH, 13 May 1791, F1/2168, 2179,CF. There was a further twist, since it was subsequently discovered that Ward's departure from the Wesleyans had been prompted by suspicion of 'conduct unnatural in itself and too indelicate to mention—that described in Rom. i. 27' (Young to LH, 11 Apr. 1791, F1/2175,CF).

[114] John Glascott to Lady AE, 22 Apr. 1794, F1/975,CF. The motive for his application at this stage is unclear, though it appears that he had latterly been attempting to raise money to build a chapel for a group that had formed under his preaching (Ford to LH, 11 Apr. 1791, F1/2179,CF).

[115] J. F. Cower and J. M. George to Lady AE, 9 Aug. 1792. F1/2226,CF.

[116] See below, Ch. 7.

[117] Giles to LH, 8 Oct. 1777; members of Maidstone congregation to LH, 5 Dec. 1782, F1/1790, 495,CF.   [118] Leggett to LH, 9 Apr. 1783, F1/1884,CF.

the 1770s, who received Dissenting ordination in 1778, supplied for a period at the Connexional chapel in Cheltenham.[119] Prominent Dissenting ministers were rare in her pulpits, however, although at the very end of her life she extended an invitation to John Newton's friend William Bull of Newport Pagnell. It was an invitation which Bull was too ill to accept.[120] Andrew Kinsman of Plymouth, a friend of the Revival since the 1740s, and a minister for whom Walter Shirley and some of the students supplied, is known to have preached at Whitefield's chapels in London, but there is no record of his doing the same thing for the Connexion.[121] One Dissenting minister who does seem to have preached for Lady Huntingdon was Thomas Grove, one of the St Edmund Hall students expelled from Oxford in 1768. After leaving Oxford he provided land for the erection of a chapel at Bourne End, Buckinghamshire, near his family home at Wooburn. Over the following years he worked with Whitefield's congregations, with Lady Glenorchy in Edinburgh, and with Edwards of Leeds, as well as with other Dissenting congregations; he offered assistance to Lady Huntingdon and on at least one occasion did actually preach for her.[122]

Students and former students

The major source of manpower in the Connexion, once its potential had been recognized, was Trevecca College. Once the step had been taken of using students for itinerant

---

[119] Meldrum to LH, 6 Nov. 1773, F1/258(a),CF; Aveling, *Claytons*, 153.

[120] Bull to LH, 19 Nov. 1789, F1/2112,CF. Bull's broad-mindedness was demonstrated by his presidency of the Newport Pagnell Academy, an institution planned and financed by John Newton and the Anglican evangelical businessman, John Thornton (Lovegrove, *Established Church, Sectarian People*, 70; M. Lewis, *A Town of Two Bridges* (Newport Pagnell, 1999), 85 ff).

[121] Shirley to LH, 27 May 1774; Molland to LH, 15 Apr. 1775; Clayton to LH, 23 Jan. 1773, E4/1(21); F1/325, 1632,CF; Seymour, ii. 173, 175–6; Tyerman, *Whitefield*, ii. 216.

[122] Inscription on the chapel at Bourne End, Bucks. T. S. Jones, *The Life of Willielma, Viscountess Glenorchy* (London, 1822), 347; Grove to LH, 11 May 1774 and 4 Mar. 1777, F1/290, 383,CF.

preaching, there was pressure to continue doing so. It was in the vicinity of the college that, as noted above, outside preaching was originally undertaken, and that tradition was to continue, even while more distant calls were being answered. Preaching from college fell into two categories: to congregations near enough to Trevecca to be served directly from college each Sunday,[123] and to those further afield which required overnight stays, albeit with the student in question still being based at college. John Clayton's biographer described how Clayton regularly went out at weekends, starting on 'the Saturday, and sometimes on the Friday, in every week', and being 'strictly enjoined to return to the College on Monday'.[124] How soon college preaching rounds became formalized in the same way as elsewhere[125] is not clear, though it is likely to have happened substantially earlier than the reference to 'College Rounds' which occurs in a letter of 1783.[126]

Not all the student body was liable for preaching duties throughout their time at college. Anthony Crole wrote in December 1773 that his studies were progressing better than on his previous occasion in college, since this time he had no stated preaching.[127] A decade later there is a reference to the 'preaching students' at college, with the clear implication that there were some who did not come into this category.[128]

Sometimes students might be allowed to choose between continuing preaching or resuming study: in 1783, for example, Edward Porter was asked by Lady Huntingdon when he wished to return to college.[129] Just occasionally students might be given a say in where they were sent, though the final decision seems to have been Lady Huntingdon's.[130] The instance just quoted also provides evidence of the moral pressure to which she was prepared to subject the students, even when purporting to let them chose between preaching and study. The reply from the college on this occasion was

---

[123] Meldrum to LH, 7 May 1774, F1/289,CF. [124] Aveling, *Claytons*, 17.
[125] See below.   [126] S. Phillips to LH, 31 Oct. 1783, F1/562,CF.
[127] Crole to LH, 17 Dec. 1773, F1/261,CF.
[128] E. Parsons to LH, 10 July 1783, F1/1892,CF.
[129] Porter to LH, 30 Apr. n.y. (but marked 1783), F1/518,CF.
[130] W. Aldington to LH, 31 Mar. and 7 Apr., n.y. (? 1774), F1/1290–1,CF.

that, although most students had been determined to continue feeding on Greek and Latin 'husks', they had dropped their objections to going out on reading her description of the calls received.

THE ORGANIZATION OF THE CONNEXION

The organization of preaching

The Connexion's preparedness to respond to calls for preaching made it necessary, from an early date, to evolve formalized preaching circuits so that the responsibility which had been accepted could continue to be met. Wesleyan Methodism had adopted circuit arrangements from the 1740s, when England and Wales were divided into seven circuits. These were subsequently subdivided and further subdivided so that there were some ninety circuits (including America) by 1770.[131] There is no evidence that Lady Huntingdon attempted a continuous process of dividing up the country; more probably, the creation of 'rounds' (as they were called in the Connexion) occurred pragmatically, in recognition that some congregations fell into certain natural geographical groupings, particularly when they owed their origins to itinerant preaching from a common central location. Thus, though students would generally be sent to an individual congregation (unlike Wesleyan Methodism, where preachers were posted to a circuit, not to any individual society),[132] it was not unknown for them to be given responsibility for a wider area. Indeed, if a group of Connexional causes had been started by preaching from a specific place, then it was natural for subsequent preachers to be expected to serve the whole group.[133] But this did not mean, even when rounds had become clearly defined, that no new places could be added: as noted, calls continued to

---

[131] Baker, 'Polity', 232.   [132] Ibid.
[133] An example falling between these two types was that of Joseph Cook in 1771, who supplied Dover on Sundays and Margate during the week (C. and M. Spencer to LH, 21 Dec. 1771, F1/157,CF).

be received, and the existence of preaching rounds provided a convenient means for them to be answered. So, when the student Christopher Hull left college in 1771, preaching through Herefordshire and Worcestershire, he was clearly following in the footsteps of others, even if not observing a set route; but this did not prevent him from turning aside to answer a call to a 'new place' on the way.[134]

When rounds became formalized throughout the country if not clear. Reference to the 'long round' occurs in March 1772; this included places between Birmingham and Wolverhampton and may, at that date, have been the only one of its kind.[135] If so, it was a concept that quickly spread. By 1774, a 'long round' existed from Weymouth to the western parts of Bridgewater, a distance (it was said) of one hundred miles, and too much for the four students who were allocated its supply—especially as the area comprised many towns held to be destitute of the Gospel, from which invitations had been received.[136] Another round appears to have extended eastwards from Dorchester into the New Forest area, including the Isle of Purbeck.[137] Evidence of large rounds occurs in various parts of the country over the following years, sometimes occasioning complaints that they placed a strain upon those expected to serve them. It is doubtful whether Lady Huntingdon organized the appointment of preachers to rounds with the degree of precision that appears in Wesleyan Methodism.[138] In 1776 Lady Huntingdon was told that the large rounds in Pembrokeshire were too big for the two people on them, with the result that some places were unvisited for six weeks; in 1780 she was thanked for sending help to a student working an area of Cornwall seventy miles across.[139] Nor is evidence of such rounds confined to the southern parts of the country—in 1788

---

[134] Hull to LH, 16 Sept. 1771, F1/135,CF.
[135] Glazebrook to LH, 15 Apr. 1772, F1/176,CF.
[136] S. Clark to LH, 21 May 1774, F1/297,CF.
[137] Crole to LH, 13 July 1774, F1/311,CF.
[138] Baker, 'Polity', i. 232–3. Baker quotes an instance of detailed instructions, passed on from preacher to preacher, about the route to be followed and where to stay, eat, and preach.
[139] J. Jones to LH, 8 Feb. 1776; Wills to LH, 2 Aug. 1780, F1/345, 1852,CF.

for example, a student at Haxey in Lincolnshire described to Lady Huntingdon the eight places he was serving in that county, Nottinghamshire and Yorkshire.[140] The size of Connexional rounds may possibly have been the reason why they did not develop beyond being simply convenient geographical arrangements for organizing supplies. They do not seem to have developed any formal equivalent to the quarterly meetings established in every Wesleyan circuit from 1749, with the job of monitoring the temporal and spiritual state of the societies within the circuit, and reporting developments to London.[141]

The Connexion, like itinerant Dissenters later in the century,[142] used the device of preaching rounds in remoter areas, as well as that of preachers based in major centres of population. There was a danger, however, that areas outside the reach of a Connexional centre or preaching round, would remain permanently untouched. It was to meet this lack of universal coverage that a group of Connexional clergy set out in 1781 on a series of extended preaching tours in different parts of the country. The intention, as Pentycross explained when an account of these efforts was published in the following year, was that at least once a year the Gospel should be preached in every city, town and large village, as a means of creating centres of influence in each area and of demonstrating that 'the New Reformation, started more than forty years ago, does not yet stagnate'.[143] This initiative was doubtless valuable both as a general stimulus in the places visited, and in establishing new areas of work. It ensured that some of the Countess's ablest ministers were heard in areas where the Connexion's presence was not yet established, rather than leaving the initiation of new congregations to inexperienced students, as more usually happened. But there is no evidence that it altered radically the thrust of the Connexion's activities—nor, indeed, that it could have done so, even if it had been possible to continue the experiment on a regular basis, as originally planned.

[140] R. Ellis to LH, 27 Aug. 1788, F1/2034,CF.
[141] Frank Baker, *John Wesley and the Church of England* (London, 1970), 115–16.
[142] LH to Langston, 18 Feb. 1784, Rylands MS, 346/338; Lovegrove, *Established Church, Sectarian People*, 90–1. [143] *Extracts of the Journals*.

It was against this background of Connexional causes and rounds that Lady Huntingdon sought to organize the preaching manpower at her disposal. This rapidly became a complex operation, approached for the most part on an ad hoc basis, but there were certain constraints under which she was obliged to work. One of these was in regard to those clergymen with posts in the Established Church who agreed to serve her and who, unless they had curates or were able to make alternative arrangements, needed someone to supply their own churches in their absence. This was an issue from the moment Lady Huntingdon had pulpits of her own. There is, for example, evidence from 1763 of arrangements being made to free a clergyman, probably John Berridge, for service at Ote Hall.[144] Nearly twenty years later, in September 1782, similar arrangements were made to release Thomas Pentycross for the Bristol chapel.[145]

The cost of moving preachers round the country, whether these were ordained men or students, was another obvious constraint, which is considered further below in the broader context of the financing of the Connexion. Another major consideration was the location and supply of horses. Upon the availability of mounts depended crucially the maintenance of preaching supplies; if the available animal were too decrepit to make the planned journey, or if there were no money to hand locally to hire one, then the trip in question had to be deferred, however imperious the command of the Countess, or insistent the call for a fresh supply. Thus it was that a student reported in 1771 that he had been delayed at Bath, en route for Bridgewater, because his horse had gone lame; a decade later a student in Cornwall wrote that he had been held up returning to college for a similar reason.[146] Horses were bought or hired, depending on the amount of travelling that preachers needed to do;[147]

---

[144] Letter of 2 July 1763, E4/8(13),CF. The author and recipient are not named, but the letter appears to link with that to Berridge quoted in Seymour, i. 358. LH seems not to have noticed the irony that using beneficed clergymen in her chapels increased parochial absenteeism.
[145] Pentycross to LH, 18 Sept. 1782, E4/13(1),CF.
[146] Barliss to LH, 24 Oct. 1771; Parish to LH, 4 Dec. 1782, F1/319, 494,CF.
[147] Peckwell to LH, 14 May 1774, F1/293,CF. Sometimes the temptation to steal a horse was too great for a student to resist (Schlenther, 114).

sometimes horses were bought by the organizers of the preaching rounds.[148] It was an issue in which Lady Huntingdon herself took an interest, so central was the mobility to the effectiveness of the work: in 1784 she wrote that she had no objection to congregations preferring to hire horses, if this were less of a financial burden, so long as the students' labours were not restricted thereby.[149]

Another factor not to be ignored by young men travelling the country in the eighteenth century, was the press gang. Writing from Frome in 1777, the student William Thresher indicated that he would not be taking the direct route back to college across the Severn because of the activities of the press; in 1779 a student at Dover decided that it would be prudent to give up open-air preaching because of the press then active in the town.[150] A further potentially important constraint was accommodation. The most natural solution for itinerant preachers, whether they were responding to new calls or returning to an established area, was residence with a member of the congregation—though on at least one occasion the student in question decided that this would be an imposition, and boarded at an inn instead.[151] There might, however, be drawbacks in the close identification with an individual family in the congregation that regular residence with them could imply—especially if there were divisions or factions of any kind within that congregation. Considerable store, financial as well as in terms of prestige, could come to be attached to providing the preachers' accommodation. John Cave of Brecon expressed considerable concern in 1773 when it was proposed ending the three-year practice of boarding the students with him, part of his concern being (it is clear) the fear that people would suspect

---

[148] Peckwell to LH, 14 May 1774; S. Clark to LH, 21 May and 10 June 1774, F1/293, 297, 299,CF.

[149] LH to Langston, 18 Feb. 1784, Rylands MS, 346/338. The availability of horses was not only an issue for the Connexion. An accusation against itinerant Dissenting preachers at the end of the century was that they hired all the available horses and left curates to walk to their churches (Lovegrove, *Established Church, Sectarian People*, 125).

[150] Thresher to LH, 31 Jan. 1777; J. Griffiths to LH, 28 July 1779, F1/1749, 437,CF.

[151] Glazebrook to LH, 29 Oct. 1770, F1/104,CF.

indecencies between the students and his daughters.[152] There was also the problem of a suitable venue for those coming for counselling.[153] In the longer term, and before the congregation reached the stage of acquiring a minister's house, the best solution was generally to hire lodgings. But though difficulties occurred from time to time, they seem generally to have been manageable: there is no evidence that want of appropriate accommodation ever stood in the way of the prosecution of the work.

It is impossible to estimate with any degree of confidence how many congregations were being supplied by Lady Huntingdon's Connexion at any given date in the 1770s and 1780s.[154] No comprehensive list exists, and it is unlikely that Lady Huntingdon herself knew how many small causes were being served from the centres which she supplied—the implication of the reports she received is that preachers were free to respond to local invitations whenever they wished to do so. But this ignorance of the scale of the work did not inhibit her from keeping in her own hands a great deal of the day-to-day direction of the Connexion. Wesley once said 'It is I...that station the preachers' and Lady Huntingdon might have said much the same, although in her case there was no annual conference to rival her in this role.[155] A number of the letters sent to her carry annotations in her own hand, indicative of the processes through which she went in attempting to match preachers to congregations, and her correspondence demonstrates, time and again, that the decision whether a preacher should move or stay came from Lady Huntingdon herself. A letter to Wills in 1777, for example, concluded, 'Have wrote to Hall to go to Harwich,

---

[152] J. Cave to LH, 30 Sept. 1770 and 25 June 1773, F1/110, 232,CF. It is an interesting comment on his view of the students that he dismissed such a possibility on the grounds that the girls had been brought up 'in the Paths of Virtue'.

[153] H. Mead to LH, 15 Nov. 1771, F1/139,CF.

[154] Only once is there anything available approaching a full list of major chapels: that in regard to the abortive Plan of Association for the perpetuation of the Connexion in 1790 (D3/2,CF; see below and Ch. 8). This lists 64 chapels, but does not include any of the minor causes likely to have been associated with them; it includes some places recently added to the Connexion, but omits many that had figured prominently in preachers' reports, a decade earlier.

[155] JW to Z. Yewdall, 4 Oct. 1780, Wesley, *Letters*, vii. 40.

and others are to be in Cornwall. Eyre may stay as I have written to Brown of Plymouth and Pease is not quite the thing, but time will tell.'[156]

In 1789 she wrote to the student Robert McAll, then serving the chapel at Wallingford, that he was to succeed the present preacher at Brighton on 'Sunday the tenth *without fail*, then Mr. Jones to Reading and Mr. Williams to Wallingford this prevents the expense of more distant removes.' Nor did she ignore the route that McAll would have to take in going from Wallingford to Brighton; he was to set out for London immediately 'as you may serve on your way'.[157]

This last example occurred little more than two years before her death, and is a vivid illustration of the close control she kept right to the end. In her last years, some of the daily control did pass into the hands of her friend Lady Anne Erskine and her secretary, George Best,[158] but she does not seem to have given up any specific functions. It was rather that some of the more mundane decisions were taken for her, such as the location of an ordination in 1790, which appears to have been agreed between Best and John Bradford, a clergyman who had seceded to join the Connexion.[159] Preachers were left, as a result, in some uncertainty where authority lay. Thus it was to Best that a preacher wrote about a move in August 1789, but Lady Huntingdon herself replied with detailed instructions.[160]

Some degree of delegation did in fact take place throughout the 1770s and 1780s, although not according to any clearly defined plan. The college, for example, seems to

---

[156] LH to Wills, 1 Apr. 1777, Rylands MS, 346/338.
[157] LH to R. McAll, 5 May 1789, E4/17(3),CF.
[158] Lady Anne Erskine (*c*.1738–1803) was the eldest daughter of the Earl of Buchan. She spent her early years in fashionable society before moving with her father to Bath, where she came into contact with LH. She became LH's companion on the death of her father in 1766, and was at her side for many of the remaining years of the Countess's life, effectively taking on the running of the Connexion at LH's death (T. Gibbons, G. Jerment, and S. Burder, *Memoirs of Eminently Pious Women* (London, 1815), iii. 257–64; on Best, see below, Ch. 8).
[159] Bradford to Best, 17 Apr. 1790, F1/903,CF; on Bradford, see below, Ch. 5, n. 228.
[160] L. Jones to Best, 18 Aug. 1789; Jones to LH, 26 Aug. 1789, F1/852, 856,CF.

have had certain functions in regard to the organization of preachers, though possibly only in the rounds for which it was directly responsible.[161] Senior ministers of the Connexion seem to have enjoyed some degree of delegated authority from time to time, and in respect of certain areas. It was apparently arranged in the middle 1770s, for example, that Henry Peckwell would have as his 'department' London, Kent, and Sussex; there were doubtless similar arrangements for other ministers in other parts of the country, giving them some say over where the available manpower was used within the area.[162] This seems to have been the case with William Taylor in 1783, in respect of preaching in London, Brighton, and Tunbridge Wells;[163] there is evidence in the same year that Wills had some say over deployment to the north-west of London.[164] Five years later, John Bradford, then at Bath, directed an exchange between the students serving Birmingham and Evesham.[165]

Despite these instances of delegation, however, the overall picture is one of continuing central control, usually by Lady Huntingdon herself. Only at Bath, and then only in the 1760s, is there any evidence of authority being delegated to chapels themselves to arrange preaching supplies.[166] In 1768 the Countess's friend, John Lloyd, who resided in Bath and was a prominent member of the chapel during its early days, clearly carried considerable responsibility for finding

---

[161] Molland to LH, 19 Oct. 1773; S. Phillips to LH, 31 Aug. 1783; J. Williams to LH, 26 June 1788, F1/253, 562, 738,CF.

[162] Shirley to LH, n.d., F1/1364,CF. This allocation cannot, however, have entailed much long-term planning for the area, since Shirley, despite his Irish commitments, proposed himself as Peckwell's substitute in London while the latter was away. It is not clear whether Peckwell's duty in regard to the students' money flowed from this responsibility (and was thus confined to the South-East) or was undertaken nationally (Peckwell to LH, 14 May 1774, F1/293,CF).

[163] Taylor to LH, 6 May 1783, F1/1886,CF. Perhaps typical of the ad hoc approach adopted was Taylor's letter to LH in 1789, approving the preaching allocations she had devised, but hoping that she would leave over the one outstanding decision until he saw her (Taylor to LH, 3 Aug. 1789, F1/2092,CF).

[164] Berkhamsted congregation to LH, 17 Dec. 1783, F1/1920,CF.

[165] J. Smith to LH, 12 Mar. 1783; T. Hughes to LH, 2 Sept. 1788, F1/513, 2037,CF.

[166] That is to say, other than when the organization broke down (see below), and congregations were forced to make what arrangements they could or go unsupplied.

supplies, both for the Bath chapel and for the clergy who preached there.[167] Such delegations did not last, however; there are no comparable later instances, and when Lady Huntingdon came to grant power of attorney to the Bath chapel organizers in 1783, she specifically kept back the appointment and removal of ministers.[168] In her hands, therefore, remained a substantial say over the most significant aspect of the life of the congregations which bore her name. Upon the maintenance of preaching supplies, and their quality, depended crucially a congregation's ability to pay its way and to survive at all.

Given such central control, it was inevitable that mistakes should sometimes occur, and arrangements be made that were less than perfect. In 1767, for example, she sent Glascott to supply John Fletcher's parish at Madeley, only for Glascott to discover, on arrival, that Fletcher was still there.[169] There are frequent instances of congregations being left unsupplied: like Dorchester who complained that they had been unsupplied for a month in 1775, or Maidstone who went for two months in 1782 on the basis of read sermons and occasional help from a neighbouring minister.[170] Sometimes there was confusion between Lady Huntingdon and Lady Anne Erskine. In September 1790, Lady Anne had promised an able supply for Swansea by the beginning of October, yet on 2 October Lady Huntingdon told the student Robert McAll that in view of his health he was to swap immediately with 'whoever' had arrived in Swansea.[171] The problem, very often, seems to have been Lady Huntingdon's tendency to react on impulse, regardless of what longer term plans might be disturbed in the process: Glascott

---

[167] T. Lindsey to LH, 29 Apr. 1768; Lloyd to LH, 22 Sept. and 13 Oct. 1768; Glascott to LH, 25 Feb. 1768, F1/27, 35, 38, 41, 1414,CF.

[168] Power of attorney from LH to Bath chapel organizers, 12 July 1783, F1/533,CF. In 1788 a member of the Birmingham committee resigned in protest at the whole chapel cost falling on the committee, while Lady Huntingdon 'reserved the Presentation to the Pulpit in her *own hands*' (Seager to Best, 12 Nov. 1788, F1/782,CF).   [169] Glascott to LH, 3 July 1767, F1/1402,CF.

[170] Molland to LH, 11 Dec. 1775; Maidstone cong. to LH, 5 Dec. 1782, F1/342, 495,CF.

[171] J. Ford to LH, 27 Sept. 1790; LH to McAll, 2 Oct. 1790, F1/2149, E4/17(4),CF.

complained in 1776, for example, of having to make long journeys at short notice, while the student Thomas Suter objected in 1782 that to obey her command to go to Reading would mean breaking engagements made three weeks earlier.[172] More serious still was for a preacher to be ordered on his way at the start of a chapel's financial quarter, when prospective purchasers of chapel tickets[173] would be looking for some guarantee of the quality and permanence of the preaching for which they were paying: the Hereford congregation complained in March 1789 that a preacher had been ordered away on the very day the new quarter started, and that this was the third time this had happened.[174]

Hand in hand with strict control of the Connexion went an expectation of total loyalty from those who served it. After differences had occurred with those running Whitefield's former congregations,[175] Lady Huntingdon ruled that no student should enter any pulpit previously occupied by any Whitefieldite minister, lest they be associated 'with those whose life or doctrine is not altogether what I require of them'.[176] Students who failed to follow instructions on where to go could generally expect a stern response. Of one student, for example, she wrote in 1783 'he...must leave the Connexion, if he does not leave Whitehaven *directly*'.[177] It was thus with a note of understandable surprise that another student that year queried the claim of one of his fellows that Lady Huntingdon had given him freedom of choice as to where he should go; this, he said, was something she did not allow, even to the oldest and ablest students.[178] This is not to imply, however, that the students were denied that degree of

---

[172] Glascott to LH, 1 June 1776; Suter to LH, 14 Sept. 1782, F1/1729, E4/4(12),CF. [173] See below.
[174] J. Williams and others to LH, 30 Mar. 1789, F1/819,CF. Contemporaries perceived Wesley's control of his preachers as similarly tight, and this gave his critics a sense of powerlessness in respect of the preachers: 'You cannot lay hold of them' was one comment, 'Mr. Wesley says depart, and they go' (quoted in Walsh, 'Methodism and the Local Community in the Eighteenth Century').
[175] Below, Ch. 6. [176] LH to Langston, 18 Feb. 1784, Rylands MS, 346/338.
[177] Seymour, ii. 472. See also the *Evangelical Magazine*, (1838), 210 for an example of her anger with a student who remained out preaching rather than returning to college, as instructed. [178] E. Parsons to LH, 10 July 1783, F1/1892,CF.

day-to-day discretion which was essential if full use were to be made of evangelistic opportunities as they arose. It is clear from the description sent her of work at Devizes in 1774, for example, that she could have had no say over where, within the area, the students preached, what new places they opened, and which towns they decided that it would be politic for the moment to abandon.[179]

Other aspects of Lady Huntingdon's control of the Connexion

Though the organization of preachers was clearly a major aspect, it was not the only element in the life of her congregations over which Lady Huntingdon exercised control. She was, as seen,[180] naturally concerned to keep a watch on expenditure for chapel building undertaken in her name. But she interested herself also in the practical aspects of chapel building and the alteration of premises, and she was regularly consulted or informed about the progress of construction work in different parts of the country.[181] Her congregations clearly regarded her as the source of authority on a range of issues. A letter from Ote Hall, for example, probably written in the mid-1770s, sought her permission for a change in the rules of the society, in order to allow them to meet to discuss their spiritual states.[182] In 1777 the society at Monmouth referred back for her approval the grudging agreement they had reached with the local Wesleyans on the joint use of premises in the town.[183] In 1788 the Brecon Society, evidently on the prompting of one of the students, sought her instructions on the sale of the chapel tickets and how the church service should be read.[184]

---

[179] J. Newbon to LH, 17 June 1774, F1/301,CF.   [180] See above p. 74.
[181] For example, Lady AE to LH, 9 Feb. 1772; Birmingham committee to LH, 14 July 1787; J. Browning to LH, 17 Apr. 1789, F/1584, 643, 825,CF.
[182] T. Humphries to LH, n.d., F1/1202,CF. Humphries is known to have preached in Sussex in 1774 (Peckwell to LH, 28 May 1774, F1/1697,CF).
[183] I. Billings to LH, 10 Nov. 1777, F1/1799,CF.
[184] P. Valentine to LH, 15 Jan. 1788, F1/699,CF.

Brecon were clearly right in believing that she was likely to take an interest in how services were conducted. It was evidently not until 1772 that she gave up choosing the hymns to be sung at Bath during the periods when she was away.[185] She was apparently responsible for choosing the hymns at Spa Fields in 1787, and a member of the chapel committee was dismissed for complaining about them.[186] The committees of the main chapels were in fact kept under tight control. Their membership was chosen by Lady Huntingdon, and though Spa Fields were left free to choose a new member in 1782, Birmingham found it necessary to seek her consent to the appointment of someone they regarded as a useful additional member in 1787.[187] A dispute developed between Lady Huntingdon and the Bath committee in 1788 over changes imposed by her which, the committee argued, would seriously have harmed the chapel school. As a result of this the whole committee resigned.[188] The Spa Fields committee found, however, that solidarity in the face of their patroness sometimes paid off. Other members resigned, following the dismissal of the hymn protester, and although new committee appointments were made by Lady Huntingdon, the complaints were such that she was eventually forced to reinstate all the original members.[189]

One of the remarkable features of Lady Huntingdon's personality was her ability to combine this kind of authoritarianism, and the critical response it inevitably occasioned, with a sweetness of character that won her an undoubtedly wide circle of loving admirers. She was clearly not short of critics. The dismissal of Pentycross from the Connexion in 1784, for example, occasioned some sharp comments.

---

[185] Lloyd to LH, 15 Feb. 1772, F1/1586,CF.
[186] Spa Fields minute book, entry for 26 Sept. 1787, D1/1,CF. The minute book is transcribed in E. Welch, *Two Calvinistic Methodist Chapels* (London Record Society, 1975).
[187] Spa Fields minute book, entry for 27 Jan. 1782; Birmingham committee to LH, 17 Nov. 1787, D1/1; F1/670,CF.
[188] R. Carpenter to LH, 25 and 31 Mar., 10 Apr., and 1 May 1788, F1/717, 719, 722, 725,CF.
[189] Spa Fields minute book, entries from 7 July to 7 Aug. 1788, D1/1,CF. The incident coincided with Wills's dismissal from the Connexion which added fuel to the feelings which were aroused (see below, Ch. 8).

According to an anonymous letter at the time it was said that she 'would not rejoice at any good done out of *your* chapels and that it is the love of fame and not the Salvation of Souls out of your line that you wish to promote'.[190] Thomas Perry, writing to resign from the Bath chapel committee over the same issue, stated his belief that, 'Such disguise and duplicity in a person of your high character is astonishing' and concluded, cuttingly, with the hope that her life 'would be prolonged to retrieve every past failing'.[191] She could, however, give as good as she got. Bitter were the recriminations when Glascott accepted a living in 1782, with the implicit assumption in her letters that the Lord's will and service in her own Connexion were one and the same thing.[192] When James Glazebrook decided in the same year to continue work in the Established Church, rather than accept her offer of a settled ministry in the Connexion, she respected his choice, but her letter contained a distinct note of sarcasm: 'Great faith and great patience are wanting to support ministers truly devoted to God in the real labours that his love and power call upon them for; and unless this is the case, the smaller field of usefulness must be submitted to, and, indeed, your point seems yet to remain as you are...'[193]

Yet evidence survives of another side to her character, and of its impact upon the Connexion she sought to organize. Warm expressions of affection run through many of the letters she received from preachers, friends, and others with whom she was associated in the work. Not all of this can be due to deference to her rank in society. Presents were occasionally sent by Lady Huntingdon to her preachers,[194] and she demonstrated a concern for their well-being, at times of difficulty or ill health, that must have done much to reconcile them to her authority.[195]

---

[190] ? to LH, 25 Feb. 1784, E4/13(29),CF.
[191] T. Perry to LH, 5 Mar. 1784, E4/13(30),CF.
[192] Glascott to LH, 16 July to 8 Nov. 1781, E4/11,CF; Seymour, ii. 458–63.
[193] LH to Glazebrook, 13 Sept. 1782, Seymour, ii. 89–90.
[194] Shirley to LH, 30 June 1770; T. Charles to LH, 8 Mar. 1790; Mrs Pentycross to LH, 11 Feb. 1784, F1/1560, 890; E4/13(10),CF.
[195] J. Fletcher to LH, 18 Mar. 1777; Mrs Taylor to LH, 6 Dec. 1782, F1/1756, 1874,CF.

There is evidence, too, that they genuinely valued her advice. Thomas Maxfield wrote in 1772 of his desperate desire to talk to her;[196] Mrs Taylor informed her in 1782 that her letters had been a cordial during her husband's illness;[197] and John Bradford, in the following year, said he felt like a weaned child, when he was separated from her.[198] Similar feelings appear from congregations, and there was sometimes an almost superstitious desire for physical proximity to her: the members at Frome apparently planned a journey over to Bath to see her in 1783,[199] while the Spa Fields congregation, later the same year, were said to be grateful at her staying in her closet a little after the service, so that they might get a glimpse of her.[200] Most congregations, however, never had the chance of such contacts, and had to content themselves, through their committee or their preachers, with writing to her of their affection. The term 'a Mother in Israel' summed up much of what they felt about the woman who had been the main instrument in their salvation, and it appears in various guises: 'Nursing Mother in Israel', 'a very ancient Mother in Israel', and 'Dear Mother in the Lord' were amongst the variants used.[201] The Broadstairs congregation simply called her 'Mother Huntingdon', while that at Dover went one better by devising a hymn of thanksgiving for their foundress, which they sang at society meetings:

> Give reward of grace and glory
> To thy faithful handmaid dear,
> Let the incense of our hearts be
> Offered up in faith and prayer
> *Bless,* O *Bless* her, *Bless,* O *Bless* her
> Now henceforth, for evermore.[202]

It is perhaps inevitable, if the cult of personality is taken to such lengths, that there will be a reaction. Twelve years after

---

[196] Maxfield to LH, 4 July 1772, F1/1607,CF.
[197] Mrs Taylor to LH, 6 Dec. 1782, F1/1874,CF.
[198] Mrs Wills to LH, 23 Oct. 1783, F1/1914,CF.
[199] T. Shinton to LH, 21 Feb. 1783, F1/510,CF.
[200] Wills to LH, 8 Nov. 1783, F1/1915,CF.
[201] J. Newbon to LH, 17 June 1774; Daines to LH, 18 June 1774; Valentine to LH, 15 Jan. 1788, F/301, 302, 699,CF.
[202] J. Cook to LH, 21 Dec. 1771, F1/158,CF.

that hymn was sung it was reported, amidst attempts by the Dover congregation 'to throw off my Ladys Government' that 'Lady H. has been call'd Old Pope'.[203]

Itinerancy in the Connexion

The centralized control described in this chapter was largely necessitated by the fact that the Connexion was organized on the basis of an itinerant ministry. Had the Connexion consisted simply of a group of congregations, each under its own minister, the need to match preachers and people would have occurred far less often. At the start, Lady Huntingdon had no choice but a rotating ministry for the congregations she had founded: the great majority of her preachers were either men with responsibilities to churches elsewhere, who could give her only a limited period of the year, or they were students with at least a nominal commitment to a course of study. The situation changed, however, as the early intakes of Trevecca students completed their training and became available for full-time service. Then the steady pressure began on Lady Huntingdon to allow her ministers to settle with individual congregations. An early example of this was the student John Harris, who wrote to Lady Huntingdon in 1773 of his hope of settling with a congregation in Dagger Lane, Hull, which had seceded from a Dissenting meeting some years previously. Harris's hope was to do this through Church rather than Dissenting ordination, and he offered as much occasional service in the Connexion as his studies (and, presumably his new congregation) would permit.[204] A similar combination of settled ministry with occasional Connexional help seems to have been in the minds of the Lincoln congregation who proposed in 1778 that John Eyre should settle with them.[205] Nor were such invitations

---

[203] T. Cannon to Wills, 15 July 1783, F1/534,CF.
[204] G. C. Bolam, *The English Presbyterians* (London, 1968), 209; J. Harris to LH, 11 Sept. 1773 and 20 Jan. 1777, F1/247, 380,CF. Though Dagger Lane was not regarded as part of the Connexion when Harris wrote, it was subsequently to become so, with Lady Huntingdon as principal trustee (*List of Trustees and Guardians of the New Chapel in Dagger Lane, Hull*, F1/1332,CF).
[205] J. Eyre to LH, 23 Feb. 1778, F1/429,CF.

necessarily confined to congregations already being supplied by the preacher in question: in 1776 William Dunn reported that an unnamed congregation in Sussex had invited him to become their minister.[206]

There must often have been attractions in a settled ministry, so far as preachers themselves were concerned. John Harris, for example, had been open about his preference for a settled ministry when telling Lady Huntingdon of his aspirations at Hull. And it was with some poignancy that Glascott commented to her in 1776 that he had by then been itinerating for ten years without house or home and would like somewhere settled in the winter, while continuing to 'ramble' in the summer.[207] That there were not more such requests from preachers was probably due to the reaction they knew they could expect from Lady Huntingdon. William Dunn, in the example previously quoted, was clearly left in no doubt of her views, for in his next letter he assured her that he would not mention settling again; if he were asked, he would refuse.[208] John Honeywell, who suggested settling with the Melksham congregation at around the same time, received an equally sharp response.[209] In this, Lady Huntingdon's attitude was not dissimilar to that of Wesley's to preachers who preferred family ties to the life of a Methodist itinerant. Writing to the Moravian Francis Okeley in 1758, Wesley suggested that there were five reasons (none of them the claimed theological ones) why he would not join the Methodists: '(1) a wife; (2) a mother; (3) children; (4) cowardice; (5) love of ease'.[210]

---

[206] W. Dunn to LH, 19 Mar. and 6 Apr. 1776, F1/349, 355,CF.

[207] Glascott to LH, 1 June 1776, F1/1729,CF. He also wanted a wife, though he had not yet fixed on anyone. Both desires were to be satisfied during his lengthy period as rector of Hatherleigh, Devon (Seymour, ii. 458–64; Haweis and Mrs Haweis to LH, 27 June 1789, F1/2084,CF).

[208] W. Dunn to LH, 6 Apr. 1776, F1/355,CF.

[209] *Evangelical Magazine* (1838), 20.

[210] JW to F. Okeley, 4 Oct. 1758, Wesley, *Letters*, iv. 35. Professor Ward comments on the attitude of some Wesleyan preachers to Wesley's authoritarian rule: 'Many thought (not unnaturally) that if life in the Church was not to be available to them, life outside, on the model of the dissenting ministry, offered advantages which their present state did not' (*Evangelical Awakening*, 350). Some in LH's Connexion doubtless felt the same.

Lady Huntingdon's attitude was not without some justification. She had been responsible for her students' training, and had some right to expect them to serve the Connexion for a while after. The problem was that no clear understanding seems to have existed as to what *was* expected. In 1776 a correspondent argued, after the departure of another student, that she should in future tie them formally for three years,[211] but no firm agreement seems to have been established. Thomas Green, once he had settled at Banbury in 1781, clearly changed his mind on the principle of itinerant ministry, and reacted vigorously against her suggestion that he had bound himself to serve her for four years; he did not, he asserted, feel himself obliged to refuse a call to feed the people of God, in favour of roaming the country, disturbing settled churches.[212] Green was arguing for freedom to settle permanently with a congregation, and effectively to leave the Connexion. Doing so seemed to Lady Huntingdon to restrict a preacher's potential usefulness, quite apart from the loss itself. When the students Molland and Adams were ordained in 1777, she lamented their 'narrow...sphere of action...which must render a labourer in these days...but a miserable prisoner at best'.[213] A separate, but related, concern on Lady Huntingdon's part was to preserve the principle of regular rotation between congregations of those whose services she did retain in the Connexion. In 1783, for example, she wrote to the Berkhamsted congregation to justify her removal of their then student 'as I have found a succession of both ministers and students to be most for the edification of the people and the improvement of the ministerial gifts'.[214]

Some students did in fact share Lady Huntingdon's belief in the advantages of an itinerant ministry. Some welcomed

---

[211] G. Smith to LH, 4 July 1776, F1/365,CF.

[212] T. Green to LH, 14 Mar. 1781, F1/1860,CF. Some students clearly did serve for a fixed four-year term, however. The student Samuel Eyles Pierce was preaching in Cornwall in 1779 when 'my term of four years, with her Ladyship, expired'. He wrote to her that he had been invited to settle, whereupon 'she gave me her full consent, and expressed her real regard for me' (S. E. Pierce, *A True Outline and Sketch of the Life of Samuel Eyles Pierce, written by himself* (London, 1824), 64).

[213] Aveling, *Claytons*, 37.

[214] LH to Berkhamsted congregation, 16 Oct. 1783, Seymour, ii. 475.

the challenge and invigoration that came with a change of congregation; one at least expressed the view that remaining with the same congregation was actually more demanding than travelling (a view that John Newton expressed from the perspective of parish ministry), while another asked to go back to itinerancy despite the damage it might do to his health.[215] There were even a few instances of congregations who went against the norm and favoured a rotation of preachers, though this could simply have represented a desire to be rid of a particular individual. In 1789 a man who had been at Worcester only ten months reported that the congregation liked regular changes of ministers;[216] it is possibly significant that the same man reported from Norwich the following year that they too were a congregation that favoured changes.[217]

The overall thrust, however, was towards a settled ministry, and there are signs, despite her general opposition to settled ministries, that Lady Huntingdon was prepared to look favourably on the idea in individual cases, even at quite an early date. As early as 1775, she herself appears to have suggested to William Aldridge the idea of settling with a congregation in the Sussex area, if an appropriate opening offered.[218] During the 1770s the idea was discussed with her of treating the major chapels as a separate entity within the Connexion, preserving a more distinctively Anglican character, and with a consistency of supply whether by one man or a small team.[219] It was apparently a settled ministry that Lady Huntingdon was seeking to arrange for Woolwich in 1777, in the special circumstances created by the absence in

---

[215] J. Newbon to LH, 15 Oct. 1777; Molland to LH, 28 Aug. 1777; R. Herdsman to LH, 17 Apr. 1787, F1/410, 402, 621,CF; Hindmarsh, *Newton*, 216. In Newton's view, itinerants might only be good for a dozen sermons; more skill was needed to be a 'burning, shining, steady light' in one parish year after year.

[216] L. Jones to LH, 18 Aug. 1789, F1/852,CF; but see below for evidence of a different kind from Worcester seven years later.

[217] L. Jones to LH, 16 July 1790, F1/928,CF.

[218] Aldridge to LH, 29 Apr. 1775; Bryant to LH, 1 Aug. and 5 Oct. 1775, F1/1715, 1717, 1720,CF. In contrast to this (and perhaps more indicative of her views at the time) was Wills's assumption in 1776 that she would object to a student suspected of wanting to settle (Wills to LH, 18 Nov. 1776, F1/1735,CF).

[219] Haweis to LH, n.d., F1/1191-2,CF (below, Ch. 6).

America on her behalf of the Revd William Piercy, who had ministered there previously.[220] Nor was settling ruled out in less glamorous locations. In 1779, for example, she responded positively to a former student who asked if there were a congregation with which he might settle, although in this case the man concerned concluded that the congregation offered was too small to provide adequate support, and he went to look elsewhere.[221] Three years later, the Worcester congregation wrote that they had heard of her preparedness to let men settle with certain congregations for a year at a time, and enquired how much they would have to raise to be supplied in that way.[222] Some other instances of long-staying at this time, however, may have been due more to a failure to remember to move the man in question than to deliberate policy. This seems to have been the case with Joseph Sowden, who by 1780 had done two years with the Haxey congregation.[223]

As time went on, and organizing the Connexion became more complex, longer stays became increasingly common. Robert Ellis, for example, had done fifteen months at Haxey (perhaps a place which it was particularly easy to forget) by August 1788; Robert Caldwell had been at Sleaford for two years by November 1788; and Thomas Young had done seventeen months at Newark by October 1789.[224] In this there are parallels with Wesleyan Methodism, which in 1784 moved from Wesley's previous limit on lengths of stay in any one place of 'usually one year, two years in exceptional cases', to a new maximum of three years.[225] Other factors, too, combined to make the Connexion a more static organization. In a number of instances, links once established between individual ministers and congregations were to be

---

[220] Woolwich chapel to LH, 26 Sept. 1777, F1/408,CF.
[221] T. Davies to LH, 22 July, 18 Aug., and 9 Oct. 1779, F1/435, 443, 450,CF.
[222] Skinner to LH, 12 Oct. 1782, F1/486,CF.
[223] Glascott to LH, 25 July 1780, F1/1850,CF.
[224] Ellis to LH, 27 Aug. 1788; Sleaford society to LH, 1 Nov. 1788; Young to LH, 17 Oct. 1789, F1/2033, 780, 2107,CF. By May 1792 Caldwell had completed five and a half years at Sleaford, but his stay ended soon after (Caldwell to Lady AE, 27 May and 3 Nov. 1792, F1/2220, 2232,CF).
[225] Baker, 'Polity', 226.

preserved over time, and to lead eventually to more permanent relationships. This was the case with Richard Herdsman, whose first visit to South Petherton is reported in 1774, and who is recorded as having settled there ten years later.[226] A similar pattern emerged later in the century within Dissent, where a natural transition often occurred from itinerant preacher to pastor of the church raised.[227] Most important of all was the fact that both preachers and congregations began to recognize the clear advantage of a more settled relationship between pastor and people, not only for purely 'pastoral' reasons, but also in the minister's own interests, and because the regular service of a known minister was often a significant factor in maintaining a congregation.[228] This might not necessarily mean the appointment of a single man to a congregation for the whole year, however. Some sort of 'team ministry' was clearly in mind when the acquisition of the Portland chapel in London was under consideration in 1783: the suggestion was for three or four ministers to be settled at the chapel while giving occasional service elsewhere.[229] At Bath and Spa Fields there was developed for periods the pattern of a resident assistant, coupled with a rotation of more distinguished 'stated' ministers; it was something on the same lines which the Birmingham congregation thought might aid their recovery from a difficult patch in 1788.[230] The more frequently applied model, which still preserved links with the Connexion, was that which was proposed for Walsall in 1788, for their minister to be settled on a resident basis, but performing occasional services outside.[231] A similar arrangement was mooted for Evesham in the following year. Here the proposal was for the minister to serve between six and

---

[226] S. Clark to LH, 21 May 1774 and 5 Apr. 1784, F1/299, 611,CF.
[227] Lovegrove, *Established Church, Sectarian People*, 54–5.
[228] One congregation that tried unsuccessfully to achieve a settled ministry was Berkhamsted, which after four years of effort, left the Connexion in 1788 to look elsewhere for a minister (Taylor to LH, 2 Mar. 1784; E. Hill to LH, 2 Mar. 1788, F1/1933, 712,CF). [229] Taylor to LH, 31 May 1783, F1/1890,CF.
[230] Birmingham committee to LH, 18 July 1788, F1/746,CF.
[231] J. Holmes to LH, 12 Sept. and 24 Nov. 1788, F1/2039, 790,CF.

twelve weeks a year in the Connexion at large, apparently paying for his supply during that time out of his stipend from the congregation.[232] The possibility of combining a settled ministry with participation in the fuller life of the Connexion may actually have been a positive attraction for independent congregations considering a link with the Countess: Handsworth, Birmingham (in 1788) and Holywell-Mount, Shoreditch (in 1789) were both congregations which joined the Connexion subject to an agreement on these lines.[233]

Just as the Connexion had developed into a large-scale itinerant mission with little deliberate planning, following the foundation of Trevecca College, so the move away from itinerancy was effected with a similar lack of conscious decision. Indeed, what emerges most clearly from a study of this aspect of the Connexion is not simply the lack of a coherent policy on Lady Huntingdon's part, but the absence of any clear message to her followers as to what was, and what was not, permitted. Despite the pressures towards settled ministry discernible in the earlier period, and the encouragement of the idea which Lady Huntingdon gave in individual cases, it was still possible as late as 1782 for a student to believe that settling might mean leaving the Connexion.[234] More striking still was the division reported at Worcester in 1784 between those in the congregation who supported continued membership of the Connexion, and those who wanted 'a settled ministry on the dissenting plan'.[235] It seems unlikely that a system of general itinerancy could have been maintained indefinitely, even though moves towards the general acceptance of settled ministry in the Connexion coincided with a rediscovery of the value of the itinerant preaching among Dissenters.[236]

---

[232] J. Dawson to LH, 20 May and 26 Dec. 1789, 26 Apr. 1790, F1/2077, 2114, 907,CF.
[233] Ford and Shepherd to LH, 31 Dec. 1788; Agreement between LH and trustees of the Holywell Mount chapel, 2 Sept. 1789, F1/799, E4/15(47),CF.
[234] G. Meller to LH, 26 Oct. 1782, F1/491,CF.
[235] *Life of Wills*, 117.
[236] Lovegrove, *Established Church, Sectarian People, passim*.

The forces undermining itinerancy were obvious. Even the most zealous minister was likely to feel the call of a settled home eventually, and the choice was bound to be between depriving the Connexion of the services of its more mature preachers (by forcing them out when that call came) or adapting the Connexional plan to accommodate them. Weakening the itinerant principle, however, had drawbacks for Lady Huntingdon. Settled ministers, even if willing to give occasional service elsewhere in the Connexion, were a less immediately available resource than itinerants. Nor could Lady Huntingdon retain the same influence over congregations served by settled ministers as she could over those dependent on her to maintain the supply of itinerants. Lady Huntingdon's itinerants did not have the status of Wesley's lay preachers, his 'other self' as Frank Baker called them, whose purpose, in part, was to sustain the unity of the movement.[237] Yet even in the Connexion, itinerants had a vital role in creating and preserving a sense of cohesion and common identity between the congregations. The itinerant principle thus retained its hold for a considerable time.

Although the idea of eventual settlement had become generally accepted by the early years of the 1780s, this seems to have been something for the older and more experienced who had, as it were, gone through the 'curacy' stage of an itinerant ministry first.[238] The reported concern of a student in 1796 that he might not be given immediate employment with a settled congregation indicates the further erosion of the principle of itinerancy that was to take place.[239]

Popular opposition

It was not to be expected that the range of activities described in this chapter would escape altogether the violently expressed opposition that characterized so much of

---

[237] Baker, *Wesley and the Church of England*, 81, 108–9. If LH had any who might be described as her 'other self' it was her clerical assistants for so long as they remained in favour.   [238] E. Parsons to LH, 10 July 1783, F1/1892,CF.
[239] Apostolic Society minute book for 6 Apr. 1796, C1/2,CF.

the early history of Methodism.[240] Although the Connexion's experiences did not differ radically from those of other groups within the Revival, they are worthy of mention, both for the contribution they make to the general history of popular resistance to Methodism, and because they were bound to leave some mark on the subsequent ethos of the group.[241] In two respects some difference of emphasis might have been expected. Because the Connexion's period of expansion came much later than that of Wesleyan Methodism, its preachers were unlikely to be suspected, like Wesley's in the early years, of being agents for Jacobite infiltration. And expansion came also at a stage when Wesley's policy of going to law over cases of violent opposition had built up a body of case law that removed much of the earlier uncertainty over whether Methodists could expect legal protection.[242] The fact that the pattern of opposition appears broadly the same for the Countess's Connexion suggests that it was principally the novelty of visiting preachers in an area, or of an unfamiliar form of religious presentation, that generated the suspicion and fear that led to violence.[243] Thus it was that the main examples of opposition to the Connexion tend to be grouped in the earlier 1770s, when the Connexion was first beginning to expand. A few examples do occur in the previous period, as when Glascott experienced eggs and 'huzzas' at Arundel in 1768,[244] and

---

[240] e.g. in R. Wearmouth, *Methodism and the Common People of the Eighteenth Century* (London, 1945).

[241] This section draws upon J. D. Walsh, 'Methodism and the Mob in the Eighteenth Century', *Studies in Church History*, 8 (1971), 213–27, for a background picture of mob opposition to Methodism, and attempts to indicate the extent to which the situation he describes (largely from the records of Wesleyan Methodism) applied also in the case of the Connexion. See also M. F. Snape, 'Anti-Methodism in Eighteenth Century England: The Pendle Forest Riots of 1748', *Journal of Ecclesiastical History*, 49/2 (Apr. 1998), 257 ff.

[242] Walsh, 'Methodism and the Mob', 226; David Hempton, *The Religion of the People: Methodism and Popular Religion, c.1750–1900* (London and New York, 1996), 151–2.

[243] Ibid. 222. See also, Walsh, 'Methodism and the Local Community in the Eighteenth Century', 142.

[244] Glascott to LH, 28 July 1768, F1/1440,CF. Eggs were obviously a convenient missile in such circumstances, being capable of producing the maximum unpleasantness with the minimum risk of significant injury. Amongst other examples were the goose egg thrown into the congregation at South Petherton in 1773, and the collection of addled eggs thrown at John Clayton in 1776 'till the young minister's

when he was mobbed out of 'Tunbridge Town' in the following year.[245] There were troubles too at the Bath chapel in 1768, when a mob tried to disturb the evening preaching,[246] and the beginning of the following year another of Lady Huntingdon's clerical correspondents reported that he had suffered the more sophisticated indignity of having been burned in effigy.[247] But it is around 1774 that a cluster of incidents is reported. Glascott was a target again, during a preaching campaign designed to extend the Connexion's influence and presence in the Leicestershire/Lincolnshire/Northamptonshire area. In February stones were thrown at the windows of a Dissenting meeting house in which he was preaching in Lincoln.[248] In May he was pelted and forced to retreat from Grantham, and he received similarly rough treatment in the streets at Oundle, though in each of these cases he experienced no trouble when he returned to preach indoors.[249] One of the students working with him, William Dunn, experienced opposition in the Stamford area at the same time. Glascott's advice to him to preach only on Sunday mornings, coupled with the fact that indoor preaching appeared on balance less likely to arouse hostility than addresses on the streets, adds to the impression that it was what was unusual that was most likely to provoke an adverse reaction.[250]

Violence was experienced in other areas of the country in 1774. In West Sussex, when Peckwell was engaged in a campaign not dissimilar from Glascott's, to establish a number of new Connexional causes, he reported violence at Midhurst,

---

face, apparel and preaching robes...became as yellow as gold' (Glascott to LH, 8 June 1773, F1/1646,CF; Aveling, *Claytons*, 19).

[245] De Courcy to LH, 8 July 1769, F1/73,CF.

[246] Maxfield to LH (stamped 19) Dec. 1768, F1/1450,CF.

[247] E. Davies to LH, 17 Jan. 1769; Fletcher to LH, 10 Feb. 1769, F1/45, 1457,CF.

[248] Glascott to LH, 18 Feb. 1774, F1/274,CF.

[249] When he returned in June, he managed to preach on two occasions without disturbance. By that stage plans for the setting up of a place of worship for the Connexion were already well advanced, possibly marking thereby the change from mere itinerant preaching to being a more permanent part of the local religious landscape (Glascott to LH, 24 May and 11 June 1774, F1/1696, 1698,CF).

[250] The hostility to Dunn was so strong, however, that he was forced to desist (Glascott to LH, 11 July 1774, F1/308,CF).

which he thought worse than that at Marylebone.[251] Further west, in Dorset, the student John Holmes was mobbed out of Weymouth.[252] In Dorset it was not the case that familiarity led to tolerance: at Dorchester, in early 1777, Molland wrote that the opposition he was facing had increased ten times over what it had been before.[253] Although spasmodic instances of opposition were to be reported to Lady Huntingdon for the remainder of her life, there does not appear to have been the same concentration of violent outbreaks after the mid-1770s. Glascott, for one, thought that by the early 1780s prejudice against field and street preaching was wearing off, recalling after a peaceful visit to Newark in 1781 that Glazebrook had escaped with his life from there some years before.[254] Wills, on the other hand, during his preaching tour of the same year, experienced varying degrees of opposition, ranging from overt physical violence through to noisy interruptions and petty vandalism (breaking the hinges of his chaise door and scratching the panels).[255] His biographer, writing in the early years of the nineteenth century, dated the decline of popular hostility from a little later than the Glascott comment implied; in his view it was the late 1780s before the novelty of Methodism had sufficiently worn off in London, with country districts falling some way behind the metropolis in displaying a similarly accepting attitude.[256]

In the nature of things it is impossible to tell the extent to which popular opposition was a spontaneous expression of indignation and hostility. What is clear is that other elements were present in at least some of the instances of violence that the Connexion experienced. The clergy were an obvious group whose influence within their own communities was

---

[251] Peckwell to LH, n.d. (stamped 3 Mar.), F1/1246,CF.
[252] J. Holmes to LH, 16 May 1774, F1/295,CF.
[253] T. Molland to LH, 14 May 1777, F1/377,CF.
[254] Glascott to LH, 20 Aug. 1781, E4/11(5),CF.
[255] *Life of Wills*, 132–4, 84, 130.
[256] Ibid. 222. He was, however, over-optimistic, for the early decades of the next century were to witness mob violence against Primitive Methodism that had many features in common with eighteenth-century persecutions (Joseph Ritson, *The Romance of Primitive Methodism* (London, 4th edn. 1909), 165–8).

threatened by the coming of itinerant preachers. The latter's presence was an implicit rebuke to a community's existing pastors, and the Connexion, like other groups in the Revival, experienced instances of opposition directly fomented by clergymen.[257] From Pershore, in an undated letter probably written in the summer of 1773, came a story of sustained persecution under clerical leadership. With the encouragement of the vicar and curate, it was said, the mob had twice wrecked the building set up for worship, and had engaged in a policy of bonfires, bells, window-breaking, and burning in effigy. With some satisfaction, however, Lady Huntingdon's correspondent was able to report the sudden deaths of both the curate and the vicar.[258] Peckwell was convinced that it was Parson Atkins of Midhurst who was behind the pelting (with eggs, apples, and tiles) which they experienced in that town in March 1774. When a room was found for preaching, Atkins succeeded in getting them locked out, and he subsequently attempted to persuade the poor of the town of their landlord's displeasure if they persisted in attending.[259] Vicars and rectors clearly had greater potential influence with local people than did their curates, who may generally have confined themselves to verbal opposition. When Glascott preached in a house at Westham, Sussex, in 1771, the curate of the place challenged him to a debate in the churchyard before the assembled congregation; in July 1774, Anthony Crole reported that he had been preached against in three churches by the curate of Corfe.[260]

Another motive for clerical opposition is suggested at Harwich in 1776. The church there was a chapel of ease supported by voluntary contributions, and the student William Dunn was especially apprehensive of the anger of the vicar and curate if his preaching drew away their congregation.[261] A similar monetary factor, as will be seen, was important in the battle over the Spa Fields chapel in

---

[257] Walsh, 'Methodism and the Mob', *passim*.
[258] W. Aldington and W. Brown to LH, 5 June n.y., F1/1102,CF.
[259] Peckwell and Mrs Peckwell to LH, 1 Mar. 1774, F1/275,CF.
[260] Glascott to LH, 3 June 1771; Crole to LH, 13 July 1774, F1/125, 311,CF.
[261] Dunn to LH, 8 July 1776, F1/366,CF.

London that culminated in secession by the Connexion in the following decade.[262] Even when financial considerations were not involved, clergy were unlikely to welcome the loss of their congregations to evangelical causes. A threat of this kind led the Revd Richard Graves to compose his anti-Methodist parody *The Spiritual Quixote*. There is evidence in 1788 of hostility from Church people at Stowbridge, from whose congregation (along with that of the Dissenters) the Connexional congregation had been drawn.[263] Persecution may indeed, as some believed,[264] have become alien to the Church's leaders by the end of the century, but it was bound to be a different matter for clergy placed in direct competition with Connexional (or any other) preachers. A student at Castle Donnington in 1794 reported that the vicar of a neighbouring parish was sending over men to kick about a football during his preaching—a ploy which revealed (even if by less violent means) an attitude and a spirit not dissimilar from that of Parson Atkins, two decades earlier.[265]

The clergy were not the only ones prominent within the local community, however, who had a role in fomenting opposition to the Connexion. Three local squires were thought to be behind the burning in effigy of one of Lady Huntingdon's clerical helpers in 1769, for example,[266] while at least one of the violent episodes which Wills experienced in 1781 had a 'local gentleman' behind it. In the latter case the man had succeeded in getting the mob drunk in anticipation, but when Wills was late in arriving they began pelting each other instead.[267] Churchwardens and overseers could also be obstructive, as Peckwell found, again in Sussex, in the early 1770s.[268] When it came to the magistracy and the mayoralty, there is no evidence of direct involvement in violence. But such people were likely to colour quite considerably the attitude of the local populace by the response they made to

---

[262] See below, Ch. 7.
[263] Stourbridge chapel to LH, 27 May 1788, F1/729,CF.
[264] See below, Ch. 8.   [265] J. Garrett to Lady AE, 17 May 1794, F1/999,CF.
[266] E. Davies to LH, 17 Jan. 1769, F1/45,CF.   [267] *Life of Wills*, 132–4.
[268] Peckwell to LH, n.d. (stamped 9 Jan.), F1/1350,CF.

outbreaks of hostility, as well as being themselves influenced by the attitudes of the clergy. The Connexion may not have faced, as Wesley did with the dean of Ripon in 1766,[269] many instances of clergy who were also magistrates.[270] But in small local communities the views of the various representatives of the established order were likely to be known to each other, and to have some reciprocal influence. Thus the clergy and magistrates were said to be united in their antipathy to the Connexion in Lincoln in 1774.[271] In the same year, at Chichester, it was said to be fear of offending the clergy that decided the mayor to deny the Connexion the use of the town hall.[272] On the other hand there may have been little more than alcohol behind the opposition which Wills encountered from a drunken magistrate at Tenby in 1780.[273]

Overall, however, the Connexion does not appear to have fared badly in its dealings with local authority. The disturbances at the Bath chapel in 1768, for example, occasioned a remarkable demonstration of support from the lady mayoress who happened to be present; not only did she return the following Sunday with a group of officers to preserve the peace, but she instructed them to be present on subsequent Sundays as well.[274] The mayor of Stamford in 1774 showed himself prepared to defend the Connexion's legal rights, provided they themselves acted lawfully,[275] while in the same year the recorder of Chichester, before whom Peckwell brought the issue of the Midhurst riots, stoutly defended Peckwell's right to pursue his lawful calling, and warned the populace against disturbing the Connexion's preachers.[276] Nearly twenty years later, when the chapel at Monmouth was 'driven...to a Tribunal of temporal justice' to defend its position, it was noted that no attorney need be engaged as the mayor and town clerk had been kind enough

---

[269] JW to the dean of Ripon, 9 July 1766, Wesley, *Letters*, v. 22.
[270] In 1761 more than a thousand justices were in orders; by 1831, a quarter of the total bench were clerics (Peter Virgin, *The Church in an Age of Negligence* (Cambridge, 1989), 256).   [271] Glascott to LH, 28 Feb. 1774, F1/274,CF.
[272] Peckwell to Lloyd, 23 Feb. 1774, F1/1676,CF.   [273] *Life of Wills*, 23.
[274] Maxfield to LH, Dec. (stamped 19) 1768, F1/1450,CF.
[275] Glascott to LH, 11 July 1774, F1/308,CF.
[276] Peckwell to LH, n.d. (stamped 16 Apr.), F1/1247,CF.

to offer all necessary help.²⁷⁷ Attitudes varied inevitably from person to person, and place to place, as Wills found at Walsall in 1784, when the current mayor stopped him from being announced by the crier—whereupon the previous year's mayor, a magistrate, offered him the use of his own doorstep as a preaching place.²⁷⁸

The decision to go to law against its opponents was not one that the Connexion necessarily took without question. Involving the civil power could be seen as a failure to live up to the Gospel message of love and forgiveness, as well as an acknowledgement that the message itself had failed to win over the recalcitrant. In 1775 a correspondent wrote to Lady Huntingdon that he knew she disapproved of their having resorted to law, justifying the decision on the grounds that otherwise the rioters in question would have burned down the new preaching place and broken open the people's houses.²⁷⁹ The Monmouth decision to involve the law, referred to above, had initially been opposed by Lady Anne Erskine. In December 1791, when she had only recently assumed the mantle of the Connexion from her friend, and with no sense of departure from established practice, she wrote that she hoped that proceedings would not be necessary; a high fine or imprisonment would be repugnant to her, and she hoped she was not more severe than the gentleness which the Gospel demanded.²⁸⁰

Such hesitation did not, as the earlier instances quoted indicate, inhibit periodic resort to the protection of the law. Wesley had argued that swift action by the magistracy would always bring disorder to a rapid end,²⁸¹ and there must have been sympathy amongst some members of the Connexion at this more pragmatic approach. Such seems to have been the attitude of Walter Shirley, who in 1771 informed Lady Huntingdon of an incident at the Bath chapel which had a number of parallels in the wider history of Methodism, a disturbance occasioned by the husband of a woman who had

---

[277] Lady AE to the Monmouth chapel committee, n.d., F1/1315,CF.
[278] *Life of Wills*, 126–7. [279] E. Bryant to LH, 1 Aug. 1775, F1/1717,CF.
[280] Lady AE to 'Sir', 28 Dec. 1791, F1/2197,CF.
[281] JW's Journal for 15 Mar. 1768, *Works*, xxii. 120.

become a regular attender. Shirley himself, as a former JP, drew up the charge (lest the clerk be too lenient to one of the mayor's tenants), although he subsequently speculated whether they should leave the man in prison until his fine was paid, or adopt a compassionate attitude.[282] Even less reticence is apparent in the request from Norwich in 1784 for Lady Huntingdon's prayers for the success of their action against those rioters committed to appear at the quarter session.[283] These must, however, have been comparative isolated instances, for in 1792 a preacher expressed surprise that the Connexion had not made a more concerted effort to defend its legal privileges, instancing the way the Protestant Dissenters employed the services of a particular attorney to present their claims before the King's Bench under the Act of Toleration.[284] Compared with Wesley's readiness to appeal to King's Bench, both against magistrates reluctant to afford Methodists the protection of the Toleration Act, and directly against rioters, the Connexion's attitude appears uncharacteristically reticent.[285]

THE LIFE OF CONGREGATIONS

Authority within the congregation

No matter how strong a centralized leadership Lady Huntingdon might attempt to exercise, sources of authority were also bound to emerge within individual chapels and congregations. Mention has already been made of the significant role played by individuals in both the initiation of

---

[282] Shirley to LH, 19 Dec. 1771, F1/1556,CF. See Walsh, 'Methodism and the Mob', 223–4 for other examples of disturbances caused by resentful families.
[283] Norwich chapel committee to LH, 27 Feb. 1784, F1/604,CF.
[284] J. Jones to Lady AE, 7–12 July 1792, F1/2224,CF.
[285] In 1766 Wesley claimed that he had never lost any of his 'many' (potentially expensive) suits in the King's Bench, although this may not have been quite true (Hempton, *Religion of the People*, 152). Wesley was later to advise his followers to use the Riot Act in the face of mob violence since the Toleration Act allowed damages only up to £20 (JW to the dean of Ripon, 9 July 1766, and to J. Winscom, 9 May 1785, Wesley, *Letters*, v. 22, vii. 270; Baker, *Wesley and the Church of England*, 198).

Connexional congregations, and the admission to the Connexion of existing causes. This was only to be expected. Someone had to take it upon himself to issue invitations to preachers, to provide or arrange preaching places, to maintain contacts with the Countess, and to organize building projects; and in most places one or more leading individuals are identifiable in those roles. Sometimes that influence might stem from the circumstances surrounding the start of the congregation. Where the origins of a cause lay in the efforts or influence of a prominent local individual (perhaps the one who had invited in preachers or made premises available) it was not unnatural for him subsequently to play a leading role in shaping its affairs. One example of this was the Gainsborough grocer, John Fletcher, who had initiated the town's first contacts with Connexional preachers, and who appears as a key figure in the congregation's affairs for some years thereafter.[286] The Connexion appears to have had no formal system of stewards responsible for the business affairs of each congregation as in Wesleyan Methodism.[287] Occasionally, however, authority might be vested in chapel managers, or even in a single manager. There appears, for example, to have been a recognizable individual who was known as manager of Barton-upon-Humber at the end of the 1780s.[288] The term manager does not seem, however, to have been in general use within the Connexion, though the concept would not have been foreign to it—as shown by the sad case of an applicant to the Connexion in 1782 who reported that his previous services, with an independent chapel in Sussex, had come to an end when his rival for the pulpit married the lady chapel manager.[289]

The more normal model for Connexional chapels was of shared leadership through a committee. Committees appear to have been regarded as responsible for preserving the life of a congregation, and furthering its objectives, as well as undertaking the necessary day-to-day tasks. Thus members

---

[286] 'A Brief Historick Record'; Fletcher to LH, 16 June 1773, F1/1647,CF.
[287] Baker, 'Polity', 240. A few Connexional causes did have stewards, however.
[288] T. Watson to LH, 22 July 1788, F1/748,CF.
[289] J. Bartholomew to LH, 23 Dec. 1782, F/1878,CF.

of the Norwich congregation wrote in 1778 to thank Lady Huntingdon for ordering a committee 'as the people's voice for regulating the Chapel'.[290] That regulation might extend to the morals of the congregation, as a couple (married, but not to each other) found at Spa Fields in 1781, when they were summoned for interrogation by the committee, and advised not to sit together in future.[291] Or a committee might be the means of maintaining ecclesiastical order. At Chichester in 1783, one prominent member—previously reported to have given up as manager, hearer, and subscriber in protest at ministers distributing the sacrament too freely—was said to support a committee being appointed to defend the chapel rules against any minister who might seek to bend them.[292]

The latter episode is illustrative of the tension that was implicit in the relationship between preachers on the one hand and those in positions of influence locally. In a sense, indeed, there were three potential areas of authority within the Connexion, without any articulated theory of church government to spell out the intended relationship between them: the Countess and her close confidants at the centre, local leaders out in congregations, and ministers and preachers in some ill-defined position in the middle. Within such a set-up, tension was inevitable, especially as the Connexion had no system of conferences or associations— akin to those of Wesleyan Methodism or the Welsh Calvinistic Methodists—to act as a point of reference on matters of faith and practice. Strong local leadership, for example, was not easily compatible with decisive ministerial direction, and there were occasional instances of resentment by men who had been active in the foundation or development of causes at the assumption of authority by a preacher. One such was William Simpson, who had played a prominent

---

[290] J. Ivory and others to LH, 17 Jan. 1778, F1/423,CF. Wills expressed a similar sentiment in 1782 (Wills to LH, 10 Oct. 1782, F1/1868,CF). Dr Welch believed, however, that committees were still being appointed (rather than directly elected) long after LH's death (Welch, 197).

[291] Spa Fields minute book for 31 July 1781, D1/1, 11,CF.

[292] Bains and Tuff to LH, 27 Apr. 1783; Prichard to LH, 14 Nov. 1783, F1/515, 567,CF.

part in the opening of Mulberry Gardens chapel in 1777, and who apparently had a significant financial stake in the undertaking. Simpson was not pleased to be termed a 'cypher' by a preacher who then proceeded, without his authority, to make wide-ranging changes in the weekly pattern of services.[293]

The resentment might, however, be as strong the other way. In 1782 William Taylor reportedly accused some committees of usurping control, 'like dissenting deacons'.[294] This was a serious charge in a Connexion that seems generally to have fought shy of what was seen as the hallmark of independency. The Gainsborough congregation, for example, specifically decided against deacons, as too great a symbolic departure from the Established Church.[295] No such reticence affected the Morpeth congregation, who by the later 1780s had deacons, elders, trustees, *and* a committee,[296] although they appear very much the exception. For all Taylor's fears, most committees, though they might occasionally flex their muscles in regard to individual preachers, claimed limited independence. In respect of the major chapels, at least, committees appear to have seen themselves as much Lady Huntingdon's lieutenants as tribunes of the congregation. The Spa Fields committee, for example, may well have been typical in having been appointed by Lady Huntingdon.[297] Even in the last months of Lady Huntingdon's life, when the Mulberry Gardens committee were offered the chance of choosing some new names to add to their numbers, they still opted to leave the decision to her.[298] A committee's relationship with Lady Huntingdon might break down, as it did at Bath over the affair of the chapel school,[299] and in that case resignation—though it deprived the congregation of

---

[293] Miss Scutt to LH, 13 Dec. 1777, E4/2/17,CF *et seq*. During building it was by no means certain that Simpson and his colleagues would place the chapel under LH's control (Peckwell and Mrs Peckwell to LH, 24 Dec. 1776; W. Simpson Jnr. to LH, 3 Jan. 1778, F1/1921, 421,CF).
[294] Wills to LH, 10 Oct. 1782, F1/1868,CF.
[295] 'A Brief Historick Record'.
[296] Morpeth to LH, 10 Apr. 1788, F1/753,CF.
[297] Spa Fields minute book for 25 Jan. 1780, D1/1, 2,CF.
[298] Mann to LH, 9 Mar. 1791, F1/965,CF. [299] See above.

their spokesmen and representatives—was seen as the natural means of registering their protest against her.

Not infrequently, direction of a congregation's affairs might include legal responsibility for the chapel buildings. When an emerging cause reached the stage where a permanent place of worship could be contemplated, it would be necessary to formalize the ownership of the buildings concerned, and the principles upon which they were to be operated. The establishment of a trust was often the means employed to achieve these ends, and it was a process in which Lady Huntingdon took as close an interest as in other aspects of the life of her congregations. In 1783 the Newark congregation, in the process of acquiring a site, informed Lady Huntingdon that they were placing land and buildings in the hands of trustees, as she had directed, in accordance with a trust deed that would provide that 'no Ministers are to be admitted...but such as preach the pure Gospel and the true Calvinist Doctrine.'[300]

Establishment of a trust offered a means of keeping ministers in their place more generally than just in matters of doctrine. Wrangles at Norwich in 1777 over the dominant influence which the Revd Walter Shirley was perceived to be seeking, were checked by Lady Huntingdon's promise that a trust would be established to regulate the chapel's affairs.[301] No organization, however constituted, could hope to avoid disputes, especially when loyalties to individual preachers were involved. There is evidence at Hereford in 1788, for example, of disagreement between the trustees on the one hand, and on the other the supporters of the student William Holland—the latter claiming to speak on behalf of the principal inhabitants of the city, as well as the congregation, in arguing for him to stay.[302] Whether or not

---

[300] Newark to LH, 9 Sept. and 15 Nov. 1783, F1/548, 569,CF. LH does not seem to have made the same systematic attempt as Wesley to ensure through standardized trust deeds that chapels established in her name admitted only doctrinally sympathetic preachers, a policy which, even in Wesley's case, was not universally successful (Baker, 'Polity'. 229). The very fact of appointing local trustees, of course, increased the danger of congregations developing a policy and mind of their own (Baker, *Wesley and the Church of England*, 108).

[301] Glascott to LH, 18 Nov. 1777; LH to Norwich chapel, n.d., F1/1802, 1235,CF.

[302] T. Silvester and J. Sharp to LH, 21 July 1788; Hereford chapel members to LH, 4 Aug. 1788, F1/747, 750,CF.

trustees were representatives of the popular will, however, vesting control of a chapel in their hands might lead to less contention in the ordering of its affairs than more democratic processes—or so Wills hoped at Worcester in 1785, when the decision was taken to transfer direction to the trustees, instead of determining questions by the vote of the whole society.[303]

If trustees were to perform a role in the day-to-day affairs of a congregation they, like committees, would have to be close to the cause concerned. Such close involvement was not always expected of the trustees, however. For the Dagger Lane chapel in Hull, in the 1770s, the list of those approached to be 'Trustees and Guardians' (with Lady Huntingdon as 'primary trustee') reads like a roll-call of the Calvinist evangelical great names.[304] And it is striking that three out of four of the original proposals for the Hereford trustees in 1783 were for men from outside the city—the only Hereford man named being subsequently deemed inappropriate as he was not a householder.[305]

At the other end of the spectrum from those who directed the affairs of a congregation, or constituted its trustees, were those whom it employed to serve its domestic needs or to perform functions in the context of worship. The grander the chapel, the more likely it was that such office-holders would be employed. Tunbridge Wells, for example, was employing a gowned chapel clerk in 1769; Bath employed a singing master in the early 1770s; and in 1780 the salaried employees of Spa Fields chapel included a cleaner, an apprentice footboy, and five doorkeepers—though two of the latter were to be dismissed on grounds of economy.[306]

---

[303] *Life of Wills*, 152–3.

[304] List of Dagger Lane trustees and guardians, F1/1332,CF. The names include Shirley, Piercy, Venn, Rowland Hill, and Edwards of Leeds. Trustees for Wesleyan Methodist preaching houses, at least in the early years, were rarely drawn exclusively from local worshippers (Baker, 'Polity', 228).

[305] Mrs Paul to LH, 26 Oct. 1783; S. Phillips to LH, 1 Nov. 1783, F1/564, 565,CF.

[306] Mrs Godde to LH, 6 Dec. 1769; Shirley to LH, 6 Feb. n.y.; Spa Fields minute book, 4 Apr. to 25 Aug. 1780, F1/82, 1366; D1/1, 4–7,CF. The Bath singing-master was presumably unpaid, since it was suggested to Lady Huntingdon that the introduction of a salary might help to keep him in his place.

But much less significant causes also engaged help. Newark, who before they acquired their chapel in 1783 had only an upstairs room in which to meet, nevertheless employed a man to clean the room and snuff the candles, and were indignant when the 'Pestilent Man' had the audacity to think he might have been chosen as a trustee.[307] The appointment of some office-holders could be a significant matter in the life of a congregation; an earlier complaint against Shirley at Norwich had been his handling of the appointment of chapel stewards.[308] Stewards, indeed, might exercise an influential role within the life of a congregation. The Chichester steward in 1779, for example, as well as administering the finances of the chapel, clearly saw himself as responsible for ensuring observation of the chapel rules as well—a role that, as he found, could lead to conflict with preachers reluctant to be bound by them.[309]

The employment of someone to read prayers does not appear to have been much considered in the early years. Spa Fields put the idea to Lady Huntingdon in 1781, as a means of relieving the burden on whoever preached, but were told that this would have been unprecedented in the Connexion. The Countess's objections appear to have veered between economic considerations—that it would be cheaper to buy any needed help ad hoc, rather than making a permanent appointment—and the fear that having a paid reader would give preachers an undue sense of their personal importance.[310] She does not appear to have pressed her objections, however. Eighteen months later when, following his secession from the Church of England, Wills was more regularly at Spa Fields and (by implication) stimulating the chapel income, the committee informed Lady Huntingdon that they could afford to pay a reader to give him the help his health demanded.[311]

---

[307] Newark to LH, 9 May and 9 Sept. 1783, F1/521, 548,CF.
[308] B. Nickalls to LH, 3 Apr. 1776, F1/354,CF.
[309] J. Lane to LH, 7 Aug. 1779, F1/440,CF.
[310] Copy of LH to the Spa Fields committee, 16 May 1781 (Spa Fields minute book, D1/1, 11,CF).
[311] Ibid. Copy of the committee to LH, 13 Aug. 1782, D1/1, 21–2,CF.

Societies

The formation of societies, where the faithful could meet to develop their faith, outside the context of worship, was a key to the spiritual life of Connexional congregations. In this the Connexion, like other groups in the Revival, stood in a great tradition. It was in the later decades of the seventeenth century that the phenomenon had emerged within Anglicanism of groups meeting in a formal way to foster religious development of their members through study and prayer, and through mutual commitment to a disciplined religious life. The model, a merging in some sense of the Puritan conventicle tradition with High Church piety,[312] was said by John Wesley to have inspired the Oxford Holy Club[313] and though such societies declined from the early eighteenth century, traces of them continued to appear. 'The Assembly for Christian Improvement' in which James Hervey was involved in the Northampton area from the late 1740s, for example, was constituted on lines very similar to those which had appeared in London seventy years before, and it is possible that a few instances of traditional Anglican religious societies survived throughout the eighteenth century.[314] Wesley himself, in Georgia in the 1730s, found that the society model could be made the vehicle, in a more popular setting, for building up the religious life of a congregation—in Curnock's phrase, 'a Moravian graft upon the Oxford Methodist stock'[315]—and from these beginnings grew the organizational structure that was to be the hallmark of Wesleyan Methodism. But there were differences between the old and the new societies. Whitefield suggested in 1739 that these lay not only in their theology, but in their practice of extempory prayer and the sharing of spiritual experience between members.[316] It is not in fact necessary to seek

---

[312] Henry Rack, 'Religious Societies and the Origins of Methodism', *Journal of Ecclesiastical History*, 38/4 (1987), 587.
[313] J. S. Simon, *John Wesley and the Religious Societies* (London, 1921), 1–27.
[314] James Hervey, *A Series of Letters from the late Rev. J. Hervey* (1760), pp. xxxii–xliii; Rack, 'Religious Societies', 583.   [315] Curnock, i. 198 n.
[316] Tyerman, *Whitefield*, i. 317–19.

continuity with earlier manifestations of the idea in every case, since the society model is a natural one for any group of like-minded individuals seeking to deepen their religious life. There are not infrequent instances which show how spontaneous this could be: for example, during the Cambuslang revival in Scotland in the 1740s, where contemporary accounts describe converts immediately forming themselves into societies 'for prayer and Christian conference'.[317] The expelled St Edmund Hall student Thomas Jones had been involved in a Staffordshire group that met for Bible study, prayer, and hymn-singing—described as 'family worship to which the neighbours were invited'—and in 1774 Glascott had come across a group in Lincolnshire that met privately for prayers and hymns.[318] Nor were such groups found only among evangelicals. There were some instances in the 1730s and 1740s of devotional groups forming within Dissenting congregations untouched by the Revival; later in the century a religious society formed at the Unitarian chapel at Essex Street in London.[319]

Despite all of this, Lady Huntingdon was initially cautious about the principle of religious societies. In 1748 she had expressed her reservations to Howel Harris 'from see^g ye Bigotry...coming in wth them'; in the following year she again 'spake her mind ag^t private societies'.[320] But she could not hold out against so self-evidently useful an institution. Within less than a decade the evangelical curate of Smisby in Leicestershire informed her, in terms which imply confidence in her approval of what was described, of the sixty people meeting in society at his church between morning and evening service.[321] By the time of the great expansion of

---

[317] Gillies, *Historical Collections* (Glasgow, 1754–61), ii. 342, 349.

[318] Richard Hill, *Pietas Oxoniensis; or a Full and Impartial Account of the Expulsion of Six Students from St. Edmund Hall, Oxford* (London, 1768), 23–4; Glascott to LH, 14 Mar. 1774, F1/279,CF.

[319] Rack, 'Religious Societies', 585; H. MacLachlan, *Letters of Theophilus Lindsey* (Manchester, 1920), 30.

[320] Harris's Diary for 5 July 1748, and 29 Apr. 1749. Whitefield was said to have had doubts about the society formed in Dublin in 1752 (Tyerman, *Whitefield*, ii. 287).

[321] Walter Sellon to LH, 5 Nov. 1757, F1/4,CF. There are many other instances of the society model operating in evangelical parishes. Newton held meetings in the parlour of Olney vicarage (transferring later to larger premises) and saw his prayer

Connexional activity from the end of the 1760s, she clearly had no doubts about the key importance of meetings outside worship in developing the faith of believers. 'Preaching they may hear and yet be miserably ignorant,' she wrote in 1773, 'whereas prayer meetings must bring them on in the examination of the heart.'[322]

Although some who joined Connexional congregations may already have known the benefits of participation in a private religious meeting of some kind, it is likely that for most such an opportunity came as a new experience. Sometimes the decision to form such an inner cell within a congregation, which would constitute the 'members' of the church as against the broader mass of casual attenders at worship, appeared the natural means of consolidating a new foundation. This was what the student Thomas Molland evidently felt at Dorchester in 1775, when he described the congregation he had raised and his intention soon to settle societies among them.[323] James Glazebrook sought Lady Huntingdon's advice on how to start a society at Ashby, a month after the chapel there had opened; and Wills, at Newark some eighteen months after the opening there, clearly felt that a society would deepen its religious life.[324] But there could sometimes be a significant gap before a society was added to a congregation's spiritual resources. The Gainsborough chapel, for example, was built in 1776, but it was not until the following decade that it gained a society;[325] similarly, Bristol opened in 1775 and waited for its society until 1784.[326] Nor did societies necessarily remain in continuous existence. In 1782 Spa Fields lost both its Monday society

---

meetings with parishioners as the nerve centre of his ministry (Newton to Lord Dartmouth, 16 Feb. 1768 and 9 Aug. 1769, HMC. (Dartmouth), iii. 186, 191; Hindmarsh, *Newton*, 198–200). In 1783, Pentycross had Friday evening meetings in his rectory at Wallingford (Lloyd to LH, 4 Mar. 1783, F1/512,CF). Nor were parsonage prayer meetings a new phenomenon: earlier in the century Susanna Wesley had held services and prayers for large numbers at Epworth rectory while her husband was away (V. H. Green, *The Young Mr. Wesley* (London, 1961), 49).

[322] LH to Hawkesworth, 13 Oct. 1773; Seymour, ii. 169.
[323] Molland to LH, 15 Apr. 1775, F1/323,CF.
[324] Glazebrook to LH, 20 May 1772, F1/181,CF; *Life of Wills*, 195.
[325] 'A Brief Historick Record'. [326] Taylor to LH, n.d., F1/1367,CF.

(following indecency accusations against a committee member who had been one of its principal superintendents) and had its Tuesday society turned into an open preaching evening. It was not till 1785 that its 'long-wished for society' was re-established.[327]

Practice varied, at least initially, over the criteria for admission to membership. Wesley set no test of spiritual progress for those joining his societies,[328] and the same may have been the case in some parts of the Connexion. The reference in 1771 to a member of the Bath society having been set at liberty shortly before he died suggests that membership there extended more widely than only to those who were already confident of their conversion.[329] But that did not mean that the expectations placed on members were lax. In Brighton in 1770 Shirley rescinded the ticket of a society member who came drunk to a love-feast, being clearly worried at the maintenance of good order in the society. He eventually proposed a scheme of inspection of society members, and weekly reports to the resident minister by five or six of the most solid members, an arrangement which has overtones of Wesley's class leaders.[330] Admission to the re-established Spa Fields society was by ticket, for which previous examination was the requirement, and tests of this kind were not uncommon. In 1774 a group of new members was admitted into fellowship at Lincoln, after having given 'a pleasing and satisfactory account to the church of the gracious dealings of God with them'.[331] The 1791 rules of the Chichester society were framed in very similar terms, with the additional requirements to 'answer a few Questions as the Minister shall think fit to ask'.[332] Admission to a society was clearly seen as a sign of spiritual maturation, whether or not any formal test was imposed; a student at Marlborough,

---

[327] Spa Fields minute book for 13 Aug. 1782 and 21 Jan. 1785, D1/1, 18–20, 28,CF.   [328] Baker, 'Polity', 221.
[329] G. Hull to LH, 22 Nov. 1771, F1/147,CF.
[330] Shirley to LH, 7 and 23 July 1770, F1/1503,CF. Shirley's inspection scheme allowed for anyone of superior condition, if they wished, to be visited by the minister instead (cf. Baker, 'Polity', 222).
[331] Glascott to LH, 18 Apr. 1774, F1/285,CF.
[332] West Sussex County Record Office, Add. MS 2458.

for example, lamented in 1777 that though many attended, few heard and none had recently been added to the society.[333]

The establishment of a society signalled that a distinction had been made between the public ministry of a congregation and the internal nourishment of its own members. Sometimes this would be reflected in the weekly round of activities. In 1773, for example, the weeknight pattern at Woolwich was of two public services (one for praying and singing, and the other for preaching), and one evening kept private for the society.[334] Lyme Regis, a decade later, was broadly similar, with a society meeting, preaching, and a prayer-meeting on three weeknight evenings.[335] Another model, in the summer at least, might be for the society to remain on after public worship for fellowship together—as in an instance reported from Wales in 1771.[336] Public weeknight services were clearly seen as a key element in the ministry of a congregation, even though the response to them might vary: weeknight congregations at Tunbridge Wells in 1771, for example, were 'deplorable', whereas at Brighton, three years later, they nearly filled the chapel.[337] There were fears at Brecon, in that same year, that ending the Wednesday sermon would lead to the break-up of the congregation.[338] Where the society was large enough to be subdivided into separate groups, the mix of private and public meetings might fill the whole week. At Bath in 1767 there were men's and women's meetings on separate nights and a full meeting of the society on a third, as well as two public-preaching evenings.[339] Two years later the women's meeting had itself

---

[333] J. Griffiths to LH, 19 May 1777, F1/1759,CF.

[334] Woolwich chapel to LH, 16 Oct. 1773, E4/2(6),CF. Simon shows how the religious societies gave impetus to the practice of weekday prayer meetings at the end of the eighteenth century (Simon, *Wesley and the Religious Societies*, 24).

[335] R. Satchel to LH, 29 Oct. 1782, F1/492,CF.

[336] Mrs Thomas to LH, 26 June 1771, F1/127,CF.

[337] Mrs Godde to LH, 7 Aug. 1771; Peckwell to LH, 28 Mar. 1774, F1/1543, 283,CF.

[338] Brecon society to LH, 1 May 1774, F1/1689,CF.

[339] E. Sheppard to LH, 29 Jan. 1767, E4/2(1),CF. In dividing up the society in this way the Connexion differed from Wesleyan Methodism, which made only limited attempts to organize classes by age or sex (Baker, 'Polity', 222). On the other hand, Cornelius Winter records how Whitefield had the Tabernacle society meet together, but separated into different groups, and then addressed each group individually (W. Jay, *Memoirs of the Life and Character of Cornelius Winter* (Bath, 1808), 32).

split, into the single and married,[340] and a group of young men had committed themselves to meeting for prayer at the chapel each morning before going to work.[341] The latter example had some parallels at Tunbridge Wells in the same year, when six or seven young men were reported meeting in the vestry three times a week to learn the hymns.[342]

Although a standard pattern for the organization of societies appears to have emerged as time went on,[343] initially there was considerable room for variation over how societies were organized and what they did—depending in part on the gifts of society members and the availability of ministerial help. Examples from Bath illustrate this. In 1769 it was commented that the single women appeared able to pray on their own, though their married sisters were likely to need ministerial help.[344] It was nevertheless worthy of mention to Lady Huntingdon the following year that a girl at the 'damsels' meeting had been drawn out to pray.[345] Examining the spiritual state of the society, three years later again, Shirley needed to make clear that nobody was bound to speak.[346] If such reticence had to be recognized in the environment of Bath, it was very likely to have been so also in less cultured parts of the country. Though society meetings might enable some new Christians to develop their own ministerial gifts, the majority of members would probably have found public speaking difficult. At the same time, Bath members may have been lulled by their regular supply of able ministers, not to mention the able wives of ministers: Mrs Shirley, for example, exercised a leadership role in the society while in Bath, and other wives may have done the

---

[340] E. Sheppard to LH, 19 Jan. 1769, F1/46,CF.
[341] Glascott to LH, 28 Jan. 1769, F1/1456,CF. Seventeen young men signed the letter to LH informing her of this fact.
[342] Mrs Godde to LH, 26 Nov. 1769, F1/80,CF.
[343] In 1790, for example, the student serving at York applied to the Countess's secretary for a copy of the rules for the ordering of societies which he understood were in general use in the Connexion (Cureton to Best, 4 Nov. 1790, F1/2154,CF). There are references to printed society rules and confessions of faith for societies in LH's accounts for Jan. and Oct. 1785 respectively (Satchell to LH, 28 Sept. 1782, E4/15(43),CF). [344] E. Sheppard to LH, 19 Jan. 1769, F1/46,CF.
[345] J. Godde to LH, 15 Jan. 1770, F1/85,CF.
[346] Shirley to LH, 22 May 1773, E4/1(18),CF.

same.³⁴⁷ In remoter areas, where ministerial support was less gifted and less regular (and possibly shared with a round of other congregations) societies would often have had to run their own meetings, doubtless discovering unsuspected talents in the process. The hope of stimulating lay leaders, either to operate within their own congregations, or as the means of extending the Gospel in their immediate vicinity, or on a larger stage after a spell at college, seems to have been a continuing concern. Planning the trip of a student to supply the Dublin congregation in 1773, for example, Lady Huntingdon suggested that the man need not be confined to that city; if only the society would unite in prayer-meetings exhorters would emerge to cover for him while he preached elsewhere.³⁴⁸ Similarly in 1787, Lady Huntingdon encouraged the Norwich congregation to identify what she termed 'simple hearted young lads' to read and pray in the villages.³⁴⁹

Sometimes, however, the problem was not reticence but the reverse, and the Connexion had occasionally to discourage too much discussion of members' spiritual experiences. To the extent that it did so, it differed from the generality of evangelical religious societies, like Whitefield's, and particularly from the confessional atmosphere that marked Wesley's bands and classes.³⁵⁰ The Ote Hall society asked Lady Huntingdon for a change in their regulations, to allow those who wished to do so to describe their religious experience; this, it was suggested, would prevent many from leaving for the Baptists.³⁵¹ The Bristol society, however, met resistance from their minister in 1792 when they sought the opportunity for 'speaking experience'—on the grounds, as he told them, of the unfittedness of some to speak and the prolixity of others.³⁵²

---

³⁴⁷ J. Godde to LH, 15 Jan. 1770, F1/85,CF.
³⁴⁸ LH to Hawkesworth, 13 Dec. 1773, G2/1(9),CF.
³⁴⁹ LH to John Bidwell, 10 Apr. 1787, B4/3,CF.
³⁵⁰ John Lawson, 'The People called Methodists: Our Discipline', in R. Davies and G. Rupp (eds.), *A History of the Methodist Church in Great Britain* (London, 1965), i. 189.
³⁵¹ T. Humphreys to LH, n.d., F1/1202,CF.
³⁵² R. Caldwell to Lady AE, 3 Nov. 1792, F1/2232,CF.

The worshipping life of the Connexion

The sacraments

Just as religious societies were part of the Revival's spiritual heritage, so too was respect for the sacraments. Regular reception of Holy Communion had been a hallmark of the London religious societies in the late seventeenth and early eighteenth centuries; indeed, there is a sense in which preparation for receiving the sacraments was one of their principal objectives.[353] Wesley had lighted upon a weekly observance early in his own religious quest,[354] and the Holy Club followed him in that pattern,[355] although outside Oxford and the major centres of population they would have found it difficult to do so with anything like that regularity. In some parts of the country, monthly Communions occurred with some frequency, even in quite small centres of population, but in others the pattern was much less: of the 836 churches in the York diocese in 1743, for example, only 72 managed a monthly Communion, and 208 fell short of even quarterly celebrations.[356] Various factors may have caused this state of affairs, such as the discouragement that the practice of frequent Communion had received during the Protectorate, or the daunting demands for proper preparation and the dangers of unworthy reception.[357] By contrast, evangelicals of all persuasions laid stress upon the sacraments as a fundamental part of their Christian nourishment. Whitefield wrote that there was 'nothing that so much be-dwarfs us in religion

---

[353] Simon, *Wesley and the Religious Societies*, 13, 16, 24; John Spurr, 'The Church, the Societies and the Moral Revolution of 1688', in John Walsh, Colin Haydon, and Stephen Taylor (eds.), *The Church of England, c.1689–1833: From Toleration to Tractarianism* (Cambridge, 1993), 138–9.

[354] JW's Journal for 24 May 1738, *Works*, xviii. 244.

[355] Samuel Wesley to JW, 1 Dec. 1730, John Whitehead, *The Life of the Revd John Wesley* (London, 1793–6), i. 425–7.

[356] F. C. Mather, 'Georgian Churchmanship Reconsidered: Some Variations in Anglican Public Worship, 1714–1830', *Journal of Ecclesiastical History*, 36/2 (Apr., 1985), 270; N. Sykes, *Church and State in England in the Eighteenth Century* (Cambridge, 1934), 251.

[357] J. C. Bowmer, *The Sacrament of the Lord's Supper in Early Methodism* (London, 1951), 3–5.

as starving our souls by keeping away from the heavenly banquet',[358] a view which Lady Huntingdon may well have shared: in 1750, Whitefield reported that life at her 'court' included the sacrament each morning, and there is the suggestion of at least a weekly celebration at her London house, two decades later.[359] The Revival, it appears, tapped into a substantial latent desire for sacramental worship. Evangelical clergy sometimes found themselves faced with Communion numbers in the hundreds (sometimes many hundreds),[360] while the desire for the sacraments was a regular theme in Lady Huntingdon's Connexion as much as in Wesley's.[361]

For Wesley, the sacraments became a touchstone of his societies' relations with the Church of England. In Bristol and London, from as early as 1743, the brothers maintained a regular pattern of sacramental worship within the Methodist chapels.[362] But except in those two places, Wesley sought for many years to preserve the principle that preaching houses were for preaching, not worship; Methodists were expected to attend their parish churches, and to communicate there if they could.[363] Not until the 1780s did Wesley begin to realize that he had lost the battle against the celebration of Communion in the societies. Thereafter, though many Methodists continued to communicate in parish churches, sacramental services on the Methodists' own premises became increasingly common.[364] Even so, while Wesley remained alive their frequency was severely limited by the lack of ordained men, since Wesley held firmly to the principle that laymen should not celebrate.[365]

---

[358] Tyerman, *Whitefield*, i. 31.   [359] Ibid. ii. 265; Seymour, ii. 126.
[360] Bowmer, *The Lord's Supper*, 3 quotes Romaine's experience of several hundred Easter communicants at Blackfriars and nearly twelve hundred communicated by William Grimshaw at Haworth in Yorkshire.
[361] e.g. W. Aldridge to LH, 29 Apr. 1775, F1/1715,CF; Bowmer, *The Lord's Supper*, 69.   [362] Ibid. 66.
[363] Ibid. 69, 72; Rack, *Wesley*, 409.
[364] Bowmer, *The Lord's Supper*, 72, 75, 78. Pressure for this may have stemmed as much from Methodist desire for self-sufficiency and antipathy to the Church of England, as from pure sacramental zeal (Rack, *Wesley*, 507).
[365] Bowmer, *The Lord's Supper*, 150–2. Apart from an apparent breach in this principle in the 1750s, when lay preachers in Norwich began to administer the sacraments,

Within the Connexion, the picture was rather different. Lady Huntingdon made no attempt to persuade her congregations to worship in church, nor did she show any reticence about the administration of the sacraments in her chapels. In the 1770s, for example, there is evidence of weekly celebrations at Bath,[366] and of a monthly cycle (with the suggestion that it might be improved to fortnightly) at the chapel at Woolwich.[367] In 1782 the norm for the congregations of the Connexion was said to be a Communion every two months, though this could not always be sustained: in that year the Reading congregation reported a six-month gap.[368] Before the inauguration of the Connexion's own ordination in 1783, the constraint was lack of ordained manpower, for there seems never to have been any suggestion in the Connexion that laymen might administer the sacraments. In this respect too, the Connexion differed from Wesleyan Methodism, where the periodic pressure from societies was for laymen to be allowed to give Communion. In the Connexion the priority was reversed, with requests for ordination frequently made on the grounds that only so could the congregation in question enjoy the sacraments—or, as it was revealingly put from Petworth in 1775, the 'Gospel privileges'.[369] This automatic assumption that administration of the sacraments required ordination may reflect the different roles and status of the Countess's students, compared with Wesley's lay preachers. Being a student was only a temporary phase, leading to the expectation of ordination once the student had developed sufficient ministerial gifts. By contrast Wesley's preachers were often men of long service and experience.

---

the principle was maintained until after Wesley's death, when the pressure for preachers to take over the full pastoral and sacramental responsibility of congregations became too difficult to resist (ibid. 147, 75; Rack, *Wesley*, 301, 418–19).

[366] E. Sheppard to LH, 9 Oct. 1777, F1/409,CF.
[367] L. Coughlan to LH, 13 Jan. 1774; Smith to LH, 23 Apr. 1774, F1/266, E4/2(4),CF. [368] T. Suter to LH, 7 Oct. 1782, F1/483,CF.
[369] Aldridge to LH, 29 Apr. 1775, F1/1715,CF. A late example of an appeal for their minister's ordination, solely on the grounds that thereby they could have the sacrament, came from the Wincanton congregation in 1790 (Wincanton Society to LH, 24 Apr. 1790, F1/905,CF).

In general, participation in the sacraments appears to have been reserved for society members, though practice varied as to whether or not the service was held in private. Norwich in 1776 had four hundred communicants and four hundred 'spectators', which suggests that Communion was held there in the context of public worship.[370] By contrast, at St Agnes four years later, Wills preached before the chapel door, and then retired inside with the society to give them Communion.[371] There were, however, other views current on how widely participation in the sacrament should extend. Wesley's position was that it could be a converting ordinance, and that the invitation to communicate should in principle extend to all who were sincerely seeking faith—though in practice, to preserve the sanctity of the ordinance, admission was confined to those in possession of a class-membership ticket or a Communion note from the minister in charge.[372] A friend of the Connexion, the Dissenting minister and former protégé of Whitefield, Cornelius Winter, counselled his people not to make admission 'narrower than that which is referred to in this language, "behold I have set before you an open door"'.[373] Lady Huntingdon herself may have leaned towards the more open policy, though the evidence is not wholly conclusive. The row at Chichester in 1783, over this very issue,[374] appears to have stemmed from the then minister offering the sacrament to any who presented themselves, contrary to society rules. Yet the minister in question, Samuel Beaufoy, had previously informed Lady Huntingdon that according to her direction they were administering the sacrament in the way that they had started.[375]

It was important for those receiving Communion to be in the right spiritual state to do so, whatever the admission policy might be in operation, and the Connexion's leaders

---

[370] Coughlan to LH, 15 Mar. 1776, F1/348,CF.
[371] *Life of Wills*, 42.
[372] Bowmer, *The Lord's Supper*, 106, 110. In 1740 Wesley had preached that 'no fitness is required at the time of communicating, but a sense of our state, of our utter sinfulness and helplessness.' (JW's Journal for 28 June 1740, *Works*, xix. 159).
[373] Jay, *Memoirs of Cornelius Winter*, 431–2.   [374] Above p. 119.
[375] Beaufoy to LH, 7 July 1783; Prichard to LH, 14 Nov. 1783, F1/2025, 567,CF.

seem to have taken seriously their duties in this regard. Fletcher, for example, while still president of Trevecca College, made a point of being back there in good time before Easter 1769, so as to be able to instruct his communicants.[376] Dorchester chapel had the sacrament postponed in 1777, when the minister concluded that they were deficient in 'Evangelical knowledge...to discern the Lord's Body'. A programme of examination and instruction was established to precede admission.[377] In Bath in the same year, after a period of friction, church members were counselled not to come to Communion if there were still strife in their hearts.[378] Inevitably less is known of the views of the Connexion's members themselves, though there are occasional insights. In 1774, for example, a member of the Haverfordwest congregation wrote of her desire for the sacraments, but of her fear at the thought of receiving unworthily; interestingly, she comforted herself by applying to the sacraments Jesus's words in John 6: 54, 'Whoso eateth my flesh...hath eternal life.'[379]

Though the proper state for receiving the sacraments was important, however, no special significance seems to have been attached to Sunday celebrations. Friday nights were fixed as a convenient time for the sacrament at Bath in 1770, for example, and the request for a Sunday celebration at Frome in 1783 appears simply to have been to avoid market-day.[380] The impression given, indeed, is that members of the Connexion adopted a pragmatic approach in matters to do with the sacraments, even on aspects made sensitive by the doctrinal conflicts of earlier ages. When Wills celebrated Communion at Wednesbury chapel in 1784, for example, some of those present 'had been brought up by dissenters, and desired liberty to sit, which I consented to, whilst myself, the students and others, received the ordinance in the usual (and what I think most reverent) posture of kneeling'.[381]

---

[376] Fletcher to LH, 10 Feb. 1769, F1/1457,CF.
[377] Molland to LH, 28 Aug. 1777, F1/402,CF.
[378] Haweis and Mrs Haweis to LH, 12 (? Feb.) 1777, F1/1801,CF.
[379] Samuel Nash to John Milbrum (*sic*), 18 May 1774, F1/296,CF.
[380] Shirley to LH, 10 Dec. 1770; Shinton to LH, 21 Feb. 1783, F1/1522, 510,CF.
[381] *Life of Wills*, 126.

Love-feasts

Love-feasts, revived by the Moravians from the fellowship meal of the early Church, and adopted by both the Wesleyans and the Whitefieldites, were also held occasionally within the Connexion. They appear, however, to have been confined largely to the principal chapels and the college, suggesting that they were a device favoured by Lady Huntingdon and her senior ministers, but which her congregations did not think of for themselves without central prompting. From a central perspective, however, they offered a way of marking special events and of symbolizing the Connexion's unity of purpose, much as they served to heighten the self-identification of Wesleyan Methodism.[382] Love-feasts are recorded, for example, as a feature of the college's anniversary celebrations on a number of occasions, and there is evidence of chapels planning love-feasts expressly to coincide with the college's anniversary, as happened in Brighton in 1770 and Bath in 1772.[383] Love-feasts might occasionally have a wider objective in terms of the general work of the Connexion: that held at Lady Huntingdon's request at Bath in July 1774 reportedly prayed for the Countess, 'the College, the societies of our Connexion and the whole Church'.[384] At other times a love-feast might be held to achieve precisely what its name implied, the settling of differences—which was Walter Shirley's object in planning one at Brighton in June 1770, and Bath in 1776.[385]

The Prayer Book

The Anglican Prayer Book provided the basis for public worship in many chapels of the Connexion, though there is

---

[382] Baker, *Wesley and the Church of England*, 87. There is no evidence in the Connexion of love feasts being regarded as a substitute for the sacraments, for want of the real thing, as they may sometimes have been in Wesleyan Methodism (Rack, *Wesley*, 411).

[383] Shirley to LH, 10 Aug. 1770; Maxfield to LH, 2 Sept. 1772, F1/1507, 1614,CF.

[384] Sheppard to LH, 9 July 1774, E4/2(3),CF. The occasion lasted from 7 until 10 p.m.   [385] Shirley to LH, 7 July 1770 and 3 Apr. n.y., F1/1503, 1263,CF.

not a consistent picture, either as to practice or to attitudes.[386] References to the use of the Church prayers are found in many parts of the country, and are not confined to the more populous and fashionable centres.[387] Use of the prayers was often seen both as a distinguishing feature of the Connexion and one likely to gain it support—even though, in at least some instances after secession, an amended version of the liturgy appears to have been used.[388] The trustees of the chapel at Rotherhithe, which applied to join the Connexion in 1783, for example, thought that the combined attraction of Connexional ministers and the Church prayers would fill their twelve hundred seats.[389] In Worcester, two years later, the decision was taken to reintroduce the prayers for an experimental period, specifically to try to remove the prejudices of Church people against coming to the chapel.[390] Another motive for using the Prayer Book was shown in 1789, when the Coleford chapel chose the set prayers in order to convince doubters that they remained loyal to the Church's doctrines.[391]

Against this were tendencies the other way. If the use of the Prayer Book guaranteed continuity and orthodoxy for some ex-Anglican members of the Connexion, there would

---

[386] I have argued that the picture of the Connexion using the Prayer Book during LH's lifetime, but being free to abandon it thereafter, is too simple an account of the position, both before and after her death ('The Anglican Prayer Book and the Countess of Huntingdon's Connexion', *Transactions of the Congregational Historical Society*, 20/12 (1970)). The Connexion published no formal revision of the Prayer Book, though some unofficial revisions appeared after the Countess's death (Welch, 200).

[387] Examples include Hull, Brecon, Maidstone, Wigan, and Guernsey (J. Bryant to 'Rev. Sir', 21 Apr. 1789; P. Valentine to LH, 15 Jan. 1788; H. Godde to (? Wills), 31 July 1777, F1/829, 699, 339,CF; B. Nightingale, *Lancashire Nonconformity* (Manchester, 1892), iv. 76; T. Jones to LH, 12 July 1790, F1/2138,CF).

[388] Bristol chapel in 1785 was 'using the church services with alterations' (Bristol Archives Office, Diocesan Survey for 1785, MS EP/A/2/2). Changes may have amounted to no more than the omission of prayers for bishops and the absolution (J. Adams to LH, 18 Feb. 1784, F1/1927,CF).

[389] Wills to LH, 9 Sept. 1783, F1/1901,CF.   [390] *Life of Wills*, 117.

[391] R. Trigg Jnr. to Best, 28 Mar. 1789, F1/818,CF. Even where the Prayer Book was the norm for public worship, however, freer prayer was likely within society meetings, for example, at the early Sunday morning service at Bath in the 1760s 'designed only for the Saints, wherein none of the Church Prayers are used' (quoted in Schlenther, 80, n. 10).

be others for whom conversion came as a liberation from the formalism that had marked their earlier religious experience—like the couple at Margate in 1771 who, in writing of their conversion, reported how the student serving the town had advised them to throw away their book of prayers and entreat the Lord.[392] Another sign that ministers of the Connexion were not themselves always the most enthusiastic for the Prayer Book, even when they were Anglican clergymen, occurred in Peckwell's report on the opening of the Maidstone chapel in 1775. The prayers were read, according to his account, to please the prejudices of the people, who were 'bigotted' to the Church of England.[393] Nor did there seem much natural affection towards the Prayer Book on the part of the student Robert McAll, who reported from Star Cross in 1787 that it was the worldly who wanted the Church prayers.[394] In some cases ministers seem to have been allowed some discretion whether or not to use the Prayer Book. In 1783 the Norwich committee stated that they had always gone along with those who used the Prayer Book, though they were patently reluctant to comply with what appears to have been a suggestion from Lady Huntingdon that they should get their current minister to start doing so.[395] Sometimes there might be resistance to the Prayer Book from within a congregation. A group at Dover in 1783, for example, was reported to have dismissed as popery the use of the Prayer Book at their student's ordination. The student himself saw this as symptomatic of their resistance to Lady Huntingdon's authority, and he may have been right (in this instance, at least) in associating hostility to the Prayer Book with general disloyalty to the Connexion; in 1789 a majority of the congregation withdrew from the chapel, leaving behind a rump of Connexional loyalists of whom only one or two were said to be opposed to the Church services.[396]

---

[392] C. and M. Spencer to LH, 21 Dec. 1771, F1/157,CF.
[393] H. and B. Peckwell to LH, 1 Nov. 1775, F1/339,CF.
[394] R. McAll to LH, 19 July 1787, F1/1952,CF.
[395] Norwich committee to LH, 2 May 1783, F1/520,CF.
[396] T. Cannon to Wills, 15 July 1783; Watkins to LH, 16 July 1789, F1/534, 845,CF.

What the Star Cross example also indicated was the belief that in order to use the Church prayers some sort of special furnishing was needed in the place of worship. Amongst McAll's reasons for not using the prayers was that the size of their place—seating not many more that two hundred—was too small to permit the (unspecified) alterations that would be needed.[397] Possibly he had in mind a reading desk. Fifteen years before, Glazebrook, who was holding services in the laundry of Lady Huntingdon's house at Ashby, indicated that preaching caused no problems, but that the place lacked what was necessary for reading the prayers.[398] Nor did use of the prayers have implications only for the fabric of the building: Coleford chapel's 1789 decision to use the Prayer Book meant the necessary acquisition of a surplice, with a gown as a desirable addition.[399]

Although some saw the use of the Prayer Book as a distinguishing mark of the Connexion, the Connexion was not alone among those outside the Anglican fold who made some use of the liturgy. Thomas Wills, after his expulsion from the Connexion in 1788, for example, continued using the Prayer Book at the Silver Street chapel on which he centred his subsequent ministry.[400] Rowland Hill did likewise at his Surrey chapel.[401] Nor was respect for the Prayer Book confined to those who had started their ministry as Anglican clergymen. One of the paradoxes of the Revival was that, though superficially a reaction against the formalism of the beliefs and practices of the Established Church, it entailed for some of those it touched a rediscovery of the spiritual possibilities of the Church's liturgy, and of the witness which the latter contained to key tenets of Reformation theology. The fact of sin, and the chance to escape its consequences which Christ offered, were very clearly stated in the Church's prayers, and could exercise a powerful converting

---

[397] R. McAll to LH, 19 July 1787, F1/1952,CF.
[398] Glazebrook to LH, 9 Mar. 1772, F1/1591,CF. The incident came at a time when Glazebrook was seeking Anglican ordination, and an added fear on his part was that reading the prayers without the necessary furnishings might alienate any clergyman he approached for a testimonial.
[399] R. Trigg Jnr. to Best, 28 Mar. 1789, F1/818,CF.   [400] *Life of Wills*, 227.
[401] Seymour, ii. 319.

influence—as evidenced, for example, by the role in Howel Harris's conversion played by the confession prayer in the Communion Service.[402] The liturgy offered a firm bastion against heterodoxy, in an age when both the Trinitarian faith and the scheme of salvation seemed under regular threat. Thus it was that amongst some Dissenters the use of the liturgy became associated with fervency of religious practice, and there were some instances of Dissenting congregations adopting the liturgy—even if, in the course of time, they were to revert to older practices.[403]

Clerical dress

Use of a gown and preaching bands appears to have been pretty general amongst the ministers and students of the Connexion. Since they were worn out of doors and in other formal settings, as well as in chapel, the implication is that their use was not confined to occasions when the Prayer Book service was being read.[404] Like the use of the Prayer Book, adoption of clerical dress added an element of authority and respectability to the Connexion's task. James Glazebrook, in Sussex in 1770, ascribed his success against local opposition to his gown and bands: although he was frank in declaring that he was not ordained, the leader of the mob still addressed him as a clergyman and acknowledged the unlawfulness of their having threatened him.[405] Similarly, Anthony Crole, preached against by the curate of Corfe in 1774, found that his gown and bands validated his status in the people's eyes.[406] Such a response did of course presuppose a general sympathy with Anglican practice, and such sympathy could not always be relied upon—as in the

---

[402] *Memoirs of Howel Harris from Papers Written by Himself* (Trevecca, 1791).

[403] R. Tudor Jones, *Congregationalism in England* (London, 1962), 165; R. Halley, *Lancashire: Its Puritanism and Nonconformity* (Manchester, 1869), ii. 437–8.

[404] The wearing of gowns was not confined to those exercising a ministerial role. As noted, chapel clerks were often required to gown, though on occasions they might be reluctant to do so (Mrs Godde to LH, 6 Dec. 1769, F1/82,CF).

[405] Glazebrook to LH, 1 June 1770, F1/1498,CF.

[406] Crole to LH, 13 July 1774, F1/311,CF.

Dover revolt against the liturgy, noted above, where the student was told he looked like a player in his robes.[407]

Wearing a gown seems in some quarters to have been taken as a mark of the Connexion. Application was made to Lady Huntingdon in 1774 for a student's gown, in the belief that if the writer appeared in it, he would be accepted as one of her students.[408] Conversely, removal of the gown appeared to symbolize expulsion from the Connexion, as was clearly felt by a correspondent in the following year who wrote to her plaintively that another had been sent to take away his gown and to preach in his place.[409] A similar instance occurred in 1779, with a student informed that he was to return horse, bags, and gown to college, and that there were no more services for him in the Connexion— though the association of the gown with other elements of Connexional property suggests that the requirement may have been as much practical as symbolic.[410] The logistics of ensuring that gowns, like horses, were in the right place at the right time, were matters of some significance for an itinerant Connexion, and ones in which Lady Huntingdon herself occasionally became involved, as when she instructed John Clayton in 1775 to leave his gown with the student who was succeeding him, and collect the new one she was having made for him, on his way to college.[411] The implication, moreover, is that the dress of those ordained into the Connexion was a matter of some importance to the Countess. In February 1783 William Taylor wrote to her to query the satin scarves she had proposed for the coming ordinations; nobody wore satin, he told her, and it was twice the price of good silk. But on this, as on other matters, Lady Huntingdon may have got her own way, since a quotation for satin scarves (at least two guineas each and nearly the price of a gown) was already on its way to her a week before Taylor wrote.[412]

---

[407] H. Spurrier to LH, 11 Oct. 1775, F1/334,CF.
[408] J. Brewer to LH, 12 Apr. 1774, F1/1685,CF.
[409] Jehoiada Brewer to LH, 29 May 1775, F1/328,CF. The correspondent in these two cases may have been the same person.
[410] T. Davies to LH, 22 July 1779, F1/435,CF.   [411] Aveling, *Claytons*, 20.
[412] Taylor to LH, 31 Feb. 1783; F. Stone to LH, 24 Feb. 1783, F1/1883, 511,CF.

Hymns

Like other branches of the Revival, the Connexion set considerable store by the singing of hymns. Hymns gave colour and variety to worship, and they reinforced the doctrines that were delivered more directly from the pulpit. The latter factor made it important that congregations had access to hymn collections which properly reflected the doctrinal standpoint of the group in question, and Lady Huntingdon devoted considerable efforts to ensuring that the Connexion had such a book continually available.[413] A book of hymns for use in the Connexion was in existence by the time the spread of new congregations began in the later 1760s. The book was on public sale by at least 1768, although its primary object was and remained the domestic one of satisfying congregational needs.[414] In response to those needs, the book passed through a number of editions over the following decades. Reprinting, for example, was planned in 1769, with a print run of at least two thousand copies.[415] In 1770 Lady Huntingdon was collecting contributions from her ministers for what was clearly a more substantial revision of the work.[416] A supplement was added to the book when it went into a further edition in Bath in 1773. At that stage Lady Huntingdon saw the same text as serving the needs of the Connexion in England, Wales, America, and Ireland, although she offered Hawkesworth, then serving in Dublin, the option of a separate Irish edition if that seemed preferable.[417]

Lady Huntingdon herself contributed some hymns to the Connexion's common stock. One of her compositions, sung at the opening of the Bath chapel and used at the chapel

---

[413] Other leaders of the Revival who produced their own hymn collections included Madan, Venn, Berridge, and Toplady (Rupp, *Religion in England*, 485). Wesley's book consciously set out the Methodist plan of salvation, and, after the Bible, provided the principal means for instructing ordinary Methodists in their faith (Rack, *Wesley*, 414).

[414] In that year LH was consulted on whether to leave sales with the commercial bookseller who was retailing copies at Tunbridge Wells, or whether the Connexion should plan direct sales in view of the expected demand for copies once the chapel was opened (T. Mills to LH, 19 May 1768, F1/30,CF).

[415] J. Donaldson to LH, 7 Apr. 1769, F1/58,CF.

[416] Piercy to LH, 10 Jan. 1770, F1/1484,CF.

[417] LH to Hawkesworth, 15 June 1773, G2/1(7),CF.

thereafter, was 'Blow ye the Trumpet, blow'. It is a traditional statement of the Calvinist message ('Ye who have sold for nought| Your heritage above, |Shall have it back unbought, |The gift of Jesus' love.') but it is a good instance of its kind and with a strong chorus ('The year of Jubilee is come; |Return, ye ransom'd sinners, home') that must have suited it well for congregational use. Its popularity was not confined to Connexional congregations.[418] Another hymn ascribed to Lady Huntingdon, with some similar features, opened with the lines: 'O, when my righteous Judge shall come| To call this ransom'd people home, |Shall I among them stand?'[419] And there may well be others by her of which the authorship has not been recorded or is uncertain. As late as the 1860s a controversy occurred over whether she or Robert Robinson (a convert of Whitefield and a Dissenting minister in Cambridge) had written the hymn 'Come thou fount of every blessing'.[420]

Maintaining uniformity of practice in the use of hymns in the Connexion did not prove easy, any more than it did to secure agreement on which hymns were acceptable. In 1770 John Wesley volunteered the view to Lady Huntingdon that some of her hymns were doggerel ('equally an insult upon poetry and common sense').[421] But he was not alone in this perception. Indeed, the question how far artistic standards mattered in hymn-writing was later to provoke a curious internal quarrel in the Connexion. Walter Shirley, who was responsible for editing the 1773 edition, had attempted to cut out a number of Moravian hymns the poetry of which he found insufferable, together with some of Charles Wesley's on Christian Perfection. Lady Huntingdon, who demanded to know in detail what was proposed, was not easily persuaded. Shirley stood firm on those he believed doctrinally

---

[418] The verses are quoted from the supplement to Watts's *Psalms and Hymns* first published in 1807 for the use of the chapel attached to the evangelical Dissenting academy at Hoxton. The authorship is revealed in J. Lloyd to LH, 7 Feb. 1772, F1/1583,CF.
[419] M. Bickerstaff, *Our Children's Heritage* (Caernarvon, 1934), 41.
[420] *The Christian Witness* (1866), 373. That hymn is also in the Hoxton Chapel collection.   [421] JW to Benson, 30 Nov. 1770, Wesley, *Letters*, v. 211.

objectionable, but was forced to restore what he patently regarded as 'vile doggerel and hum-drum tunes'.[422] Given this exchange, it was unfortunate, six months later, that Henry Peckwell should propose producing a separate collection of hymns for the chapels at Wapping and Westminster, and in so doing told Lady Huntingdon that he would not sacrifice truth to fine poetry.[423] Shirley, by then engaged on another edition, took this as a direct allegation that just such a sacrifice had taken place, and saw the plan to publish a separate book as a repudiation of the Connexion's own. Peckwell defended his proposal on the grounds that these were a few hymns of special personal significance, but he remained initially suspicious of using the new Connexional book in the London chapels.[424] He appears to have become reconciled to using it, however.[425]

Peckwell was of course not the first Evangelical clergyman of the period to think of producing his own hymn collection, and at least one other such set gained access to the Connexion. In 1772 the munificent Evangelical layman John Thornton bought up and sent to Lady Huntingdon a thousand copies of a hymn collection produced for the congregation at St George's, Southwark by a former associate of Whitefield named Dyer.[426] It was an act of charity on Thornton's part, since Dyer himself was in financial difficulties, but it was also of practical value to the Connexion where the demand for hymn books was continuous. Through the Countess's correspondence run regular requests for further supplies of books, requests which (like Peckwell's) were not always immediately successful—as in the case of Glazebrook at Ashby, who first asked for copies in February 1772 and who was still asking, at least five letters later, in the following June.[427] For the book to be of any value, congregations had

---

[422] Shirley to LH, June 12 and 28, 1773, E4/1(19–20),CF.
[423] Peckwell to LH, 12 Jan. 1774, F1/1669,CF.
[424] Peckwell to LH, 24 Jan. 1774, F1/1672,CF.
[425] Peckwell estimated a need for thirty dozen copies each at Brighton and Chichester. Peckwell to LH, 16 Mar. and 31 Jan. 1774; J. Lloyd to LH, 25 Apr. 1774; Peckwell to LH, 28 May 1774, F1/281, 1673, 1688, 1697,CF.
[426] J. Thornton to LH, 28 May 1772, F1/183,CF.
[427] Glazebrook to LH, 22 Feb., 15 Apr., 11 and 20 May, and 12 June 1772, F1/173, 177, 178, 181, 184,CF.

The Life of the Connexion 145

to have access to reasonable numbers of copies. Five hundred were sought for Wales in 1774, and one to two hundred for South Petherton in the same year.[428] In 1780, signs of awakening at Wallingford led William Taylor (supplying the parish for Pentycross) to ask for extra copies in addition to the ten dozen he had already.[429]

Wallingford was not the only instance of the Connexional hymn book in use at a parish church; in 1784 Lady Huntingdon sent Glascott one hundred copies for use in his new parish of Hatherleigh.[430] But Wallingford did provide an insight into how the book was seen in some quarters as a hallmark of the Connexion. Pentycross's account of his first interview with his new bishop in 1782 makes clear that his use of the Connexion's hymns was regarded by the bishop as indicative of questionable loyalty to the Church of England.[431] The book also served as a definition of the Connexion's doctrinal position: in 1788 the Birmingham congregation, defending their orthodoxy, asserted that they had no other doctrine than that contained in the preface to the hymns.[432] Nor did the book serve simply as a cold theological statement. That the hymns could also have an impact upon the spiritual life of members of the Connexion was shown in 1780 in the account of a dying woman who had been helped by studying them.[433]

It was the words of the hymns that mattered most, and though it was clearly important to find good tunes to which to sing them—Shirley's objection to humdrum tunes showed a clear recognition of that point—there seems to have been no early attempt to provide the Connexion with an equivalent musical resource. The tunes in use at the Bath chapel were printed in 1774,[434] but it was not until 1788 that the Countess's friend John Lloyd mentioned to her a proposal to

---

[428] Lloyd to LH, 4 May 1774; S. Clark to LH, 10 June 1774, F1/1691, 299,CF.
[429] Taylor to LH, 16 Aug. 1780, F1/1855,CF.
[430] Glascott to LH, 24 Feb. 1784, F1/1929,CF.
[431] Pentycross to LH, 18 Sept. 1782, E4/13(1),CF.
[432] Birmingham committee to LH, 17 Dec. 1788, F1/798,CF.
[433] Glascott to LH, 2 Aug. 1780, F1/1851,CF.
[434] Lloyd to LH, 12 July 1774, F1/310, CF.

publish music for the whole Connexion.[435] He may have been inspired in this by the leader of the singing at the Reading chapel, who the previous year had selected some original tunes for hymns in the Connexional book. Lady Huntingdon agreed to the suggestion that the set of Connexional tunes should be dedicated to her.[436] Thomas Haweis was another member of the Connexion who composed; one tune at least, 'Richmond' remains in regular use today. An earlier instance of a singing master composing tunes for use in Connexional worship was Benjamin Milgrove at Bath, to whose work there are references from the early 1770s.[437] Some of his music, too, has retained a permanent place in English hymnody,[438] and it may well have been staple fare in many parts of the Connexion; Lloyd's view in 1788 was that any collection of Connexional tunes would need to include some of Milgrove's compositions. By then, however, Milgrove had long since separated from the Connexion. The events of his departure, early in 1772, are well documented, although the precise reason remains uncertain; his own explanation to Lady Huntingdon was the inadequacy of the chapel singers, who were mangling his music, but there was also an argument with the principal singer at Bath over which of them had written particular tunes. It was suggested, too, that he had Wesleyan sympathies, and had opposed the singing of certain Calvinist hymns, including Lady Huntingdon's.[439]

Producing a hymn book in the numbers needed for the Connexion was a significant commercial undertaking. Lady Huntingdon herself seems to have carried the initial costs,

---

[435] Lloyd to LH, 26 Mar. 1788, F1/1997,CF.
[436] Lloyd to LH, 24 Dec. 1787, and 18 and 25 Jan. 1788, F1/1977, 1983, 1989,CF.   [437] Shirley to LH, 27 Jan. 1770, F1/86,CF.
[438] For example, tunes by Milgrove (1731–1810) appear in *Hymns for Today's Church* (1982) and *The New English Hymnal* (1986).
[439] B. Milgrove to LH, 15 Jan. 1772; Shirley to Milgrove, 3 and 5 Feb. 1772; Lloyd to LH, 7 Feb. 1772; Shirley to LH, 6 and 21 Feb. 1772, F1/1577, 1381, 1383, 1583, 1366; E4/1(9),CF. Four years later there was to be another row among the Bath singers, again related in part to the authorship of tunes; it was resolved with a mutual declaration that they would stop bickering, and not give away tunes (or parts) without the composer's consent (Shirley to LH, 3 Apr. (? 1776); articles signed by the singers at the Bath chapel, n.d., F1/1263, 1296,CF).

which would then be recouped from sales. Thus it was that Glazebrook hesitated about giving copies to the four or five people who had been particularly kind to him in the West Country in 1770, since this would have been a direct charge on Lady Huntingdon's generosity.[440] Pricing policy appears to have reflected production costs, possibly with a profit margin as well,[441] and allowed purchasers to choose the quality of binding they wanted. In 1771 calf-bound copies sold at one shilling and sixpence, with the cheaper (probably sheepskin) edition at one shilling.[442] Once congregations became established, it would fall to them to budget for the acquisition and sale of hymn books; hymn books appear in the Gainsborough chapel accounts in 1777, and in 1780 the Spa Fields committee decided to purchase one hundred hymn books from the Communion collections, to give to those of their stated hearers who could not afford to buy them.[443] There were always likely to be members of congregations in this position, even though Walsh the printer, discussing the price for the new edition in 1783, suggested that with most congregations now supplied, there was less need than formerly to hold down the price for the sake of the poor.[444]

On at least one occasion, there was an unintended free distribution. The complaint reached Lady Huntingdon from Birmingham in 1787 that many copies had not been paid for by members who subsequently withdrew when a rift occurred in the congregation, in addition to which there were students who had 'borrowed' copies during their stay in

---

[440] Glazebrook to LH, 13 Dec. 1770, F1/114,CF. There was some central demand for copies, for example from the college, which would not be covered by sales. Hughes and Walsh, who handled the Connexion's printing in the 1780s, also acted as LH's agents in the acquisition of books and other requirements; thus their 1786 account offset the provision *inter alia* of oysters, medicines, and newspapers against the sale of hymn books (E4/15(43),CF).

[441] This is the implication of the quotations that LH was sent in 1769, compared with the selling price for books from the same source two years later (J. Donaldson to LH, 7 Apr. 1769; Glascott to LH, 13 June 1771, F1/58, 125,CF).

[442] Glascott to LH, 13 June 1771, F1/125,CF.

[443] W. Thresher to LH, 27 Aug. 1777; Spa Fields minute book for 20 June 1780, F1/1782; D1/1, 5,CF.   [444] W. Walsh to LH, 13 May 1783, F1/524,CF.

Birmingham and had never brought them back.[445] Given the size of the financial commitment implicit in the production and supply of hymn books, there was understandable concern in 1780 at the news that a pirated edition was being advertised, underselling the official version. The offending printer was Gye of Bath, to whom the Connexion had given the sole Bath agency for the 1774 edition, because of his rival's Wesleyan sympathies. Walsh urged Lady Huntingdon against compromising with Gye, proposing instead that they should undersell him and institute proceedings in Chancery.[446] The indications are that the affair was still dragging on some years later, though it was to have no detectable impact upon what was clearly a vital element in the Connexion's ministry.[447]

Although some sections of the Revival remained suspicious, like their Puritan forebears, of the use of organs to accompany worship,[448] there appears to have been no such reticence on Lady Huntingdon's part. In more fashionable places, indeed, having an adequate source of musical accompaniment would have been essential to the maintenance of the Connexion's appeal, given the availability of attractive alternatives if standards were not maintained. The Bath chapel is likely to have had an organ from an early date; in 1783 a new organ was installed which produced effects that impressed even the Countess's son.[449] Attention to the musical arrangements for the new Swansea chapel in 1787 included the hire of an organ (as well as a month's visit from the principal singer at Bath); hiring was only a temporary expedient, however, and the following year found Lady Huntingdon personally concerned in considering the suitability of different organs for Swansea.[450] By the end of the

---

[445] Adams to LH, 15 Oct. 1787, F1/665,CF.
[446] Pentycross to LH, 3 July 1780; Walsh to LH, 18 July 1780, F1/457, 463,CF.
[447] LH to Carpenter, 17 Feb. 1787, Meth. Arch. (LH), 121.
[448] On the resentment that Rowland Hill caused by the introduction of an organ at the Surrey chapel, see P. E. Sangster, 'Rowland Hill'. In Lancashire, Scottish influence discouraged many independent congregations from introducing organs (Halley, *Lancashire: Its Puritanism and Nonconformity*, ii. 434–5).
[449] Mrs Carteret to LH, 26 May 1783, F1/528,CF.
[450] LH to Carpenter, 10 Feb. 1787; J. Lloyd to LH, 4 May 1788, Meth. Arch. (LH), 135. F1/2010,CF. Among those whom John Lloyd suggested might advise her was Charles Wesley.

1780s (if not before) organs were so commonplace in some parts of the Connexion that application could quite naturally be made to Lady Huntingdon for any organist post that might fall vacant at any of her chapels in the London area.[451]

The religious instruction of children

The religious needs of children were a natural concern of the Revival, though not of course exclusive to it. Sundays had long been used for catechizing children in England,[452] and there were many examples, in England and on the Continent, of systematic attempts to teach Christian doctrine to children.[453] In the eighteenth century such initiatives occurred more frequently. One of Wesley's Holy Club associates, William Morgan, gave religious instruction to the children of the poor families in the villages,[454] while the Holy Club itself established a school to teach children reading and the Catechism.[455] Instruction on the Catechism was not uncommon in the Church at large. In the York diocese in the 1760s, for example, all but a few parishes made some attempt at catechizing children prior to Confirmation.[456] Thus James Hervey may not have been unusual among parish clergy in questioning children on their understanding of the Catechism, although his concern was very clearly to establish an evangelical approach from an early age.[457] John Newton established a class of nearly ninety children at Olney in 1765 and seems to have made this an early priority of his ministry there.[458] In the same year (showing the

---

[451] R. Munn to LH, 16 Dec. 1789, F1/875,CF.
[452] Rupp, *Religion in England*, 526.
[453] The earliest of these appears to have been Cardinal Borromeo of Milan, who in the late sixteenth century established a confraternity to teach Christian doctrine to the children of his diocese (D. H. Farmer (ed.), *The Oxford Dictionary of Saints* (Oxford, 1982), 50). Seventeenth-century examples include Sunday schools started by the Little Gidding community in 1625 and by Jean Baptiste de la Salle in Paris in 1669 (T. W. Laqueur, *Religion and Respectability, Sunday Schools and Working Class Culture, 1780–1850* (Newhaven and London, 1976), 24).
[454] JW to R. Morgan, 19 Oct. 1732, *Works*, XXV. 335–44.
[455] Bowmer, *The Lord's Supper*, 20.
[456] Judith Jago, *Aspects of the Georgian Church* (London, 1997), 115–18.
[457] *Life of Hervey* (1770), p. iii; S. Brown, *Memoir of James Hervey* (Edinburgh, 2nd edn., 1809), 101.
[458] Newton to Lord Dartmouth, 11 Feb. 1765, HMC (Dartmouth), ii. 176. Newton recognized that Sunday schools could be an indirect means of addressing

wide-ranging appeal of work with children) the future Unitarian Theophilus Lindsey set up a children's meeting at Catterick which was actually called a Sunday school.[459] By then the pace was quickening. In 1769, Wesley's friend Hannah Ball began her Sunday school at High Wycombe[460] and there were to be other examples of lay-inspired Sunday schools over the following decade.[461] Robert Raikes's founding of a Sunday school in Gloucester in 1781, committed to general education as well as religious instruction, was thus by no means the first such initiative, though the publicity it gained proved the inspiration for a general expansion of such schemes.[462] By 1784 Wesley wrote that he found such schools 'springing up wherever I go'.[463]

The Connexion fits into this pattern of developing concern for children's work, even recognizing that children themselves could have an evangelistic role. In 1765 Lady Huntingdon reported that she had a group of some thirty children at Brighton who acted as her agents in seeking to reach the most poor and miserable children of the town.[464] Despite this innovative approach, however, the references to specific children's work are quite sparse,[465] possibly because it was regarded as such a natural part of ministry, that it was not worthy of special mention. It may have been the new impetus provided by Raikes's school which led to the attaching of a charity school to the Bath chapel in 1784—the initiative here coming from the chapel itself in the face of Lady Huntingdon's doubts about the financial implications of its maintenance. The objective was doubtless philanthropic,

---

parents; his initial technique was to give the children small rewards so that they would then show their parents, although he soon realized that some were coming just for the gifts (Hindmarsh, *Newton*, 196–7).

[459] H. MacLachlan, *Letters of T. Lindsey*, p. xi.   [460] Curnock, v. 104 n.
[461] Laqueur, *Religion and Respectability*, 24.
[462] Laqueur shows how the establishment of Sunday schools became a favourite middle-class charity; at the same time, many Sunday schools were working-class in origin and ethos (*Religion and Respectability*, 25, 29).
[463] JW's Journal for 18 July 1784, *Works*, xxiii. 323.
[464] LH to Mrs Wadsworth, 7 Mar. 1765, Bridwell Library MSS, 2.
[465] J. Godde to LH, 10 Jan. 1770; J. Panton to LH, 3 Jan. 1774, F1/84, 263,CF.

though there may have been a desire to meet the needs of the chapel's own poorer members, since it was later reported that the Bath clergy and charity school governors had refused charity school admission to the children of chapel members. By 1788 the Bath committee noted with satisfaction that seventy poor children had been educated through the school. But its days as an adjunct to the chapel were numbered. Lady Huntingdon's suspicions over the funding arrangements—specifically that it was drawing off money that would otherwise have passed to the general financing of the Connexion—were to lead that year to the committee's resignation over her insistence on the separation of the two institutions.[466]

Despite this apparent setback, it is likely that concern for the secular and religious education of children remained a permanent element in the Connexion's ministry. In 1786 Matthew Dupont, a founder member of the Spa Fields committee, established a Sunday school on what appears to have been his own initiative. By 1788 he could claim that eighty little 'vagabonds' had been given basic education and Gospel instruction.[467] In 1787 a subscription was set up to fund a Sunday school to be associated with the planned Swansea chapel; a decade later it was reported that the students at the new Cheshunt College had asked to establish a Sunday school there.[468]

Size and geographical spread of the Connexion; numbers in congregations and societies; catchment areas

From an early date, the annual conference of Wesleyan Methodism preserved a full record of its societies and preachers, and of where they were stationed.[469] No equivalent

---

[466] LH to R. Carpenter, 31 Mar. 1785, MS in the possession (in 1969) of the former Huntingdon Chapel, Vineyards, Bath; Carpenter to LH, 25 and 31 Mar., 10 Apr. and 1 May 1788; Sam. Jones to LH, 2 May 1788; Lloyd to LH, 14 and 27 May 1788, F1/717, 719, 722, 725, 726, 2014, 2021,CF.
[467] Dupont to LH, 13 Aug. 1788, F1/2130,CF.
[468] W. Jernegan to LH, 3 Nov. 1787; Apostolic Society minutes for 6 Dec. 1797, E4/14(4); C1/2,CF.   [469] Baker, *Wesley and the Church of England*, 228.

record has survived for the Connexion.[470] For that reason it is difficult to determine at any one time which congregations were officially part of the Connexion, and which individuals were deemed to be on active service within it. One extensive list of the chapels of the Connexion has been preserved, however: that compiled in 1790 when plans were being drawn up for the organization of the Connexion after Lady Huntingdon's death. These proposals, the so-called Plan of Association,[471] listed twenty-three districts[472] comprising a total of sixty-four chapels,[473] as shown in the list at Annex A and map at p. xvi. What this demonstrates is both the wide geographical spread of the Connexion's work (there are few significant areas of England in which no Connexional presence at all is recorded in the 1790 list) but also the extent to which the Connexion's strength was concentrated in a few main areas. The Midlands were a major focus of activity; other significant areas were Lincolnshire, Herefordshire, Huntingdonshire, and London and the Home Counties. At the same time there were some apparently very isolated chapels, of which Morpeth in Northumberland is most striking.[474]

Only in two instances, Wincanton and St Columb, does the Plan refer specifically to a series of preaching places in addition to the named chapels. The absence of such references elsewhere could possibly reflect the more settled state which the Connexion had reached by this date, with efforts focused more on established congregations than on serving scattered groups of adherents, although the evidence of the lost 1788 list[475] suggests that a good deal of the latter may still have gone on. It seems that in the years following

---

[470] In particular, we do not have the list of 116 'Chapels and preaching places in the Connexion' which LH is reported to have passed to the recently founded Apostolic Society in 1788 (C1/1, 17,CF; on the Apostolic Society, see below).

[471] The proposals are discussed below.

[472] There is no evidence to suggest that these districts represented real administrative units at the time the Plan was drawn up; more probably they were the invention of those who devised it.

[473] The difference between this figure and that mentioned two years earlier may be explained by the inclusion of 'preaching places', as well as chapels, in the former.

[474] There were ten cathedral cities in the Plan but this need not imply (in Edwin Welch's words) that she was 'more willing than John Wesley to challenge the Church of England in its strongholds' (Welch, 191).   [475] Above, n 470.

the first flush of Connexional activity many congregations either severed their links with the Connexion or ceased to be viable.[476] Sussex provides an example of this process of concentration upon a few main centres. Only four Sussex chapels are listed in the Plan of Association (Brighton, Ote Hall, Lewes, and Chichester), although at least six other congregations (Angmering, Ditchling, Heathfield, Midhurst, Petworth, and Ringmer) had been served by the Connexion at some stage in the 1770s.[477] Another Sussex congregation, Arundel, continued its Connexional links until at least 1792,[478] although it is not mentioned in the Plan of Association. This shows that the Plan cannot be regarded as a complete picture of the Connexion's activity, even at the date at which it was drawn up.[479] Nevertheless, the list does provide some indication of the broad size and spread of the work in the last years of Lady Huntingdon's life. Given the known omissions from it, it suggests that the Connexion might have been supplying seventy or more congregations in the final decade of the century, while there was a significant further number of causes or preaching places (whether or not still in existence) which had been initiated or served by the Connexion over the previous years. Even so, the scale of the Connexion's work was still substantially less than that of Wesleyan Methodism, which had some four hundred and seventy preaching houses in England alone by the date of Wesley's death.[480]

---

[476] Only occasionally has evidence survived of moves by whole congregations to leave the Connexion. In 1788 Newark and Barton-upon-Humber threatened to leave, although in both these instances the congregations decided to remain under her patronage (J. Stevenson to LH, 19 Apr. and 11 May 1788; Barton trustees to LH, 14 June and 9 July 1788, F1/2007, 2013, 734, 743a,CF).

[477] See in particular T. French to LH, 12 Nov. 1777; Peckwell to LH, 12 and 31 Jan., and 25 Feb. 1774; Lloyd to LH, 14 Oct. 1771; T. Davies to LH, 9 Oct. 1779, F1/1800, 1669, 1673, 1677, 2200, 450,CF.

[478] E. Irish to Lady AE, 23 Dec. 1792, F1/2235,CF. Ad hoc links with the Connexion may have continued up to 1797 (C. H. Valentine, *The Story of the Beginnings of Nonconformity in Arundel* (Harpenden, c.1925), 21).

[479] Barton and Sleaford in Lincolnshire were other examples of congregations being served by members of the Connexion at the time of the Plan of Association, but which were not included in the list (Barton Trustees to LH, 9 July 1788; J. Wilson to Lady AE, 23 May 1792; Sleaford Chapel to LH, 1 Nov. 1788; R. Caldwell to Lady AE, 27 May 1792, F1/743a, 2218, 780, 2220,CF).

[480] Baker, 'Polity', 228.

It is not possible to say precisely how many men the Countess had available to service work on this scale. In the later 1780s some thirty or forty names of ministers and students appear annually in her correspondence, though the total may well have been more than this. Most, if not all, of the congregations listed in the Plan of Association would have expected a full-time supply, even though there were often gaps between supplies. The fact that congregations were occasionally left unsupplied suggests that the Connexion had somewhat fewer preachers than congregations, though possibly not by much: perhaps a total manpower of fifty or sixty in all, including those who only gave part-time service.

The wide variation in the size and type of Connexional causes makes it difficult to generalize about the numbers who might normally be found in congregations or societies. There was obviously a major difference between the casual congregations that might be attracted to itinerant preaching, and the numbers who would attend worship regularly, once a chapel had been built. It was notoriously difficult, too, to judge the size of an outdoor gathering, and some of the very high figures that were quoted—two thousand near Corfe in 1774, for example, or the three thousand in morning and eight or nine thousand in evening congregations at Birmingham the previous year[481]—should not perhaps be taken too literally.

Indoor estimates could be rather more certain. And there were some premises that could and did accommodate very large numbers. One such was the meeting house at Frome, recorded as holding twelve hundred and fourteen or fifteen hundred in 1774 and 1777 respectively.[482] Figures in the hundreds were more common. Glascott anticipated a 'standing congregation' of six or seven hundred at South Petherton in 1773; Chelmsford had 'upwards of eight hundred' in the following year; Chatteris, with seating for

---

[481] Crole to LH, 13 July 1774; Glascott to LH, 12 Mar. 1773, F1/311, 1636,CF.
[482] Lloyd to LH, 4 May 1774; J. Chapman to LH, 5 Sept. 1777, F1/1691, 403,CF. The pulpit was so high off the ground that the student Samuel Pierce got vertigo when he preached (Pierce, *Life of Samuel Eyles Pierce*, 61).

five hundred, was said in 1778 to be constantly crowded.[483] Congregations of three or four hundred in Sussex in the latter year were regarded as slender.[484] Some strikingly high figures for weekday services were occasionally recorded: Barton-upon-Humber claimed attendances of two or three hundred at their 'despised Barn', and Evesham a figure in the order of five to seven hundred—both in 1787.[485] If numbers dropped into double figures the cause might well be at risk. Chichester, after the divisions referred to in 1783, was down to forty or fifty attenders, and was clearly past the margins of viability.[486] A similar picture emerged at Weymouth, which in 1779 was down to morning and evening congregations of around twenty, and Whitehaven, which in 1787 mustered only thirty or forty.[487]

Double figures for the membership of societies were much more the norm. There were seventy communicants at Dover in 1773, for example, and thirty at Dartford the following year.[488] Dorchester recorded forty society members in 1777; Bath had seventy or eighty in 1777; Lyme Regis thirty-three in 1782; and Worcester forty-nine in 1788.[489] The striking exception appears to have been Norwich which recorded four hundred communicants in 1776, and eight hundred in society the following year. Lady Huntingdon clearly thought the size of the Norwich society remarkable and mentioned it in correspondence.[490]

People sometimes travelled a substantial way for the ministrations of the Connexion, reflecting the distance over

---

[483] Glascott to LH, 12 Mar. 1773 and 19 Feb. 1778; E. Bryant to LH, 12 Dec. 1774, F1/1636, 1819, 1711,CF.   [484] J. Giles to LH, 3 Feb. 1778, F1/426,CF.
[485] Barton-upon-Humber congregation to LH, 24 Aug. 1787; T. Hughes to Bradford, 3 Dec. 1787, ibid., F1/649, 1971,CF.
[486] D. Pritchard to LH, 14 Nov. 1783, F1/567,CF.
[487] T. Davies to LH, 18 Aug. 1779; Whitehaven congregation to LH, 12 June 1787, F1/443, 634,CF.
[488] Aldridge to LH, 20 Nov. 1773; Coughlan to LH, 4 Feb. 1774, F1/1666, 271,CF.
[489] Molland to LH, 28 Aug. 1777; Sheppard to LH, 9 Oct. 1777; Satchell to LH, 29 Oct. 1782; J. Child to LH, 3 June 1788, F1/402, 409, 492, 731,CF.
[490] Coughlan to LH, 15 Mar. 1776, F1/348,CF. LH to Wills, 1 Apr. 1777, J. Rylands Library, Eng. MS. 338.

which the influence of active causes might extend. One remarkable instance was the twenty-eight miles (and back) that two men were said to have travelled to a love-feast at Brighton in 1770.[491] Brighton, indeed, was a chapel that seemed to attract energetic travellers: one society member was from Westerham, some twenty-five miles away, while in 1774 it was reported that young men from Lewes were walking to Brighton every night and back again after preaching.[492] But there were equally impressive distances covered in other parts of the country. In 1773 Glascott encountered a group at Somerton who were going fifteen or twenty miles to hear the Gospel; some people came eighteen miles for the opening of the Maidstone chapel in 1775; and in 1787 a group regularly walked eight miles for Sunday worship at Dorchester.[493]

The financing of the Connexion

As indicated earlier[494] there were occasional instances, at least in the early 1770s, of direct financial contributions by Lady Huntingdon to the establishment of new causes. Throughout the last decades of her life she also made substantial contributions towards the continuing support of individual congregations. The original chapels had depended from the start on her liberality, and they seem for some time to have gone on receiving money from her. Bath, for example, was submitting regular quarterly accounts of some size in the early 1770s, that for £25 in April 1770 being regarded by the congregation as sufficiently small to be a cause of satisfaction.[495] Brighton appeared to turn to her as a matter of course when there were large bills to be paid, and their accounts evidently embraced Ote Hall as well. In 1774, two years' rent and other bills at Ote Hall amounted to £67.[496]

---

[491] Shirley to LH, 27 Aug. 1770, F1/1562, CF.
[492] Glascott to LH, 3 June 1771; R. Harman to LH, 8 Jan. 1774, F1/125, 320,CF.
[493] Glascott to LH, 23 June 1773; Peckwell and Mrs Peckwell to LH, 1 Nov. 1775; J. Hopkins Jnr. to LH, 3 Oct. 1787, F1/1648, 339, 1962,CF.
[494] Above pp. 73-4.   [495] Lloyd to LH, 1 Apr. 1770, F1/1490,CF.
[496] Harman to LH, 8 Jan. 1774, F1/320,CF.

Newer causes received money also. In 1777, for example, Lady Huntingdon paid off the outstanding £10 debt with which the Gainsborough trustees had been saddled since the chapel was opened.[497] Two years later £10 went to Chichester, evidently as part of a spasmodic series of donations from her.[498] There are, inevitably, more instances of appeals for her support than firm evidence that money was forthcoming.[499] There appear, however, to have been firm expectations of support from West Bromwich, Kidderminster, and Worcester in 1787,[500] and there is evidence of payments made to Llangadog and Coleford in 1788.[501] Sometimes Lady Huntingdon contributed specific items to the needs of a congregation, like the Communion vessels she sent to Bristol in 1776, the plate sent to Birmingham in 1787, or the candles for the Union Street chapel, Whitechapel, in 1788.[502]

The overall impression is that Lady Huntingdon's instinct was to respond generously to the needs of her congregations, but in a disorganized and unplanned way that could lead to commitments, or assumed commitments, that she could not subsequently deliver. The acrimonious dispute which occurred with members of the Birmingham committee in 1788, over which of their debts Lady Huntingdon had undertaken to meet, probably witnesses more to the confusion with which Connexional finances were conducted, than to a wilful failure to honour promises with which some were ready to credit her.[503] Her employment of the surveyor

---

[497] W. Thresher to LH, 27 Aug. 1777; Glascott to LH, 18 Nov. 1777, F1/1782, 1802,CF.   [498] J. Lane to LH, 7 Aug. 1779, F1/440,CF.

[499] For example, it is not clear what happened to the appeal to her to help York back to viability in 1782 (G. Meller to LH, 26 Oct. 1782, F1/491,CF).

[500] West Bromwich congregation to LH (stamped 2 July 1787); Pockin Lister to LH, 22 Sept. 1787; T. Skinner to LH, 26 Sept. 1787, F1/642, 655, 658,CF.

[501] H. Jones to LH, 16 Feb. 1788; E. Hodgkinson to LH, 26 Feb. 1788, F1/705, 708,CF.

[502] E. Shepperd to LH, 16 Jan. 1776; Birmingham committee to LH, 15 Nov. 1787; 'Expenses for candles at the Riding School, Union Street, Whitechapel', F1/343, 670; E4/15(19),CF. The gift to Birmingham was of limited significance, however, compared with the debts of nearly £500 that they were facing at the time.

[503] S. Seager to Best, 12 Nov. 1788, F1/782,CF. The correspondents' complaint was that whenever they called on her to honour her promise of help, 'the utmost we get is a letter none of us can well understand'.

John Case, whom she used in connection with a number of building and maintenance projects in the 1780s, was a sign of the practical interest she took in such issues, but it was further evidence of her financial disorganization as their relationship soured into recriminations by Case at her failure to settle his bills.[504] Lady Huntingdon's continued but undisciplined liberality was illustrated again in the concern expressed by the Spa Fields committee in 1789. Faced with her fading health and the prospect of having to assume responsibility for running the Connexion, they sought an undertaking from her not to enter into any new engagements without their agreement.[505]

The cost of students

In addition to occasional support for congregations, Lady Huntingdon contributed directly to the expenses of ministers and students.[506] As the ministry expanded in the early 1770s, detailed accounts of expenditure become an increasingly prominent part of her correspondence, either with requests for reimbursement, or to account for her money. So far as the students were concerned, the indication from the Gainsborough account in 1773—which included board, travelling, clothes, and apothecary bills—was that it might cost around £1 a week to maintain an itinerating student.[507] Exceptional circumstances could add to costs. Mead and Glazebrook, in pursuit of ordination in 1771, incurred additional expenses, which they had to defend to Lady Huntingdon. Mead's account included travel 'in the Machine' to London, in view of the poor state of his horse, and the purchase of a hat before he could call on the bishop.[508]

---

[504] LH's account with Case, to Aug. 1786; Taylor to LH ('Saturday' and 'Tuesday night'); Case to LH, 6 May, 11 and 28 June, and 20 and 25 Sept. 1787, E4/15(14); F1/1368, 1370, 626, 632, 636, 654, 657,CF.
[505] Spa Fields minutes for 23 Nov. 1789, D1/1, p. 30,CF.
[506] Her comment to Hawkesworth in 1773 that she would support his Dublin ministry, but not the costs of the building, suggest indeed that she saw the support of ministers as a more natural charge upon her than assistance in the provision of places of worship (LH to Hawkesworth, (? 9) Feb. 1773, G2/1(5),CF).
[507] Fletcher (of Gainsborough) to LH, 6 July 1773, F1/1651,CF.
[508] Mead to LH, 5 Aug. 1771, F1/131,CF.

Glazebrook's included his ordination licence and the purchase of books, the latter possibly contributing to the charge for excess weight on his baggage which was also on his bill.[509]

In the early days at least students appeared to have enjoyed considerable freedom in incurring debts, even if they might have to face critical questions from Lady Huntingdon afterwards. In 1774, for example, Ellis ran up a bill of over 6 guineas for a suit and coat, the need for which he had apparently determined for himself;[510] the following year Lady Huntingdon was less than pleased to learn that Molland had undertaken the publication of a pamphlet, part of the cost of which might fall on her.[511] Sometimes students' expenses were handled locally, by ministers serving in the area, or prominent lay people, but vigilance was still needed to prevent the students from running up more extensive bills than was justified. In 1774 Peckwell proposed relinquishing his responsibility for the students' monies in Sussex in favour of Richard Harman, a leading member of the Brighton congregation, and in Peckwell's eyes less likely to be imposed upon.[512] In the same year Samuel Clark of South Petherton, who handled the expenses of the students serving in that area, asked the senior student William White to check the account of over £12 which he (Clark) was submitting to Lady Huntingdon in respect of students' clothes.[513] With sums of this magnitude involved, strictness was obviously increasingly important as the work expanded. When Richard Slaughter asked for a further trial at college in 1777, he was warned that if he proved unsuitable, he would have to bear his own travelling costs.[514] And in 1785 Lady Huntingdon informed the students attending an ordination that they must walk to save the expense falling on the people.[515]

---

[509] Glazebrook to LH, 24 Dec. 1771, F1/159,CF.
[510] J. Sparke to LH, 28 June 1774, F1/305,CF.
[511] Molland to LH, 20 Apr. 1775, F1/325,CF.
[512] Peckwell to LH, 14 May 1774, F1/293,CF.
[513] S. Clark to LH, 10 June 1774, F1/299,CF.
[514] Slaughter to LH, 12 Sept. 1777 (with the master's reply on the reverse), F1/404,CF.
[515] LH to Carpenter, 31 Mar. 1785, MS letter of Lady Huntingdon in the former Huntingdon chapel, Vineyards, Bath.

Financial support for the clergy

There are some examples of clergy in direct receipt of financial support from Lady Huntingdon. In 1781, while still itinerating for the Connexion, Glascott was receiving occasional payments from Lady Huntingdon that appear unconnected with any submitted accounts.[516] In the same year, she supported Taylor's ministry at Tunbridge Wells,[517] and there is evidence in the following years of regular quarterly payments to certain of the Welsh clergy.[518] When beneficed clergymen like Pentycross (and soon Glascott) served the Connexion, support of another kind might be forthcoming from Lady Huntingdon in the form of funding for curates to serve in their place. In 1782 Pentycross told his bishop that he could afford a curate because of the liberality of Lady Huntingdon;[519] in the following year it was agreed that he and Glascott would share a curate, with Lady Huntingdon making up the deficit in the salary they could afford between them.[520]

Local funding and central influence

Despite these instances of help from Lady Huntingdon, the cost of ministry fell increasingly upon those who received its benefits. The pressure for this may partially have been local pride in a congregation's readiness and ability to support its own ministry—as in the report from Gainsborough in 1773 that the member of the congregation responsible for handling the students' expenses would prefer these to be met locally, rather than by Lady Huntingdon.[521] It was clearly right that congregations should aim to become self-supporting, rather than remaining dependent upon central provision, and the scale of the expanding work made it inevitable that local funding should become the norm. One instance of this among many was the correspondence in 1777 about the best

---

[516] Glascott to LH, 4 Sept. 1781, E4/11(6),CF.   [517] Seymour, ii. 324.
[518] e.g. to Nathaniel Rowlands on 17 Mar., 11 June, 10 Sept. and 29 Dec. 1783, and 8 Mar. 1784, E4/16(22, 6, 51, 88, 73),CF.
[519] Pentycross to LH, 18 Sept. 1782, E4/13(1),CF.
[520] Glascott to LH, 7 Dec. 1783, F1/580,CF.
[521] Crole to LH, 17 Dec. 1773, F1/261,CF.

and most economic means of getting clergymen to serve at the Bristol chapel; this was clearly premised upon the assumption that it was the chapel that would bear the costs incurred.[522]

There appears to have been considerable diversity during these years, not only over the circumstances in which Lady Huntingdon would make a financial contribution, but also in the degree of influence she exercised over local funding arrangements. The provision of curates for clergy serving the Connexion was a case in point. In addition to occasional instances of direct funding by Lady Huntingdon as mentioned, there was a centrally prescribed system for the supply of churches, albeit based upon local funding. In 1782 Lady Huntingdon wrote to the ordained ex-Trevecca student James Glazebrook:

> in this Connexion there is a rotation of *Clergy*, throughout the large chapels and congregations. They serve some eight, some ten weeks in a congregation. Some of these have livings, and such are allowed two guineas a week, a lodging, and travelling charges (finding their own board), according to the time they serve in each congregation. Should you like to make a trial of being one of these, by way of trial only, at any time, you can have your Church supplied...[523]

That facility did not apply universally, however. In the same year that Lady Huntingdon described these arrangements, Bristol refused to pay for the curate of a visiting clergyman, on grounds that this was not normal practice and would create a precedent they could not sustain.[524]

Lady Huntingdon's correspondence with Glazebrook also indicated that she had firm views on scales of remuneration. Describing the congregation with which he might settle permanently, as an alternative to temporary spells in the Connexion, she wrote that she would require from them 'one hundred a year, and a house'.[525] Where there was no fixed rate, guidance from her might be welcome. Worcester,

---

[522] J. T. Jones to LH, 18 Dec. 1777, F1/1629,CF.   [523] Seymour, ii. 90.
[524] Bristol committee to LH, 29 Oct. 1782, F1/1873,CF.
[525] Seymour, ii. 88.

negotiating for supplies in 1782, were anxious that Lady Huntingdon should fix a figure for the students' pocket money that they were expected to pay, so that they would not be exposed to pressure to pay more.[526]

Set against these examples, however, were congregations who clearly saw themselves as on their own in devising remuneration arrangements. In 1783, for example, Norwich appear to have been working on their own initiative towards a system in which they would bear the salary of an individual minister throughout the year, even while he was serving elsewhere, in the expectation that whoever supplied for them at such times would be similarly supported by his home congregation.[527] There could be wide variations, too, in the level of financial support that congregations could provide. At the other end of the scale from the £100 plus chapels[528] were causes like Lakenheath, able in 1789 to pay only 8 shillings a week, or Dover who paid 16 shillings a week in 1792.[529] Gravesend, who in 1779 were offering £60 a year, a house and expenses, lay somewhere in the middle, and were clearly regarded as an attractive option.[530]

Ministers' stipends and their day-to-day expenses were not the only demand on congregational resources. Purchase of hymn books, candles, and cleaning formed a regular part of many chapels' running costs. Bath's outgoings in 1787 totalled nearly £300, set against an income almost £30 less.[531] Where extensions or improvements were undertaken, there could be consequential expenses in addition to the direct cost of the work, as in the case of the 'Shandelier for the (new) Gallery' at Birmingham in 1787.[532] The initial building work might saddle the congregation with debt repayment and interest charges over the coming years; in

---

[526] T. Skinner to LH, 12 Oct. 1782, F1/486,CF.
[527] Norwich committee to LH, 2 May 1783, F1/520,CF.
[528] Also in 1782 Tunbridge Wells were said to be paying 'two guineas a week and travelling charges' (Seymour, ii. 147).
[529] J. Child to LH, 23 July 1789; E. Stead to LH, 10 Sept. 1783, F1/2090, 985, CF.   [530] T. Davies to LH, 9 Oct. 1779, F1/450,CF.
[531] Carpenter to LH, 12 Mar. 1788, F1/715,CF.
[532] Birmingham committee to LH, 17 Nov. 1787, F1/670,CF.

1782, for example, Worcester reported interest payments of £25 a year.[533] Compared to this, renting premises might appear an easier option. The £3 a year rent that Stourbridge were paying in 1785[534] seems to have been particularly low, but Chichester, Grantham, Brecon, and Whitehaven all record rents in the £7–8 range during the 1770s and 1780s.[535]

The source of finance
The funds that Lady Huntingdon was able to contribute to the support of the work came from a variety of sources. Two elements in this were her personal property and the American estates she had inherited from George Whitefield. The latter was potentially significant and the prospect of losing it following the American War of Independence meant that increased effort would be needed to raise central Connexional revenue, if its ability to proselytize new areas was not to be diminished.[536] Her family wealth seems to have been limited. Effectively, she received only debts from her husband's estate (once she and Francis had sorted out their respective entitlements, following her misguided building work at Donnington), and she had a long-running battle with her blood relations over monies on the Ferrers side.[537] Rent from property appears to have made a frequent contribution to her income. Houses of hers at Brighton, Tunbridge Wells, and Ashby were all let at various times—that at Tunbridge Wells, for example, being let for six weeks in 1780, for a total of 55 guineas.[538] At Ashby the rent of the house went to support the work there, and this was not the only instance of revenue being earmarked for specific areas of work;

---

[533] T. Skinner to LH, 12 Oct. 1782, F1/486,CF.   [534] *Life of Wills*, 156.
[535] Peckwell to LH, 24 Jan. 1774; Glascott to LH, 11 June 1774; J. Lewis to LH, 26 Nov. 1787; Joseph Fletcher to LH, 15 Dec. 1787, F1/1672, 1698, 692, 695,CF.
[536] LH to John Bidwell, 10 Apr. 1787, B4/3,CF. At an earlier stage Lady Huntingdon had apparently considered devoting the whole of her American income to work on that side of the Atlantic (Wills to LH, 7 Dec. 1783, F1/1918,CF).   [537] Schlenther, 143.
[538] Mrs Wills to LH, 28 June 1779; LH to Lord Donnegal, 13 Dec. 1780, F1/1825; E4/10(1),CF. LH to Mr. Dawson, 29 June 1790, Hastings MSS, HA, 5862.

in 1781 Lady Huntingdon described how 'the income from an estate of mine has been ever freely given to support the Gospel' in the Tunbridge Wells area, in view of the poverty of the local people.[539] Additionally, there were her personal effects. The possible sale of jewels to finance the Brighton chapel has been mentioned; in 1787 she sold over 140 oz. of silver plate, presumably again to support the work.[540]

A further source of income was the generosity of her friends. John Thornton was in correspondence at various times over financial arrangements designed to be of benefit to her.[541] Lady Glenorchy, sending her £400 in 1771, assured her that 'my purse is always at your command'.[542] In 1774 a Mrs Ann Power proposed an arrangement whereby Lady Huntingdon would receive the £200 with which Mrs Power had been going to purchase an annuity, in return for Lady Huntingdon paying her a small annual income.[543] In 1783 there is evidence of a large legacy to Lady Huntingdon for the continuation of the college.[544]

Congregations, whether faced with debts to pay off, or simply maintenance of their buildings and ministry, had four principal means of raising revenue: by regular contributions from their members, by periodic collections, by the sale of admission tickets, or by donations from outside. For smaller congregations, in particular, maintaining the flow of members' contributions to meet their commitments may have been a largely informal (and possibly nerve-racking) process—as in the case of the small congregation at Milton in Kent, which in 1790 was struggling to raise the ten shillings and sixpence a week they paid their minister, since they had only one 'gentleman' among them who subscribed two shillings and sixpence.[545] Holding a collection for congregational funds appears to have been regarded as a more formal step, and not one which—in the early days of the

---

[539] Seymour, ii. 324.
[540] Above p. 49; E4/15(31-3), CF.
[541] Thornton to LH, 30 Oct. 1772 and 11 Mar. 1774, F1/197, 278,CF.
[542] Lady Glenorchy to LH, 10 Jan. 1771, Seymour, ii. 110.
[543] Ann Power to LH, 2 Mar. 1774, F1/277,CF.
[544] Wills to LH, 7 Dec. 1783, F1/1918,CF.
[545] J. Child to LH, 23 June 1790, F1/924,CF.

Connexion's expansion—could necessarily be guaranteed Lady Huntingdon's support. In 1771, for example, the Dublin congregation had a collection each Sunday to defray the expenses of their hall, but there was uncertainty whether Lady Huntingdon would allow the practice to continue.[546] Her permission was needed nine years later for Spa Fields to hold a twice-yearly collection at the chapel to meet their expenses and the debt.[547] The use of collections to meet domestic needs may have become more accepted as time went on, however. As described below, there was a faction at Bristol in 1777 who, though a collection had been held the previous year, were firmly opposed to another—whereas ten years later a quarterly collection appears to have been the norm.[548] And in 1789 Birmingham proposed a scheme for paying off their debt which was premised upon them being able to raise £300 in three years by collections.[549]

Amongst established chapels the sale of reserved seats seems to have been a regular means of raising revenue. Tickets for seats were often sold for a fixed period, and the quarterly renewal point could become a key date in the life of the chapel, since it was vital to avoid anything around that time that might depress sales.[550] In 1778, for example, the Bristol chapel signalled a wish to delay the arrival of a less popular preacher until after the next quarter day renewal.[551] In a rather similar way John Bradford reported in 1783 that he would defer the confrontation for which he was heading with the Rotherhithe chapel committee, until after the tickets had been renewed.[552] In 1789 Hereford complained that for the third time they had had their minister removed on the first Sunday of a new quarter.[553]

---

[546] Mead to LH, 16 Nov. 1771, F1/140,CF.
[547] Spa Fields minutes for 17 Oct. 1780, D1/1, 7,CF.
[548] H. Godde to LH, 20 Dec. 1777; A. Gadd to LH, 12 Sept. 1788, F1/420, 766,CF.   [549] Birmingham committee to LH, 12 Jan. 1789, F1/806,CF.
[550] For the Connexion the quarterly renewal of tickets seems to have been a purely financial process, unconnected (as in Wesleyan Methodism) with an assessment of continued suitability for membership of the Society (Baker, *Wesley and the Church of England*, 78).   [551] H. Godde to LH, 1 Mar. 1778, F1/430,CF.
[552] Bradford to LH, 10 Dec. 1783, F1/1919,CF.
[553] J. Williams and others at Hereford to LH, 30 Mar. 1789, F1/819,CF.

There does appear to have been some flexibility, however, over the precise day on which renewal would take place. In 1784 Bristol picked upon a particular (week) day on which to change the tickets, because it was one on which no services were being held elsewhere in the city, and because it was a popular day for attendance by the better classes.[554] Sometimes there would be different grades of ticket, according to the quality of the seating on offer.[555] What the sale of tickets inevitably meant was that the space available for poorer and casual attenders was reduced. It was reported of the Mulberry Gardens chapel in 1779, for example, that the effect of having paid seats was to turn hundreds of would-be worshippers away, a fact that was particularly irksome while many of the paid seats were left unoccupied.[556] Valuable as ticket sales might be in providing regular financial support for chapels, they did imply a restriction on free access to the Gospel which some found uncomfortable. Wesley, years before, had expressed satisfaction that at the Foundry 'the poorest have frequently the best places, because they come first'.[557] Haweis voiced his distaste for the practice, which apparently occurred sometimes in the Connexion, of making ministers the direct beneficiaries of ticket receipts.[558] In 1777 the idea of increasing the revenue of the Bristol chapel by extending the ticketed area to embrace seats that were currently free occasioned bitter representations to Lady Huntingdon from members of the chapel society. Those in favour saw it as the means of avoiding a collection and encouraging more regular hearers. Those against argued that it was a sad departure from the traditions of Whitefield and the other founding fathers to do so little to accommodate the poor and casual visitor.[559]

---

[554] Mrs Wills to LH, 27 Mar. 1784, F1/1937,CF.
[555] H. Godde to LH, n.d.; R. Parsons to LH, 16 May 1772, F1/1177, 180,CF.
[556] Glascott to LH, 11 Aug. 1779, F1/1835,CF. Norman Sykes commented on the similar effects of large family pews in parish churches in *Church and State in England in the Eighteenth Century*, 236.
[557] JW to Mrs Hutton, 22 Aug. 1744, *Works*, xxvi. 113–14.
[558] Haweis to LH, n.d., F1/1192,CF.
[559] H. Godde to LH, 20 Dec. 1777; J. T. Jones to LH, 18 Dec. 1777; Bristol society to LH, 4 Feb. 1778, F1/420, 1629, 1816,CF.

Self-sufficiency, whether founded upon ad hoc giving by members, or more formally through collections or the sale of tickets, was beyond the grasp of some congregations. One remedy in such circumstances, where a congregation could not support a minister on its own, might be to link with another cause and perhaps have services on alternate Sundays—as the Wincanton congregation contemplated doing in 1787.[560] Another device might be for the minister to augment his stipend by running a school: Morley, at Partney in 1789, reported that he and his wife had 'lived pretty decent' by these means.[561] Or (more frequently) congregations might appeal to their richer brethren for assistance.

One congregation, which thought more than once of this expedient, was Kendal. In 1783, their then minister suggested that if Lady Huntingdon would lend them their outstanding purchase money he would go to London the next summer and beg for it.[562] Five years later, still in need of £50, the society sought permission for their minister to beg for them through the Connexion.[563] Their wants, however, were more modest than those at Banbury in 1792, where it was suggested that the congregations of the Connexion might help them with the £600 they needed.[564] Sometimes neighbouring chapels might provide help at moments of special need, as in 1787 when Chatham promised a collection in support of the new Dover chapel.[565] In that instance Dover's minister, Samuel Beaufoy, was considering going to London on a similar errand, and it was to London that congregations most frequently looked for help. Back in 1783, when the Dover congregation needed to clear their debt, their minister Thomas Cannon spent some months in London trying to raise funds. The London pavements might prove to be less

---

[560] Wincanton congregation to LH, 20 June 1787, F1/635,CF.

[561] T. Morley to Best, 22 July 1789, F1/846,CF. The Methodist conference had continuing difficulties with preachers augmenting their income (for example, by travelling in patent medicines), but there is no sign that this was seen as a problem in the Connexion (Baker, 'Polity', 236).

[562] D. Gray to LH, 4 Dec. 1783, F1/579,CF.

[563] W. George to LH, 2 Apr. 1788, F1/720,CF.

[564] J. Jones to Lady AE, 27 Aug. 1792, F1/2227,CF.

[565] S. Beaufoy to LH, 27 Apr. 1787, F1/623,CF.

extensively gilded than congregations supposed, however, especially if their representative came without any special recommendation. In the latter instance Cannon had managed only £25 by private subscription when he informed Lady Huntingdon that he was thinking of a house-to-house collection in Bath, unless, he hinted, she were to write round the London chapels to require a public collection.[566] Possibly he hoped that Lady Huntingdon would give the sort of lead in encouraging and heading individual chapel appeals that Wesley made a frequent practice.[567]

Of the London chapels, Spa Fields was likely to be uppermost in congregations' minds when thinking of help. In 1785 the Spa Fields committee resolved to respond to a petition from Wigan that was circulating round the London chapels, though with the comment that they received many such requests.[568] How they were viewed was demonstrated by the Birmingham committee, three years later, when they sought Lady Huntingdon's agreement to a collection at Spa Fields, a facility which they claimed had been granted to many other congregations.[569] But even Spa Field's resources were not unlimited. Shortly after the Birmingham request (and possibly in connection with it) the Spa Fields committee met in special session to consider a request from Lady Huntingdon for help for another congregation; this they hoped she would withdraw, given that they found themselves with a deficiency rather than a surplus.[570]

As well as the support forthcoming through these spasmodic appeals for help, there was a more formalized system for distributing resources from wealthier congregations. This was the so-called Travelling Fund, a central pool (somewhat akin to the series of central funds, which Wesley had established much earlier for the support of his societies)[571] from which grants could be made to initiate new work or

---

[566] T. Cannon to LH, 10 Feb. 1784, F1/596,CF.
[567] Walsh, 'Methodism at the end of the Eighteenth Century', in Davies and Rupp (eds), *History of the Methodist Church in Great Britain*, i. 252.
[568] Spa fields committee to LH, 21 Jan. 1785, D1/1, 28,CF.
[569] S. Seager to Best, 6 Sept. 1788, F1/765,CF.
[570] W. Hodson to LH (on behalf of the committee), 2 Dec. 1788, F1/794,CF.
[571] Walsh, 'Methodism at the end of the Century', 251.

sustain it in poorer areas. In 1787 Lady Huntingdon was to describe it as the only means available for carrying the Gospel to 'dark places' whose poverty meant that they could not initiate preaching themselves,[572] as instanced by the trip to the Isle of Wight which it supported that year 'to arrange for a new call for the Gospel'.[573] From 1780 Spa Fields had maintained a charitable fund that made payments to ministers and students, as well as to needy individuals and for the discharge of certain chapel expenses.[574] It may well have been from this that the idea developed of a separate fund to support new initiatives within the Connexion. In August 1781 Spa Fields established a separate account book for the Travelling Fund, in what looks like the formal launch of the new arrangements, with a contribution of over £64 from Lady Huntingdon and sermons in the morning and evening that together raised nearly £90.[575] Administration of the Fund rested initially in the hands of William Hodson, secretary to the Spa Fields committee and treasurer of the chapel school. It was a resource on which Lady Huntingdon could draw, but she clearly saw it as distinct from her own income; in 1784 she felt it necessary to enquire about her authority in respect of the Fund.[576]

An example of the part the Travelling Fund came to play by the end of the decade in supporting the circulation of ministers upon which the Connexion depended, is to be found in the agreement with the trustees of the Holywell Mount chapel, Shoreditch, into which Lady Huntingdon entered in 1789. This provided for a settled minister who would spend six weeks a year elsewhere in the Connexion, and as the agreement was originally drafted it left the minister's travelling expenses (but not those of his supply) to be met by

---

[572] LH to Bidwell, 10 Apr. 1787, B4/3,CF.
[573] Receipt from the Travelling Fund, 28 Dec. 1787, E4/15(8),CF.
[574] Spa Fields charity book, D1/3,CF.
[575] Spa Fields committee to LH, 9 Aug. 1781; Travelling Fund account to 20 July 1787, D1/1, 12; E4/15(39),CF. What suggests continuity with the earlier arrangements is that the Travelling Fund accounts, made up in 1787, show payments from the Fund slightly earlier than Aug. 1781.
[576] Spa Fields minutes for 25 Jan. 1780; Hodson to LH, 12 May 1781; Wills to LH, 24 Feb. 1784, D1/1, p. 2; D1/2, p. 10; F1/1930,CF.

the trustees. This was subsequently amended to an agreement to hold an annual Travelling Fund collection, based upon three sermons in the chapel on any Sunday that Lady Huntingdon should appoint.[577] The Fund, moreover, was to support work overseas as well as at home. Before a collection sermon in 1790 Lady Huntingdon was asked for 'the letter from Nova Scotia' (apparently about people walking in snow shoes to hear the Gospel) in order to enhance the appeal.[578] What is difficult to determine is the distinction that Lady Huntingdon perceived between work supported by the Travelling Fund, and that covered by the 'Augmentation Fund' which she and Wills established in 1783 to supplement the income of those working in poorer areas.[579] Possibly this was 'the fund' from which John Hornby hoped for 'a few shillings' in 1790, in view of the work done at his own expense to the Hereford chapel.[580] But there are no further references to the Augmentation Fund by name after the report of its inception, and it may be that the functions of the Travelling Fund came to be regarded as insufficiently different to justify separate accounts.

Maintaining the Travelling Fund's income was a continuing concern. Although donations and profits from hymn book sales appear in the Fund accounts, it depended principally upon special collections.[581] In June 1784 committee members from Spa Fields, Mulberry Gardens and Princes Street chapels, with certain Connexional ministers, agreed together over dinner on an annual collection for the Fund at each of their chapels, and to recommend the same to all other Connexional chapels that could afford it.[582] Despite this, the Spa Fields committee recorded the next January that Bristol had been the only other chapel to have contributed during 1784.[583] There was inevitably a conflict between calls on a congregation's generosity for external

---

[577] Agreement between LH and the trustees, 2 Sept. 1789, E4/15(47),CF.
[578] D. Jones to LH, 22 Feb. 1790, F1/887,CF.
[579] Spa Fields minutes for 3 Nov. 1783, D1/1, 25,CF.
[580] J. Hornby to LH, 19 Jan. 1790, F1/880,CF.
[581] Travelling Fund account to 20 July 1787, E4/15(39),CF.
[582] Spa Fields minutes for 8 June 1784, D1/1, 27,CF.
[583] Spa Fields committee to LH, 21 Jan. 1785, D1/1, 28,CF.

causes, however worthy, and the needs of the congregation itself. In 1788 Bristol complied reluctantly with a request for a Travelling Fund collection, although the date Lady Huntingdon had set coincided with their own quarterly collection.[584] A similar situation would have occurred there in February 1790, had not the minister concerned taken it upon himself to defer the Travelling Fund appeal for some weeks.[585] Expectation evidently differed over the frequency of Travelling Fund collections. Bath were apparently receiving special treatment from Lady Huntingdon in 1785 when she promised them no more than one such collection a year.[586] Bristol chapel clearly imagined themselves in an annual cycle by 1790, and suggested that the requests from the Countess's secretary for a November collection was premature, rather than late as he had thought. Nevertheless, a further Travelling Fund collection *was* held that month, as it happened, clashing once again with their quarterly collection.[587] That Bristol collection raised some £17, and was broadly in line with what might be raised at chapels other than Spa Fields. In 1786, for example, Brighton had raised £21.16s, Tunbridge Wells 15 guineas, and Lewes £10.[588] The previous year a Spa Fields collection had raised nearly £150, which corresponded with a similar figure following sermons by David Jones in 1784.[589] In the first six years of its life the Fund had a turnover of more than £1,000, of which nearly half is known for certain to have come from Spa Fields.[590]

Travelling Fund collections were not the only support that Spa Fields was called upon to give to the wider work of the Gospel. As noted, the chapel was the frequent recipient of appeals from individual congregations, and there were also occasional requests for help with charitable causes. One such, on behalf of the Finsbury dispensary in 1783,

---

[584] A. Gadd to LH, 12 Sept. 1788, F1/766,CF.
[585] David Jones to LH, 8 Feb. 1790, F1/882,CF. Jones no doubt felt on stronger ground than some in modifying Lady Huntingdon's instructions.
[586] LH to Carpenter, n.d., Meth. Arch. (LH), 133.
[587] J. Ford to LH, 1 and 15 Nov. 1790, F1/2152, 2156,CF.
[588] Travelling Fund accounts to 20 July 1787, E4/15(39),CF.
[589] Spa Fields minutes for 8 July 1784, D1/1, p. 28,CF.
[590] Travelling Fund accounts to 20 July 1787, E4/15(39),CF.

raised £63.[591] The committee were wary of a hostile reaction from the congregation if they permitted too many appeals, as they told Lady Huntingdon in 1781 when informed that she had promised support for what may have been the same dispensary.[592] The fact that they could respond on such a scale, however, is testimony to the pre-eminence and prosperity which Spa Fields rapidly attained. After the establishment of Spa Fields, the centre of gravity within the Connexion appears to have swung there from Bath, just as, earlier still, it had focused more on Brighton. Lady Huntingdon's own choice of principal residence was undoubted a major factor in this, though it was inevitable that once a major chapel was established in London, it would become the central influence in the Connexion.

The diversity that existed within the Connexion is one of its striking features. At the opposite extreme from Spa Fields, with its ability to attract the most eminent of the Connexion's preachers and make such a significant contribution to the wider work, were congregations of the sort described in this chapter, meeting in rented accommodation and able only with difficulty to scrape together the most meagre of stipends. Diversity may not in itself be surprising. It is the extent to which all of these very different causes shared together in the concern—and the usually benign, if not always very efficient oversight—of their patroness, that is one of the striking features of the Countess of Huntingdon's Connexion in these decades.

[591] Spa Fields minutes for 23 Nov. 1783, D1/1, p. 26,CF.
[592] Spa Fields committee to LH, 22 Dec. 1781, D1/1, 16,CF. In 1788 Dupont asked for a charity sermon on behalf of his charity school, though it is not clear what response he received (M. Dupont to LH, 13 Aug. 1788, F1/2030,CF).

5
Trevecca College

ORIGINS AND ESTABLISHMENT

It is not certain when Lady Huntingdon first came to the idea of the college that she was to open at Trevecca in 1768, but it is clear that she had for some time been contemplating an institution that would help satisfy the requests for ministers which she was increasingly receiving. In June 1764, for example, in response to an approach for help in finding suitable curates, she expressed a wish for some kind of 'nursery' for turning Wesley's lay preachers into clergymen.[1] It is possible that at this early stage she was thinking simply of an institution that would provide the equivalent of a university education for godly young men unable to gain admission to Oxford or Cambridge. If so, she may have had in mind building upon the support which, a decade before, she had shown towards some of the more godly Dissenting academies. In the early 1750s she had contributed towards a scheme to establish an expressly evangelical academy in London, as well as providing direct financial support for students at Philip Doddridge's Northampton Academy.[2] The date of the 'nursery' remark fits with the statement that Howel Harris made, years later, about having told Lady Huntingdon of the vision he had nursed since 1740 of a 'School of the Prophets' near to his own home in Trevecca. The term nursery is in itself significant, denoting as it does nurturing and training.[3] It is clear that by the stage of detailed planning for her college, the emphasis was firmly upon the preparation of

---

[1] LH to CW, 9 June 1764, Meth. Arch. (LH), 75.
[2] Seymour, i. 143, 146.
[3] Tom Beynon (ed.), *Howel Harris's Visits to London* (Aberystwyth, 1960), 287. The idea clearly remained with Harris: in 1764 he attempted to persuade John Fletcher

men for the ministry; the acquisition of learning was definitely a secondary consideration. Lady Huntingdon's object was not to turn out scholars, nor even scholars who might discover ministerial gifts along the way.

For this, there seems to have been no direct precedent. The universities, though the standard route to Church ordination for most men, were in the business of education, not vocational training: neither their curriculum nor their *raison d'être* were expressly geared to developing ministerial gifts. This remained the case for the Anglican ministry into the following century. Although the early decades of the nineteenth century witnessed the founding of some institutions dedicated to the training of non-graduate ordinands,[4] this still left graduates without vocational training for the role they were to fulfil after ordination. As late as 1832 (the decade which, at its close, saw the first of the colleges like St Bees designed to provide professional training for graduate ordinands) one commentator observed that 'the clergyman is the only member of any of the learned professions who has strictly no regular provisions for an education suited to the office to which he aspires.'[5]

It was not a dissimilar story with the Dissenting academies, which for more than a century from the Restoration filled the gap created by the exclusion of Nonconformists from the universities. Although a major part of their significance lay in the maintenance through these years of an educated Dissenting ministry, the concern of the generality of academies up to this time (some notable exceptions were to appear later in the century) was as much with the provision of a general education—principally, though not exclusively,

---

to lead a theological school at Trevecca (Patrick Streiff, *Reluctant Saint? A Theological Biography of Fletcher of Madeley* (Peterborough, 2001), 140). Dr Schlenther suggests that Trevecca should be understood more as a missionary organization than a college, but this may be a false distinction: a training college for mission (principally at home, but abroad where necessary) would be a better description (Schlenther, 83).

[4] e.g. St Bees Theological College, founded in 1816. See Alan Haig, *The Victorian Clergy* (London and Sydney, 1984), 116.

[5] (Anon.), *On Clerical Education: A Letter by a Clergyman* (1832), quoted in Haig, *Victorian Clergy*, 73. Even at the end of the nineteenth century, half the graduate clergy had not been to a theological college (ibid., 88).

for the sons of Dissenters—as with direct preparation for future ministry. Many of the academies admitted students who were not destined for a ministerial career; had they not done so, Dissenters' sons without a ministerial vocation would have been driven to the universities and conformity to the Established Church.[6] Francis Okely, who was offered the tutorship of the proposed college in 1765, identified the distinction between this traditional approach and that which Lady Huntingdon now envisaged: '...there are Schools and Academies enough, both on the Establishment, and in the dissenting Way, but a School of the Prophets, that's the Thing.'[7]

That phrase, a 'School of the Prophets', can be regarded as symbolic of the new college's role.[8] Lady Huntingdon cannot claim to have been the initiator of the concept. In the 1740s Wesleyan Methodism had speculated about the possible provision of college training for its preachers; in the 1750s the Dissenter James Scott of Heckmondwike was supervising an academy for training evangelical ministers; and in 1760 a proposal was put to Wesley for a college as a source of travelling preachers.[9] Nevertheless, it is important to keep in mind both the relative novelty of the concept and

---

[6] E. G. Rupp, *Religion in England, 1688–1791* (Oxford, 1986), ch. 12; M. R. Watts, *The Dissenters, from the Reformation to the French Revolution* (Oxford, 1978), 367. There are some instances of theological students in academies spending a longer period than their brethren who were destined for secular callings, though this does not necessarily mean that the focus of their education changed during this further period, (Rupp, *Religion in England*, 177).

[7] G. M. Roberts (ed.), *Selected Trevecka Letters* (Caernarvon, 1962), ii. 102. For the dating of the relevant Trevecca letters (nos. 74 and 72) see G. F. Nuttall, *The Significance of Trevecca College* (Cheshunt College Bicentenary Booklet, 1968), 22, n. 5. I have followed the implications of his dating (which differs from that of Roberts) in the following description of the planning of the college. Okely (1719–94) of Bedford was a member of the Cambridge equivalent of the Oxford Holy Club and a friend of JW. He joined the Moravians, left them in 1757, and resumed ministry with them a decade later. In 1763 the bishop of London refused him Anglican ordination, despite the fact that he was a Moravian deacon. His mixed ecclesiastical pedigree made LH's choice of him for Trevecca a striking one (Colin Podmore, *The Moravian Church in England, 1728–1760* (Oxford, 1998), 49, 115, 287–9).

[8] Nuttall, *Significance of Trevecca*, 21.

[9] Frank Baker, 'Polity', in R. Davies and E. G. Rupp (eds.), *A History of the Methodist Church in Great Britain* (London, 1965), i. 248; Bruce Hindmarsh, *John Newton and the English Evangelical Tradition* (Oxford, 1996), 85; Tyerman, *Wesley*, ii. 360.

the fact that the justification for such an institution was by no means self-evident to all Lady Huntingdon's circle.

Had Lady Huntingdon established a Connexional equivalent of a Dissenting academy, she might well have been criticized both for the distraction of effort and resources which this represented, and for the encouragement thus given to secular learning. Howel Harris, despite his longstanding enthusiasm for the right sort of ministerial training, once expressed the view that 'nothing is more dangerous than letter-learning and head or book knowledge'.[10] George Whitefield, towards the end of his life, expressed a rather similar opinion,[11] though he himself was criticized, by Wesley and others, for his decision to turn the Orphan House which he had founded in America into an academy.[12] Lady Huntingdon, however, had chosen a potentially more controversial course—the establishment of an institution whose objective of making men into ministers could be seen as usurping God's role, as well as questioning the sufficiency of their spiritual calling as an adequate basis for future ministry. John Berridge articulated the fear that an institution established for this purpose signalled a lack of faith in God's power to call whom he wanted, and to give them the gifts they needed: 'Will not Jesus choose and teach and send for his ministering servants now as he did the disciples aforetime? ... We read of a School of Prophets in Scripture, but we do not read that it is God's appointment.'[13]

Berridge's view was perhaps understandable in the light of his own background; like some other leaders of the Revival he had pursued a distinguished university career, and was nearly forty when he went through the spiritual crisis that brought him into the ranks of the Church Evangelicals.[14] He indeed could claim that he had been called without human

---

[10] *Memoirs of Howel Harris, from papers written by himself* (Trevecka, 1791), 120.

[11] W. Jay, *Memoirs of the Life and Character of Cornelius Winter* (Bath, 1808), 70.

[12] Wesley's concern was that the original charitable purpose of the institution had been perverted; John Berridge was more blunt and described the new academy as a 'lumber-house for human learning' (JW to Whitefield, 21 Feb. 1770, and to LH, 16 Sept. 1773, Wesley, *Letters*, v. 184; vi. 42, Seymour, ii. 263).

[13] Seymour, ii. 92.   [14] Rupp, *Religion in England*, 480.

agency, and he was not alone in expressing such misgivings. The Bristol Education Society, which was formed in 1770 to support the work of the Bristol Baptist Academy, found it necessary in its constitution to respond to the objection that providing learning was an improper attempt to perfect the work of the Spirit. Their conclusion was the opposite of Berridge's. Since, they argued, the age of miracles had passed, 'it seems rather to be tempting the Spirit of God to expect that in an extraordinary which we are authorised to expect only in an ordinary way'.[15] There were others, as well, who believed with Lady Huntingdon that the religious state of the country was dire enough to warrant human intervention into the process of making ministers. In 1777, George Burnett, a former curate of Henry Venn in Huddersfield and by then vicar of Elland, Yorkshire, founded the Elland Clerical Society to provide financial support for the education of evangelical ordinands. Burnett, however, was a stricter exponent of Church order than Lady Huntingdon. His concern was specifically to ease the path to Anglican orders, and thereby to prevent evangelical young men being tempted into Methodism or Dissent. Although the original rules of the Elland Society envisaged support for non-graduates, its principal object appears to have been to assist those following the orthodox route of a university education prior to ordination.[16] But there was a common strand here in the recognition that something positive needed to be done to assist godly but impecunious young men to realize their

---

[15] Quoted in D. W. Lovegrove, *Established Church, Sectarian People: Itinerancy and the Transformation of English Dissent, 1780–1830* (Cambridge, 1988), 67. The attitude, to which the Bristol Society was responding, survived into the following century. When the Revd Joseph Philpot resigned his Oxford fellowship and seceded from the Church of England in 1835, part of his objection was to 'the whole principle of a University, as needful to qualify men to become ministers of Jesus Christ' (J. H. Philpot, *The Seceders* (London, 1964), 190).

[16] *Evangelical Magazine* (1793), 83; Haig, *Victorian Clergy*, 64, 103, n. 147. Burnett's description of the Society to Lord Dartmouth in March 1782 indicated that all their young men had so far been sent to Cambridge, where they had trusted academic mentors (HMC (Dartmouth), iii. 256–7). Later institutions following a similar path to the Elland Society were the Bristol (1795) Creaton (1812) and London (1816) Clerical Education Societies (Charles Smyth, *Simeon and Church Order* (Cambridge, 1940), 243–4; Haig, *Victorian Clergy*, 64).

calling, rather than waiting passively for men with the right skills to appear.[17]

The indications are that Lady Huntingdon had fixed on Trevecca for the location of her college by the end of 1765, and that Howel Harris was by then actively involved in planning the institution.[18] Although Trevecca (in Breconshire, near Hay-on-Wye) was remote from the centres of Connexional activity in England at that time, its advantage lay in its proximity to the 'Family' of craftsmen, artisans, and labourers, which Harris had established in the village (on Moravian lines) in 1752. Help was thus to hand in the physical task of setting up the college, and there was the prospect of continuing oversight and support thereafter. The building chosen for the college was a short walk from the Harris settlement, and was leased to Lady Huntingdon by Howel Harris's brother Thomas, of nearby Tregunta.[19]

Francis Okely turned down the offer of the tutorship after a few months' deliberation.[20] Lady Huntingdon's alternative choice was John Fletcher,[21] although it was not until November 1767 that this was agreed.[22] By this stage Lady Huntingdon had drawn up a plan for the examination of potential students, which she circulated to Fletcher and Berridge and others of her friends.[23] She was now actively

---

[17] There was a sense in which Wesley approached the problem from the other side, in the way he used and organized his lay preachers, effectively by taking his more articulate converts and developing their skills (and testing their vocations) on the job.

[18] In January 1766 Okely was in correspondence with Harris about arrangements for the college, including the furnishings of the 'Tutors House' (Okely to Harris, 5 January 1765/6, Roberts, *Trevecka Letters*, ii. 100). Roberts quotes no evidence for his claim that it was during LH's visit to Wales in July 1764 that she decided to establish her seminary at Trevecca (ibid. ii. 96).

[19] The negotiation of the lease was not concluded until January 1769 (Lloyd to LH, 21 Jan. 1769, F1/47,CF). The house itself shows signs of Strawberry Hill gothic windows in what had been the college chapel.

[20] Okeley to Harris, 10 April 1766, Roberts, *Trevecka Letters*, ii. 102.

[21] For a moving account of Fletcher's saintly ministry at Madeley—and, by implication, of the calibre of the man in whose hands the early life of the college was placed—see Rupp, *Religion in England*, 429–32.

[22] With characteristic modesty Fletcher indicated that he was ready to throw his 'mite into the treasury that your Ladyship may find in other persons' (Fletcher to LH, 24 Nov. 1767, Seymour, ii. 82).

[23] Ibid. 81, 92. Seymour suggests that Wesley, Venn, and Romaine were also consulted (ibid. 82).

seeking students also. Fletcher had just one candidate from Madeley, the twenty-three-year-old 'collier and getter of iron stone', James Glazebrook.[24] By December Lady Huntingdon had seven names, including two suggested by Dr Conyers (vicar of Helmsley, Yorkshire, and brother-in-law of John Thornton), and others proposed by Whitefield.[25] The pace was clearly quickening, with a broad spread of interest making the college project symbolic of the Revival's underlying unity of purpose. Lady Huntingdon set aside a day of prayer for the college in December, and there was hope that in this initiative, at least, all factions within the Revival would be united.[26]

Despite forwardness of planning in some areas, however, Lady Huntingdon had evidently not yet thought out what her students were to do at college. In January 1768 Fletcher told her there must be a 'plan of study', with suggestions for the subjects that this might cover.[27] It is striking that such a long time after Lady Huntingdon had determined on the idea of a training college, she had given so little thought to how the institution might work in practice. What makes this lack of a clear curriculum particularly striking is that at that stage an opening date substantially earlier than August was still envisaged.[28]

It was the preparation of the building that caused delay over the coming months. Substantial structural work was necessary to adapt it for use as a theological college, and progress was not helped by the fact that Lady Huntingdon was not on hand to take decisions as they arose (including

---

[24] Glazebrook had by then been awakened seven years, and had recently told Fletcher of his belief that he was called to the ministry (Fletcher to LH, 24 Nov. 1767, Seymour, ii. 81).

[25] LH to Harris, 17 Dec. 1767, Roberts, *Trevecka Letters*, ii. 115.

[26] Maxfield to LH, 24 Dec. 1767, F1/1412,CF. At least in its early years Trevecca College was to prove a meeting place for many of the disparate strands in the Revival. Dr Nuttall wondered whether 'in these years any other place in the country drew together so many religious leaders' (G. F. Nuttall, *Howel Harris, the Last Enthusiast* (Cardiff, 1965), 36).

[27] Fletcher to LH, 3 Jan. 1768, Seymour, ii. 84–6.

[28] In February it was decided to put back the opening till June; by April the talk was of LH coming to Wales in August (Mrs Leighton to LH, 8 Feb. n.y., F1/1210,CF; Harris to Easterbrook, 7 Apr. 1768, Roberts, *Trevecka Letters*, ii. 118).

on such key issues as her own accommodation and the decoration of the chapel).[29] It was an arrangement which invited delay, and in late July a clear view had still not been obtained from Lady Huntingdon on aspects of the work on the chapel which had first been raised two months before.[30]

By now there had been a change in the planned teaching arrangements for the college. Late in 1767 Lady Huntingdon had recommended to Fletcher the seventeen-year-old Joseph Easterbrook, who had been educated at Kingswood School and who was hoping for a ministerial career. Fletcher apparently envisaged him as some sort of senior student, who would be 'captain of the school and a great help to the master as well as a spur to the students'.[31] The intention was evidently that he should study and instruct at the same time. Fletcher was delighted with Easterbrook's preaching, when the latter came to stay with him at Madeley, prior to the opening of the college. By late April, however, something had occurred—the implication is a moral lapse, rather than any theological differences—which shattered the good opinions which had been forming of him;[32] he is heard of no more in relation to the college or the Connexion at large.[33] That left a gap to be filled, since Fletcher could only give a limited time to the college, and by early June Lady Huntingdon had found a Welshman, John Williams, who had been converted under Howel Harris, and who 'on account of his religious principles' had left the boarding school where he had been an usher. Williams was said to be capable of teaching Welsh and English

---

[29] Mrs Leighton to LH, 13 Mar. n.y. and 12 May 1768, F1/1213, 29,CF; LH to Harris, 4 June 1768, Roberts, *Trevecka Letters*, ii. 120. One of the second-order issues that had to be resolved was whether brewing utensils should be procured as a cheaper alternative to buying beer for the students (Mrs Leighton to LH, 12 May 1768, F1/29,CF).

[30] Harris to ?, 21 July 1768, Roberts, *Trevecka Letters*, ii. 124.

[31] Fletcher to LH, 3 Jan. 1768, Seymour, ii. 84. Telford describes him as 'son of the bellman at Bristol' (Wesley, *Letters*, v. 82 n.).

[32] Lloyd to LH, 23 Apr. and 5 May 1768; Glascott to LH, 11 May 1768, F1/1421, 1424, 1427,CF.

[33] The statements by Telford and Curnock that he became assistant master at Trevecca—and of Seymour that he was 'headmaster'—are wrong. Although Glascott hoped that Easterbrook would now give up thoughts of the ministry, he did gain ordination, dying as vicar of Temple Church, Bristol, in 1791. Wesley preached

grammar and Latin; if they needed someone more gifted in due course to complete the educational process, Lady Huntingdon would attend to that when the time came.[34]

In the midst of the preparations for the college there occurred an event that seemed to underline the need for such an institution. This was the expulsion of six undergraduates from St Edmund Hall, Oxford, in March 1768. The offences with which the six were charged before the Vice-Chancellor were 'holding Methodistical tenets, and taking upon them to pray, read and expound the Scriptures, and singing hymns in private houses'.[35] The factors which led to the case being brought were complex; academic ability and social origins figured in the hearing, as well as Methodist doctrines and irregular ecclesiastical practices.[36] The personal venom of the vice-principal of the Hall appears to have been a major factor in the case being brought to trial,[37] although there were contemporaries who believed he had acted in the affair as the tool of more eminent men; certainly the majority of the assessors who heard the case had already shown their hostility to evangelicals in the University.[38] What the affair did arouse, as well as stimulating by a side wind renewed conflict between the Arminian and Calvinistic wings of the Revival,[39] was the spectre of clandestine attempts to infiltrate Methodist sympathizers into the universities, thereby to subvert the order and authority of the Church. At the public hearing of their case the undergraduates were pressed as to whose support had enabled them to come to Oxford;[40] a contemporary wrote of the Hall as

for him on a number of occasions (Wesley, *Letters*, v. 82 n, Curnock, vii. 47 n. Seymour, ii. 96; Glascott to LH, 11 May 1768, F1/1427,CF.

[34] LH to Harris, 16 June 1768, Roberts, *Trevecka Letters*, ii. 122. Williams was paid 25 guineas a year, 'with board, room and washing' (Fletcher to LH, 1 July 1769, Seymour, ii. 97). See also LH to Whitefield, 17 April 1768, Meth. Arch. (LH), 115.
[35] Nuttall, *Significance of Trevecca*, 3. Dr Nuttall quotes the summary of the charge given in the *St. James Chronicle*—'having too much religion'.
[36] Rupp, *Religion in England*, 476–8.
[37] Rupp calls him 'a psychological case' (ibid. 476).
[38] J. S. Reynolds, *The Evangelicals at Oxford, 1735–81* (Oxford, 1953), ch. 2.
[39] See below, ch. 6.
[40] S. L. Ollard, *The Six Students of St. Edmund Hall expelled from the University of Oxford in 1768* (London, 1911).

'the place where a certain person sends all those who have a mind to skulk into orders';[41] another asserted that all the students had been admitted 'by the recommendation of Lady Huntingdon'.[42]

The evidence is inconclusive on whether there was a prior link between Lady Huntingdon and the undergraduates—although Dr Nuttall quotes what he regards as a reliable source to the effect that all six were connected with her.[43] So far as possible financial backing was concerned, her earlier support for the Doddridge students[44] shows that this would not have been out of character; ten years after the St Edmund Hall affair she provided financial support for a former Trevecca student, John Eyre, to go to Oxford—as it happens, to St Edmund Hall.[45] By the same token, moreover, there was an established tradition of providing such support; the early religious societies had done so; so had Lady Betty Hastings; and the Elland Society had, as noted, recently been established for a similar purpose.[46] If any or all of the students had had outside backing, it need not necessarily have come from Lady Huntingdon. What is known is that within a fortnight of the expulsions one of the six, Joseph Shipman, a twenty-one-year-old former apprentice draper, had written to Lady Huntingdon to seek her help in his 'readmission into the University & C. of Eng^d.'[47]

Shipman had been told by James Matthew that she wanted him to write. Matthews was another of the six who was charged with having been associated with John Fletcher.[48] Lady Huntingdon's response was to invite Shipman to

---

[41] The passage in question comes from a series of *Letters from Oxford* transcribed (in an 18th-century hand) in the Bodleian copy of *Pietas Oxoniensis*, Sir Richard Hill's defence of the undergraduates. It is quoted in part in Seymour, i. 425.

[42] Ibid. 423.   [43] Nuttall, *Significance of Trevecca*, 6.

[44] Above p. 173.   [45] J. Eyre to LH, 30 Aug. 1779, F1/446,CF.

[46] J. S. Simon, *John Wesley and the Religious Societies* (London, 1921), 20; T. Gibbons, G. Jerment, and S. Burder, *Memoirs of Eminently Pious Women* (London, 1815); Tyerman, *Whitefield*, i. 58. Welch (p. 112) doubts that she provided funding.

[47] Shipman to LH, 26 Mar. 1767, E4/5(1),CF. Shipman told her that he had at one stage assisted Lawrence Coughlan, the former Wesleyan preacher irregularly ordained by the Greek Bishop Erasmus (see Curnock, iv. 297 n).

[48] Seymour, i. 425. This may have been the group's only prior, and indirect, link with LH. Certainly Shipman's letter did not read as from someone already well known to her.

Trevecca to continue his studies,[49] and she appears to have given similar invitations to the other five. In May John Newton wrote that 'two of them have accepted Lady Huntingdon's invitation'.[50] The two were Shipman and Matthews.

The substitution of Trevecca for Oxford doubtless seemed a natural exchange to Lady Huntingdon, as well as an answer to what appeared the start of a policy of barring the road to higher education and ordination to those suspected of Methodist sentiments. In the same month as the expulsions the SPCK had resolved 'to accept no recommendation for... missionaries, but such as have had a literary education, and have been bred up with a design to dedicate themselves to the Ministry'[51]—a clear threat to those shut out from the universities and those who, despite not being born into the classes from which the clergy were usually drawn, had found their vocation through the Revival. But if Trevecca was a natural response to such moves, so far as Lady Huntingdon was concerned, it may not have appeared in quite that light to the expelled undergraduates. A South Wales farmhouse (even on a fine day) may not have had the same appeal as an Oxford college, and admission to it made a ministerial career no more certain. It is perhaps not surprising that four of the six chose other routes to ministry, or opted for other vocations,[52] while Shipman explained to Lady Huntingdon that it was only his financial circumstances which had decided him to accept her invitation 'which doubtless was for the distressed only'.[53]

Part of Lady Huntingdon's motive in inviting the expelled students to Trevecca may have been concern that the new college would not have sufficient students with which to start. The initial intake had been pretty haphazard, but towards the end of 1767 the search for candidates became more purposive. Thomas Maxfield, for example, was actively

---

[49] Shipman to LH, 13 Apr. 1768, E4/5(2),CF.
[50] Newton to Lord Dartmouth, 10 May 1768, HMC (Dartmouth), iii. 188.
[51] Quoted in Nuttall, *Significance of Trevecca*.
[52] Seymour, i. 424–5. Two of the other four subsequently obtained episcopal ordination. [53] Shipman to LH, 13 Apr. 1768, E4/5(2),CF.

seeking names. At the end of the year he told Lady Huntingdon about three or four possibles;[54] the following April he had come upon a promising former pupil of a Dissenting academy who had given up his studies there for want of money.[55] The following month Glascott reported that he was making all the enquiries he could for possible students, but concluded that suitable young men were thin on the ground.[56]

Shipman and Matthews were given shelter by Lady Huntingdon at her house in Tunbridge Wells until the college was ready to receive them;[57] Shipman, for one, was with her at Trevecca by the end of July. By this stage final plans were being made to bring the other recruits to Wales in time for the eventual opening of the college.[58] George Whitefield performed the dedication ceremony on Lady Huntingdon's sixty-first birthday, 24 August 1768.[59] Over the next few years the date was observed as a special festival at some of the major chapels of the Connexion, as well as Trevecca itself.[60]

RECRUITMENT TO THE COLLEGE

Once the college had actually started, the recruitment of students settled into a more coherent pattern. There were

[54] Maxfield to LH, 15 and 24 Dec. 1767, F1/1410, 1412,CF.
[55] Maxfield to LH, 16 Apr. 1768, F1/1419,CF.
[56] Glascott to LH, 30 May 1768, F1/1433,CF.
[57] Seymour, ii. 126 n. The statement is confirmed by Maxfield to LH, 14 May 1768, F1/1429,CF. According to Seymour it was while they were there that LH forced them to try out their preaching skills by causing a crowd to be assembled before her house, and then thrusting them out of doors to address it.
[58] Maxfield to LH, 16 July 1768, F1/1438,CF.
[59] Seymour, ii. 92. Whitefield's account of the festivities that marked the opening is quoted in J. Gillies, *Memoirs of the Life of George Whitefield* (London, 1772), 254 n. See also Nuttall, *Howel Harris*, 75–6 n. 112. Early in August 1768 Wesley had told LH that he would try to attend the opening if free; in the event he left Bristol around 20 August, but went to the South-West, rather than to Wales (JW to LH, 9 Aug. 1768, G2/1 (Add),CF). He was present at the celebrations of the college's first anniversary (JW's Journal for 20–2 Aug. 1768, and for 23 and 24 Aug. 1769, *Works*, xxii. 153, 200–1).
[60] For example, Maxfield to LH, 2 Sept. 1772; Shirley to LH, 10 Aug. 1770, F1/1614, 1507,CF. The anniversary celebrations at college in 1776 were particularly well attended; according to one report, some three thousand people were present, with over thirteen hundred horses being turned into one field near the

broadly three sources of supply. One was through the students themselves, as they embarked on their ministry outside the college. The preaching of Trevecca students, often men of obviously humble origins, clearly inspired some of their hearers to the thought that they might take the same route to ministry. One such instance was the approach made to Glazebrook at Ote Hall in 1770, by a man who had harboured thoughts of ministry for the past year.[61] Another was the young man whom the student William Dunn sought permission to bring to see Lady Huntingdon in 1774.[62] The pattern continued through the period. An example in 1789 amounted to more than merely passing on a name: the student in question interviewed the would-be student and then arranged for him to expound the Scriptures to him and others, before he wrote to recommend him to Lady Huntingdon.[63] Further evidence of selectivity in passing on applications is found in 1791, in the comment that the recommendation being forwarded was the first of many such approaches that the student in question had thought it right to bring to Lady Huntingdon's attention.[64]

Another route was direct application to the Countess. Examples of this were the man (converted some years earlier under the London Baptist minister, Dr Giffard), who in 1770 looked to Trevecca to help sort out his thoughts of ministry; another was the former cabinet-maker with a persistent sense of vocation, who applied in 1772.[65] Happily less typical was the man whose undated application to Lady Huntingdon, after he had already been seen by her, ran to three and a-half foolscap sides of quotations from the psalms on the necessity of wisdom.[66] Distinct in a different way was

---

college. The celebrations nearly ended in disaster when the scaffolding erected outside the college buildings for a succession of open-air sermons collapsed under the weight of some forty ministers (Seymour, ii. 122–3).

[61] Glazebrook to LH, 1 June 1770, F1/1498,CF.
[62] Dunn to LH, 14 Jan. 1774, F1/268,CF.
[63] J. Wright to LH, 24 Sept. 1789, F1/861,CF.
[64] J. H. Browning to LH, 30 May 1791, F1/2181,CF.
[65] N. de la Symonds to LH, 25 Oct. 1770; W. Newton to LH, 23 Oct. 1772, F1/109, 196,CF. [66] J. Symes to LH, n.d., E4/4(18),CF.

the father in 1779 who wrote on behalf of his son (and plainly at the behest of his wife) to see if she would admit the boy to Trevecca 'in order to make my family less'.[67]

The third source of recommendations was from persons known to Lady Huntingdon, or otherwise of some standing. Samuel Clark of South Petherton made at least two recommendations, in 1774 and 1784.[68] John Eyre, referred to already, was recommended for Trevecca by an occasional correspondent of Lady Huntingdon, a Mr Brown of Plymouth.[69] A Welsh curate near Brecon recommended a recently converted parishioner in 1774,[70] and recommendations have been preserved from some prominent leaders of the Welsh Revival. In 1788 the Revd Peter Williams, a long-standing friend of the college, sent a young man from the Carmarthen society—apparently without consulting Lady Huntingdon first.[71] In 1790 David Jones of Llangan gave his support to a young man from near Llandovery.[72]

There appears to have been no set age of admission at Trevecca, but a broad pattern emerges from the ages of new entrants and applicants that are recorded. Two of the original students whose ages are known, Mead and Glazebrook, were both in the region of twenty-three or twenty-four, so that had Easterbrook come to Trevecca as senior student as planned, he would (at seventeen or eighteen) have been distinctly their junior. Late teens to early twenties was probably the norm for young men considering such a path to ministry; applications received in 1773, 1780, and 1791, for example, were from young men respectively of eighteen,

---

[67] B. Lewis to LH, 16 July 1779, F1/434,CF. The father, having done his duty, undermined any impact the letter might have had with the comment that the boy was not really fit for college, but would be useful to him in his business!

[68] Clark to LH, 21 May 1774, and 12 Apr. 1784, F1/297, 612,CF.

[69] J. Brown to LH, 29 March 1776, F1/353,CF; see also LH to Wills, 1 Apr. 1777, J. Rylands Library ENG. MS 338.

[70] J. Williams to LH, 19 Jan. 1774, F1/1671,CF.

[71] John Williams to LH, 21 Apr. 1788, Gloucester Record Office, D. 2538, Ebley Chapel Records, 8/1. no. 4.

[72] D. Jones to LH, 28 Dec. 1790, F1/948,CF. David Jones (1735–1810) was vicar of Llangan, Glamorganshire from 1788, and of Maenornawan, Pembrokeshire from 1794; he was prominent in the Revival in Wales and opposed separation from the Established Church.

nineteen, and twenty years.⁷³ There seem, however, to have been some older entrants. Samuel Eyles Pierce was just over thirty when he was admitted in 1775; George Brown, was apparently approaching thirty when he arrived in 1788.⁷⁴

Numbers fluctuated considerably. Sixteen students are listed at the college in 1769, and it is not impossible that they were all original members.⁷⁵ The highest recorded number at any one time was in 1773, when two dozen students were said to be present.⁷⁶ A lower figure appears, however, to have been more normal. Fourteen were present in 1775, for example, and seven in 1783.⁷⁷ In 1787 the master regarded the college as 'rather full' with twelve students; the following year he described eleven as a 'great number'.⁷⁸

It would doubtless have been difficult to keep student numbers constant, even if that had been regarded as desirable. Nominations for the college might be made at any time, and not necessarily in respect of men able to go to Trevecca as soon as accepted: the earlier of Samuel Clark's recommendations, for example, was on behalf of an apprentice with more than a year still to serve.⁷⁹ The number of men on the waiting list for the college might build up to such an extent that the phasing of admissions became necessary: in 1772, for example, there is a reference to the current date for admissions having passed.⁸⁰ Added to

---

⁷³ W. Jones to LH, 11 June 1773; Glascott to LH, 12 Aug. 1780; W. Chealy to Lady AE, 2 Nov. 1791, F1/228, 1853, 2193,CF.

⁷⁴ S. E. Pierce, *A True Outline and Sketch of the Life of Samuel Eyles Pierce, Written by Himself* (London, 1824), 54. Article in the *Nottingham Guardian*, 23 Oct. 1933. (I am grateful to Brown's great-great niece for this reference.)

⁷⁵ Fletcher to LH, 12 Apr. 1769, F1/1464,CF. The 16 were: Glazebrook, Waite, Davenport, Rowley, Aldridge, Cosson, Hull, Ellis, Hewer, Pecore, Mead, Goodrick, Cook, Gibbons, Roberts, and Cheek. The St Edmund Hall students were not mentioned. ⁷⁶ LH to Hawkesworth, 13 Oct. 1773, G2/1(8),CF.

⁷⁷ W. Aldington to LH, 31 May 1775; S. Phillips to LH, 31 Oct. 1783, F1/1716, 562,CF.

⁷⁸ J. Williams to LH, 9 Aug. 1787 and 29 May 1788, F1/680, 730,CF. He did not succeed (if that were his object) in reducing average numbers; figures over the following twelve months remained between 9 and 12. Williams to LH, 23 Aug. and 29 Sept. 1788, and 16 May 1789, F1/760, 769, 2076,CF.

⁷⁹ Clark to LH, 21 May 1774, F1/297,CF.

⁸⁰ Maxfield to LH, 7 Nov. 1772, F1/1621,CF.

the uncertainty caused by the irregular inflow of new students was the regular coming and going among the students occasioned by sometimes lengthy absences on preaching tours. It was generally the needs of the Connexion which determined the pattern of student preaching, rather than the interests of the college.[81] Thus it must have been difficult for the college authorities to monitor who was still on the books of the college, and to anticipate who was likely to be around at any given time.

Some two hundred and twelve students can be identified as having passed through Trevecca College in the twenty-three years of its existence,[82] a substantial number which (since the great majority went into a ministry of some kind) is an indication of the wide-ranging influence that the institution was able to achieve.[83] It is difficult to estimate the average number of students itinerating from the college at any one time, not least because of the problem of determining whether individuals still counted as students or not. At a rough estimate around a dozen to fifteen students may have been engaged in preaching in the course of each year, defining as student those who expected to return for further study.[84]

No consistent picture emerges as to the background or previous history of those who sought to enter Trevecca.[85] Glazebrook, as noted, had been a collier—and was taunted on the point during the controversies with the Wesleyans in

---

[81] One exception to this was the suggestion to LH in 1775 that it would be helpful for a student who had quarrelled with the master to be sent on a preaching tour (Aldington to LH, 31 May 1775, F1/1716,CF).

[82] Dr Nuttall lists 170 Trevecca students. 'The Students of Trevecca College', *Transactions of the Hon. Society of Cymmrodorion* (1966–7). To this figure can be added the further 43 students listed in Annex B.

[83] Earlier in the century the largest of the Dissenting academies produced only 110 pastors out of a total of 303 students (M. R. Watts, *The Dissenters, from the Reformation to the French Revolution* (Oxford, 1978), 367). In the last nine years of the century the evangelical Hoxton academy produced 67 future ministers, a ratio that falls a little short of Trevecca's (Lovegrove, *Established Church, Sectarian People*, 84).

[84] Annex C lists those known to have been out preaching in 1777, 1783, and 1787, and who can, with some confidence, still be regarded as students at the time in question. It is almost certainly incomplete.

[85] Dr Welch suggested that some 20% of the students were Welsh in origin, but the evidence does not permit any very confident calculation (Welch, 178).

the early 1770s.⁸⁶ John Eyre, like Samuel Clark's nominee, had been an apprentice,⁸⁷ and as such was probably most typical of the strata in society from which Trevecca drew. If so, there are parallels with the St Edmund Hall students, who included among their number a barber, a draper, and a tapster.⁸⁸ But the picture is mixed. William Morley was a 'poor farmer's son' who chose a ministerial calling in preference to work as an attorney's clerk;⁸⁹ George Brown was the son of a framework knitter;⁹⁰ Edward Barry was the son of a Bath apothecary⁹¹ and Samuel Davenport was the son of a curate.⁹² A few of those who applied had already tried out their ministerial gifts. Eyre had been preaching for twelve months before his application;⁹³ an applicant in 1772 had previously been supplying what was described as an Independent Methodist cause in Glamorganshire;⁹⁴ and Mosely Cheek had been a Wesleyan itinerant.⁹⁵

TREVECCA AS AN EDUCATION AND TRAINING

In outlining his scheme of study in January 1768, Fletcher had shown that he envisaged a process of some academic rigour, even if not all the students would be able to tackle the full range of subjects: 'Grammar, Logic, Rhetoric with Ecclesiastical History, with a little Natural Philosophy, and Geography, with a great deal of practical divinity, will be sufficient for those who do not care to dive into languages.'⁹⁶

---

⁸⁶ Wesley's associate Thomas Olivers (himself a former cobbler) called him a 'novice just come out of the coal pits' (Glazebrook to LH, 12 June 1772, F1/184,CF).   ⁸⁷ J. Eyre to LH, 29 March 1776, F1/353b,CF.
⁸⁸ Rupp, *Religion in England*, 477.
⁸⁹ W. Thomas to LH, 11 June 1773, F1/228,CF.
⁹⁰ *Nottingham Guardian*, 23 Oct. 1933.
⁹¹ Seymour, ii. 62 n.; E. Barry to LH, 3 Dec. 1776, F1/1740,CF.
⁹² Davenport to LH, 25 Sept. 1770, F1/103,CF. Overall, the backgrounds of Trevecca students stand comparison, for variety and lowliness of social origin, with the 'shoemakers, joiners, dyers, tailors, weavers and farmers' which the Independent pastor of Rothwell in Northamptonshire sent out as lay evangelists in the 1690s—scandalizing many of his Dissenting brethren in the process (Watts, *The Dissenters*, 293).   ⁹³ Eyre to LH, 29 Mar. 1776, F1/353b,CF.
⁹⁴ J. Thomas to LH, 12 Jan. 1772, F1/166,CF.   ⁹⁵ Curnock, v. 29 n.
⁹⁶ Fletcher to LH, 3 Jan. 1768, Seymour, ii. 85.

Beyond this outline proposal there are only odd hints as to the scope of studies which the students were expected to undertake; indeed, it is doubtful whether anything approaching either a formal curriculum or formal standards was ever laid down. A document of some kind was put together by the following spring, however, and though this may have been principally a statement of the college's general philosophy, it doubtless reflected educational aims as well. This was presumably the 'Apostolic Plan' which one of the original students was to describe as fully enshrining the intentions of their foundress for the institution, and which (he later implied) was meant as a regular object of study among the students. It may also have been what a prospective student was shown as the 'articles of the College' in 1773.[97] Wesley was scathing of the implications of this document for the success of what he termed (to Charles) 'our college': 'Did you ever see anything more queer than their plan of institution? Pray, who penned it, man or woman?'[98] Wesley's respect for the educational standards at Trevecca was not enhanced by early experience of it in operation; the following January he determined to let his own school at Kingswood go if he could not get a 'proper master'; 'I will have another kind of school than that at Trevecca or none at all.'[99]

There are occasional glimpses of what Fletcher wanted for his students. The master, in his view, had to be able to teach Greek and the 'harder classics' (Cicero and Horace) and give the students 'some idea' of divinity and the sciences.[100] A more detailed indication of his expectations, in terms of both academic ability and what was needed of prospective ministers, is contained in the letter he addressed to the student body in 1770, while the master was away. His letter implicitly acknowledges the importance of basic classical skills and a grasp of doctrine, but it is striking also for its emphasis on their own spiritual development and the skills

---

[97] Aldridge to the 'Brethren at College', 20 Apr. 1774; J. Nicoll to LH, 3 May 1773, F1/2202, 221,CF.   [98] JW to CW, 14 May 1768, Wesley, *Letters*, v. 88.
[99] JW to Benson, 2 Jan. 1769, ibid. 123.
[100] Fletcher to LH, 1 July 1769, Seymour, ii. 97.

they would need in defending the faith. His requirement was that they should write:

- a translation of the Thirty-Nine Articles into as good classical Latin as they could manage;
- a parallel between John's baptism and Christ's, demonstrating the superiority of the latter;
- an English letter to a deist on the truth of the Scriptures;
- an essay on the mischief of unsanctified learning;
- an address to Jesus for the coming of the Holy spirit (giving the strongest reasons they could think of for granting the request);
- an exhortation to the college as from a dead student, Gibbons; and
- a letter to one 'who has not the Kingdom set up in his soul', to convince him he is not a true Christian.

Their exercises were to be saved and shown to him on his return. In addition they were to read a set passage of Baxter's *The Saint's Everlasting Rest*, and discuss it among themselves.[101]

This suggests that a degree of rigour was maintained, at least in the Fletcher era. How far the students could measure up to these expectations was another matter. Much obviously depended upon the calibre of the students on admission, although it is unclear whether formal entry standards were generally set or enforced. In November 1767 Lady Huntingdon had, as noted, prepared a draft plan for the examination of potential students, but it is not certain that her assembled recruits were put through it, or what would have happened had any failed.[102] As late as May 1768

---

[101] Fletcher to LH, n.d., A3/3(28),CF. Such a menu appears a stark contrast to the rich diet of logic, arts, mathematics, science, politics, ecclesiastical history, and modern languages, which would have been experienced in many Dissenting academies. And there is likely to have been little prospect at Trevecca of enforcing the requirement to 'speak Latin always, except when below stairs among the family' which applied at at least one such institution. But the practice described at another academy, of requiring the students to prepare orations and epistles upon prescribed subjects (for example, ambassadorial reports) has some parallels with the spiritualized role-playing exercises that Fletcher devised (Rupp, *Religion in England*, 174–5).

[102] Fletcher to LH, 24 Nov. 1767, Seymour, ii. 81.

Glascott wrote to her about ways in which the men might be examined, but there is no evidence that his principal suggestion, that he and Whitefield should examine those who were in London, was ever followed through.[103] Possibly Lady Huntingdon was content to rest upon satisfactory evidence of spiritual development: back in December, for example, Maxfield had promised to send her the 'experiences' of the young men he was enquiring into.[104] One instance that has survived of an applicant being put through a prior examination was James Nicholl, who offered himself in 1772. According to his own account he was examined by two students and told he would have the next vacancy, only to be notified months later (again by a student) that he was not acceptable.[105] The doubts about him may have been as much spiritual as academic, since there is no suggestion that further study would improve his chances.

When potential students were recommended to the college by someone of standing, their letters of introduction might themselves serve as testimonials to their character and religious development. William Platt's application in 1779, for example, was accompanied by a testimonium said to be signed by several 'serious persons'.[106] Otherwise a separate testimonium might be required before a provisional acceptance could be confirmed. One such example was Edward Burn who was offered a place in 1777, following which his referee wrote to confirm both his spiritual state and his intellectual potential.[107] Some students were interviewed by Lady Huntingdon herself before admission,[108] but her involvement in the selection process was not consistent—there is at least one instance in the 1770s of a student who appears to have begun his studies at Trevecca without any prior contact with her.[109] Suitably rigorous standard were not always

---

[103] Glascott to LH, 30 May 1768, F1/1433,CF. For the rest they would ask the religious friends who had recommended them to do it.
[104] Maxfield to LH, 24 Dec. 1767, F1/1412,CF.
[105] J. Nicoll to LH, 3 May and 5 July 1773, F1/221, 235,CF.
[106] Glascott to LH, 11 Aug. 1779, F1/1835,CF.
[107] J. Fisher to LH, 16 Jan. 1777, F1/1746,CF.
[108] T. W. Aveling, *Memorials of the Claytons* (London, 1867),15; T. Williams to Mr Phillips, 27 Sept. 1777, F1/1789,CF.
[109] J. Griffiths to LH, n.d., F1/1182,CF.

maintained, however: in 1783 the then master expressed the hope that future admissions would be tested by some proper person for 'Character, Abilities, Motives etc'.[110] By 1790 it had apparently become normal practice for all would-be students to be seen in London.[111]

A probationary period after first arrival at college seems to have been normal. Thus in 1773 three new students were formally admitted as 'probationers' during the celebration of the college anniversary.[112] Burn went to college in 1777 with the expectation of a three-month probationary period, and that sort of time might well have been necessary to judge suitability for a preaching ministry.[113] The promise of future effectiveness as a preacher was clearly the key test and this meant, at one stage at least, that the master would hear the probationers preach in order to assess their developing capabilities.[114] There is little direct evidence of probationers failing their trial. One example of a student judged to have no ministerial calling occurred in 1775—a judgement that Lady Huntingdon was told came from the collective student body, including those out preaching as well as those in college.[115] In another case a student was allowed an

---

[110] Phillips to LH, 31 Oct. 1783, F1/562,CF. Possibly he regarded LH herself as insufficiently objective in her assessments. Her enthusiastic comment in 1784 that 'many new and Very Promising Students are come' suggests a readiness to see all geese as swans (LH to Mr Green, 8 Oct. 1784, Nat. Library of Wales MSS 7005.C).

[111] Dr Ford to LH, 15 Nov. 1790, F1/2156,CF.

[112] Glascott to LH, 27 Aug. 1778, F1/1656,CF.

[113] J. Fisher to LH, 16 Jan. 1777, F1/1746,CF. Even so, some were sent out sooner. Thomas Suter complained in 1782 that he had not spent in college three months of the nearly three years he had been in the Connexion (Suter to LH, 14 Sept. 1782, E4/4(12),CF). William Roby, a man of exceptional gifts, as his subsequent career in Lancashire was to show, spent only six weeks at Trevecca before being sent out; he was evidently disappointed by the institution, though at the time he appeared keen to stay longer (R. Halley, *Lancashire, its Puritanism and Nonconformity* (Manchester, 1869), ii. 452–3; Lovegrove, *Established Church, Sectarian People*, 69; T. Price to LH, 16 Aug. 1787, F1/1959,CF).

[114] Best to LH, 2 July 1789, E4/4(17),CF. This may have been 'live' preaching, or simply practice sessions. Samuel Pierce was required to preach before the other students within days of his arrival at college in late 1775; he was overcome by nerves and dried up, but he was still sent out preaching the next Sunday (Pierce, *Life of Samuel Eyles Pierce*, 54). In 1776 the dean of Norwich suggested to LH that the students would improve their prospects of ordination if they stuck to practice preaching only (P. Lloyd to LH, 17 Sept. 1776, E3/2(10),CF).

[115] Aldington to LH, 31 May 1775, F1/1716,CF. It is not clear how long the man concerned had been a student.

extended trial, following his representations, despite the view of Glascott and most of the other students that he was not called to such a ministry.[116] Probation appears to have been for a fixed period. In 1788 the master referred to a poor student who had, however, completed his probation; the implication was that they were now stuck with him.[117]

There is some evidence of would-be students who were judged not yet up to the requirements of the college going through a preliminary course of study with a minister (a practice also followed with some of the men sent to the universities by the Elland Society, and by some of the more evangelical academies founded in the latter part of the century).[118] In 1771, for example, the Revd Edmund Leigh of Llanedy had a young man under his tuition who was due to enter the college in twelve months' time, but whom he hoped to 'qualify' in half that time, because the youth lacked the means to support himself for so long.[119] A different instance of pre-college preparation occurred in 1777, when a prospective student expressed relief that Lady Huntingdon was not displeased at his decision to defer entry for a year, in order to learn some Latin and Greek first.[120]

Beyond these examples, the picture of students' previous schooling and achievements is a mixed one. William Morley had been studying under his Glamorganshire vicar for some two and a half years before applying to the college in 1773.[121] He had gained some Latin in that time, an attainment

---

[116] R. Slaughter to LH, 12 Sept. 1777, F1/404,CF.

[117] This contrasted with another student, disobedient both as to his preaching duties and his persistence in entering the housekeeper's room. The master concluded he would have to leave (Williams to LH, 21 Apr. 1788, Gloucester Record Office, D2538.8/1(4)).

[118] J. D. Walsh, 'The Yorkshire Evangelicals in the Eighteenth Century', Ph.D. thesis (Cambridge, 1956), 267; Lovegrove, *Established Church, Sectarian People*, 76. Newton acted as mentor to prospective ordinands who lodged with him at Olney (Hindmarsh, *Newton*, 211).

[119] Leigh to Harris, 21 Nov. 1771, National Library of Wales, Trevecca Letters, no. 2701.   [120] J. Davies to William White, 30 Jan. 1777, F1/381,CF.

[121] William Jones to LH, 11 June 1773, F1/228,CF. He appears to have applied for admission earlier in his period of preparatory study, but failed the initial interrogation. (Morley to LH, n.d., F1/1231,CF).

claimed by a number of applicants over the years.[122] Possibly less typical was George Brown, who had some knowledge of Greek as well as Latin by the time he went to Trevecca in 1788,[123] or John Derbyshire whose mechanical and musical genius was praised by Glascott in 1777.[124] Despite the suspicion voiced by Bishop Brownlow North in 1771 that there were some students who came to college wholly illiterate,[125] some previous education, however rudimentary, seems to have been the norm. The student who arrived in 1788 with not a day's previous schooling was unusual.[126]

Nevertheless, a good deal of basic education must have been necessary for some new entrants before they could tackle more advanced work. It was in part to meet this problem that William Williams of Pantecelyn, the hymn-writer and theologian, and one of the leaders of the Welsh Revival, suggested in 1769 that a school be attached to the college to teach grammar to those with insufficient skills, or whose calling was insufficiently clear.[127] The proposal (which seems to have come to nothing),[128] was designed to leave the master free for academic teaching, as well as providing a more leisured opportunity to assess the vocations of those who were intending to go on to the college proper. This latter was particularly important in the early days of the college, while some people clearly regarded Trevecca simply as a new educational opportunity. Williams told Lady Huntingdon that Trevecca was seen as a free education for those who wanted to get on in the world, and a number of the applications Lady Huntingdon received seem to bear this out. There was

[122] e.g. W. Gough to LH, 10 Jan. 1774; J. Brown to LH, 29 Mar. 1776; T. Williams to LH, 2 Dec. 1776, F1/265, 353a, 1739,CF.
[123] *Nottingham Guardian*, 23 Oct. 1933.
[124] Glascott to LH, 2 July 1777, F1/1769,CF.
[125] Glazebrook to LH, 16 Dec. 1771, F1/153,CF.
[126] J. Williams to LH, 29 Sept. 1788, F1/769,CF.
[127] Williams to LH, 9 Aug. 1769, MS, F1/1475,CF. This was evidently Williams's first contact with her.
[128] There is, however, a reference to the fact that Morley had been schooled by his vicar 'and at your college' prior to his application to be a student (Morley to LH, n.d., F1/1231,CF). Similarly, one Owen Bowen was apparently already at college but still uncertain of his calling when he wrote to LH in 1776 to ask if she would let him be a student (F1/346,CF).

no stated ministerial intention, for example, in the application reported from a member of the Bath congregation in 1768, whose wish was said to be 'to cultivate an acquaintance with human learning'.[129] Nor was there in the approach to Lady Huntingdon in 1770 from the father of an ex-Kingswood boy who, having exhausted all that that institution had to offer, turned to Trevecca in preference to a grammar school as the next stage in his education.[130]

The overall impression of the college's years at Trevecca is of a body of young men, not naturally given to scholarship, who battled with mixed success at the subjects supposed necessary for the exercise of ministerial office. Early in the college's existence, Fletcher suggested that they should be selective in what they required of their students. Analysing the progress of the sixteen students in college in April 1769, he identified two that he thought should no longer puzzle with Latin, as well as a number of others who clearly found academic studies hard going.[131] The students' standards appeared to be improving in 1773, but it was clearly an uphill struggle.[132] One of the two men (presumably Trevecca students) for whom Lady Huntingdon sought ordination in 1779 must, she said, 'be a little dispensed with for literary attainments'.[133] In 1783 Thomas Wills argued that the college was not worth the trouble and expense it caused the Countess. The preaching demands to which the students were subject meant that they could make only limited academic progress; in many cases (he thought) all they acquired was a little knowledge and much self-conceit.[134]

The academic picture did not change greatly over the following years. 1788 appears to have been particularly dire.

---

[129] J. Lloyd to LH, 18 May 1768, F1/1430,CF.
[130] M. Ling to LH, 7 June 1770, F1/96,CF. There is no evidence that the boy was admitted.
[131] Fletcher to LH, 12 Apr. 1769, F1/1464,CF. When Fletcher left the college two years later, it was said that he feared the admission of students of low ability (Tyerman, *Fletcher*, 181). [132] T. Molland to LH, 19 Oct. 1773, F1/253,CF.
[133] LH to the Revd Mr Beale, 6 Apr. 1779, G2/2(c),CF.
[134] Wills to LH, 7 Dec 1783, F1/1918,CF. Wills's solution was to leave prospective preachers in their secular employment, practising their English and their ministerial gifts with a suitable clergyman until they were ready to be sent out.

In February the master concluded, from the quality of the students he had been receiving, that 'This a great disgrace to the English nation that they bring up their children so';[135] in April he reported that his senior students were the most stupid he had ever had;[136] and in August he commented that the damage done to the college books was unhappily to be expected in men trained only in the use of mechanical instruments.[137] Against this background it was with satisfaction that in the following March he could report four students with respectable New Testament Greek.[138] The Unitarian Theophilus Lindsey once expressed the hope that the college would be 'a place for more rational inquiries after she (Lady Huntingdon) drops into her grave'[139]—but it was clearly more than just the attitude of their foundress that kept the students from scaling the heights of intellectual discovery.

Some of the students (like some of the early critics of the college) would clearly have preferred to trust to the leading of the Holy Spirit, rather than to secular learning. The student who warned her in 1771 of the danger of man's wisdom in the college, probably tells us more about his own suspicion of academic study than any overcommitment to such work on the part of the students generally.[140] Another student, two years later, spoke of his 'dead' books; he worked, he said, 'with a Latin trowel in one hand, & the sword of faith and prayer in the other'.[141] Typical of not a few who passed through Trevecca must have been the student said in 1788 to be convinced 'that Learning is not the Essential Qualification of a Minister'[142] or another, the same year, said to have had no capacity for learning and to have hated the place.[143]

The concern of the college authorities was not to produce great scholars—the student in 1787 who talked of nothing

---

[135] J. Williams to LH, 21 Feb. 1788, F1/706,CF.
[136] J. Williams to LH, 3 Apr. 1788, Gloucestershire Record Office. D.2538. 8/1(3).
[137] J. Williams to LH, 23 Aug. 1788, F1/760,CF.
[138] J. Williams to LH, 2 Mar. 1789, F1/2063,CF.
[139] T. Belsham, *Memoirs of the late Revd Theophilus Lindsey M.A.* (London, 1873), 2 n.
[140] C. Hull to LH, 29 Nov. 1771, F1/150,CF.
[141] A. Crole to LH, 17 Dec 1773, F1/261,CF.
[142] Members of the Broadoak congregation to LH, 17 Jan. 1788, F1/700,CF.
[143] J. Williams to LH, 15 Nov. 1788, F1/2049,CF.

but the great classical authors was as much of a problem as the most ignorant[144]—but men whose education gave them sufficient presence to make them a recommendation for the Gospel, and not the opposite. They needed to understand the basic tenets of the faith and be able to articulate them, so the likely effectiveness of their future preaching was the ultimate test by which progress was judged.[145] If they were of Welsh origin they needed to develop a decent command of English for outside the principality.[146] Though many of their hearers might be of humble origins, preachers still needed a basic level of social presentability if they were to commend the Gospel to them, and still more if they were to have a chance of reaching more exalted levels of local society. For those in sympathy with the Connexion's aims, there must have been something winsome about these simple but earnest young men; Lady Buchan, mother of Lady Anne Erskine, was said, for example, to have been 'charmed' by the students.[147] But attaining and maintaining social acceptability was not easy. In 1769, responding to Lady Huntingdon's concerns on this point, Fletcher set himself the limited objective of ensuring that 'some of them will learn how to make a bow without bespeaking the clown at once'.[148] Twenty years later the then master lamented of one of his students, that 'the Articulation of his Person deviates in some Degree from the Rules of common Proportion'.[149]

The fact was that the college had to make the best of the raw material that came its way, whether in terms of spirituality, academic ability, or social skills. Only if prospects of advancement were very low indeed would Trevecca have very much to offer men of intellectual ability. Archbishop Cornwallis once told Lady Huntingdon that he thought her college unlikely to produce 'very able or judicious

---

[144] J. Williams to Best, 16 Oct. 1787, F1/1965,CF. The fact that he knew no Latin or Greek appeared to make matters worse.
[145] See, for example, the progress report on the students then at college that was sent to LH in 1789 (Best to LH, 2 July 1789, E4/4(17),CF).
[146] e.g. J. Williams to LH, 13 Oct. 1787, F1/1964,CF.
[147] Lady AE to LH, 18 Nov. 1772, F1/1624,CF.
[148] Fletcher to LH, 12 Apr. 1769, F1/1464,CF.
[149] J. Williams to LH, 2 Mar. 1789, F1/2063,CF.

divines'.[150] It is difficult to think of an epithet more obviously inappropriate for the young men which Trevecca was attempting to turn out.

LENGTH OF STAY AT TREVECCA

How much instruction could be got through at Trevecca depended on how long the students spent there. This in part (though only in part) turned on the overall length of the course to which they were entitled. In 1777 Lady Huntingdon informed the Archbishop of Canterbury that she had originally hoped to give each student three years, but that opportunities for service had cut across this.[151] There is other evidence that three years was the original intention,[152] but it is doubtful whether any student spent anything like that time within the college. A shorter period almost certainly became the norm, though with no set period that the students could expect. One Trevecca career whose boundaries can be plotted with some exactness was that of Richard Hurdsman, who arrived in November 1772 and set out for the last time in May 1774.[153] A number of examples, all from the 1780s, suggest that very short stays occasionally occurred: Job Hupton, for example, was said to have been there for only three months, and William Roby, as noted, did only six weeks.[154] Another student claimed in 1783 that he had never been in college a fortnight together.[155]

In most instances, however, it is difficult to determine when a student had formally completed his period at college.

---

[150] Cornwallis to LH, 3 Sept. 1777, E3/2(2),CF.
[151] Copy of LH to the Archbishop, 24 June 1777, E3/2(1),CF.
[152] James MacDonald, *Memoirs of the Revd Joseph Benson* (London, 1822), 15; Meldrum to LH, 6 November 1773, F1/258a,CF. Dr Nuttall quoted a student at Trevecca in the mid-1770s of whom it was said (at his funeral) that it was intended he should study for four years. But it seems unlikely that such a commitment was made to any Trevecca student (Nuttall, 'The Students of Trevecca College', 252).
[153] *Evangelical Magazine* (1816), 124. Manuscript references fit with the departure date quoted, e.g. S. Clark to LH, 10 June 1774, F1/299,CF.
[154] Nuttall, 'The Students of Trevecca College'.
[155] Lloyd to LH, 21 Nov. 1783, F1/1916,CF.

Indeed, the uncertainties of ordination and of opportunities to settle with congregations meant that students must often have set out on preaching tours not knowing whether they would be returning to Trevecca or not. Hurdsman's (Dissenting) ordination, for example, took place eleven months after he had left the college.[156] One example of a student who was evidently unclear whether his course had ended was William Dunn who in 1777—five years after first joining Lady Huntingdon and two and a-half years since he had last been resident at college—asked whether he could return to 'headquarters' for the winter.[157]

Such irregular and unpredictable attendance at college was not compatible with an effective education programme, a fact clearly recognized among the group of evangelical Dissenting academies that appeared in the latter decades of the century. The English Evangelical Academy, for example, which was founded in 1778, established clear rules in respect both of length of course and student preaching, allowing students progressively more and more time away on preaching duties as their courses went on.[158] Rules of this kind clearly made sense. When plans were drawn up in 1787 for the continuation of Trevecca after Lady Huntingdon's death, it was specifically provided that students should spend four years in college, or at least two years before being allowed to preach other than in the vicinity.[159]

INVOLVEMENT IN PREACHING AND MISSION

As we have seen, Trevecca was recognized from the start as a source of preaching manpower.[160] From October 1768 it was reported that the students were making 'excursions' into the neighbourhood,[161] thus establishing a tradition of contacts

---

[156] Adams to LH, 20 Apr. 1775, MS, F1/1714,CF.
[157] Dunn to LH, 22 Sept. 1777, F1/407,CF; there is no evidence that his request was granted. [158] Lovegrove, *Established Church, Sectarian People*, 82.
[159] Plan of the Apostolic Society, 17 Oct. 1787, C4/26,CF.
[160] This was not in itself too revolutionary a step. Back in the 1730s the young men at Doddridge's academy were sent out preaching, in what has been described as 'almost the beginning of an evangelical itinerancy' (Rupp, *Religion in England*, 166).
[161] Glascott to LH, 13 October 1768, F1/1448,CF.

with the surrounding area that was to continue throughout the twenty-three years the college remained in Wales. Dr Nuttall found evidence of students preaching at some nine locations within a dozen or more miles of the college,[162] and the signs are that a regular pattern of Sunday supplies was developed.[163] Provided there were reasonable numbers at college, not all the experienced resident students would necessarily be involved in this ministry: a student who had recently returned to college in 1773 commented that he hoped to make better progress with his studies on this occasion, as he had no fixed preaching duties.[164] But local preaching requirements could be as much a factor in keeping students in college as their academic needs: at one stage in the 1770s Lady Huntingdon was told that she was ordering out too many students for them to continue to meet their local commitments.[165] The college was in a similar predicament in 1787.[166] One danger was that the local congregations would get only the less experienced students; in 1783 the master asked leave to bring back some of those away on preaching tours, in order to change the personnel on the college's home preaching rounds.[167]

The college was also a focus for the religious life of the neighbourhood. There is evidence of local people attending the college chapel as early as November 1768,[168] and this pattern continued. There is a reference in 1788, for example, to an exhorter who had been a regular attender at the chapel;[169] the chapel was said that year to be well attended, and the master had baptized a young woman there.[170]

---

[162] Builth, Cregrina, Hay, Clifford, Cwmyoy, Crickhowell, Llanbedr, Llangrwyney, and Brecon (Nuttall, 'The Students of Trevecca College', 264–5). There was also substantial work at Talgarth, the nearest significant village to Trevecca (F1/672,CF). Requests from Usk and Hereford in 1783 seem to have envisaged supplies coming from the college (S. Phillips to LH, 31 Oct. 1783, F1/562,CF).
[163] Meldrum to LH, 7 May 1774, F1/289,CF; see also R. Lane to LH, 20 May 1775, F/223,CF for evidence of Sunday duties.
[164] Crole to LH, 17 Dec. 1773, F1/261,CF.
[165] Aldington to LH, 7 Apr., n.y., F1/1291,CF.
[166] Williams to LH, 20 Sept. 1787, F1/1959,CF.
[167] S. Phillips to LH, 31 Oct. 1783, F1/562,CF.
[168] Fletcher to LH, 10 Nov. 1768, F1/1449,CF.
[169] Williams to LH, 29 May 1788, F1/730,CF.
[170] Williams to LH, 31 and 10 Jan. 1788, F1/1991, 1980,CF.

The college was a source of medical help also, through the distribution of medicines to the poor of the area.[171]

A system of weekend preaching tours, involving the absence of students from the Friday or Saturday each week, and a requirement to return on the Monday, was a regular feature of life at Trevecca in the early days.[172] Doubtless such expeditions served as a transition from less daunting local preaching to the nationwide mission in which students were soon to be involved. Preaching over a wide area quickly became established as a regular feature of the college's life. Early in 1769 Lady Huntingdon thought of employing some of the better students at Bath—not, it appears at the main chapel, but at a second, smaller chapel, which she then had thoughts of acquiring. Fletcher's advice was to do nothing until after the college anniversary in August, to allow more time for study and for assessment of the students' capabilities.[173] Nothing further seems to have come of the idea. But in the course of the year, the students' work led to the opening of a chapel in Brecon, one of the first places, it appears, where students remained away from college overnight.[174]

Before the end of 1769 Lady Huntingdon turned the students into fully-fledged itinerant preachers by sending two of them, Glazebrook and Mead, to the West Country. They were in Bridgwater early in January 1770 and back in college, after a spell in Herefordshire, by the middle of February.[175] Glazebrook was out again in the late spring, this time to Brighton to join another student, William Aldridge, and with him to make expeditions to neighbouring congregations.[176] The pattern had thus been established, and thereafter continuous periods away from the college became a normal part of the students' lives.

[171] Mrs Powell to LH, 22 Nov. and 16 Dec. 1787, F1/671, 1975,CF.
[172] Aveling, *Claytons*, 17; Aldridge to LH, 20 Apr. 1774, F1/2202,CF.
[173] Fletcher to LH, 12 Apr. 1769, F1/1464,CF.
[174] Williams to LH, n.d., Congregational Library MSS, II.c.7(8); Cosson to LH, 1 Dec. 1769; Cave to LH, 30 Sept. 1770, F1/81, 110,CF.
[175] Glazebrook to LH, 5 Jan. 1770; Mead to LH, 15 Feb. 1770, F1/1482, 87,CF.
[176] Goodrick to LH, 7 Apr. 1770; Glazebrook to LH, 16 May and 1 June 1770, F1/90, 1495, 1498,CF.

Lady Huntingdon sought initially to moderate the amount of travelling the students undertook. In March 1770, for example, she signalled that she might have to rob the college of a further student, though she would try to avoid doing so.[177] She became less reticent as time went by. The persistence of calls for preachers[178] became, indeed, a regular theme of Lady Huntingdon's correspondence, so that one measure of the college's success became its ability to respond to such demands. In 1775 she reported (not with any sense of regret) that she had emptied the college of all but four students; in 1778 the college 'still goes on well', but 'does not fill equal to our calls'.[179] Three years later again she wrote that though the college was full, 'yet such amazing calls they are dragged out by the people, that we live ever in want'.[180] Such were the demands that on at least one occasion a prospective student was ordered off to preach before even arriving at college.[181] Only once, in 1773, is it recorded that the supply of students had temporarily outstripped demand, the college reporting that it had at that stage more preachers than places to send them.[182]

It was not surprising, given this pressure for preachers, that some students were sent out before they were ready. Complaints reached the college, both in regard to the general abilities of the students, and on specific points of doctrine. Howel Harris complained to Wesley in 1772 of 'those pert, ignorant young men, vulgarly called students', whose brash hyper-Calvinism he had felt forced to oppose 'to the face'. Wesley, in turn, wondered what could be expected from 'raw lads of little understanding, little learning and no experience'.[183] It was in the later 1780s, however, that criticisms became most marked. The congregations at Partney and Peterborough, for example, both complained

---

[177] LH to Benson, 26 Mar. 1770, Meth. Arch. (LH), 119.
[178] For the source of calls for student preachers, see above, Ch. 4.
[179] LH to Haweis, 7 Sept. 1775, Bridwell Library MS, 85; LH to Hawkesworth, 5 Dec. 1778, G2/1(19),CF.
[180] LH to Hawkesworth, 21 Oct. 1781, Seymour, ii. 187.
[181] Bryant to LH, 5 July 1774, F1/1701,CF.
[182] Molland to LH, 19 Oct. 1773, F1/253,CF.
[183] JW's Journal for 14 Aug. 1772, *Works*, xxii. 346.

in 1789 that the students supplying them might make good preachers in time, but that that time was not yet.[184] This inevitably reflected upon the institution, and a regular theme of the master's correspondence in the 1780s was the need to keep students in college for longer. In his view four months was the absolute minimum.[185] His patience must have been sorely tried when a student solemnly informed him that in England it was not considered fashionable to know anything of the Old Testament or to speak grammatically.[186]

Within the student body there were mixed feelings about time spent away preaching. Some were anxious to be out testing their calling,[187] or, having had a taste of preaching, were not keen to return to college.[188] But others recognized their needs for training and there is at least one instance of a student pleading inexperience and shortness of time at college, in response to an instruction from Lady Huntingdon to set out.[189] Not a few were conscious of the conflict between preaching and study. Mead and Glazebrook saw the danger of this on their original preaching tour in 1770,[190] and it is a recurrent theme of student letters. In January 1777, for example, John Eyre asked to have three months back in college to tackle some of the reading for which he had had no time as an apprentice.[191] In 1785 Edward Porter asked to return to college after a year's absence, in the hope that better acquaintance 'with Letters and Things' might improve his usefulness.[192] Two comments in the 1780s showed how major a demand preaching might be. In 1782 Thomas Suter

---

[184] Lewis to LH, 22 Jan. 1789; members of the Peterborough congregation to LH, 2 Feb. 1789, F1/808, 811,CF.
[185] Williams to LH, 20 Sept. 1787, F1/1959,CF.
[186] Williams to LH, 26 June 1788, F1/738,CF. For other instances of his anxiety about the students' abilities, see Williams to LH, 13 Oct. 1787, 12 Jan. and 21 Feb. 1788, F1/1964, 1981, 706,CF.   [187] Williams to LH, 4 Oct. 1783, F1/1908,CF.
[188] Glascott to LH, 23 June 1773; Green to LH, 5 July 1780, F1/1648, 1846,CF.
[189] Jones to LH, 18 June 1791, F1/2185,CF.
[190] Mead and Glazebrook to LH, 15 Feb. 1770, F1/87,CF.
[191] Eyre to LH, 14 Jan. 1777, F1/376,CF. He could not have had long in college since his original application the previous March.
[192] Porter to LH, 5 Sept. 1785, F1/616,CF.

complained that out of nearly three years in the Connexion, he had not been in college three months;[193] the following year Edward Parsons calculated that he had spent only six months in college out of his three years.[194] Such absences might have mattered less had it been easier to keep up with study while away. But there is no evidence of the college authorities attempting to set work for the students while they were out, and their uncertain periods of absence would in any case have made this difficult. One instance of a student who did keep studying was Thomas French in Sussex in 1777, who sometimes worked at the classics (he said) till 12.00 or 1.00 in the morning.[195]

FOREIGN MISSIONS

Preaching expeditions of an altogether more adventurous sort were the occasional foreign missions in which members of the college were involved. The first was very early. Howel Harris noted in his journal for Christmas 1769: 'This morning two out of seven were chosen by lot in the college to go to the East Indies to preach the Gospel.'[196]

Behind this lay an approach to Lady Huntingdon for help with a scheme to found a settlement of Protestant families on the island of Bencoolen in the East Indies. An ordained schoolmaster was needed for the project, and when the initiator of the scheme failed to find anyone to go, he turned to Lady Huntingdon.[197] The two students chosen, Hewar and Pecore, were evidently among the more promising of the student body,[198] and Lady Huntingdon made a rapid request to the bishop of London for them to be ordained. Time was short before the ship was due to sail, and in regard to Pecore the bishop set aside his usual requirement of three

---

[193] Suter to LH, 14 Sept. 1782, E4/4(12),CF.
[194] Parsons to LH, 10 July 1783, F1/1892,CF.
[195] French to LH, 12 Nov. 1777, F1/1800,CF.
[196] Tom Beynon (ed.), *Howel Harris, Reformer and Soldier* (Caernarvon, 1958), 234.
[197] LH to (? the bishop of London), n.d., E3/1(6),CF.
[198] Fletcher to LH, 12 Apr. 1769, F1/1464,CF.

weeks in which to enquire into character.[199] But he refused to ordain Hewar, who was under age; a projected appeal to the Archbishop of Canterbury was either unsuccessful or never sent, and Hewar sailed without ordination. The fate of the two students was very different. Pecore was reported in 1771 to be minister of a church on Bencoolen worth nearly £600 a year;[200] Hewar, on the other hand, was back at college that October, believing that he had achieved nothing by the expedition.[201]

An expedition of more central significance to the Connexion and the college occurred in 1772. This focused upon Whitefield's Orphan House and College in Savannah, Georgia, which Lady Huntingdon learned, early in 1771, had been bequeathed to her in Whitefield's will.[202] She was initially uncertain what to do with this possibly unwelcome benefaction. Some thought that she should relinquish it to the province, as Whitefield had apparently contemplated doing,[203] and this might have been the best course, given the burden which the institution was to prove over the coming years. Instead she decided to use her inheritance as a centre for missionary activity in the area. Initially she pursued the idea simply of a clerical presence at the Orphan House, and she wrote to the bishop of London in 1771 about his willingness in principle to consider further ordinations.[204] During 1772, however, the idea developed of sending over a team of students, under clerical leadership. The principal idea seems to have been to establish a missionary base, but continuing training was also envisaged, since she drew up a partial plan of study for the students of the Orphan House College.[205] There may also have been the hidden agendum

---

[199] LH to 'Rev'd Sir', n.d.; the bishop of London to LH, 3 Jan. 1770, E3/1(10), (1),CF.
[200] LH to the bishop of London, 30 Aug. 1771 and 9 Jan. 1770, E3/1(5), (8),CF.
[201] Harris's Diary for 22 Oct. 1771, Beynon, *Harris's Visits to London*, 287. Hewar had been advised by Harris not to go without ordination, and he was regretting going by the time the ship reached the Cape of Good Hope (Hewar to LH, 25 May 1770, F1/95,CF). [202] J. Habersham to LH, 31 Dec. 1770, A3/1(2),CF.
[203] R. Keen to LH, 13 June 1772 and 28 July 1773, A1/4(10), A1/7(11),CF.
[204] The bishop of London to LH, 2 and 27 Apr. 1771, E3/1(2-3),CF.
[205] C. S. Eccles to LH, 12 Apr. n.y., A3/5(12),CF.

of wresting the American initiative away from Wesley. Thomas Rankin, Wesley's General Superintendent in America, wrote later that some of the party had declared before the expedition set out, that 'they will soon drive all the Methodist preachers from the continent of America'.[206]

Early in October 1772, a great gathering of clergy and students was called at Trevecca to dedicate the undertaking and commission the students chosen. Such was the significance of the undertaking ('Lady Huntingdon supposes this the most important event of her whole life') that she had printed a circular notice to her clergy, students, and congregations, inviting participation in the gathering and their prayers.[207] It was a feast of worship and preaching, with a special place in the chapel for the students who were going, and much comparing of notes afterwards in preparation for a published account of the events.[208] Eight students were intended for the expedition: John Cosson, Joseph Cook, Thomas Hill, Thomas Jones, Daniel Roberts, Lewis Richards, Henry Mead, and William White. With them were to go two clergymen: William Piercy,[209] and an Irishman, Charles Stuart Eccles.

---

[206] Rankin's Journal, transcribed in the Tyerman/James Everett transcripts, Meth. Arch., vol. ii, 91–2.

[207] Seymour, ii. 257–8 n. The copy sent to Mead and Hawkesworth is enclosed with LH to Hawkesworth, 10 Sept. 1772, G2/1(3),CF.

[208] Lady AE to LH, 8 and 13 Nov. 1772, and n.d.; Lloyd to LH, 13 Nov. 1772; LH to Hawkesworth, 4 Nov. 1772, F1/1622, 1623, 1313, 203; G2/1(4),CF; *Some Account of the Proceedings at the College of the Right Hon. The Countess of Huntingdon, in Wales, Relative to those Students called to go to her Ladyship's College in Georgia . . . in Three Letters, by One who was Present* (London, 1772).

[209] Piercy had been curate of West Bromwich in the late 1760s, leaving in 1770 for the Lock Hospital, where he combined his duties with preaching at Whitefield's London chapels. When he was dismissed from the Lock (chiefly for field preaching) in 1771, LH invited him to become involved in the work of the Connexion. He did so on an occasional basis during 1772, while a chapel was being built for him in Woolwich. His possible involvement in the Georgia mission was under discussion from June: he was a scholar, a good preacher, single, and had a commercial background, all of which made him appear particularly suitable. The expedition was not planned round him, however, and as late as September it was still uncertain whether he would agree to go (H. Godde to LH, 25 Aug. 1772; Mrs Godde to LH, 6 Sept. 1771; Piercy to LH, 7 Sept. 1771; Lady AE to LH, 21 Apr. 1772; Glazebrook to LH, 11 and 20 May 1772; Keen to LH, 13 June and 29 Sept. 1772, F1/1546, 1548, 133, 1599, 178, 181; A1/4(10), A1/5(1),CF). Piercy's brother Richard was also in the party.

After the send-off from Trevecca there were to be further celebratory services in London while the ship was waiting to sail.[210] Then began a trail of disaster. One of the students, White, developed smallpox and remained in England. Then the ship's unexpected departure left behind all but two students, Cook and Cosson, plus the Trevecca maid, Elizabeth Hughes—the rest of the expedition (except for Mead, who never set off at all)[211] had to follow on later. Cosson married Betty Hughes on their arrival in Savannah in December 1772; early the following April a baby was born and Cosson was duly sent back to England in disgrace.[212] Finally, the Orphan House, which the expedition had found in a state of dereliction, despite the thousands of pounds Whitefield had spent on it, was devastated by fire at the end of May.[213]

The worst feature of the whole affair was the legacy of recrimination that flowed from it. The students doubted each other's motives, and expressed their reservations openly to Lady Huntingdon.[214] Differences appeared between Piercy and Eccles, and Lady Huntingdon was eventually to fall out with both of them.[215] Most striking of all was the hostility between Piercy and the students. They described him on various occasions as arrogant, pompous, violent, and extravagant, neglectful of them and uninterested in the native population.[216] He, in turn, lamented their worldliness, and claimed they were only interested in

[210] *Some Account of the Proceedings*; Seymour, ii. 259–61; Welch, 136–7.
[211] By contrast, his luggage did reach America (B. Page to LH, 19 Feb. 1773; Mead to LH, 22 Apr. 1773, A3/5(17),CF).
[212] Cosson claimed that they had in fact undergone a secret marriage the previous May, though he later acknowledged that the ceremony had been performed by a layman in one of the parlours at college (Cosson to LH, 14 Apr. 1773, A3/5(24),CF). He returned to America (and to his wife) in 1774 (Keen to LH, 27 Sept. 1774; Piercy to LH, 15 Apr. 1773, A1/12(6), A4/1(6),CF).
[213] Cosson to LH, 9 Jan. and 2 Feb. 1773; Cook to LH, 8 Jan. 1773; Roberts to LH, 16 Feb. 1773; Keen to LH, 14 May and 24 July 1773; Piercy to LH, 8 June 1773, A3/4(3, 5, 8, 12), A1/7(4, 10), A4/1(9),CF. The fire could have been arson, coming as it did in the midst of local complaints about LH's Church of England takeover of an institution which had been largely financed by Dissenters (Schlenther, 88).
[214] Cosson to LH, 9 Jan. 1773; Cook to LH, 26 Dec. 1772, A3/4(3, 7),CF.
[215] Keen to LH, 5 Feb. 1774; Piercy to LH, 27 May 1773; Keen to LH, 22 Jan. 1774, A1/9(9), A4/1(8), A1/9(4),CF.
[216] e.g. Keen to LH, 15 Dec. 1773; Cosson to LH, 14 Apr. 1774 and 25 Mar. 1785, A1/8(5), A3/5(24), A3/12(24),CF. They were not alone in commenting on

preaching to Europeans.[217] It was not totally wasted effort, however: although the students quite quickly dispersed, at least four survived the traumas of the War of Independence and were still in America in 1785, engaged in ministries that touched all sections of the population.[218] But it was ministry for which Lady Huntingdon paid a high price in terms of money and anxiety over the years.[219]

Doubtless it was the trials and limited success of the Orphan House expedition that dissuaded Lady Huntingdon from repeating what she had attempted in 1772. Apart from a black student, David Margate, who went to America with Cosson on the latter's return in 1774,[220] there were no further expeditions from Trevecca to Georgia.[221] Trevecca was however invited to participate in one further North American initiative—an expedition to New Brunswick in Nova Scotia in 1788. Two men went: John James from Pembrokeshire, who had come to college on the recommendation of Richard de Courcy in September 1787, and Charles William Milton.[222] One of the factors which, in retrospect, was seen to have

---

his pretended grandeur. A Wesleyan observer in 1775 wrote of him 'going through the continent with his phaeton and pair of fine horses, with his black boy to fan him in the pulpit while he was preaching, and all at the expense of Lady Huntingdon' (Rankin, Journal). LH's dispute over Piercy's stewardship of the Orphan House estate continued into the 1780s—see especially A4/4 and A4/5,CF.

[217] Piercy to LH, 25 Mar. 1774, A4/2(17–19),CF.
[218] The four were: Cosson, Cook, Hill, and Richards (Cook to LH, 24 Mar. and 27 May 1785; Hill to LH, 12 Apr. 1785, A3/12(22, 23, 25–28),CF). The first three were certainly still preaching; Richards may have been. Cosson had at one stage sought to join the Wesleyans (Rankin, Journal).
[219] There is no evidence that LH had any serious doubts about the morality of keeping slaves, despite the arguments put to her in the mid-1770s by the Quaker anti-slavery campaigner, Anthony Benezet (Benezet to LH, 25 May 1774 and 10 Mar. 1775, A3/1 (38–9)). LH's dispute with Piercy over his stewardship continued for more than a decade (Welch, 165–8, 175).
[220] Keen to LH, 27 Sept. 1774, A1/12(6),CF. Margate proclaimed himself a second Moses, who had come to liberate his people, and he narrowly escaped lynching (Schlenther, 91 and n.).
[221] Two former students went over, in 1788 and 1790, principally in an attempt to secure LH's assets, although also with some hope of forwarding LH's more recent ambition of a mission to the American Indians (Welch, 173–5).
[222] Williams to LH, 13 Oct. 1787, F1/1964,CF. The master was evidently so impressed with James's abilities that he sounded him on the American idea within three weeks of his arrival in college. Milton was younger and needed more attention from the master, but both set out with high approbation (Williams to LH, 7 Feb. 1788, F1/704,CF).

undermined the effectiveness of the Georgia mission, was the low status of the students, resulting from their lack of ordination, whether episcopal or Dissenting.[223] By the time of the New Brunswick venture, however, events had moved on. The Connexion now had its own ordination,[224] and James and Milton were duly ordained before they set out. It was symptomatic also of the shift in the geographical centre of the Connexion that the ordination and commissioning took place not at college, but at Spa Fields chapel in London.[225] The ordination was performed by the Revd John Bradford[226] and three others (two of whom were alumni of Trevecca). At Lady Huntingdon's request, Bradford wrote an address to the people of New Brunswick, which was printed as a pamphlet to accompany the expedition.[227]

The nature of the undertaking is not clear. Possibly the mission was a response to an influx of loyalists from the south, following the American War of Independence. The progress of the two men was followed with interest within the Connexion, and collections were taken in its support.[228] But the experience of James and Milton may not have been much happier than that of their brethren in Georgia a decade earlier. In 1792 James wrote sadly from what he described as a wicked and dismal place; Milton had gone off to New England; the country was overrun with Wesleyan preachers; and he himself wanted to be allowed home.[229]

There were plans for the involvement of Trevecca students in one further overseas venture during Lady Huntingdon's lifetime. This arose from Thomas Haweis's long-held vision (inspired by the writings of Captain Cook and others) for

---

[223] Keen to LH, 20 June 1774, A1/10(3),CF. [224] See below, Ch. 7.
[225] Spa Fields minute book for 17 Feb. 1788, D1/1, p. 29,CF.
[226] Bradford (1750–1805) matriculated at Wadham College, Oxford, in 1767 (BA 1771). Curate of Felsham, Berkshire, from which he was subsequently dismissed. Bradford was preaching in the Connexion by 1783, and seceded from the Church of England. His hyper-Calvinism appears to have been a factor in his dismissal from the Connexion in 1790. After leaving the Connexion he preached in various chapels in Birmingham and London, for a period supplementing his income by making watch chains (Seymour, ii. 76; *Alum. Oxon; DNB*).
[227] A copy is preserved at Cheshunt as A3/14,CF; it is dated 18 Feb. 1788.
[228] D. Jones to LH, 22 Feb. 1790; Dr Ford to LH, 1 Nov. 1790, F1/887, 2152,CF.
[229] James to Lady AE, 18 Oct. 1792, F1/2230,CF.

a mission to the island of Tahiti. Late in 1789 Haweis persuaded Lady Huntingdon to allow two Trevecca students, Michael Waugh and John Price, to be prepared for an expedition there. Haweis determined that the students should be properly trained for the venture, and 1790 was spent teaching them practical skills such as first aid and gardening, as well as further theology. After some difficulty, Haweis succeeded in persuading Captain Bligh (of the *Bounty*) to allow the young men to travel with him on his planned return to the Pacific, only to find, early in 1791, that the men refused to go without episcopal ordination. Haweis was unsuccessful in his efforts to persuade the Archbishop of Canterbury to ordain them, and he was disappointed in his hopes that Lady Huntingdon might live to see such an expedition set out.[230]

AUTHORITY IN THE COLLEGE

Lady Huntingdon had, as noted, had some initial doubt whether John Williams would prove adequate for the post of master. Those reservations were confirmed by experience. By April 1769 Williams accepted that he was being outstripped by the brighter students, and that more help was needed.[231] The course of William's later career at the college is uncertain. In September 1769 Harris recorded that Lady Huntingdon had 'turned Williams away from the College and Hannah'—implying, it is to be supposed, a relationship with Hannah Bowen, housekeeper to the Trevecca family.[232]

---

[230] Wood, *Haweis*, 170–2, 177–81; Haweis to LH, 25 April, (?) May and 25 Nov. 1790, F1/2129, 2131, 2159,CF. Haweis's efforts with Waugh and Price anticipated the pressures which the London Missionary Society came under, later in the 1790s, to establish a proper scheme of preparation for missionary service (Stuart Piggin, *Making Evangelical Missionaries 1789–1858* (Abingdon, Oxford, 1984), 156–7). Haweis himself was a major force in mounting an expedition to the South Seas, five years after the abortive Tahiti mission (Wood, *Haweis*, 198–203, 208–11, 217–19).

[231] Glascott to LH, 13 Oct. 1768; Fletcher to LH, 10 Feb. and 12 Apr. 1769, F1/1448, 1457, 1464,CF.

[232] Harris's Diary for 19 Sept. 1769, Beynon, *Harris's Visits to London*, 281. The original plan had been for Hannah to serve the college, but LH concluded she was too young to be in close proximity to the students (LH to Harris, 4 June 1768, Roberts, *Trevecka Letters*, ii. 119; see also R. Evans, 'The Eighteenth Century Welsh

There are further references to a 'Mr. Williams' later in 1769, in 1770, and in 1771.[233] If this was the same Williams, he was to suffer Lady Huntingdon's displeasure a second time: in September 1772 Harris recorded 'Williams the Master is dismissed and gone away'.[234]

During 1770 Lady Huntingdon ran the college under two masters, subject to Fletcher's oversight.[235] The new man was twenty-two year old Joseph Benson, whom Wesley had appointed classics master at Kingswood four years earlier. Benson's early education had come from a Presbyterian minister in his home parish; subsequently Wesley took on the direction of his reading. In 1769, with Wesley's approval, he had entered as an undergraduate at St Edmund Hall, Oxford.[236] He combined this with continued service at Kingswood, but in November 1769 determined to leave the school for a post at Trevecca.[237] This he took up early in 1770,[238] though he had to leave for a period in May to return to Oxford.[239] Benson's coming evidently pleased the students and their parents, for standards were felt to have risen.[240] Whatever Williams's role at this stage, Benson was

Revival, with its Relationship to the Contemporary Evangelical Revival', Ph.D. thesis (Edinburgh, 1956), 178, which suggests that the later coldness between LH and Harris stemmed from the latter's displeasure at what he regarded as her precipitate judgement on Williams and Hannah. But, as shown below, the relations between LH and Harris remained cordial for some time *after* this affair).

[233] Cosson to LH, 1 Dec. 1769; Hull to LH, 10 June 1770 and 22 Nov. 1771; Cook to LH, 21 Dec. 1771, F1/81, 98, 147, 158,CF.

[234] Harris to E. K. Wilson, 18 Sept. 1772, Roberts, *Trevecka Letters*, ii. 141.

[235] Confirmation of the dual mastership is contained in Fletcher's reference in July 1770 'masters and students' (Tyerman, *Fletcher*, 164).

[236] R. Treffry, *Memoirs of the Rev. Joseph Benson* (London, 1840), 5, 13, 18–20; Wesley, *Letters*, v. 79 n.; Seymour, ii. 101.

[237] Wesley was not pleased (JW to Benson, 19 Nov. 1769 and 27 Jan. 1770, *Letters*, v. 157, 178).

[238] Telford says that he kept his promise to stay at Kingswood until March, but Harris appears to have met him at Trevecca early in January (Wesley, *Letters*, v. 178 n.; Harris's Diary for 9 January 1770, Beynon, *Harris's Visits to London*, 282).

[239] Benson to LH, 9 May 1770, F1/1493,CF.

[240] G. Goodrick to LH, 7 Apr. 1770; T. and M. Davenport to LH, 1 Aug. 1770, F1/90, 100,CF. JW to Benson, 4 and 22 Dec. 1768, Wesley, *Letters*, v. 115–16, 118. He may have had some other academic help at the college, since there is an account of the infant prodigy and ex-Kingswood boy, John Henderson, teaching Latin and Greek at Trevecca at the age of only twelve (Tyerman, *Fletcher*, 145–8). There is a separate reference to the 'learned boy Henderson' which lends some weight to this story (Peckwell to LH, 23 Jan. 1771, F1/118,CF).

clearly in the lead. When Fletcher set the students exercises during his own absence, he was careful to stipulate that these should not cut across anything Benson might require them to do.[241]

When Benson took up the post, Lady Huntingdon had hoped that 'opinions' (that is to say differences over non-core doctrines) would not destroy their relationship.[242] Such hopes were not to be realized. The renewed doctrinal dispute between the Countess and Wesley, triggered by the Minutes of Wesley's conference in August 1770, quickly spilled over into Lady Huntingdon's dealings with her college.[243] Benson was dismissed at the turn of the year, and in March Fletcher resigned his own links with Trevecca.[244]

This dual departure left a significant gap. Fletcher himself, though he was at college only infrequently, had provided a wise and steadying influence, not only on the students themselves, but on the development of the institution. No one was to replace him in that role. Williams seems to have soldiered on alone until his dismissal in September 1772, and then there was no master at all for a significant period.[245] Once he had gone the students were supervised by one of the more senior students, Thomas Molland. He performed a wide range of domestic and administrative duties: his letters to Lady Huntingdon are filled with accounts of horses, gardeners, glaziers, and bills. He also played some part in the organization of student preachers.[246] But he had no direct authority, and he and his brethren lamented the lack of anyone to make them attend to their rules and studies.[247] It was

---

[241] Fletcher to LH, n.d., A3/3(28),CF.
[242] LH to Benson, 26 Mar. 1770, Meth. Arch. (LH), 119.   [243] Below, Ch. 6.
[244] Seymour, ii. 238. LH wrote Benson a testimonial to his 'capacity, sobriety and diligence' at Trevecca, but his association with her and Wesley effectively terminated his Oxford career and hopes of Anglican ordination (Treffry, *Benson*, 35).

[245] Williams's rule must have been light; in September 1772 a correspondent commented that the rebelliousness shown by one of the students was the result of leaving 'inexperienced lads' to their own devices (Maxfield to LH, 2 Sept. 1772, F1/1614,CF). LH failed to persuade Henry Peckwell to superintend the college (Peckwell to LH, 31 Oct. and 29 Dec. 1772, and n.d.; Peckwell and Miss Blosset, n.d., F1/1618, 1630, 1631, 1350, 1352,CF).

[246] Molland to LH, 6 Nov., 17 Sept. and 16 Nov. 1773; J. Cave and family to LH, 25 June 1773, F1/258b, 249, 259, 232,CF.

[247] Crole to LH, 17 Dec. 1773, F1/261,CF.

to another Kingswood master, Isaac Twycross, that Lady Huntingdon next turned for help, although the circumstances both of his coming and going are unclear. He was at Trevecca in November 1773, and still there in March 1774;[248] but in the following July Wesley's friend at Brecon, Walter Churchey, wrote that 'Mr. Twycross, I hear, is gone from the college. Why, I know not—it is a mysterious Seminary!'[249] Possibly he had only come as a temporary arrangement, for a month earlier Lady Huntingdon had received a letter from the Revd Samuel Phillips accepting the Trevecca mastership.[250]

Phillips was to introduce an element of continuity that had been lacking so far in the college's life. He remained at Trevecca for at least a decade,[251] combining care for the college with an extensive role in the direction of the students while they were out preaching.[252] He was absent himself on occasions, serving as Haweis's curate and preaching at Connexional chapels.[253] In 1783 he was actively involved in a legal dispute over the Hereford chapel.[254] During his mastership the practice of student leadership was developed, and for a period authority was shared with some of the more senior students. John Clayton and William Aldington performed this role at various times in 1775, corresponding about bills, domestic arrangements, and the organization of student preachers.[255] In 1777 William White appears to have

[248] Molland to LH, 16 Nov. 1773, F1/259,CF; Wesley to Twycross, 17 Mar. 1774, *Letters*, vi. 78.   [249] Meth. Arch. (Letters to CW), vi, no. 15.
[250] Phillips to LH, 19 June 1774, A3/6(29),CF. It is not clear what previous contact he had had with LH. He appears to have resigned a living to come to Trevecca.
[251] Phillips may have considered moving on from Trevecca in 1781—in that year LH received an application from a clergyman who had heard she was looking for a tutor (J. Neale to LH, 17 Sept. 1781, F1/478,CF).
[252] For example, Phillips to LH, 31 Oct. 1783 and 19 Mar. 1784, F1/562, 609,CF.
[253] LH to ?, 10 July 1781; Seymour, ii. 318; Phillips to LH, 9 Dec. 1782, F1/496,CF. Phillips appears in the Aldwincle parish register as Haweis's curate in July 1776, and he served in this role during Haweis's absences preaching, for part at least of the period of his mastership (Wood, *Haweis* 167; Haweis to LH, 10 Apr. and 2 June 1777, F1/1757, 1760,CF). Phillips was one of the clergy present at the Spa Fields ordination in 1784 (Spa Fields minute book for 30 May 1784, D1/1, 26,CF).
[254] Phillips to LH, 11 and 18 Nov. 1783; Mrs Paul to LH, 11 Dec. 1783; Phillips to LH, 12 Dec. 1783, F1/565, 571, 582, 583,CF.
[255] Clayton to LH, 20 Oct. 1775; Skinner to LH, 17 June 1776; Aldington to LH, 31 May 1775, F1/336b, 364, 1716,CF.

held a similar position.²⁵⁶ Beyond this there are no strongly marked features of Phillips's mastership. Despite his long tenure, there is no sense in the surviving papers of a distinctive academic or spiritual leadership. But he did hold the organization together during a period when the college, though remaining important as a source of manpower, became less the centre of the Connexion's life than it had been earlier.

Effectively the last master of Trevecca College was another John Williams, the clergyman son of Williams of Pantycelyn. The first reference to him in the post is in February 1786.²⁵⁷ From the evidence of his correspondence, much of his preoccupation (as Phillip's had been) was with domestic affairs and the arrangements for the student preachers.²⁵⁸ He too got drawn into the business of the Hereford chapel;²⁵⁹ he, if anything, found the students' limited abilities even more depressing than his predecessor had done. He was, however, not wholly on his own, either in regard to the organization of the students, or in assessing their abilities, for the Countess's secretary, George Best, appears to have taken a distinctive part in both activities (by letter, and in person at college) as the decade went on.²⁶⁰ Williams's tenure of the post ended early in 1791, when the death of his father took him back to Pantycelyn. The trustees of the Apostolic Society, which assumed oversight of the college following the Countess's death in June 1791, invited him back later in the year to supervise the institution's final months in Wales,²⁶¹ but he did not accept. John Jones of Birmingham served for some months as a temporary tutor, and supervised the exodus from Trevecca in early 1792. He was not an Anglican clergyman, and was not regarded as sufficiently qualified for a permanent post.²⁶²

---

²⁵⁶ *Evangelical Magazine* (1854), 756; (1814), 458 n.; Leggett to LH, 27 Aug. 1777; Giles to LH, 8 Oct. 1777, F1/1781, 1790,CF. ²⁵⁷ Aveling, *Claytons*, 88.
²⁵⁸ Williams to LH, 13 and 16 Oct. 1787, F1/1964–5,CF.
²⁵⁹ Williams to LH, 16 May 1789; Hornby to Best, 21 Dec. 1790, F1/2076, 949,CF.
²⁶⁰ e.g. Price to Best, 23 July 1787; Williams to Best, 16 Oct. 1787; Best to LH, 2 July 1789, F1/1953, 1965, E4/4(17),CF.
²⁶¹ Apostolic Society minutes for 3 Aug. 1791, C1/1, 36,CF.
²⁶² Munn to LH, 23 Mar. 1791; *Order for the Opening of Cheshunt College*, 1792; Apostolic Society minutes for 2 May 1792; Apostolic Society records, F1/967; C4/1; C1/1,91–2; C5/2,CF.

Apart from occasional visits from Connexional clergy and other leaders of the Revival,[263] there were two other sources of potential authority over the students: Howel Harris and his community, and Lady Huntingdon herself. Harris, as has been seen, was closely involved in the planning and establishment of the college. A year after the college's foundation Harris recorded that he was 'thankful that the Lord did incline Lady Huntingdon to set the college down here near me, thankful indeed for bringing it through my faith and prayer in any degree, but above all thankful for making us all one'.[264] For the students Harris was a source of spiritual counsel and advice. In 1769 William Gibbons reported that he had consulted Harris to helpful effect on his spiritual state;[265] a year later a student reported that 'Mr. Harris continues his fatherly visits to us.'[266] Such contacts were encouraged by the college. Harris recorded that before Fletcher left the college in January 1770, he 'gave...the students in charge to me to keep the fire and true life up'.[267] In September 1770 Lady Huntingdon asked him 'affectionately' to visit the college each Tuesday evening; the following spring she repeated her hope that he would give them his 'frequent advice'.[268]

In the summer of 1770 links were further strengthened with the preparation of accommodation for Lady Huntingdon's personal use in the Harris settlement,[269] and when Harris made facilities available in his house for the those attending the college anniversary.[270] Hospitality on an

---

[263] For example, Glascott and Jones of Llangan spent time with the students in 1773 (Molland to LH, 17 Sept. 1773, F1/249, CF; Seymour, ii. 118). Williams of Pantycelyn preached at college while his son was master (J. Williams to LH, 15 Apr. 1789, F1/2070,CF).

[264] Harris's Diary for 10 Sept. 1769, Beynon, *Harris's Visits to London*, 280.

[265] Gibbons to LH, 17 Feb. 1769, F1/50,CF.

[266] Goodrick to LH, 7 Apr. 1770, F1/90,CF.

[267] Harris's Diary for 20 Jan. 1770, Beynon, *Harris's Visits to London*, 282.

[268] Harris's Diary for 25 Sept. 1770, Beynon, *Harris's Visits to London*, 285; LH to Harris, 26 Mar. 1771; Harris to LH, 24 May 1771, Roberts, *Trevecka Letters*, ii. 134, 136.

[269] Harris noted that his answer to any who objected to the grandeur of the house would be that 'tis not too good for the Lord and for the Countess of Huntingdon's use' (Harris's Diary for 14 July 1770; Beynon, *Harris's Visits to London*, 283).

[270] 'Seventeen beds and three kept empty expecting more' (Harris's Diary for 24 Aug. 1770, Beynon, *Harris's Visits to London*, 284).

even more extensive scale was provided for the 1771 anniversary, but by then signs of strain were becoming apparent.[271] In September 1771 Lady Huntingdon announced that she was leaving Harris's house for a separate establishment, though this cooling between them did not immediately lead to a breach: Harris himself was involved in plans to build her a new house, and there was a reconciliation of some sort in January 1772.[272] By March 1772, however, a major rift had occurred. This appears to have been caused on Harris's side by the hyper-Calvinism he detected in the students, and on Lady Huntingdon's by the undue influence he seemed to be claiming over the college, both for himself and other Welsh preachers. One student, at least, was relieved that Harris's 'tyranny' over them had come to an end.[273] Harris offered accommodation for those attending the commissioning ceremonies for the Georgia expedition in October, but this was refused;[274] by March 1773, only months before Harris's death, Lady Huntingdon wrote of a total separation between the two institutions, and claimed that an ex-student was maintained by the Harris family to attend the college chapel and preach against them in the lane afterwards.[275] It was a sad end to a friendship of more than thirty years, and after the high hopes of joint endeavour with which the college had been founded.

When Lady Huntingdon was at Trevecca she played a direct part in the students' lives. She spent only a few weeks there in 1768 and 1769, but her substantially longer stays thereafter may reflect a desire to fill the supervisory vacuum left by Fletcher's departure.[276] There is evidence in 1770, for

---

[271] Harris had put up fifty guests, but complained in his diary that LH did not appreciate (or consult him about) the burdens she was placing on him (Harris's Diary for 24 Aug. 1771, Beynon, *Harris's Visits to London*, 286).

[272] Harris's Diary for 1 Oct. 1771 and 8 Jan. 1772, Beynon, *Harris's Visits to London*, 287, 288. There is no evidence that LH did acquire a house; it is likely that she used the college itself whenever she was at Trevecca.

[273] Wase to Harris, 27 Mar. 1772, Roberts, *Trevecka Letters*, ii. 139; Glazebrook to LH, 28 Mar. 1772, F1/176,CF; JW's Journal for 14 Aug. 1772, *Works*, xxii. 346.

[274] Harris to E. K. Wilson, 8 Dec. 1772, Roberts, *Trevecka Letters*, ii. 143, '... even the Ceremony of enquiring aft(er) my Health was laid aside'.

[275] LH to Cosson, 10 Mar. 1773, A3/15(1),CF.

[276] From LH's correspondence, the following pattern of visits to Trevecca emerges: 1770–1—8 months; 1771–2—9 months (including a Welsh tour), plus a

example, of her expounding texts to the students;[277] in 1773 there is an account of her taking a few students into her rooms each evening to explain a chapter of scripture and pray together.[278] On occasions she set the students written exercises;[279] in 1785 a pamphlet was printed containing Lady Huntingdon's advice to the students on the expectations of the ministry.[280] Given this degree of involvement, it is clear that Molland's hope in 1774, that she would fill the office of master herself was no empty suggestion.[281] In 1780, indeed, she did effectively run the college for a spell during the absence of Samuel Phillips.[282] The warmth of Lady Huntingdon's personal relationship with her students is often striking. They honoured her, but they had little hesitation in telling her frankly of their problems and anxieties, both spiritual and academic.[283] Sometimes the most seemingly trivial issues were brought to her attention, even when she was away from college—as with the student who wrote to ask, on medical advice, whether he could substitute water gruel with currants for beer.[284] Another wrote, 'I have not forgot before God my Ladys going down on her knee to dress my legs.'[285] The students' health in particular was a matter of continuing concern; in her eighty-second year, for example, she summoned a student back from Cornwall to London because of her anxiety for his health.[286] Nor were the students inhibited from telling her frankly of their

return for 2–3 weeks in late 1772; 1773—6 months; 1774—4 months; mid-1776 to the early months of 1778—at least 21 months; 1779—2 and a-half months; 1780—3 months; 1781-2—14 months; 1784-6—20 months; 1787—6 weeks. When she left the college in April 1787, it was for the last time.

[277] Harris's Diary for 17 and 23 July 1770, Beynon, *Harris's Visits to London*, 283, 284. [278] Nicoll to LH, 3 May 1773, F1/221,CF.
[279] Two examples of student essays addressed directly to her were on the subject 'What is Faith?' (essays by N. M. Cheek and Cosson, n.d., F1/1155, 1157,CF).
[280] Printed letter of LH, 1 Mar. 1785, A3/12(1),CF. This was evidently a response to one individual's request for advice, subsequently printed for general use in the Connexion. [281] Molland to LH, 18 Jan. 1774, F1/269,CF.
[282] LH to Wills, 26 Sept. 1780, John Rylands Library, ENG. MS, 338.
[283] Gibbons to LH, 17 Feb. 1769; Seymour to LH, 11 Feb. 1774; Goodrick to LH, 7 Aug. 1770, F1/50; E4/8(4); F1/90,CF.
[284] (? Mead) to LH, 18 Aug. 1769, F1/76,CF.
[285] Wase to LH, n.d., E4/3(6),CF.
[286] LH to McAll, 13 Sept. 1788, E4/17(2),CF.

medical conditions; one student wrote simply that he had 'a Violent pain in my Bowells'.[287]

THE THEOLOGY OF TREVECCA COLLEGE

The confessional basis of the college was likely to have been construed in fairly generalized terms, at least until the Calvinistic controversy began to affect the institution.[288] One of the original students later described the key elements on which the college rested as being a sense of pardon for sin, together with a personal knowledge of the truth. This formulation was not far removed from that proposed by the Apostolic Society (set up in 1787 to perpetuate the college after Lady Huntingdon's death) that new students should be tested for an experiential conviction of the fall of man.[289] But within these basic precepts there was originally some room for variety of interpretation. Fletcher noted in October 1769 that Calvinists were in the majority by three to one at college, implying thereby that Lady Huntingdon had admitted a third of the student body who were not. Fletcher's approach was to try to make the students think critically about their presumptions.[290] Whether or not due to his and Benson's influence, a change of outlook seems to have occurred; by the following August Harris thought the college in the grip of Arianism, legalism, and 'the spirit of J. We'.[291]

These references may imply a catholicity of outlook, but they could also betray a suggestible frame of mind among generally ill-educated and perhaps naïve young men, in which doctrines were apt to be taken up to, and beyond, their reasonable conclusions. There was no room for non-Calvinists after the controversy, and this removed the college's ability to serve the Revival at large.[292] Moreover, there was a danger that the students would distort the principles of

---

[287] Hull to LH, 29 Nov. 1771, F1/150,CF.   [288] See Ch. 6.
[289] Aldridge to LH, 20 Apr. 1774; Plan of the Apostolic Society, 17 Oct. 1787, F1/2202; C4/26,CF.   [290] Tyerman, *Fletcher*, 155.
[291] Harris's Diary for 31 Aug. 1770, Beynon, *Harris's Visits to London*, 285.
[292] Schlenther, 111.

Calvinism into a belief that the elect were no longer subject to the moral law. Only two years after Harris's lament at the students' legalism he was complaining of their 'bare-faced Reprobation and... broad Antinomianism'.[293] The exaggeration of doctrine was a continuing anxiety,[294] and just occasionally it had disastrous practical results; at one stage in the 1780s Williams had had two students voicing antinomian sentiments (for which they claimed Lady Huntingdon's authority), one of whom persuaded a girl in the society at Coleford that there was 'no manner of Sin in Fornication'.[295]

LIFE AT TREVECCA

The records give a few glimpses of life at Trevecca. One such was the account Fletcher gave in November 1768, after he had lectured the students individually on the deadness he detected within the college. Fletcher's threat was that he would ask Lady Huntingdon to pick out the six of the most earnest of the students and expel the rest. First one and then another of the students experienced a spiritual release in the course of the following day, with small groups heard in prayer in different parts of the college; in the evening the whole student body (plus the future Mrs Cosson) gathered in Fletcher's room, praying together in the dark. Tuesday started with hymn-singing (that woke Fletcher) and ended with an address from Howel Harris; Wednesday was a fast day, with the whole college—including the boy who cleaned the shoes—gathered voluntarily in the chapel during the afternoon. So it went on, and nearly a week later there were still students audibly at prayer at 11 o'clock at night.[296]

There are other indications of the spiritual authority that Fletcher wielded at college. Benson, for example, described

---

[293] JW's Journal for 14 Aug. 1772, *Works*, xxii. 346.
[294] Fletcher had been worried in the early days about the possibility of student 'enthusiasm' (Fletcher to LH, 10 Nov. 1768, F1/1449,CF).
[295] Williams to LH, 5 Feb. 1789, F1/2060,CF. Despite this, the young man concerned seems to have continued serving in the Connexion (Munn to LH, 24 July 1789, F1/847,CF). [296] Fletcher to LH, 10 Nov. 1768, F1/1449,CF.

Fletcher leading the students from the schoolroom into his own room for two to three hours' prayer.[297] Possibly Fletcher had originated the watch evenings for prayer which two of the students were continuing, three times a week, in April 1769—or the Thursday meeting referred to in 1770.[298] Under Fletcher it appears that regular teaching regimes were sustained. Some of the events that Fletcher described in 1768 took place around an afternoon lecture, following which he remained in the study to answer questions. In 1769 he suggested suspending the daily exercise for a fortnight, to allow a Whitsun break.[299]

After Fletcher's time there are fewer indications of how life was spent. John Clayton's biographer describes a strict morning regime (rising at 5 a.m., and prayers in the hall at 6 a.m.) which has some similarities to those proposed in 1787 for the anticipated successor body to Trevecca.[300] There is a reference to morning family worship during Samuel Phillips's mastership.[301] Doubtless Fletcher's successors (when there were any) attempted to preserve a regime of study and worship. But the absence of much evidence of this after the strong lead evident during Fletcher's presidency, suggests that his mastery of the student body may not have been easy to repeat.

By and large there seem to have been no serious disciplinary problems. Occasionally, as noted, there were conflicts of personality between students and the master,[302] and disagreements over the importance of academic work.[303] Sometimes differences erupted between the students; one wrote to Lady Huntingdon in 1783 that the daily strife at college was such that he wanted her either to send him out

---

[297] Tyerman, *Fletcher*, 166–7.
[298] Fletcher to LH, 12 Apr. 1769; Hull to LH, 10 June 1770, F1/1464, 98,CF.
[299] Fletcher to LH, 12 Apr. 1769, F1/1464,CF.
[300] When LH was in residence, she was always vigilant for 'she cast a searching glance around her, to satisfy herself that none appeared in negligent attire, or betrayed an inattention to the requirements of cleanliness and neatness, on which she was wont to lay great stress' (Aveling, *Claytons*, 17; Plan of the Apostolic Society, 17 Oct. 1787, C4/26,CF).   [301] Phillips to LH, 23 Dec. 1783, F1/588,CF.
[302] Phillips to LH, 23 Dec. 1783; Williams to LH, 29 May 1788, F1/588, 730,CF.
[303] Williams to LH, 26 June 1788, F1/738,CF.

or to dismiss him.[304] Possibly more difficult to deal with was the temptation to laxity and sloth: as early as 1771 a student warned Lady Huntingdon not to allow idleness and indulgence to creep into college life.[305] Very occasionally, there are indications of suspect honesty and other moral lapses—like the young man whose theology proved so convenient with the girl at Coleford. It would have been surprising, perhaps, if the college had escaped such pitfalls altogether. Indeed, the judgement of John Adams, an ex-student who subsequently became a Dissenting minister, was that fewer of the students had fallen into sin or serious apostasy than in any other connexion.[306] It is safe to say that the Trevecca students were not generally given to the 'disobedient and turbulent behaviour' which characterized some of the more liberal Dissenting academies in the last decades of the century.[307] But it was doubtless the dangers to which such bodies of young men are prone, even when all of them are destined for a ministerial career, that led to the strict timetable—regulating every aspect of the day, including Bible readings at meal times to prevent unprofitable conversation—that was proposed in the plans for Trevecca's successor organization.[308]

An institution the size of Trevecca needed domestic staff. Hannah Bowen from the Harris settlement, upon whom Lady Huntingdon originally fixed for housekeeper,[309] wanted two maids under her. Harris thought there should be a manservant as well,[310] though it is doubtful whether the college ever sustained so extensive a complement. A housekeeper was likely to have been needed throughout: there

---

[304] Dixon to LH (marked 'November 1783'), F1/572,CF.
[305] Wase to LH, n.d., E4/3(6),CF.
[306] Adams to LH, 18 Feb. 1784, F1/1927,CF.
[307] Watts, *Dissenters*, 488–9. At Warrington Academy, at a period contemporary with Trevecca, the students engaged in drunken and riotous behaviour, on one occasion swapping round the sign boards outside the town's inns.
[308] Plan of the Apostolic Society, 17 Oct. 1787, C4/26,CF. The records of the Apostolic Society are transcribed in E. Welch (ed.), *Cheshunt College, The Early Years* (Hertfordshire Record Society, 1990).
[309] LH to Harris, 17 Dec. 1767, Roberts, *Trevecka Letters*, ii. 115.
[310] Mrs Leighton to LH, 12 May 1768, F1/29,CF.

are references to a Mrs Hannah in the 1770s,[311] and a Mrs Powell appears from the late 1780s.[312] There was at least one maid (Betty Hughes) until her departure with the Georgia expedition; another Betty is mentioned in 1788 and 1789.[313] At various times there are references also to a college gardener[314] and (as noted) a boy to clean the shoes.[315] A man, William Abraham, was employed in some capacity during the 1780s.[316]

Apart from some garden produce and the pigs and poultry they were able to raise themselves—some of which, latterly, they sent to Lady Huntingdon in London[317]—the college was wholly dependent upon the Countess and the occasional liberality of her friends for its financial support.[318] This was a substantial commitment, as some examples show. In the autumn of 1773, for example, Lady Huntingdon was thanked for two £50 drafts within a month of each other.[319] In the fifteen months from April 1787 the college expenses, not including the master's salary and the servants' wages, were calculated as of the order of £337.[320] Requests for money occur from early in the college's life,[321] but in the last years became more regular and occasionally desperate.

---

[311] Clayton to LH, 20 Oct. 1775; Leggett to LH, 27 Aug. 1777; Phillips to LH, 23 June 1780, F1/336b, 1781, 454,CF. Possibly this was the Mrs Bowlling found by LH as a substitute for the more youthful Hannah (LH to Harris, 4 June 1768, Roberts, *Trevecka Letters*, ii. 119). Or perhaps she was Hannah Bowen herself, restored to favour after the Williams affair, as suggested in M. Francis, 'Selina, Countess of Huntingdon', B.Phil. thesis (Oxford, 1955), 65a.

[312] e.g. Mrs Powell to LH, 16 Dec. and 22 Nov. 1787, F1/1975, 671,CF.

[313] Mrs Powell to LH, 23 May 1788 and 5 Mar. 1789, F1/728, 2064,CF. The Jane Watkins, for whom the students wrote a testimonial on 20 July 1787, may also have been a college maid (E4/15(38),CF).

[314] Molland to LH, 17 Sept. 1773; Mrs Powell to LH, 23 May 1788, F1/249, 728,CF.   [315] Fletcher to LH, 10 Nov. 1768, F1/1449,CF.

[316] Abraham's receipt, 7 June 1790; breakdown of monies owed to Abraham from 1783; Mrs Powell to LH, 18 Feb. 1788, E4/15(17, 18, 23),CF.

[317] Mrs Powell to LH, 14 Apr. 1788; Williams to Best, 16 Oct. 1787; Mrs Powell to LH, 2 Oct. and 27 Nov. 1788, F1/2004, 1965, 2043, 2051,CF.

[318] *Order for the Opening of Cheshunt College*, 1792; Wills to LH, 7 Dec. 1783, C4/1; F1/1918,CF.

[319] Molland to LH, 19 Oct. and 16 Nov. 1773, F1/253, 259,CF.

[320] E4/15(46),CF. After her death it was calculated that Trevecca College had cost her £500–£600 a year (Apostolic Society Report for 1791, C4/26,CF).

[321] e.g. Molland to LH, 26 Feb. 1774, F1/273,CF.

Mrs Powell had to juggle between her creditors,[322] and some suppliers gave up for want of payment: in August 1788, for example, she had to send to Brecon for beef because the Talgarth butcher refused to supply the college any longer.[323] The same year she found herself under threat of the college's goods being seized if taxes were not paid. It was a threat she only avoided by borrowing the money locally.[324] It was not always possible to keep wages up to date; William Abraham left the college's employ in January 1788, but did not receive a final settlement of what was due to him until June 1790.[325] It was small wonder in these circumstances that Mrs Powell's temper was not always of the best.[326]

THE END OF TREVECCA COLLEGE

The Countess's college remained in Wales for something over twenty-three years. But for the last ten years it was effectively under notice to leave. The reasons for this were connected with the terms under which Lady Huntingdon leased the building.[327] By 1782 it was apparent that the college could not stay at Trevecca indefinitely and that new premises would be needed.[328] Lady Huntingdon's surveyor and agent, John Case, was working on building plans for a new college in Wales from at least as early as 1786, although the prospective site is not clear.[329] That plan came to nothing, though other Welsh sites were to be considered. In 1787 the architect William Jernegan, who was building a Connexional chapel in Swansea,[330] reported a couple of ideas for the new

---

[322] Mrs Powell to LH, 22 Nov. 1787, F1/671,CF.
[323] H. Howell to LH, 19 Mar. and 23 Apr. 1788; Mrs Powell to LH, 21 Aug. 1788, F1/1996, 2009, 2032,CF.
[324] Mrs Powell to LH, 27 Nov. 1788 and 8 Jan. 1789, F1/2051, 2057,CF.
[325] Abraham's receipt 5 to 7 June 1790; Mrs Powell to LH, 23 May 1788, E4/15(17, 18, 23),CF. LH herself checked the calculation.
[326] Best to LH, 2 July 1789 E4/4(17),CF.   [327] Lloyd to LH, 21 Jan. 1769, F1/47,CF.
[328] B. La Trobe to E. Roberts, 30 Jan. 1783, Roberts, *Trevecka Letters*, ii, 162; Pentycross to LH, 28 Aug. 1782, F1/480,CF.
[329] LH's account with Case to Aug. 1786; Case to LH, 6 May 1787; Case to LH, 28 June 1787; E4/15(14), F1/626, 636,CF.
[330] 'Swansea Chapel Letters', E4/14,CF. Jernegan's most noted work was Streatly Hall near Swansea (H. M. Colvin, *Biographical Dictionary of English Architects* (London, 1978)).

seminary—a house at Llanelli and one near the Mumbles—though he thought a site adjacent to the Swansea chapel would be the most convenient option.[331] In March 1789 Jernegan reported that the Swansea corporation had granted her a ninety-nine year lease on the site for a college charity,[332] but nothing came of these plans either. When Lady Huntingdon died in June 1791 the college was still at Trevecca. Well before her death, however, Lady Huntingdon had recognized the need for some more formal basis for the future management of the college. In April 1787 she noted that she was leaving half her possessions for the support of the college (and 'other things'),[333] though her subsequent actions suggested that she was doubtful whether this would be sufficient to sustain the institution.[334] That October she called together in London a group of ministers (two of whom, Samuel Barnard and Jenkin Jenkin, had themselves studied at Trevecca), and laymen (including prominent members of the Spa Fields chapel and her secretary, George Best) to discuss the plan she had put to them for a society to perpetuate the work of the college.[335] The idea found favour in principle, but the group deferred a decision to launch a subscription until they had received Lady Huntingdon's proposed plan for the college. Only when they were satisfied that there were clear ground rules for the institution did they formally resolve themselves into trustees for what was to be called the Apostolic Society—a name chosen from its primary purpose of sending out apostles.[336]

---

[331] Jernegan to LH, 1 Oct. 1787, E4/14(2),CF.
[332] Jernegan to LH, 29 Mar. 1789, E4/14(13),CF.
[333] LH to J. Bidwell, E4/3(5),CF (also indexed as B4/3,CF).
[334] In this she was absolutely right. She actually left the Connexion debts of £3,000, to meet which her freehold houses in Bath, Brighton, and Hereford had to be sold. Spa Fields minute book for 29 June 1791, D1/1, 35,CF. Her income of £1,200 p.a. was only a jointure and stopped at her death (*Order for the Opening of Cheshunt College*, 1792, C4/1, 79,CF).
[335] Minute book of the Apostolic Society for 5 Oct. 1787, C1/1, 1,CF. According to the minute book, the initiative came from LH, rather than the other way round, as suggested by Seymour, ii. 513. The Apostolic Society records, on the other hand, indicate that it was two of the stated hearers at Spa Fields who approached her with the idea (C5/2,CF).
[336] Apostolic Society minute book; Report of the Apostolic Society for 1791, C1/1, 3–6; C4/26,CF. The insistence upon clear rules may reflect the unease of

Some of the features of the planned college have been noted already. What principally distinguished the 1787 plan from Trevecca was that it made explicit what had previously been left vague.[337] The document was also an implicit recognition of the shortcomings of the Trevecca arrangements. If Lady Huntingdon drafted it herself, it was a remarkably frank acknowledgement of where Trevecca had gone wrong; more likely the hand of George Best can be detected in it. The plan provided expressly for the salary to be paid to the master (and his assistant if one were needed); servant numbers were to be limited; three local people were to be nominated as inspectors of the college; twenty students were to be admitted at any one time, with length of course and time in college before being sent out, clearly stipulated;[338] during the week students were only to be allowed preaching engagements from which they could return the same night; at weekends they could travel over ten miles, but no more than thirty miles from the college, going on Saturday and returning on Monday morning. As indicated, the daily routine was tightly prescribed, with the students engaging in prayer, preaching, and domestic chores by rotation. Divinity lectures would be given every day, with classes in English, Latin, Greek, Logic, and Sciences distributed through the week. The new institution was said to be the continuation of Trevecca, whose object in turn was described as being for the education of young men 'according to the plan (of secession)'.[339] The message was that priority would go to those planning ordination in the Connexion, though the

---

potential subscribers at the lack of firm rules at Trevecca. The later history of the Dissenting academies showed how responsive subscription income could be to public perceptions of their ethos and discipline (Watts, *The Dissenters*, 489). Despite this show of independence on the part of those LH consulted, however, it was accepted that the trustees should be appointed by her and (after some argument) that the trust should be self-perpetuating, rather than vacancies being filled by the vote of the subscribers (Apostolic Society minute book for 17 Oct. 1787, MS, C1/1, 5,CF).

[337] Apostolic Society Report for 1791, C4/26,CF.

[338] The latter was somewhat undermined, however, by the provision that students might be sent out earlier, if judged suitable.

[339] The Connexion's secession from the Church of England is described in Ch. 7. The phrase 'plan of secession' was subsequently used within the Connexion to refer to its particular organizational and theological features.

possibility of episcopal or Dissenting ordination was not ruled out.[340]

What this prescription symbolized was a striking reflection of general thinking about ministerial training which Trevecca itself had done much to stimulate. In founding Trevecca Lady Huntingdon had pioneered the principle of education for ministry, education in which the practical development of skills through itinerant preaching played a major (at times all-consuming) role. It was in part the influence of Trevecca—both as an example to be followed, and through the impact which Trevecca students had on Dissenting congregations and as Dissenting ministers— which was to lead, in the last decades of the eighteenth century, to the foundation of a number of Dissenting academies with objectives broadly similar to those of Lady Huntingdon.[341] They were, however, institutions which learned lessons from the obvious flaws in the Trevecca scheme, particularly the imprecise nature of its academic objectives, and the damaging impact which unregulated itinerant preaching could have upon a course of study. The plans of the Apostolic Society can thus be seen as a part of the process of refining the Trevecca model, which was going on in parallel within orthodox Dissent. In the new evangelical academies admission procedures and the length and content of courses became clearly defined; there were, as noted, set rules governing when students could participate in itinerant preaching; and there was a concerted attempt to

---

[340] Apostolic Society Report for 1791, C4/26,CF. The extent of the intended identification between the college and the Connexion was to prove an issue of contention into the middle of the next century and beyond. A pamphlet of 1857, for example, argued for the similarity of purpose shared by Trevecca and Cheshunt; it concluded from this that the college's prime job was to serve the Connexion, rather than to be a resource for the Christian world at large (James Bridgman, *An Address to the Ministers, Deacons and Friends of the Countess of Huntingdon's Connexion and College* (London, 1857). A copy is bound into D3/2,CF).

[341] The principal institutions identified by Dr Lovegrove in his study of the contribution of academies to the revival of Dissent in the late eighteenth and early nineteenth centuries were: Hackney, the English Evangelic academy (later Hoxton), Idle, and Newport Pagnell, together with Bogue's Gosport academy and Cornelius Winter's academy at Marlborough (Lovegrove, *Established Church, Sectarian People*, ch. 4).

raise academic standards.[342] It was in that context that the plans for the new Trevecca have to be seen.

The Apostolic Society having thus been formed, a circular letter was prepared to solicit funds; three thousand copies were printed, and the appeal had raised £156 by the end of the year. The great majority of subscribers came from London, and there were strong links in particular with Spa Fields chapel.[343] Apart from appealing for money and then investing it, however, there was little for the Society to do while Lady Huntingdon remained alive. This, indeed, may explain the limited response to their appeal.[344] Their remit was to prepare for the perpetuation of the college after her death, and Lady Huntingdon seems to have had no thought of allowing the trustees to anticipate their future role by sharing oversight of Trevecca with them while she was still alive. Despite the financial straits through which Trevecca was passing in 1788, for example, the college had no share in the money being set aside for its successor.

When the Society was formed, Swansea was still envisaged as the new location, and it was anticipated that the move might have taken place in Lady Huntingdon's lifetime. In the event, however, nothing had happened by the time of her death in 1791, when the trustees had earnestly to address the question of where the college should be relocated, and under whose tutelage. On the first point it was immediately determined to stay in Wales until a convenient place could be found within ten to fifty miles of London. The search could not be allowed to take too long, since their continued tenure of the Trevecca buildings could be

---

[342] Lovegrove, *Established Church, Sectarian People*, ch. 4. Dr Lovegrove distinguishes between those academies which saw their missionary responsibilities in predominantly local terms, evangelizing and ministering to congregations in their own area—and those like Hoxton and Hackney which had links with two home missionary societies, respectively Societas Evangelica and Village Itinerancy, who claimed a national evangelistic role (ibid. 83). As seen above, Trevecca started in the former category, providing preaching experience for its students in the immediate vicinity of the college, but quickly progressed into a resource for the Connexion at large.

[343] Apostolic Society minutes for 5 Dec. 1787; Sept., 5 Nov. and 3 Dec. 1788; C1/1, 8, 21–8,CF (Welch, *Cheshunt College*, x).

[344] So, indeed, the Society thought (C5/2,CF). There were only 382 individual subscribers between 1787 and 1799 (Welch, *Cheshunt College*, x).

measured only in months. By October 1791 the trustees had settled on a house in Cheshunt in Hertfordshire;[345] the trustees wanted to retain Trevecca until midsummer 1792, but were told they could not stay after Lady Day (25 March).[346] Lady Huntingdon had bequeathed the Society furniture, Communion plate, and library from Trevecca; early in 1792 the committee appointed by the trustees to discharge their day-to-day responsibilities, was arranging for the packing up of the books and the disposal of any items not worth the carriage. The library and the furniture arrived in Cheshunt at the beginning of April.[347]

Finding a clergyman to serve as master for the new college proved difficult. Several applicants were judged unsuitable, whether on grounds of inexperience or denomination (one was a Baptist).[348] Two candidates (one of whom was James Glazebrook) declined the mastership when offered it; another looked set to come, but then withdrew because of doubts about the security of the position.[349] Advertisements for clergymen were placed in the Oxford, Cambridge, York, and Leeds papers,[350] and at one stage the trustees contemplated a temporary appointment to bridge the gap until someone permanent could be found.[351] In the event, having asked for suggestions from a number of leading Anglican Evangelicals—including Charles Simeon, Thomas Charles,

---

[345] Apostolic Society minutes for 12 Oct. 1791, C1/1, 50,CF. Initially there was talk of renting the building at £50 p.a. but in the event they purchased it outright for £950 (minutes for 28 Sept. and 23 Nov. 1791, C1/1, 48, 57,CF).

[346] Apostolic Society minutes for 26 Oct. 1791, 54,CF.

[347] Apostolic Society minutes for 13 July and 5 Oct. 1791; and 11 Jan., 1 Feb. and 14 Apr. 1792, C1/1, 34, 43, 70, 74, 86,CF. One item from Trevecca not brought to Hertfordshire was the pulpit, Whitefield's original from Moorfields, which remains in the buildings which were then the Harris settlement.

[348] Apostolic Society minutes for 4 and 28 Dec. 1791, and 25 Jan. 1792, 61, 64, 65, 72,CF.

[349] Apostolic Society minutes for 11 Jan. 1792, 28 Dec. 1791, 1 Feb. 1792; Apostolic Society records for Mar. 1792; Apostolic Society minutes for 14 and 21 Mar. and 25 Apr. 1792, 68–9, 64, 73; C5/2; C1/1, 82–4, 90–91,CF.

[350] Apostolic Society minutes for 30 Nov. and (? 2) Dec. 1791, C1/1, 59, 60,CF.

[351] Apostolic Society minutes for 29 Feb. 1792, 78,CF. This was the Revd Dr Illingworth who had at various times preached for the Connexion and the Whitefieldites (Seymour, i. 217; Shirley to LH, 23 Apr. 1777, F1/388,CF). He declined a permanent post because of his age and infirmity—and because he was expecting a living!

Milner of Hull, Thomas Robinson of Leicester, William Cadogan, and Richard de Courcy—they settled (at the suggestion of the last named) on a clergyman then serving as curate at Coddington, near Chester, the Revd Isaac Nicholson.[352]

George Best took possession of the Cheshunt House on 3 March 1792;[353] John Jones's temporary appointment as Trevecca tutor ended, along with the college's tenure of the building on 25 March.[354] That date, effectively, marked the end of Trevecca College, although some, if not all, of the students had left before then. The trustees undertook to meet the travelling expenses of those Trevecca students who transferred to Cheshunt, but admission to the new college was not automatic—during March, for example, four of them were in London to preach to the trustees and to be examined by two Connexional ministers.[355] After Trevecca had been vacated there was a gap of some months while the Cheshunt buildings were prepared for their new use,[356] and until Nicholson could arrange his move to Hertfordshire. For a few months Mrs Powell came up from Wales to supervise the housekeeping arrangements.[357] The first students were admitted on 1 August 1792, and the opening ceremony was performed (appropriately) on 24 August—twenty-four years after the inauguration of Trevecca itself. Equally appropriately, the officiants were four former Trevecca students (Platt, Kirkman, Crole, and Eyre) who between them represented the principal options open to Cheshunt students, of Connexional, Dissenting, or episcopal ordination.[358]

---

[352] Nicholson was a non-graduate who had been ordained priest in 1785. He was said to have been converted by reading de Courcy's sermons. Retired from Cheshunt through ill health in 1803; died in 1807, aged 46. One of his previous pupils was recommended as a Cheshunt student in 1792 (Welch, *Cheshunt College*, pp. xii–xiii); Apostolic Society minutes for 8, 15 and 22 Feb.; 18 Apr.; 2, 9, 16 and 23 May; and 25 July 1792, C1/1, 74–7, 90, 91–5, 109,CF).

[353] Apostolic Society minutes for 7 Mar. 1792, C1/1, 81,CF.

[354] Apostolic Society records, C5/2,CF.

[355] Cheshunt College minute book, 24 Mar. 1792; Apostolic Society minutes for 28 Mar. 1792, C1/1, 85,CF.

[356] Apostolic Society minutes for 6 Mar. 1793, C1/1,144–5, CF.

[357] Apostolic Society minutes for 2 Mar.; and 4 and 25 July 1792, C1/1, 79, 103, 107–8,CF.

[358] *Order for the Opening of Cheshunt College*, 1792, C4/1,CF; Seymour, ii. 513–20.

Those who launched the new college were naturally conscious of the links between the two institutions.[359] But the world had moved on since Lady Huntingdon's pioneering venture in South Wales. Orthodox Dissenters had taken up the Trevecca model, and though the Church of England had still to wait some decades for the establishment of training colleges, there was some acceptance, even here, that some of those whom God called to ministry required practical assistance in fulfilling their calling.[360] Cheshunt was not an isolated example as Trevecca had been; when the trustees applied for financial help to Henry Thornton (son of Lady Huntingdon's old friend and occasional benefactor), he declined on the basis of 'other opportunities of the same kind opening to him'.[361] Even the Connexion itself had by now an alternative source of basic training in ministerial gifts, in the prayer meeting being run by a founder member of the Spa Fields committee, Thomas Weatherill. Significantly, this was termed a 'School of the Prophets' and provided an opportunity for testing and exercising 'Gifts for publick work in the Lord's service'. It was to be a route sometimes recommended to Cheshunt applicants not judged ready for the college.[362]

Despite its often ramshackle and ill-directed appearance, Trevecca deserves its place—and an honoured one—in the history of ministerial training. It was born of a new vision on Lady Huntingdon's part, and she held to that vision through nearly a quarter of a century, and despite the discouragement of friends as well as enemies. It was a tribute to all involved in the Trevecca enterprise that the concept to which it gave birth was sufficiently robust for it to be worthwhile improving upon it in the establishment of its successor.

---

[359] Crole, for example, considered using the same text as Whitefield had done for the Trevecca opening (Seymour, ii. 517).
[360] See above, on the developing tradition of clerical education societies.
[361] Apostolic Society minutes for 16 May 1792, C1/1, 93,CF.
[362] This institution seems to have become a source of Connexional manpower in its own right. In 1795 Haweis wrote that men should expect a period as lay evangelists before being considered for Connexional ordination, whether they came from the college or the 'Prophets School' (quoted in Bridgman, *An Address to the Countess of Huntingdon's Connexion and College*).

But Trevecca deserves to be judged not just for its theoretical contribution to the development of ministerial training, but for what it achieved in itself. For the impact of the student preachers on the development of the Connexion and other churches, and the subsequent success of some of the students in attaining positions of significance in the later history of the Revival,[363] showed that the college was a force to be reckoned with. Doubtless the students' experience upon the road was at least as important as any formal instruction they received. But however far short the college fell of Fletcher's aspirations in proposing his original curriculum, and however little formal teaching was done within the college walls, there was no gainsaying the stream of highly motivated young men who planned their ministry, and started out upon it, from the farmhouse at Trevecca.

[363] For example, in addition to those who participated in the Cheshunt opening, there were: Mead, Molland, Clayton, Aldridge, Hawkesworth, Glazebrook, Edward Burn, Roby, and N. M. Cheek.

6

Doctrines and Divisions

CALVINISTS AND ARMINIANS PRIOR TO 1770

The 1750s, as we have seen,[1] were a period in which Lady Huntingdon, though theologically on the Calvinistic wing of the Revival, maintained harmonious relations with the Wesleys and saw it as part of her objective to preserve the unity of the movement. She did not, for example, keep exclusive company with fellow Calvinists: at the end of the decade she was a regular attender when the Wesleys preached in London, wherever else she might worship at other times.[2] Her unifying role continued in the 1760s, against the backdrop of a continued awareness on both sides of the need for tact and restraint in order not to expose tensions lying not far beneath the surface.[3] It was a concern which events at the end of the decade showed to be all too well founded.

Lady Huntingdon was present with some of her immediate circle at the Wesleyan conference in 1762,[4] but she appears to have remained on the sidelines during the controversy that was to shake the Wesleyan societies in the following year. The issue had as its origin the doctrine of Christian Perfection,[5] which had been taken to extremes by a group within the Foundry Society in London that had gathered round Thomas Maxfield and a more recent convert, George Bell. Bell had advanced from claims of personal sanctification and immortality to predicting the immediate

---

[1] Above, Ch. 3.
[2] LH to CW (marked 1 and 7 Sept. 1759), Meth. Arch. (LH), 71, 72.
[3] Cf. Tyerman, *Wesley*, ii. 508; John Fletcher to CW, 8 Aug. 1765, Meth. Arch. (Fletcher), 29. [4] Tyerman, *Wesley*, ii. 448.
[5] On the doctrinal issues which affected relations between LH and JW, see below, pp 243–56.

end of the world. Despite Wesley's published repudiation of Bell, the prophesy caused widespread alarm not just within the Wesleyan societies but among many other Londoners as well. There was much criticism of Methodism as a result.[6] It was not difficult for Wesley to weather the Bell incident itself. But it did scare many people away from the doctrine of Perfection, and Wesley was hurt by the readiness of his Calvinist friends to use the affair as fresh grounds for criticizing it. It is symbolic of the ambivalent way in which Lady Huntingdon was still regarded that, within a few days of each other, Wesley wrote to solicit her sympathy, while Romaine wrote critically to her of the doctrines that had led to the Bell debacle.[7]

There is no evidence of bridge-building by Lady Huntingdon on this occasion. Possibly she was prevented by her daughter's fatal illness, which occurred that year; possibly too the impact of the affair passed off quickly.[8] The following year, despite some initial coolness in her relations with Wesley, she responded positively to an initiative by the latter to unite the 'awakened clergy'. The proposal, which Wesley sent to some fifty clergy, was for a meeting at which they would not attempt to resolve disputed points (that, Wesley feared, might be courting disaster) but would agree on a code of mutual respect and assistance. Lady Huntingdon's support was to be a key element: '...if your Ladyship could...be near, it might be of excellent service in confirming any kind and friendly disposition, which our Lord might implant in the hearts of His servants.'[9] Wesley's circular met with minimal response, but some thirteen

---

[6] W. Stephen Gunter, *The Limits of 'Love Divine'* (Nashville, 1989), 218–19 quotes press correspondence at the time. See also Tyerman, *Wesley*, ii. 432–41 and E. G. Rupp, *Religion in England, 1688–1791* (Oxford, 1986), 402–3 who has a characteristically colourful account of the affair. Rack sees JW's earlier slowness to move against Bell as a sign of his fear of hindering a perfectionist revival (Rack, *Wesley*, 338, 341).   [7] Tyerman, *Wesley*, ii. 463–4.

[8] In January 1764 Shirley thought there had been a retreat from extremes among both perfectionists and predestinarians (Shirley to LH, 10 Jan. 1764, E4/1(4),CF). JW may have been more affected by the loss of his old helper, Thomas Maxfield, who left the Foundry with some 100 ultra-perfectionists (Rupp, *Religion in England*, 404).

[9] Schlenther, 70; Harris's Diary for 5 and 7 May 1764; Tyerman, *Wesley*, ii. 508–9; Seymour, i. 409–10; JW's Journal for 19 Apr. 1764, *Works*, xxi. 454–61.

clergy (including Madan, Townsend, and Jesse) plus Howel Harris, did meet with the Wesleys for a general conference at Lady Huntingdon's house in Bristol in August 1764.[10] Harris, from his brief account of the gathering, seems to have regarded it as a success; other evidence suggests that having avoided doctrinal pitfalls, the meeting stuck on Wesley's unwillingness to agree to withdraw preachers from parishes where there was already an evangelical ministry.[11]

There was to be another attempt at union in 1766, on this occasion at the initiative of Lady Huntingdon. The target this time was something less than the general agreement at which Wesley had been aiming in 1764; Lady Huntingdon's objective was more narrowly concerned with harmony between herself, Whitefield and the two Wesleys. It was a sign of the regard in which Wesley held her that he was prepared, at her urgent request, to alter his planned itinerary and travel to London from Yorkshire in August 1766[12] for a meeting with Whitefield and Charles. The upshot was an offer from Wesley to supply the Bath chapel during his coming visit to Bristol,[13] and Lady Huntingdon's hope that the four of them would meet regularly 'to communicate our observations upon the general state of the work'.[14]

The harmony thus established suffered no major rupture during the remaining years of the decade. In 1767, when Lady Huntingdon opened an enlarged Brighton chapel, she hoped that the Wesleys and Whitefield, together with Howel Harris, might join her in a love-feast to rededicate their remaining days.[15] In the event, however, and to his regret, John was unable to be present.[16] Whitefield attended

---

[10] Harris's Diary for 8–10 Aug. 1764. The gathering was evidently designed to coincide with Wesley's conference at Bristol which began on 6 August (JW's Journal, for 6 Aug. 1764, *Works*, xxi. 485). [11] Tyerman, *Wesley*, ii. 511.

[12] JW's Journal for 17 Aug. 1766, *Works*, xxii. 57.

[13] CW's comment that 'all her chapels...are now put into the hands of us three' must have been a misunderstanding of what was agreed—although the report received some general credence (CW's *Journal*, ii. 247 (21 Aug. 1766); Tyerman, *Wesley*, ii. 556; Maxfield to LH, 29 Aug. 1766, F1/1394,CF).

[14] LH to JW, 14 Sept. 1766, Meth. Arch. (LH), 103.

[15] LH to CW, 4 Feb. 1767, Meth. Arch. (LH), 76.

[16] JW to Whitefield, 21 Mar. 1767, Wesley, *Letters*, v. 44.

Wesley's conference that August and preached for him thereafter.[17] Wesley commented at the end of the year, 'In every place where Mr Whitefield has been he has laboured in the same friendly Christian manner. God has indeed effectively broken down the wall of partition which was between us. Thirty years ago we were one; then the sower of tares rent us asunder; but now a stronger than he has made us one again.'[18]

Such expression of solidarity did not mean, however, that the movement was heading towards more formal reunion, or that the leaders ever achieved the co-ordinated approach to new initiatives that Lady Huntingdon envisaged in 1766. Wesley was not one of those whom Lady Huntingdon consulted on the preparations for Trevecca College, and this may partially explain his suspicions of the institution. He was not present when the college was opened in 1768, though he did come to the first anniversary, taking advantage of the opportunity to preach at the Harris settlement, as well as in the college chapel.[19] Wesley had preached for Lady Huntingdon in Bath, earlier in 1769,[20] but despite these occasional instances of co-operation, there were signs that their relationship was not seen as wholly harmonious. In November 1769 there was disagreement over the use by Lady Huntingdon's preacher of the Wesleyan room in Bath, and in the same month Mrs A. E. Goode, who with her husband acted as caretaker of the house and chapel at Tunbridge Wells, wrote to Lady Huntingdon that Wesley was in the area, but that 'I don't know if he is on such terms with yr Ladyship as wd make it proper to ask him to preach here.'[21]

Wesley's relations with Lady Huntingdon during these years were marked more by reserved respect than cordiality. It was a situation in which hasty or ill-considered comments could lead to misinterpretation or dispute. This contrasts with his relations with other moderate Calvinists: his correspondence during this period includes letters to

---

[17] Tyerman, *Whitefield*, ii. ch. 9.
[18] JW to Mrs Moon, 6 Dec. 1767, Wesley, *Letters*, v. 69.
[19] JW's Journal for 23 Aug. 1769, *Works*, xxii. 200–1.
[20] JW's Journal for 5 Mar. 1769, *Works*, xxii. 172.
[21] JW to Mary Bishop, 5 Nov. 1769, Wesley, *Letters*, v. 153–4; A. E. Godde to LH, 26 Nov. 1769, F1/80,CF.

John Newton and Samuel Furley,[22] and he makes friendly references to such people as Mrs Henry Venn and Venn's curate at Huddersfield, John Ryland.[23] Supremely, though, the theological gulf was bridged in the case of George Whitefield: the friendship of which Wesley had spoken with such pleasure in 1767 remained unbroken until Whitefield's death in 1770. In what proved to be his last letter to Whitefield in February 1770, Wesley wished him well on his voyage to America and gave him his authority to encourage the Methodist preachers over there. When the news of Whitefield's death reached England in November, Wesley was to speak of his old friend as 'that blessed man' and gave great thought to the preparation of the funeral sermon he preached for him at the end of the month.[24]

In the light of this warmth, it is difficult to avoid the impression that the real reason for the coolness between John Wesley and Lady Huntingdon lay more in the realm of personalities than of beliefs. They were people between whom the potential for tension had been long apparent, while others, equally divided in matters of doctrine, found themselves in this period on natural and friendly terms. While doctrine remained as important as it ever had been, evangelicals were content for the moment that it should not disturb their relations with one another, whatever they might say in private. Thus the apparent harmony of these years did not prevent Wesley writing to Fletcher in March 1768 to commiserate with him on the sterility of preaching founded upon notions of Irresistible Grace, and its inability to inspire devotion or self-denial. It was symptomatic of Wesley's ill-fated relations with Lady Huntingdon that she should have come to hear of this letter, for although she was not named in it, it required little perception to identify the 'genteel Methodists' about whom Wesley wrote.[25]

---

[22] 1732–95. Graduate of Queen's College, Cambridge and a Cambridge friend of Henry Venn; correspondent of JW from the 1750s; preached occasionally for LH at Bath in the 1760s; vicar of Roche, Cornwall from 1766 (Wesley, *Letters*, iii. 117 n.; Curnock, iii, 521 n.; Seymour, ii. 2–3).

[23] JW to Samuel Furley, 3 Apr. 1766, Wesley, *Letters*, v. 8.

[24] JW to Whitefield, 21 Feb. 1770; JW to Ann Bolton, 16 Nov. 1770, Wesley, *Letters*, v. 183–4 and 207.

[25] JW to Fletcher, 20 Mar. 1768, Wesley, *Letters*, v. 82–5. LH's comments on this are to be found in Seymour, ii. 235.

With others who shared Wesley's theological position, however, Lady Huntingdon enjoyed more friendly relations than she did with Wesley himself. Typical of these was Charles whose links with her remained close. Charles continued to preach for her from time to time, and on occasions rendered valuable assistance at Bath when the chapel might otherwise have been unsupplied. So important a part of his ministry did he consider this that in May 1768, he even considered moving house from Bristol to Bath to be more easily available.[26] Also striking were her contacts with the Revd Walter Sellon,[27] who was a leading proponent of Arminianism in this period. At the same time as Wesley encouraged him in his attacks on Calvinism, Sellon continued the friendly correspondence with Lady Huntingdon that had begun in the 1750s. It was not that Sellon dissembled his opinions to Lady Huntingdon: in 1765, Fletcher had spoken of the friendly dispute which he and Sellon had had with Lady Huntingdon on the issue of Perfection, and as late as November 1771, when the doctrinal dispute which broke out in 1770 was at its height, Sellon was still attacking Calvinist excesses to Lady Huntingdon in terms which suggest that he expected her broad agreement.[28] Nor were Sellon and Charles Wesley isolated examples. It can hardly be without significance that two of those to whom Lady Huntingdon gave positions of the highest responsibility at Trevecca, John Fletcher and Joseph Benson, were men who not only shared Wesley's theology, but were in regular cor-res-pondence with him.

Parallel with these contacts with Arminians are some signs that the Connexion itself was not exclusively Calvinistic in theology. The Wesleyan doctrine of Perfection was in evidence in Brighton in 1767; in January 1770, many of the

[26] J. Lloyd to LH, 13 Oct. and 5 May 1768, F1/41, 1424,CF; Seymour, ii. 109.
[27] 1715–92. One of the original masters at Kingswood School in 1748. Subsequently ordained and combined the curacies of Smisby and Breedon in Leicestershire with oversight of Wesleyan preachers in that area. Presented by Lord Huntingdon to Ledsham, Yorkshire in 1770 (Tyerman, *Wesley*, ii. 11, 201, 359–60; Walter Sellon to LH, 5 Nov. 1757 and 6 June 1770, F1/4, E4/4(5),CF).
[28] Fletcher to CW, 8 Aug. 1765, Meth. Arch. (Fletcher); Walter Sellon to LH, 6 June 1770, 20 Nov. 1771, 5 Nov. 1757, 23 Oct. 1770, E4/4(5 and 6), F1/4, 107,CF; JW to Sellon, 9 July 1768, 30 Dec. 1769, 21 Feb. 1770, Wesley, *Letters*, v. 96, 167, 183.

Bath congregation were reported as holding similar sentiments.²⁹ Bath, indeed, seems to have been particularly susceptible to Wesleyan doctrines: the director of the chapel singers, the composer Benjamin Milgrove, was strongly sympathetic and it was to this sympathy that his resignation in 1772 was attributed.³⁰ It would be difficult, in fact, to see how theological uniformity could have been achieved throughout the Connexion when its pulpits were supplied by men of such differing outlooks. Fletcher and Charles Wesley were obvious examples of non-Calvinists preaching for the Connexion, but there were others, like Thomas Maxfield. Maxfield had broken with Wesley in 1763, after the Bell Perfection fiasco and for a period was alienated from the Wesleys completely.³¹ But though he was in close contact with Lady Huntingdon in the following years, and frequently assisted in her chapels, he did not adopt a Calvinistic theology. In June 1768, he expressed his fear that the Bath clergyman, the Revd Edward Shepherd, would 'preach up certain opinions' in the chapel there, and it is clear that it was Predestination that he had in mind. Before Shepherd came to preach in Maxfield's chapel in Rope-Makers Alley in London, Maxfield made him promise to avoid the subject.³²

Another possible source for non-Calvinist influence was Trevecca College, for it was not until February 1771, when the controversy was well under way, that the Countess started to insist on doctrinal orthodoxy from her students. As already seen, a significant minority of the early students was not Calvinist.³³ One of the latter was James Glazebrook,

---

²⁹ Glascott to LH, 29 July 1767; J. Godde to LH, 10 Jan. 1770, F1/1403, 84,CF.
³⁰ Mrs Shirley to LH, 2 Mar. n.y; J. Lloyd to LH, 7 Feb. 1772, E4/1(10), F1/1583,CF.
³¹ Tyerman, *Wesley*, ii. 440–1; CW's *Journal*, ii. 248 (7 Sept. 1766).
³² Maxfield to LH, 9 June and 16 July 1768, F1/1435, 1438,CF. Maxfield found himself estranged from nearly all groups save that of LH. In 1766 he alienated both JW and Whitefield when he published a *Vindication* of his doctrinal development. Eventually Whitefield urged him to apologise to JW. Relations with the Wesleyans continued to be difficult and in July 1768 the Foundry society expelled one of its members for the crime of preaching for Maxfield. Not until 1772 was an attempt made to heal the breach, so that Maxfield could supply at the Foundry during the absences of the Wesleys and other major preachers (Maxfield to LH, 5 and 9 May 1767, and 16 July 1768, F1/1398–99, 1438,CF).   ³³ See Ch. 5.

who continued faithful to his original opinions for some time. In June 1770, a group at Ote Hall accused him of not being sufficiently explicit on the doctrine of the imputed righteousness of Christ, and it was not until the following month that Walter Shirley finally argued him away from the doctrine of Perfection.[34]

In a variety of ways, therefore, diversity of doctrine was maintained in the Countess's Connexion in the years before the Calvinistic controversy. The Connexion, though, did not speak for all Calvinist evangelicals, and there were others, more extreme than the Countess, who were less tolerant. Parallel with the attempts at co-operation just described was a continual undercurrent of bickering. Significant in this context was the posthumous publication in 1765 of James Hervey's *Vindication* of the most celebrated of his Calvinistic works, *The Dialogues between Theron and Aspasio*. Wesley had written a short attack on the *Dialogues* when they first appeared, fearful that the doctrine of imputed righteousness which they advanced would lead to neglect of holiness and thus to antinomianism. Although Hervey had completed a reply to Wesley by the time of his death in 1758, he had refrained from publishing for fear of worsening the controversy. Hervey's Calvinism was moderate in tone, yet the *Vindication*, sold bound together with Wesley's original attack, was little less than an extended review of the points at issue, as well as containing some severe criticism of Wesley's character and theological inconsistency.[35] A further sign of the conflict brewing beneath the surface came in the later 1760s, when the visits of Joseph Townsend to Edinburgh heightened latent divisions between Calvinists and Arminians and drastically reduced the size of the Wesleyan society.[36] The real clash, however, followed from the events surrounding the expulsion of the Methodist students from St Edmund Hall in Oxford in 1768.[37] The affair occasioned

---

[34] Glazebrook to LH, 21 June 1770; Shirley to LH, 23 July 1770, F1/99, 1561,CF. [35] Rack, *Wesley*, 452–3.
[36] JW to Joseph Townsend, 1–3 Aug. 1767, Wesley, *Letters*, v. 57–9; JW's Journal for 12 May 1770, *Works*, xxii. 229. Tyerman saw the virulence of Sellon's pamphlet reply to Hervey as having done major damage to the Wesleyan cause in Scotland (*Wesley*, ii. 531–2). [37] See Ch. 5.

wide interest and among the pamphlets it called forth was Sir Richard Hill's *Pietas Oxoniensis*, which appeared in June 1769. Hill was not content with a mere defence of the undergraduates, but used the occasion to assert his belief in a Calvinistic interpretation of the Church's Articles. When Dr Newell, the Oxford Vice-Chancellor, rejected Hill's assertion in a pamphlet dated early in September, the issues had been brought fully into the open. Augustus Toplady, formerly an Arminian but now a staunch Calvinist,[38] entered the contest with a reply to Dr Newell, *The Church of England Vindicated from the Charge of Arminianism*, and a translation of a work by the sixteenth-century Italian reformer Jerome Zanchius, *The Doctrine of Absolute Predestination Stated and Asserted*. The Arminian reply came from the pen of Walter Sellon, though with him the expulsions were not the immediate impetus for his controversial writings: as early as July 1768, Wesley had encouraged him in the defence he was preparing of the seventeenth-century Arminian, John Goodwin's *Redemption Redeemed*.[39] This appeared in September 1769.

Doctrinal debate was thus a live issue within the ranks of the Evangelical Revival, well before the Wesleyan Minutes of 1770 that are traditionally regarded as the start of the second Calvinistic controversy. There is little doubt where Lady Huntingdon's ultimate sympathies lay in this debate, although she was not fully identified with the Calvinists before 1770. Indeed, there may have been some distance between her and the more extreme Calvinists. One hint of this came during 1768 in the pages of the *Gospel Magazine*, frequently the mouthpiece of strong Calvinism. Discussing the St Edmund Hall expulsions, the author states the charge against the students to have been that of acquaintance with 'reputed Methodists, namely Mr. Venn, Mr. Newton, Mr. Townsend, and with Mr. Fletcher and Mr. Davies'. This separation of Fletcher and Davies from the others is in itself striking but when, in the following paragraph, the writer speaks of the blessings of God upon 'the three persons first

---

[38] 1740–78. Educated at Trinity College, Dublin, and priested in 1764. Incumbent of Broad Hembury, Devon, from 1768.

[39] JW to Walter Sellon, 9 July 1768, Wesley, *Letters*, v. 96.

mentioned', it is hard to avoid the impression of a deliberate denigration of Fletcher and Davies. Yet this is but a few months before Fletcher became president of the Countess's college and before Davies (the Revd Edward Davies, curate at Evesham with whom Joseph Shipman had stayed after his expulsion from Oxford) was presented to the living of Coychurch, Glamorgan, through the influence of Lady Huntingdon.[40] Even after the appearance of the Wesleyan Minutes, there is evidence of the Connexion holding a consciously moderate position. In August 1770 Walter Shirley wrote from Brighton of Lady Caroline Hervey having been hurt among what he termed the 'fashionable' London Calvinists and that she was glad to find a different spirit there; Mrs Shirley commented on Lady Caroline that 'not one bit of calvin remained'.[41] Two months later Shirley, who was to be the main protagonist in the Connexion's response to Wesley, described the Countess's group as a 'golden mediocrity avoiding legality on the one hand and illegality or Antinomianism on the other'.[42] At the end of the year, there is evidence of Lady Huntingdon herself attempting to moderate excessive Calvinist zeal in the students' preaching.[43]

So far as local congregations were concerned, the prevailing pattern appears as one of co-operation during this period. In January 1769, for example, Edward Shepherd, on a preaching tour through southern England, was allowed, notwithstanding his Calvinist sentiments, to preach twice to the Wesleyans in Salisbury and was accompanied on the next stage in his journey by one of their preachers.[44] Possibly some congregations could see little to distinguish between Wesley and the Countess. A newly formed congregation at Taunton in 1767, for example, indicated that it was willing to accept the protection of either.[45] Similarly in 1769, the

[40] *Gospel Magazine* for 1768; Davies to LH, 17 Jan. 1769, F1/45,CF.
[41] Shirley to LH, 27 Aug. 1770; Mrs Shirley to LH, 4 Aug. n.y., F1/1562, 1506,CF.
[42] Shirley to LH, 19 Oct. 1770, F1/1565,CF. A decade before the controversy of 1770, Shirley had been on close terms with JW (Schlenther, 107).
[43] Glazebrook to LH, 5 Dec. 1770, F1/1521,CF.
[44] E. Sheppard to LH, 19 Jan. 1769, F1/46,CF.
[45] E. K. Wilson to H. Harris, 11 Nov. 1767 (G. M. Roberts (ed.), *Selected Trevecka Letters* (Caernarvon, 1962), ii. 114).

Wesleyans in Cardiff asked Howel Harris if he would solicit financial assistance for them from Lady Huntingdon, as the Methodist conference had been less forthcoming than they had hoped.[46] Just occasionally, however, there was less cordiality: in Upton, Worcestershire, during the summer of 1769, both the Countess's society and the Wesleyans were seeking possession of the same building as a meeting house, but the former drew back from the idea of a joint purchase on the grounds that the Wesleyans would exclude Calvinists, although they themselves would allow in either.[47]

THE DOCTRINAL ISSUES

Despite the controversies that afflicted the Evangelical Revival, its leaders clung in the main to the conviction that they were at heart a single movement, more united around a common set of beliefs that marked them out from the religious world of their day, than they were divided on finer points of theology. The problem, however, was that the leaders of the Revival held between them a number of distinctive doctrines not all of which were easily reconciled. These went to such fundamental questions as whether man enjoyed any degree of free will, how (if so) that free will related to the sovereignty of God, and where God's justice ended and his mercy began. It was perhaps not surprising that these issues should lead to disagreement: Wesley brought to the Revival a High Church tradition that preserved the notion of man's free will, while others, Anglicans as well as Dissenters, had inherited a reformed theology in which predestination served to emphasize God's free grace at work in man's salvation. Differences over these issues had been notorious in the history of the Church and they were to play a significant part in the divisions that occurred within eighteenth-century evangelicalism.

The Fall of man was as much a point of departure for Wesley as it was for Calvinists. To undermine that doctrine,

---

[46] J. Harper to Harris, 23 Aug. 1769, ibid. 131.
[47] Shipman to LH, 7 Aug. n.y., E4/5(13),CF.

to think of natural man as possessed of a morality in himself which might help him attain salvation, was to all of them to strike at the very roots of the Christian revelation and make pointless the sacrifice of Christ.[48] To the leaders of the Revival, this was a basic truth which the latitudinarian churchmen of their day so frequently ignored, that man was far from being the largely rational and potentially enlightened creature that the century supposed; rather he was in a state of condemnation and corruption from which his own efforts and good works could not deliver him. Only the grace of God could do that. It was over the operation of that grace, however, that difficulties arose. Clearly it could not be 'earned' by faith, or faith would become just another good work. At the same time, grace obviously did not have an equal effect in the hearts of all men, or all would have been converted, which was manifestly not the case.

It was here that the notion of predestination was attractive. It spoke of God's absolute authority to determine who should be saved: the initiative was God's, with no room for man to substitute his own will for the divine.[49] It was a doctrine that reflected well the sense of wonder that many evangelicals felt that God should have chosen *them* as the recipients of his mercy. And it was a source of comfort also. If God's will was sovereign, and if God had chosen them, then their salvation was assured; they would not fall away, but would 'finally persevere'. Moderate Calvinists would generally have preferred to rest at this point, emphasizing the positive side of election, and the experience of grace, leaving open the question of what might happen to those who were not chosen. Some, indeed, sought to avoid specific mention of election altogether. James Hervey asserted that predestination 'makes no part of my scheme, never comes under consideration, [and] is purposely and carefully avoided', and stated that nowhere in *Theron and Aspasio* 'does he

---

[48] See, for example, JW's attack on Dr John Taylor of Norwich, *The Doctrine of Original Sin* (1757).

[49] For example, Harris to John Cennick, 27 Oct. 1740: 'I plainly see that we preach two Gospels: one sets all on God, the other on man; the one on God's will, the other on man's will' (quoted in Gunter, *Limits of 'Love Divine'*, 229).

[Aspasio] once touch upon *absolute Predestination*, much less does he plead the Articles of our Church in its Defence'.[50]

Moderate Calvinists preferred to emphasize the breadth and inclusiveness of God's love. Rowland Hill, who became an active proponent of the Calvinist position during the controversies of the 1770s, wrote that 'No-one will ever say: "I *would* have come to Christ, but he *would not let* me come".'[51] When moderate Calvinists spoke of election, their concern was to emphasize the positive and comforting aspects of the doctrine, with its message of God's love and it reassurance to the faithful of their place in God's favour.[52] The trouble was that it was difficult in logic to deny the converse of predestination, reprobation for the non-elect. If the consequence of not being chosen was damnation, then it seemed to many mere semantics to pretend that God had not actively condemned the non-elect, merely passed them by.

John Wesley was a consistent opponent of predestination.[53] It appeared repugnant to him that human beings should be damned for sins that, since grace had been withheld from them, they could not have avoided. Such cruelty was an appalling slur on God, who was made to appear the author of

---

[50] J. Brown, *Memoirs of the Life... of James Hervey* (Edinburgh, 2nd edn., 1809), 357; James Hervey, *Aspasio Vindicated: Eleven Letters to the Revd Mr John Wesley* (London, 1765), 185.

[51] Quoted in P. E. Sangster, 'The Life of the Revd Rowland Hill', D.Phil thesis (Oxford, 1964), 105.

[52] Moderate Calvinists could be embarrassed by the harshness of talk of reprobation. Richard Cecil wrote of the theology of the Erskines, 'I want a more kind-hearted and liberal sort of divinity' (Josiah Pratt (ed.), *The Works of the Revd Richard Cecil* (3rd edn., London, 1828), ii. 559). I am grateful to Dr Walsh, in this context, for sight of his sequence of unpublished essays 'The Moderation of Moderate Calvinism', 'Moderate Calvinism Criticised', and 'Antinomianism and "Immoderate" Calvinists'.

[53] At the time of his ordination, faced with subscription to the 39 Articles, including Article 17 on predestination, Wesley considered a compromise position: that salvation of the elect need not rule out some of the non-elect securing salvation also. Gunter, *Limits of 'Love Divine'*, 237. The idea of election without reprobation was not new; it remained occasionally attractive to Wesley, as it did to many moderate Calvinists. Told in 1771 of a preacher who held this position, Wesley commented: 'If I was resolved to understand all God's dispensations, I should embrace his opinion; because it in a manner accounts for some things which otherwise are unaccountable. But this I do not expect; I am content to understand exceeding little while I am in the body' (JW to Mrs Bennis, 20 July 1771, Wesley, *Letters*, v. 268).

sin and injustice; and it made nonsense of the scriptural witness that Christ had died for all. Wesley also believed that predestination was unhelpful in developing the life of congregations, since it risked encouraging spiritual pride on the one hand, or despair on the other.[54] Wesley needed a solution to this dilemma that did not imply that man had regained control of his own salvation. So he sought to hedge round man's choice in such a way that the initiative still lay with God. Man in his natural state—man, that is, after the Fall of Adam—cannot will anything good and is incapable of accepting any offer of salvation held out for his choosing. It was this total hold of sin that Wesley believed God had broken by giving man the divinely imparted talent to respond to the drawing of the Spirit, and thus the ability to choose good rather than evil. It is this 'prevenient' grace, the 'light that enlightens every man' (in St John's phrase) that restores to mankind the moral accountability that the absence of choice in the Calvinist system had appeared to deny. It is not so much *free* will, as *freed* will, which creates in every man the conditions in which he is able to respond positively to the offer of salvation, yet leaving him a free agent to accept or reject.[55] If man, by his own will, gives a sufficiently free rein to the promptings of prevenient grace, then he will be led on to the faith which justifies.

Wesley thus developed a theory of *conditional* election: all are potentially salvable, because God has given everyone the opportunity to respond to grace. In this way he sought to square the circle of preserving Divine initiative without forfeiting man's responsibility.[56] Arguably he had given the Calvinists all they wanted, by making God the author both of man's initial conversion and of his continuation in the faith. The trouble, in Calvinist eyes, was that Wesley still allowed man the opportunity to refuse the gift that was offered: that meant that the final outcome was man's choice, not God's.[57]

---

[54] H. B. McGonigle, 'John Wesley: Evangelical Arminian', Ph.D. thesis (Keele, 1994), 435–7; Albert C. Outler (ed.), *John Wesley* (New York, 1946), 426.
[55] Rack, *Wesley*, 389; Gunter, *Limits of 'Love Divine'*, 239; McGonigle, 'Evangelical Arminian', 451, 454.   [56] Gunter, *Limits of 'Love Divine'*, 242–3.
[57] Alan P. F. Sell, *The Great Debate, Calvinism, Arminianism and Salvation* (Grand Rapids, Mich., 1983), 75, 71.

Though the sacrifice of Christ had provided the means of salvation, there was no certainty in the Wesleyan system that *anyone* would actually accept it. That, for Calvinists, denied God's sovereign authority, and meant that Christ could have died in vain. As Howel Harris had put it, as early as 1740, 'Christ saith, "All that the Father hath given to me shall come to me"...But Man says, "God draweth all alike, but some resist him".'[58]

Differences of emphasis on the sovereignty of God might have mattered less if there had not also been disagreement on the weight to be attached to Christians' moral behaviour. For high Calvinists, the issue was clear-cut. Christ had imputed his righteousness to the elect, and their salvation was complete.[59] Nothing could add to it, so nothing more was needed. Conversion was validated by inner conviction and no degree of external goodness was required, even as proof that redemption had taken place. No external rules were necessary, because the saints were so closely grafted into Christ that they would be guided by an internal principle of love within the heart. If the moral law prescribed the life of the Christian, that meant he was back in legalism: indeed, for the Christian to strive for righteousness would imply that Christ's sacrifice was not in itself sufficient for salvation.

Such views could lead, at least in theory, to antinomianism, the belief that the moral law did not apply to the elect: indeed, that sin was almost to be welcomed in the believer, because it emphasized the amazing grace of God in having saved him. Theoretical antinomianism may have led to less 'practical' antinomianism (actual sinful behaviour justified by the claim that it was not inconsistent with one's religious profession) than the critics of the Revival liked to suggest. Such attributed beliefs were, however, a gift to the satirists: the brothel-keeper in Samuel Foote's play *The Minor*, for example, chose Whitefield's religion, rather than Roman Catholicism, because the former, by preaching salvation by

---

[58] Quoted in Sell, *Great Debate*, 62.
[59] Some of what follows draws on the analysis in Walsh, 'The Moderation of Moderate Calvinism', 'Moderate Calvinism Criticised', and 'Antinomianism and "Immoderate" Calvinists'.

faith and not by works, allowed her to continue in her profession.[60] There were, moreover, real fears within the ranks of the Revival that antinomianism would lead to immoral conduct. In 1771, for example, Dr Thomas Gibbons (an eminent Dissenting minister and friend of Whitefield) wrote to Lady Huntingdon about the need to preach grace without giving encouragement to licentiousness; later the same year Walter Sellon informed her of a man leading a lewd life because, as he said, 'I am for my Lady's Gospel'.[61] Nor were the Connexion's preachers immune from the seductions of antinomianism. The student in 1783 who rested on the text 'who shall lay anything to the charge of Gods elect?' clearly regarded himself as exempt from the moral law. This was a theological perspective akin to that from which James Hogg's *Justified Sinner* started upon his career of crime and murder.[62]

Some Calvinists had laid themselves open to misinterpretation by unguarded expressions. Whitefield, for example, had said that 'God loves sinners as sinners'; Hervey, in *Theron and Aspasio*, wrote: 'believers who are notorious transgressors in themselves have a sinless obedience in Christ.'[63] Moderate Calvinists rejected antinomianism, however, not just because it brought the Gospel into disrepute, but because they saw growth in holiness as the determining sign that conversion was real. Emotions could be fallible and be fabricated by the Devil, but not so the evidence of a sanctified life. God ordained not only that the elect should attain eternal life, but should be fitted to enjoy it. Comments on these lines can be found on the lips of men associated with the Countess of Huntingdon. Rowland Hill, for example, said 'we prove our election no otherwise than by our sanctification'; and Walter

---

[60] Samuel Foote, *The Minor* (1760). The central character of Dr Squintum was a parody of Whitefield, and the play incurred protests from LH and others. The story line was not entirely fanciful, however: Thomas Pentycross came across some high Calvinist prostitutes in his parish at Wallingford (W. Huntington, *Tidings from Wallingford* (London, 1786), 8).

[61] Gibbons to LH, 4 July 1771; Sellon to LH, 20 Nov. 1771. F1/128, E4/4(6),CF.

[62] Lloyd to LH, 5 Feb. (marked 1783), F1/1882,CF; James Hogg, *The Private Memoirs and Confessions of a Justified Sinner* (London, 1824).

[63] Quoted in Walsh, '"Immoderate" Calvinism'.

Shirley informed the bishop of Clonfert that though he preached justification by faith alone, he did not 'consider a man as possessed of saving faith who leads an ungodly life'.[64] The life of faith was not static, but implied the need for growth. Two maxims of Thomas Scott (that so impressed the young Newman that he recorded them in his *Apologia*) might be regarded as summing up the moderate Calvinist position: 'Holiness before peace' and 'Growth is the only evidence of life'.[65]

Given this dimension to moderate Calvinism, it is perhaps surprising that its exponents should find themselves so divided from Wesley, for whom growth in holiness was also a cardinal principle of the religious life. Wesley's conversion experience did not displace his original view of the Christian life as a progression deeper and deeper into the knowledge and presence of God. It was to seek holiness that Wesley had set out on his religious pilgrimage; he never lost his conviction that the pursuit of holiness in this world was the goal, even though his perception of the path diverged from that of some of the mystical writers who had shaped his initial strivings.[66] This did not mean a return to the purely moral preaching which the Methodists objected to in the sermons of contemporary clergy; rather it was a recognition on Wesley's part that although it was through faith alone that man was freed from the consequences of his sin, this in no sense lessened his need to strive for the eradication of the sin that remained within him. In this Wesley remained consistent. In 1746 he wrote that conversion is 'the gateway to religion, but holiness is religion itself'.[67] The need for continual search after 'the whole gift of God, the entire renewal of your soul, the full deliverance from sin'[68] is a recurrent theme both of his correspondence and his published writings. In 1759, for example, he wrote to Lady Huntingdon of his desire to 'sink deeper and rise higher in the knowledge of God our Saviour... that we may the more speedily come to

---

[64] Sangster, 'Rowland Hill', 102; Seymour, ii. 180.
[65] J. H. Newman, *Apologia Pro Vita Sua* (Random House edn., New York, 1950), 37. [66] Outler, *Wesley*, 252.
[67] John Wesley, *The Principles of a Methodist Further Explained* (1746).
[68] JW to George Cussons, 18 Nov. 1768, Wesley, *Letters*, v. 113.

the measure of the stature of the fullness of Christ'.[69] The pursuit of holiness was not an optional extra: 'believers [he wrote in 1766] can hardly retain any power of faith if they are not panting after holiness.'[70] Wesley held that there was a further landmark to be looked for on the path of Christian holiness. For some believers there would come a moment when the Spirit of God intervened dramatically, once again, to effect their full sanctification, the eradication of even inner sin. Even this was not the end of the journey. 'Christian Perfection', paradoxically, was not an unimprovable state, and those who had been perfected were still expected to grow in grace. But a significant point had been passed, effecting an actual change within the believer concerned: freedom from sin, in the sense of the voluntary transgression of a known law, even if not (in this life) release from all breaches of the perfect law of God.[71] If the Christian faltered thereafter, this was simply the result of defects of understanding and perception inseparable from the human condition—'as long as you are in the body,' Wesley conceded, 'you will come short of what you would be'[72]—but what mattered was that now love and not self was in command. Was the experience of total purity of motive really to be looked for in this world? Wesley held that some could indeed expect such a moment of instantaneous sanctification between justification and death.[73] Anticipation of such a moment was a continual spur forward: 'our words,' he wrote in 1772, 'will carry little weight unless we lead people to expect sanctification *while we speak.*'[74] But vigilance was needed to sustain it. In 1767 John wrote that he retracted anything that suggested the impossibility of falling away; in 1770 he wrote sadly that

---

[69] JW to LH, 10 Mar. 1759, Wesley, *Letters*, iv. 57–8.
[70] JW to Mrs Bennis, 29 Mar. 1766, Wesley, *Letters*, v. 6.
[71] Harald Lindstrom, *Wesley and Sanctification* (Upsala, 1946), 84; Rack, *Wesley*, 399. [72] JW to Mrs Marston, 11 Aug. 1770, Wesley, *Letters*, v. 196.
[73] He worried over this, however. 'What shall we...maintain...concerning the nature, the time (now or by-and-by), and the manner of it (instantaneous or not)? I am weary of intestine war...let us *fix* something for good and all' (JW to CW, 14 June 1768, Wesley, *Letters*, v. 93).
[74] JW to CW, 26 Apr. 1772, Wesley, *Letters*, v. 316; Minutes of the Conference of 1770.

'so few...retain it [deliverance from inbred sin] one year, hardly one in ten, nay one in thirty'.[75]

The Wesleyan pursuit of holiness may not have been very different in its impact on believers from the moderate Calvinists' desire for holiness as a sign of election. But it sounded warning bells in Calvinist ears. 'Perfection,' Shirley told Lady Huntingdon in 1770, 'puts seekers into bondage and professors into Enthusiasm and spiritual pride.'[76] The idea that sin could be eradicated from man struck at the very root of the Calvinist system. Sin for Calvinists was something inseparable from man's nature, and the idea of being able, even with God's help, to find total freedom from it encouraged spiritual pride, as well as undermining the seriousness of sin. The man who believed himself without sin would, they thought (despite Wesley's acknowledgement that even those who had been perfected remained dependent on Christ to preserve them from relapse), put confidence in his own achievements and lose the vital sense of total dependence upon Christ.

There was also the danger that Wesley's system would reintroduce belief in justification by works. Calvinists feared that overemphasis on the requirement for a holy life would make such a life the necessary condition for salvation itself. Wesley was aware that an incautious development of his doctrine could lead in this direction: in 1766, for example, a report of the views of one preacher concerned him 'lest we should get back again into justification by works'.[77] Yet in the incautious wording of the Minutes of 1770, as described below, he seemed deliberately to spell out the worst fears of his critics. 'Whoever desires to find favour with God,' they state, should '*cease from evil and learn to do well...* We are every moment *pleasing* or *displeasing* to God *according to our* works.'[78] Though Wesley was careful to say that the reward was '*according*' to our works, rather than 'for the sake' of our works, he admitted

---

[75] JW to CW, 27 Jan. 1767; JW to Mrs Barton, 15 Mar. 1770, Wesley, *Letters*, v. 38–9, 185.   [76] Shirley to LH, 19 Oct. 1770, F1/1565,CF.
[77] JW to Samuel Furly, 3 Apr. 1766, Wesley, *Letters*, v. 8.
[78] Minutes of the Conference of 1770.

the fineness of the distinction and the hair-splitting it implied. If Wesley seriously thought that peace could be achieved by arguing that the Minutes were concerned with the condition 'not of obtaining but of continuing in the favour of God', it shows how far he was from understanding the extent of the issues that divided the two camps. Calvinists could accept that God was pleased or displeased by his people's actions,[79] but to speak of conditions was to go much further and imply merit in those that fulfilled them. Worse still, it made the efficacy of Christ's sacrifice less than total, an incomplete justification that needed man's efforts to make it effective. A fundamental of their faith was being called in question.

The ramifications of the two theologies led to conflict at other points. The most vexed of these was the question of perseverance and the certainty of ultimate salvation. Calvinists believed that for the elect there could be no falling away from grace. If men did lapse, it was a sign that they had never in fact been chosen by God. If the believer was saved, regardless of his own merits or lack of them, then nothing he might do subsequently could undermine that salvation; to believe otherwise was to doubt God's competence to bring his saving purposes to pass. 'Those that are sealed,' Walter Shirley wrote to Lady Huntingdon in 1772, 'are sealed to the Day of Judgement.'[80] Wesley was less sure, and his hesitations received the scathing comment of James Hervey that they made 'the heavenly Records...less faithful than the Parish Register'.[81] It was, though, as logical for Wesley to dissent from the notion of final perseverance as it was for the Calvinists to uphold it. Not only was final perseverance difficult to reconcile with man's freedom to choose or reject the salvation held out to him, but, more basically, a denial of the possibility of falling back challenged the urgency of his insistence on the need for continual striving forward—to yet greater heights and in order to preserve what was already achieved.

---

[79] Edward Spencer, a convert of Whitefield, and curate of Bradford-upon-Avon, said as much in the attack on the Minutes that he sent to Shirley. Spencer to Shirley, 20 June 1771 (E4/7(3),CF).   [80] Shirley to LH, 15 Apr. 1772, E4/1(13),CF.
[81] Hervey, *Aspasio Vindicated*, 48.

Which of these conflicting theologies was more attractive to congregations? Predestination (in the words of the Anglican Article XVII, a doctrine 'full of sweet, pleasant, and unspeakable comfort to godly persons') could certainly claim to be. It reminded the believer that his destiny was secure in God's hands, free from the vicissitudes of human chance.[82] For high Calvinists it should certainly not have been a gruelling doctrine, for no demonstrable signs of holiness were required, and there was nothing that human effort could add to a salvation that was already complete. The Calvinist message generally could be presented in highly dramatic and challenging terms. It presented a stark contrast between man's awful state and God's grace in rescuing his elect, and it may for some have had a more immediate appeal than the long road to holiness of the Wesleyan system. John Fletcher confided to Charles Wesley in 1773 that the only Calvinist argument that worried him was the claim that their preaching was more blessed than his: no sinners cried out to him, he said, 'what shall I do to be saved?'[83]

Even so, Calvinists themselves were not always free from anxiety. How did one *know* that one was among the predestined, and not in a state of self-delusion? Moderate Calvinists who believed that growth in grace was a prime evidence of election were often prone to an introspection in which feelings and states of mind could take on excessive importance. Lady Glenorchy's journal, for example, in which she reflected each year upon the state of her soul, is frequently taken up with tortuous self-examination and regret for coldness of heart.[84] Similarly, Thomas Maxfield, in the account of his late wife which he published in 1778, spoke of the restless unease in which she continued to the end of her life in spite of having been convinced of God's promise years before.[85] Lady Huntingdon herself worried over her slow progress on the path to holiness: 'the farther,' she wrote,

---

[82] Outler, *Wesley*, 426.
[83] Fletcher to CW, 24 Aug. 1773, Meth. Arch. (Fletcher), 48.
[84] T. S. Jones, *The Life of Willielma, Viscountess Glenorchy* (London, 1822). Long passages from her journal are transcribed as an appendix to Jones's work.
[85] T. Maxfield, *A Short Account of God's Dealings with Mrs Maxfield* (London, 1778).

'that he [the Lord] carries our souls into the divine life, the slower he appears in hearing.'[86] For Wesleyans, however, the position could also be anxiety-inducing. They too were called to continual striving forward, to yet greater heights and in order to preserve what was already achieved. And there was the added fear of falling away. It was a restless system that permitted no repose: when the congregation at Gainsborough abandoned Wesley's preachers for Lady Huntingdon's in 1772, the reason given was that the Wesleyans had insisted overmuch upon the doctrine of Perfection and the possibility of falling from grace.[87]

The previous discussion has referred in general terms to the beliefs of those on the Calvinistic wing of the Revival. Did the Connexion have a distinctive doctrinal stance? Discovering the details of Lady Huntingdon's own position is not easy: she appears to have made no attempt to write a systematic theology, and her letters, concerned either with the organization of the Connexion or with personal religious experience, provide little basis on which one might be constructed. She certainly worked with some high Calvinists, for example, Romaine in the earlier period, and John Bradford in her last years. Some of her students also were doubtless attracted to higher Calvinism: Fletcher found at Trevecca, for example, that he could not encourage the more slothful among them without being accused of trying to rob them of their assurance of final perseverance.[88] The majority of her clerical helpers, however, were likely to have been moderates, and from the introspection described above, and the worries she expressed at her own slow growth in holiness, it seems likely that that is where her personal loyalties lay.

There is a statement of sorts of Connexional doctrines contained in the Articles of Religion that were compiled for the Connexion's first ordination in 1783. The text of the Articles is reproduced at Appendix C. The Connexion settled on 15 Articles compared to the Anglican 39, but the Connexion's set, like the latter, bears certain hallmarks of the religious controversies and concerns out of which they

---

[86] Quoted in J. Cottingham, *A Funeral Sermon for Lady Huntingdon* (1791).
[87] 'A Brief Historick Record'. [88] Tyerman, *Fletcher*, 184–5.

were born. The Connexion had no need, unlike the Church of England two centuries before, to spell out its specific points of difference with Rome. Nor was it a State Church needing to define the Christian's civic obligations. But these differences apart, the Connexion's articles bear a close similarity to those of the Church of England, particularly in regard to the issues that were at the centre of the controversy. Indeed, a major part, proportionately, of the Connexion's articles are concerned with these aspects. On original sin, predestination, free will, justification, and good works before and after justification, the Connexion articles used passages verbatim from the Anglican Articles.

For the Connexion, like the Church of England, original sin 'is the fault and corruption of the nature of every man', and all deserve God's wrath; it has pleased God to predestine to everlasting life 'those whom he hath chosen in Christ out of mankind'; man himself cannot turn to faith, and without grace cannot please God; we are accounted righteous before God only for the merit of Christ, by faith; good works performed before justification have the nature of sin; but good works which are the fruits of faith and follow after justification, though they cannot put away sin, are pleasing and acceptable to God.[89] The departure from the Anglican text which is most striking, given the doctrinal disputes within the Revival, is in respect of justification, where the Connexion added a statement to the effect that sinful men are accounted as righteous 'by imputing the obedience and satisfaction of Christ unto us'. If this was intended to emphasize the Connexion's place in the ranks of Calvinistic Methodism, however, there was an addition of a different kind, which appeared a gesture in Wesley's direction, as well as a safeguard against antinomianism. For to the Connexion's article on good works (the latter part of which replicated the Anglican Article XII on works after justification) was prefixed the statement that those who are regenerated, 'having...a new spirit created in them, are further sanctified, really and personally...The dominion of sin is destroyed...and they [are] more and more...strengthened...to the practice of

[89] Anglican Articles, 9, 17, 10, 13, and 12.

true holiness.' Separately, the Connexion added a gloss to the Anglican statement that sin remains in the regenerate, to the effect that this is 'without dominion'. The message seems to be that the Connexion's articles positioned it clearly within the Calvinist camp, while at the same time signalling recognition of the need for holiness and for an actual break in the hold of sin over the believer, which acknowledged common ground with the Wesleyans.

THE CALVINISTIC CONTROVERSY OF 1770

It was the events of 1770 that made the issues just discussed the centre, once again, of controversy and invective. They came at the moment when the Connexion was beginning its phase of rapid expansion, and thus set the tone of the Connexion (in its own eyes, and in the eyes of the wider religious world) at a crucial point in its development. At first, however, there was little indication that the year would not follow the recent pattern. Shirley, it is true, annoyed Wesley in January, apparently by preaching against Perfection in the Wesleyan preaching house in Bristol, but it was only a 'hint' of his displeasure that Wesley asked to be conveyed to Shirley and there is no evidence of any correspondence between them on the subject.[90] April and May saw Wesley in Scotland, making a brief visit to Edinburgh on his way north and coming back there on his return. Three years earlier, Joseph Townsend had, as has been seen, been the cause of division in Edinburgh, and the first of Wesley's visits may have been for the specific purpose of dealing with the effects of doctrinal dispute. He spoke with Lady Glenorchy during the visit, but though he was able to convince her of his basic orthodoxy,[91] he himself seemed uneasy about the situation; his Journal makes no reference to his meeting with her, but laments in general terms 'that the children of God should so

---

[90] JW to J. Whitehead, 27 Jan. 1770, Wesley, *Letters*, v. 179.
[91] Jones, *Lady Glenorchy*, 147. In her journal she recorded that 'I believe him to be sound in all essential doctrines.'

zealously do the devil's work!'[92] On Wesley's return to Edinburgh, he and Dr Webster, the Calvinistic minister of the Tolbooth church, debated their doctrines in Lady Glenorchy's presence. Lady Glenorchy was unaffected but continued to attend Wesley's ministry while he remained in Edinburgh, wishing, at the same time, that 'he preached more of Christ and less of himself'.[93]

It was against this background that the 27th conference of Wesleyan Methodism met in London from 7 to 10 August, and issued Minutes that were to bring the whole doctrinal issue into the open. The Minutes surveyed the steps that might be taken to give fresh impetus to the Revival, and to spur Methodists in their zeal. In the context of doctrine, they were urged to work 'for as well as from life': 'We have received it as a maxim that "a man is to do nothing in order to justification". Nothing can be more false. Whoever desires to find favour with God should "cease from evil, and learn to do well".... And if this is not in order to find favour, what does he do them for?' This section of the Minutes concluded: 'Is not this salvation by works? Not by the merit of works, but by works as a condition.'

In talking in these terms Wesley was reverting closer to his High Church roots than he had done before. The Minutes did not pass unchallenged. Lady Huntingdon reacted strongly to them and there is even a story of her burning the copy sent her by Shirley.[94] Certainly she had seen them within about a week of the close of the conference. Wesley was due to accompany her to Trevecca for the college's anniversary on the 24th, but she apparently informed him that he was banned from her pulpits till he had recanted the doctrines of the Minutes.[95] At this stage, the dispute was

---

[92] JW's Journal for 16 Apr. 1770, *Works*, xxii. 225.

[93] Jones, *Lady Glenorchy*, 156.

[94] D. Bogue and J. Bennett, *History of the Dissenters from 1688 to 1808* (London, 1808–12), iv. 235; Gunter, *Limits of 'Love Divine'*, 252. Owen Chadwick describes how 'veering away from the old, sharp, language of *sola fide* became, in some measure, characteristic of high Anglican thought in the later seventeenth century' (*The Mind of the Oxford Movement* (London, 1963), 21). It may be giving the Connexion too much importance to suggest, as Dr Schlenther does, that publication of the Minutes 'was aimed directly at the Countess's theology' (Schlenther, 106).

[95] JW to Joseph Benson, 21 Jan. 1771, Wesley, *Letters*, v. 218; Seymour, ii. 106–7.

still an essentially personal one between him and the Countess, a rejection by her of his offensive personal doctrines rather than a general massing of the outraged forces of Calvinism.

It is not fully clear what happened in the following months to turn this rupture into a major breach, but there are hints from which a general picture can be built up. It is evident that after this demonstration of Wesley's doctrinal infidelity, Lady Huntingdon began to suspect him of disloyalty in other fields and of trying to trespass upon her work. In particular, she believed that the plan for him to attend the college anniversary had been a device to gain influence with the students. Writing from the college to Charles Wesley some time in September, Fletcher lamented 'la distance que je vois entre Lady Huntingdon et lui [John]' and wrote of his attempt to remove that prejudice by telling her that it was he and the students who had invited Wesley to visit them.[96] Even at this early stage local rivalries were also playing a part in controversy. There is evidence in Fletcher's letter of the conflict that was already developing between Wesley's preachers in Brecon and the students supplying the Countess's chapel in the town.[97] The impression that emerges from Fletcher's comments is that although doctrine was important to Lady Huntingdon—'Perfection,' he wrote... 'lui parait un *monstre* aussi terrible que dangereux'— the jealousy and suspicion that coloured much of her outlook in the latter part of her life were also at work. Already, Fletcher warned, she was listening to reports that Charles was using the chapel at Bath for his own ends.[98] This attitude

---

[96] Fletcher to CW, Sept. 1770, Meth. Arch. (Fletcher), 34. JW stressed that it had not been his own idea to visit the College—'It was of their own mere motion that the students...desired me to come and spend a little time with them. I had no thought or desire to do so...' (JW to Benson, 21 Jan. 1771, Wesley, *Letters*, v. 217). That he still needed to argue the point at this stage is a sign of the importance it had assumed in his relations with LH.

[97] Fletcher seems to have regarded the Brecon divisions as one of the significant stages in the developing rift between JW and LH (Tyerman, *Fletcher*, 180). There is evidence of continuing rivalry in Brecon, and the challenge of the Wesleyans was put to LH on more than one occasion, as a reason for sending her most skilful preachers to the chapel (see William Pitt to LH, 8 Oct. 1770; John Cave to LH, 20 Oct. 1772; Brecon Society to LH, 1 May 1774, F1/106, 195 and 1689,CF).

[98] Fletcher to CW, Sept. 1770, Meth. Arch. (Fletcher), 34.

seems early to have rubbed off on to some of the students. At the end of October Glazebrook warned that there were Wesleyans 'playing about within 3 or 4 miles' of Bridgwater who would make an entry into the town if the Connexion withdrew.[99] As noted,[100] it was not until he was at Tunbridge Wells in July that Glazebrook had been persuaded to abandon his belief in Perfection and if, as is likely, he had returned to Trevecca for the anniversary, it may have been that the personal influence of Lady Huntingdon had engendered in him—and in others—the hostility to Wesley that these remarks reveal.

Wesley's attitude at this time was equivocal. On 5 October, in a letter to Joseph Benson at college, he cautioned him to 'all possible tenderness and respect' in his dealings with Lady Huntingdon and lamented that a woman of 'a thousand valuable and amiable qualities' should be so groundlessly fearful for her authority.[101] Yet Wesley did not follow his own counsels of peace, and within a week had written to Lady Huntingdon a letter of stern personal criticism that was, at that moment, to have as decisive an effect as the Minutes themselves. No text of the letter has survived, but it is evident that Wesley made it a general indictment of her character failings. Howel Harris was the first to comment upon it, recording in his Diary for 12 October that it was: 'very bitter charg^g her wth Self and having fall^n to Pride etc. from ye Ld condeming [sic] her Hymn Book etc because she had not asked him to open her chappel and for her—[? practice] in call^g her chappels etc and despis^g her helpers.'[102]

On 19 October Walter Shirley wrote that though he knew Wesley's pride and self-sufficiency, he was surprised that it should have carried him to such lengths.[103] Even Wesley's friends doubted his wisdom in writing in such terms. Charles Wesley promised Lady Huntingdon that he would raise the matter with his brother[104] and Fletcher, writing after his resignation from the college in the spring of the following year,

---

[99] Glazebrook to LH, 29 Oct. 1770, F1/104,CF.   [100] Above p.240.
[101] JW to Benson, 5 Oct. 1770, Wesley, *Letters*, v. 202.
[102] Harris's Diary for 12 Oct. 1770.
[103] Shirley to LH, 19 Oct. 1770, F1/1565,CF.   [104] Seymour, ii. 237 n.

spoke of an 'unkind letter—written by one and received by the other as highly insulting'.[105] Wesley claimed to see the matter in a very different light, regarding his reproof as part of his duty as a Christian minister that he had put off doing for many years but which he 'did not dare to delay any longer, lest death should call one of us hence'.[106] Even if this were true, this was hardly the time to have raised it: a more tactful man would not have chosen this moment to tell her that her 'doggerel hymns' were 'equally an insult upon poetry and common sense'. Either this was a deliberate challenge to her authority or Wesley was showing a remarkable vanity in believing that so bald an assumption of his own right to criticize could produce anything but a vigorous reaction on the part of Lady Huntingdon.

It was into this setting that the news of Whitefield's death, which reached England early in November, brought a momentary appearance of unity. Whitefield had asked that Wesley should preach his funeral sermon and on 18 November, after apparently devoting considerable time to the sermon's preparation, he preached it to packed congregations at both the Tottenham Court chapel and the Tabernacle.[107] To coincide with this, Lady Huntingdon had arranged for Venn to preach in the chapel at Bath, and a fortnight later Wesley was invited to deliver his sermon again, this time by the trustees of the Tabernacle in Greenwich.[108] Yet it would have taken more than a momentary sense of common loss to heal the breach that was now opening, especially since Whitefield's death had removed an important force for unity. It did not help that Wesley's focus in his sermon on the doctrines on which he and Whitefield had agreed, was seen by some Calvinists as appearing to gloss over the latter's true beliefs.[109] On 27 November, Wesley wrote that he could not advise his followers to attend

---

[105] Tyerman, *Fletcher*, 180–6.
[106] JW to Benson, 30 Nov. 1770, Wesley, *Letters*, v. 211. A month later Wesley was still claiming that in this affair he had simply spoken 'the truth in love' (JW to Benson, 28 Dec. 1770, ibid. 215).
[107] JW's Journal for 10 Nov. 1770, *Works*, xxii. 259.
[108] Seymour, ii. 44 n; JW's Journal for 10 and 23 Nov. 1770, *Works*, xxii. 259.
[109] Rack, *Wesley*, 455.

Shirley's preaching, while on the following day Lady Huntingdon told Charles of her fear of being a cause of division between him and John and of her determination that John should not rob her of God's grace.[110]

Meanwhile, there were further signs of the practical effects of doctrinal conflict, with divisions among evangelicals at Hay-on-Wye. What made this breach particularly significant was the fact that a prominent leader of the Hay Methodists, Walter Churchey, was a friend and correspondent of John Wesley, even though the congregation was frequently served by students from Trevecca. In part, conflict at Hay seems to have been about the running and control of the society,[111] but doctrine also played a role, and by the start of December, the congregation had divided into Calvinist and Arminian factions. The situation was not helped by the differing doctrinal positions of two of the students who supplied them, Cosson and Glazebrook. In spite of the latter's expressed opposition to Wesleyans while in Somerset, Lady Huntingdon still seems to have suspected him of allying with the Arminian wing at Hay. He in turn claimed that it was Cosson who was adding to the division by the specifically Calvinist content of his addresses.[112] This difference of opinion between the students may shed some light on the 'unhappy event' at college to which a number of veiled references were made at this time.[113] More than a year had passed since Fletcher had spoken of the distinction between Calvinists and Arminians at college and though Glazebrook could still declare himself to be neither,[114] most of the students must by now have made up their minds where they stood on these issues. If the 'witch-hunt' directed by students against the moderate Howel Harris in early December was doctrinal,[115] this suggests that some of the student body had by then arrived at an extreme Calvinistic position.

[110] JW to Mary Bishop, 27 Nov. 1770, Wesley, *Letters*, v. 209; LH to CW, 28 Nov. 1770, Meth. Arch. (LH), 79.
[111] Glazebrook to Mr Thomas, 20 Dec. 1770, F1/1525,CF; JW to Mr Churchey, 29 Nov. 1770, Wesley, *Letters*, v. 210.
[112] Glazebrook to LH, 5 Dec. 1770, F1/1521,CF.
[113] For example, Glazebrook to LH, 13 Dec. and Mead to LH, 22 Dec. 1770, F1/114–15,CF.   [114] Glazebrook to LH, 5 Dec. 1770, F1/1521,CF.
[115] *Journal of the Calvinistic Methodist Historical Society*, xii, 45.

Joseph Benson's dismissal from the Trevecca mastership at the beginning of January 1771 ensured that the controversy continued to centre upon the college. Benson's support for the Minutes since the early autumn[116] and his friendship and correspondence with Wesley, cannot have made his position at college an easy one. That he survived so long is an indication that the protagonists in the conflict were not yet fully aware of the seriousness of the present rift. Matters between Benson and the Countess came to a head during December, however, when she appears to have called upon him to declare his position on the issue of free will and the offer of salvation to all men. His answer did not satisfy and in Fletcher's terse words to Lady Huntingdon, 'a master is discarded for believing that Christ died for all.'[117] The dismissal showed how the situation was deteriorating for, with the exception of John Wesley's exclusion from the Countess's pulpits, the controversy had not previously prevented co-operation between those of differing views. Fletcher was shocked at the decision and saw it as evidence of a new spirit at work in the college. On the 10th he wrote of the violence of Lady Huntingdon's reaction to Wesley,[118] and on the 19th he sought information from Benson 'whereby I may show that false reports, groundless suspicions, party spirit against Mr. Wesley, arbitrary proceedings, and unscriptural impulses, hold the reins and manage affairs in the College'.[119] Clearly he was already contemplating a publication on the dispute.

At the start of the year there was fresh evidence of trouble brewing in Scotland. Despite the tensions revealed back in 1767, a measure of contact between the parties had been maintained, and Lady Glenorchy still allowed Wesley's preachers one evening a week at the new chapel she opened in March 1770. She could hardly have been unaware of the controversy developing in England, but it appears that Lady Huntingdon made a determined effort in December 1770 to

---

[116] JW to Benson, 5 Oct. 1770, Wesley, *Letters*, v. 202.
[117] Fletcher to LH, 1 Jan. 1771, Seymour, ii. 238.
[118] Letter quoted in J. E. Hull, 'Lady Huntingdon and John Wesley', Ph.D. thesis (Edinburgh, 1959). [119] Tyerman, *Fletcher*, 171–7.

brief her on the position and to enlist her support. Replying on 10 January, Lady Glenorchy undertook to bear her testimony against the Minutes, adding that although she still respected Wesley, she could no longer countenance his preachers. It was evidently Lady Huntingdon's intervention at this critical time that precipitated the final break between Lady Glenorchy and the Wesleyans.[120]

Although Lady Huntingdon remained at Trevecca till late in March 1771, there were signs of continuing friction between her and Wesley. On 8 March, for example, he wrote to a correspondent in Bath that if 'that well-meaning (though not always well-judging) woman... continues to show scraps of my letters, I shall be obliged to give you a copy of the whole.'[121] What is difficult to determine at this stage is how far Lady Huntingdon was alone in recognizing the implications of the Wesleyan Minutes. Certainly it was some time before the Calvinist mouthpiece, the *Gospel Magazine*, got round to a condemnation of the Minutes. In January 1771, it carried a respectful attack on Wesley by Romaine, but this was concerned solely with the sermon on Whitefield and made no reference to the Minutes. In March, the *Magazine* was much more violent, this time in a denunciation of Sellon's *Defence of God's Sovereignty*, but it was not until May, under the title of *Popery Unmasked*, that it printed the Minutes. Even then a comment upon them had to wait until the following month. This could simply reflect a publishing backlog, but it seems likely that space would have been found for a piece on the Minutes if their significance had really been recognized.

The most significant developments in the early part of 1771, however, surrounded John Fletcher's return to college on 20 February. Even before the events at Brecon and Hay he had been worried by the admission to college of pupils whom he regarded as without gifts or grace, and at the 'hasty

---

[120] Lady Glenorchy to LH, 10 Jan. 1771, Seymour, ii. 111; D. P. Thomson, *Lady Glenorchy and her Churches* (Crieff, 1967), 27. Lady Glenorchy's decision to end the arrangement with Wesley was thus taken *before* Richard de Courcy's arrival to preach for her in Edinburgh the following month, although it was de Courcy who was popularly blamed for the breach.

[121] JW to Mary Bishop, 8 Mar. 1771, Wesley, *Letters*, v. 227.

admitting of subjects that did not appear to me proper'. These factors, along with Benson's dismissal, implanted in him 'a disgust to the College' even before he got back.[122] Although he attempted to keep an open mind on his return, he felt heaviness in his preaching. He also sensed a reserve on the part of the students, which he attributed to the influence of Walter Shirley, who had so alerted them to the errors of Perfection that any attempt by Fletcher at spiritual encouragement was seen as undermining their own assurance of salvation.

Fletcher was now out of place in the college and within a week of his return he made it known that he would resign the presidency once a new master had been found. Thus might matters have continued had not, according to Fletcher, Lady Huntingdon been sent a fresh copy of the offending Minutes. If this means that she had previously been without a copy,[123] it gives weight to the story of her burning her original copy and may show why it took so long for the Countess to issue any direct challenge to Wesley. At the end of May Wesley referred to the point of contention between him and the Countess being no longer his offending letter, but the resolution of the conference.[124] It was, moreover, quite in keeping with Lady Huntingdon's volatile character that the sudden arrival of the half-remembered document should have produced a strong if sorrowful reaction that convinced her that none who shared its sentiments should continue members of the college.[125] Each student was called upon, therefore, to state freely his attitude to the Minutes, the Countess subsequently informing Fletcher that anyone 'who did not *absolutely* disavow and renounce' them would be turned out. Whether she said as much to the students is uncertain, though it is reasonable to suppose—especially as there is no evidence of anyone actually being expelled—that they were under no illusion as to the

---

[122] Tyerman, *Fletcher*, 177–9.
[123] On 9 February, Thomas Davies spoke of his failure to obtain a copy. It may have been that he was trying to get one for her, rather than for himself (Davies to LH, 9 Feb 1771, F1/119,CF).
[124] JW to Mary Bishop, 27 May 1771, Wesley, *Letters*, v. 252.
[125] Tyerman, *Fletcher*, 177–9.

displeasure which approval of the Minutes would occasion. Though not required to participate in this exercise, Fletcher felt bound to inform her that he could not give the absolute denunciation of the Minutes that she was demanding from the students—especially now, when the college, once based upon the principle of resistance to both antinomians and legalists, seemed more likely to fall prey to the former than to the latter. Accordingly he sent her on 7 March his detailed comments on the Minutes. This acknowledged that the Minutes might appear at first sight to assert salvation by works—and that there were elements in them which might have been more judiciously expressed—but then proceeded, point by point, to defend each of the key points in the Minutes, arguing that nothing in them was incompatible with salvation by faith. When the Minutes talked of works as a condition of salvation, for example, this meant no more than that they were the evidence or fruit of faith. The letter ended with his resignation.[126]

Fletcher remained at Trevecca for another ten days, and had the opportunity of further conversation with Lady Huntingdon. In view of the new form the college was taking, he advised her to entrust it to a moderate Calvinist like Richard Hill. He also got her to agree to write to Wesley for an explanation of his views. On his return to Madeley, he wrote to Wesley himself, to urge a generous answer to this and one that would 'stop the mouth of our friend' by making much of man's helplessness and dependence on the Spirit'.[127] There is no evidence that she wrote, however, and it is possible that with Fletcher's moderating influence removed she repented her agreement to make an approach of this kind.[128]

---

[126] Fletcher to LH, 7 Mar. 1771, E4/7(1),CF. Even when events had reached this stage, Fletcher was still performing the duties of his presidency, and in the covering note that accompanied this letter, he spoke of his efforts to hurry the students into the completion of their own comments on the Minutes (E4/7(2),CF). Fletcher asked that his letter should be returned to him once LH had read it, so that it could be shown to the students, but she had 'thought it too bad to be laid before the students' and had refused to return it (Fletcher to JW, 24 June 1771, Meth. Arch. (Fletcher), 36). [127] Tyerman, *Fletcher*, 177–9.
[128] Fletcher's letter to Wesley of 24 June 1771 clearly implies that LH changed her mind after his departure (Tyerman, *Fletcher*, 177–9).

Fletcher's departure from Trevecca was followed by a temporary lull in the controversy, but (according to Walter Shirley) it was the publication of the Wesleyan Minutes in the *Gospel Magazine* for May 1771 that finally convinced the Countess that a public dissociation from their tenets was necessary. The form that this should take was uncertain, however, and Lady Huntingdon called a meeting in Bath with Shirley and three prominent Calvinist laymen, Richard Hill, Thomas Powys from Shropshire, and James Ireland from Brislington, near Bristol. The meeting decided that all who disagreed with the Minutes should be called upon to attend in a body at the next Wesleyan conference to urge a retraction. It was agreed that all likely sympathizers should be sent a circular letter, canvassing their support for the planned action, and annexing both the text of the Minutes and a declaration repudiating them as 'repugnant to Scripture and the whole plan of man's salvation'.[129] It is not clear who originated the proposed deputation. Richard Hill later claimed to have been doubtful of the wisdom and propriety of such a course, and he alleged that he had not had the chance to approve the final version of the circular, although his name was included among the signatories.[130] Possibly the idea of the deputation had already been determined upon by Shirley and Lady Huntingdon in advance of the meeting, although Shirley claimed the opposite.[131]

Hill's attempt to dissociate himself from the circular may partly have been due to the mixed response it occasioned among its recipients. No list has been preserved of who these were, though they evidently extended to Scotland and included friendly Dissenters as well as members of the Established Church.[132] Among some of the Countess's own

---

[129] Seymour, ii. 239–40 n.

[130] Hill to Shirley, 4 and 10 Jan. 1772; Shirley's answer, 18 Jan. 1772; Shirley to Powys, 2 Jan. 1772; Powys to Shirley, 6 Jan. 1772, F1/1385–9,CF. Shirley, for his part, claimed that he and LH had simply followed the lead provided by Hill, Ireland, and Powys.   [131] Shirley to Powys, 2 Jan. 1772, F1/1388,CF.

[132] Walter Shirley, *A Narrative of the Principal Circumstances relative to The Reverend Mr Wesley's late Conference held in Bristol, August the 6th 1771, at which the Reverend Mr Shirley, and Others, his Friends, were Present* (Bath, 1771). Letters of support for LH's stand have been preserved from the Revd Charles Nisbet of Montrose and the Revd John Brown of Haddington (Nisbet to LH, 26 July 1771, G2/3,CF (copy of

preachers the circular seems to have had the desired effect of stiffening their attitude to the Minutes. Glascott, for example, who had written at the beginning of June of the need for charity towards the 'many good and eminent persons' with whom they differed doctrinally, wrote at the end of the month to encourage Lady Huntingdon against the 'unscriptural and pernicious errors' of the Minutes and the 'evasive cunning and sophistry of the Author'.[133] Other reactions were more mixed. Some, like the Revd Edward Spencer, the evangelical curate of Bradford in Wiltshire, agreed that the Minutes could be dangerous, but doubted the wisdom of drawing attention to them by a public protest.[134]

Others reacted more strongly and were shocked at the impropriety of the proposed action and the dictatorial tone in which it was advocated, a response which indicated the bonds that must still have been felt between those on each side of the Revival. The trustees of Whitefield's London chapels, for example, were among those who refused to participate.[135] William Romaine expressed an interest in seeing the protest,[136] but Augustus Toplady, whose opposition to Wesley was hardly in any doubt, was one who declined, and Shirley appears to have written personally to urge him to be present. It is difficult to gauge whether the reasons Toplady gave for not doing so (an expected visitor and an impending episcopal visitation) were the real cause of his absence, though his final suggestion—that a reference to the Minutes in a new pamphlet he was writing against Sellon might prove more effective than his presence in Bristol—implies at least some reservations about the procedure being proposed.[137]

---

original MS in the Library of Dickinson College, Carlisle, Pa.); National Library of Scotland MSS, vol. 1707, f. 6). The theological divisions in Scotland were as strong as in England. In July 1771, the mother of Lady Anne Erskine wrote of the 'quagmire' that now existed between 'the established Church who plump for the tenets of Mr Wesley, and those who oppose them' (Lady Buchan to LH, 24 July 1771, F1/1541,CF).

[133] Glascott to LH, 3 and 28 June 1771, F1/125 and 1535,CF.
[134] Edward Spencer to Shirley, 20 June 1771, E4/7(3),CF.
[135] Seymour, ii. 241.   [136] Glascott to LH, 23 July 1771, F1/1539,CF.
[137] Toplady to Shirley, 26 July 1771, F1/1572,CF. Toplady's letter shows that his pamphleteering was part of his on-going opposition to Arminianism, and was not occasioned by the Minutes. Elsewhere, Toplady suggested that he, Romaine and

Reaction to the circular among Wesley's confidants was naturally more marked and one of its most significant effects was to bring an end to the continuing friendship between the Countess and Charles Wesley. She had written personally to him with a copy of the circular but he reacted strongly against what he saw as an attempt to inveigle him away from John, angrily endorsing her letter 'Lady Huntingdon's LAST UNANSWERED BY JOHN WESLEY'S BROTHER'. Thereafter, cordiality between them ceased even though Charles was far from identifying himself entirely with his brother's views. It was reported later in that year that he still disapproved of the meaning that the Minutes appeared to convey.[138]

Fletcher, too, was further alienated from the Countess by the circular. After his return from Wales, she had accused him of being duped by Wesley when he sent her a passage on free grace from one of Wesley's letters; now he resented implications in the circular that only its supporters could be counted as 'real Protestants' and he wrote to Wesley on 24 June with a pledge of his support.[139]

That support was first expressed in the form of a vindication of the Minutes and it was to this that Fletcher devoted his energies during July. Wesley also felt that a defence of the Minutes would be of value and prepared a short explanatory gloss upon them, which he sent for printing on 3 August.[140] Lady Huntingdon, meanwhile, had had second thoughts about marching on his conference. Accordingly, Shirley wrote to Wesley on 2 August, to acknowledge the hastiness of the circular, to assure him that no assertion of authority had been implied by it, and to hope that as he had recanted the

---

others had stayed away in order to avoid contact with JW and his preachers (Toplady to William Linnell, n.d., quoted in A. Coppedge, 'John Wesley and the Doctrine of Predestination', Ph.D. thesis (Cambridge, 1976), 240n. Toplady's stance seems unduly purist, given the significance of the issue, and it suggests that they actually believed nothing could come of the initiative.

[138] T. Jackson, *The Life of the Revd Charles Wesley, MA* (London, 1841), ii. 255; R. Chapman to LH, 25 Nov. 1771, F1/1554,CF.

[139] Fletcher to JW, 24 June 1771, Meth. Arch. (Fletcher), 36.

[140] JW to 'Several Preachers and Friends,' 10 July 1771; JW to Mary Bishop, 20 July 1771; JW to CW, 3 Aug. 1771, Wesley, *Letters*, v. 262–5, 269, 270. The defence bears the date of 10 July.

letter, so Wesley would recant the Minutes.[141] Shirley was invited to attend the conference on 8 August and this he did with a party consisting of Glascott, Owen, Winter, Lloyd, Ireland, and two students from Trevecca. Shirley read to the conference his own letter and one that Lady Huntingdon had written to Wesley on the 5th. He then proceeded to discuss with Wesley whether the Minutes were consistent with justification by faith, and to settle the matter produced a draft Declaration which, after some minor changes, was signed by Wesley and the majority of his preachers.[142] This affirmed Fletcher's interpretation of the Minutes to Lady Huntingdon. It admitted that they were 'not sufficiently guarded' and went on to assert that 'though no-one is a real Christian believer (and consequently cannot be saved) who doth not good works...yet our Works have no part in our meriting, or purchasing, our Salvation from first to last, either in whole or in Part.' This formula satisfied all but Thomas Olivers. Lest the Declaration be thought to cast doubt on Wesley's consistency, Shirley was asked to acknowledge that he had been mistaken in his interpretations of the Minutes. This he did in a letter a few days later, though with some reluctance for, as he pointedly remarked in a subsequently published account of these events, nothing but the Declaration would have persuaded him that the Minutes were not about justification by works.[143]

There is some evidence that the conference was followed with interest in the Connexion at large and was regarded, if not as a triumph, then at least as an amicable and satisfactory settlement of the issue.[144] Hopes of peace were soon dispelled, however, by Wesley's publication of a defence of the Minutes that Fletcher had prepared the previous month. The theme of Fletcher's *First Check to Antinomianism*[145] as his vindication of the Minutes was called, was that the Minutes

---

[141] Shirley, *A Narrative*.
[142] JW's Journal for 6 Aug. 1771, *Works*, xxii. 285–6.
[143] Shirley, *A Narrative*.
[144] H. Godde to LH, 1 Aug. 1771; Mrs Godde to LH, 13 Aug. and 6 Sept. 1771, F1/1542, 1543, 1548,CF.
[145] J. Fletcher, *A First Check to Antinomianism, or a Vindication of the Revd Mr. Wesley's Minutes* (1771).

were wholly in accordance with belief in the total helplessness of man, and in man's sole dependence on Christ for salvation. Faith was, however, necessarily productive of love and obedience, so that works could indeed be said to be a condition of salvation in so far as they were the fruit and evidence of that faith. This was the same message as in Fletcher's letter to Lady Huntingdon prior to his resignation from Trevecca, but the appearance of the work at this stage looked like a deliberate attempt to keep the controversy alive.[146] In one sense, Wesley was quite justified in publishing: the Declaration he had just signed was not a recantation of the Minutes but a denial that they implied justification by works, and if they were not erroneous, then it was perfectly logical to defend them. Nevertheless, the speed with which the decision to publish was taken betrayed an insensitivity to the delicacy of the situation comparable to Wesley's authoritarian letter to the Countess the previous October. Wesley followed the publication by writing to Lady Huntingdon on 14 August, affirming again his belief in justification by faith and protesting that the Minutes (and Fletcher's defence of them) were in no way at odds with this belief. Such a letter might have been effective a year before, but at this stage in the controversy, so soon after both sides had retreated from extreme positions in the interests of peace, it was a conciliatory spirit that was required of Wesley, not the citing of God's blessing on his work as a sign that he was not the heretic she claimed.[147] Lady Huntingdon does not appear to have sent any reply but told Shirley that she could in no way explain the letter except by 'attacking his integrity or suspecting that his judgement is impaired'.[148]

Fletcher was less happy at the decision to publish, and wrote at once to James Ireland to request his help in preventing the sale of the *First Check*.[149] This intervention had no effect. The fact that Wesley had entrusted the operation to Thomas Olivers, one of the staunchest of his supporters, was a sign of the importance he attached to publication, for whatever he may have admitted about the phraseology of the

---

[146] Shirley, *A Narrative*.
[147] JW to LH, 14 Aug. 1771, Wesley, *Letters*, v. 274–5.
[148] Seymour, ii. 244.
[149] Shirley, *A Narrative*.

Minutes, he continued to believe that they were a bastion against the contagion of antinomianism.[150]

The publication of Fletcher's *Check* meant inevitably that the issues would not be allowed to rest. Wesley's followers evidently regarded the conference as a triumph for him and it was reported in September that some were even speculating that Lady Huntingdon would soon be forced to close her chapels.[151] As Wesley had published a defence of his Minutes, it followed that the Countess's followers should similarly attempt to justify the action that they had taken. Accordingly in September Shirley prepared a *Narrative* of the Wesleyan conference and of the events that had led up to it. Its tone was moderate, and as a mark of his good intentions he wrote to Fletcher, early in the month, to advise him of what was proposed. Fletcher's reply on 21 September was similarly conciliatory, even suggesting that *Narrative* be printed the same size as his own work so that he could send copies to those who had bought copies of the latter.[152] Though Shirley did not reply to this offer, he does appear to have been sincere in his desire to avoid rancour, and he expressed regret to Lady Huntingdon when the *Gospel Magazine* published Wesley's Declaration, lest it be thought that this had been inspired by him.[153]

Nevertheless, his *Narrative* made clear that the Minutes remained suspect in his eyes. His reference to Wesley's Declaration effectively accused Wesley of inconsistency or worse, and it did not endear him to Wesley's followers when he described the Minutes as appearing as 'an attack upon the foundation of our hope'.[154] Yet Lady Huntingdon for one seems to have hoped that the publication of the *Narrative* would now see the end of her involvement in dispute. Shirley

---

[150] JW to Mary Bishop, 1 Sept. 1771, Wesley, *Letters*, v. 276. Fletcher's letter to Shirley of 11 Sept. confirms the statement in Seymour, ii, 243 that it was Olivers who was given the task (Tyerman, *Fletcher*, 195).

[151] John Cosson to LH, 14 Sept. 1771, F1/134,CF. Wesleyans may not have been alone in seeing the Conference as a triumph for their leader: Henry Peckwell, writing from Scotland in December, commented that what had actually been achieved at Bristol had fallen far short of the expectations of Calvinists in that country (Peckwell to LH, 21 Dec. 1771, F1/156,CF).

[152] Fletcher to CW, 21 Sept. 1771, Meth. Arch. (Fletcher), 37.

[153] Shirley to LH, n.d., F1/1569,CF.   [154] Seymour, ii. 244.

referred in the course of it to her decision to leave off the controversy and in December spoke of her conviction that 'the Lord hath graciously suggested to Yr Ladyship to sit still' even if others were continuing the battle.[155] The fiery temperament which had done so much to keep the controversy alive earlier in the year seemed temporarily to have subsided. In October she wrote to the society at Hay of the need to avoid dispute, presenting herself, like Shirley, as one forced into taking a stand only when the very foundations of faith were challenged.[156] Far from remaining the focus of the Calvinist reaction, she had sufficiently mellowed in her attitude to Arminians in general—as opposed to the individuals from whom she was alienated on personal grounds—for Shirley to find it necessary, as late as February 1772, to urge the abandonment of what he termed her 'catholic' plan for Trevecca; she needed to decide, once and for all, whether it was an Arminian or a Calvinist institution that she wanted.[157]

But the hostile reaction to the Minutes, which the Countess had done so much to encourage, had by now gained a momentum of its own and would not be halted. It was reported to Lady Huntingdon in November that no less a person than Mrs Romaine had remarked upon the esteem which the *Narrative* had brought to Shirley in the eyes of all Calvinists.[158] Tarter productions were to follow from other pens. Towards the end of the year, for example, Richard Hill published an account of the *Conversation* which he and Madan had had in July with the head of a Paris house of English Benedictines, Father Walsh.[159] In the course of their discussion they had shown the priest the Wesleyan Minutes. To their evident satisfaction they had got him to agree that

---

[155] Shirley to LH, 19 Dec. 1771, F1/1556,CF.
[156] LH to Mrs Ingram, 5 Oct. 1771, F1/1551,CF.
[157] Shirley to LH, 17 Feb. 1772, E4/1(8),CF.
[158] R. Chapman to LH, 25 Nov. 1771, F1/1554,CF.
[159] *A Conversation between Richard Hill, Martin Madan and Father Walsh, Superior of a Convent of English Benedictine Monks at Paris, Held There on July 13, 1771, in the Presence of Thomas Powys and others.* The exact date on which the pamphlet appeared is not clear: Fletcher evidently knew of its existence in September, though it was not until December that Shirley spoke of the advertisement for the 'Conversation with the Prior of the Convent' (Shirley to LH, 19 Dec. 1771, F1/1556,CF).

these set too much store on man's righteousness and too little on Christ. This was a sign, said Hill, that the principles of the Minutes were 'too rotten even for a Papist to rest upon'. The pamphlet continued with jibes at Wesley's inconsistency, his views on tea-drinking and (with particular cruelty) his matrimonial problems, and then ended with what purported to be a verse paraphrase of the August Declaration: 'Be it known from henceforth, to each friend, and each brother, Whene'er we *say* one thing, we *mean* quite another.'[160]

Although Lady Huntingdon had withdrawn, for the moment, from active involvement in controversy, the closing months of 1771 witnessed a progressive deterioration in her relations with John Fletcher. In part this was inevitable since it was Fletcher whose writings continued for the moment to form the spearhead of the Wesleyan reply to Calvinist attacks. In December he furnished John Wesley with a draft reply to the personal attacks contained in the *Conversation*,[161] and published his *Second Check to Antinomianism*. In the *Second Check*, Fletcher defended belief in a second judgement by works: that is, that the extent of the believer's heavenly reward depended upon his good works.[162] Without that belief, Fletcher argued, there was no defence against antinomianism. The *Second Check* was moderate in tone and even contained an invitation to Shirley to preach for him at Madeley. But it was specifically described as correcting errors in the *Narrative*, and Shirley resented what he took to be its insinuation that all who opposed Wesley encouraged antinomianism in some fashion.[163]

Fletcher's relations with Lady Huntingdon were not improved by a quite separate incident that autumn when he attempted to obtain a neighbouring curacy for one of her students. When a student wrote to Fletcher asking to become his curate, it was reasonable to believe that this accorded with Lady Huntingdon's wishes, especially as the application

---

[160] LH evidently took the *Conversation* seriously enough to inform John Thornton that 'an old monk in France had declared these minutes to be the Pelagian heresy' (Seymour, ii. 242 n). [161] Meth. Arch. (Fletcher), 40.
[162] Curiously, Wesley had earlier condemned such a view (Rack, *Wesley*, 460).
[163] Shirley to LH, 9 Jan. 1772, F1/1576,CF.

purported to come with Lady Huntingdon's support. Fletcher had no need of an assistant for himself but persuaded a neighbour to provide a title after he himself had contributed a part of the salary. Instead, however, of Lady Huntingdon repaying him, as he had been led to believe she would, she 'with her usual Lordliness' (as Fletcher said) saw fit to regard his action 'as treachery, a decoying or engrossing of her students'.[164] Fletcher's is the only account of this incident to have survived and it may have been that Lady Huntingdon had no knowledge of undertakings being made in her name. Nevertheless, the incident demonstrated how frayed relations had become and how easily theological and personal differences could become merged.

It is an indication of Shirley's moderation that his only reply to Fletcher's *Second Check* was a new edition of the *Narrative*.[165] He himself does not appear to have considered engaging in controversy of a specifically theological kind, and when Richard Hill published a reply to Fletcher, Shirley regretted that, though politely written, Hill's work contained elements of high Calvinism that some would find offensive.[166] No one within the Connexion itself was prepared to take a lead in the continuing controversy. The reissuing of the *Narrative* proved to be the Connexion's final contribution and its role thereafter was a passive one. It could not fail to be affected by the bitterness that the controversy had left, but it did little as a body to shape the future pattern of events. Just occasionally, however, the Connexion was involved in contacts that showed that the divisions between Wesleyans and Calvinists were not incapable of being crossed. One such example was Thomas Maxfield's relationship with his quondam friends in the early months of 1772. Maxfield's passage from perfectionist to moderate Calvinist had left him with few friends in either camp, but he was

---

[164] Fletcher to CW, 24 Nov. 1771, Meth. Arch. (Fletcher), 38.

[165] The importance which the Connexion attached to the *Narrative* as a statement of its position is demonstrated by its systematic attempt to make copies available in Scotland as well as in England (Peckwell to LH, 21 Dec. 1771; John Lloyd to LH, 15 Feb. 1772, F1/156, 1586,CF).

[166] Shirley to LH, 23 Jan. 1772, F1/1580,CF. Shirley's comment on Hill is interesting, given Fletcher's earlier categorization of him as a moderate. Above, n. 127.

asked in February by one of the senior members of Wesley's Foundry society if he would agree to preach for them whenever Wesley was out of London. He and Wesley dined together (for the first time in nine years) and Wesley agreed that Maxfield should take no decision on the matter until he had consulted with Lady Huntingdon. Maxfield clearly believed there was no inconsistency in preaching for Wesley as well as the Countess, and for a while seemed confident that an arrangement would be worked out.[167] Nothing in fact seems to have come of the suggestion, possibly because of opposition from Lady Huntingdon,[168] and while he was at Bath in July he refused requests from Wesleyans to preach in their chapels.[169] Thus ended one attempt at a partial reconciliation and thereafter Maxfield became more and more committed to the Calvinist side. In the account of his late wife that he published in 1778, he regretted the bitterness which the controversy had caused but put the blame squarely on the Wesleyans.[170]

Meanwhile, Fletcher continued to seek an entente with the Countess. At the start of 1772 he expressed regret for the pain he had caused her, and in March had had a dream about a reconciliation.[171] But in the latter month he re-entered the debate with the publication of his *Third Check to Antinomianism*. This was a reply to Hill's pamphlet, and in it he argued that the doctrine of a prevenient grace which was present in all men and gave everyone the chance to repent, meant that it was possible to believe in a universal offer of salvation without denying that the full credit for man's salvation still belonged to God. Wesley said of the work that in it, Fletcher 'draws the sword and throws away the scabbard'.[172]

---

[167] Maxfield to LH, 27 and 28 Feb. 1772, F1/1588–89,CF.
[168] Maxfield to LH, 28 and 14 Apr. 1772, F1/1600, 1598,CF.
[169] Maxfield to LH, 20 July and 3 Aug. 1772, F1/1610, 1611,CF.
[170] Maxfield, *God's Dealings with Mrs Maxfield*. The assumptions which lay behind the contacts in 1772 are significant, however, and it is of particular interest that the Foundry society believed that when Maxfield's chapel came to be demolished during impending local redevelopment, it would be to them, rather than to the equidistant Whitefieldite Tabernacle, that his congregation would go (Maxfield to LH, 28 Apr. 1772, F1/1600,CF).
[171] Seymour, ii. 245; Fletcher to CW, 12 Mar. 1772, Meth. Arch. (Fletcher), 42.
[172] JW to CW, 17 Mar. 1772, Wesley, *Letters*, v. 311.

It was perhaps not surprising, therefore, that Fletcher's hopes of better relations with Lady Huntingdon were not realized. In August, indeed, he reported that Lady Huntingdon had ordered that he be forbidden to preach in any of her chapels.[173]

A year later, in August 1773, Fletcher commented to Charles Wesley that he thought his breach with Lady Huntingdon was irreparable. 'With some people we must be *very near*, or *quite off*. I doubt whether this is not a little the case with our Great Friend.'[174] Despite this gloomy prediction, however, the pattern that emerged over the next few years was of occasional contacts followed by lengthy periods in which they each went their own ways.[175] This continued until 1777 when Fletcher's serious illness provided the stimulus for a final reconciliation. In January that year, one of Lady Huntingdon's London friends reported that he was the 'same humble, heavenly creature that he ever was' and had been to visit all those, like Toplady and Romaine, with whom he had ever been in disagreement.[176] Fletcher was in friendly correspondence with Lady Huntingdon as the year continued, yet he was at pains, at the end of May, to deny a report, apparently emanating from the college, that he had recanted the doctrines of the *Checks*. He was as opposed as ever, he said, to the doctrines of absolute necessity and Calvinist reprobation, and he had prepared a new pamphlet, *The Reconciliation*, as a final statement of his views. This sought (according to its full title) 'to unite the professing people of God, by placing the doctrines of grace and justice in such a light, as to make the candid Arminians Bible-Calvinists, and the candid Calvinists Bible-Arminians'. Fletcher's failing health prevented him from taking forward the scheme of union which the pamphlet proposed, but he remained on good terms with Lady Huntingdon and she

---

[173] Fletcher to CW, 5 Aug. 1772, Meth. Arch. (Fletcher), 45; Glazebrook to LH, 11 May 1772, F1/178,CF.

[174] Fletcher to JW or CW, 24 Aug. 1773, Meth. Arch. (Fletcher), 48.

[175] For example, Mrs Carteret to LH, 4 Dec. n.y.; Anne Power to LH, 30 May 1775, F1/1137, 329,CF; *Letters of the Reverend Mr. Fletcher* (1791), 221, 223; Tyerman, *Fletcher*, 300–1, 306–7; Fletcher to CW, 14 Aug. 1774, Meth. Arch. (Fletcher), 50.   [176] Mrs Carteret to LH, 4 Jan. 1777, F1/374,CF.

invited him to visit her at college later that summer.[177] With Walter Shirley, Fletcher was also reconciled, and the harmony thus established was to continue through the few years of life that remained to them.[178]

The varied pattern of John Fletcher's relations with Lady Huntingdon was symptomatic of the Connexion's inability, once its original attack upon the Minutes was over, to decide what its stance towards the Wesleyans should be. Even when its members abstained from active involvement in controversy, tensions remained between Lady Huntingdon herself and John Wesley. When Wesley visited Ormiston near Edinburgh in May 1772, for example, he found that Lady Huntingdon had already written to the Earl of Hopetown[179] to warn him that the Wesleyans were 'dreadful heretics to whom no countenance should be given'.[180] Nonetheless, to preach specifically against Wesley was still sufficiently unusual in the Connexion that when Edward Sheppard did so at Tunbridge Wells, later in the same year, Lady Anne thought it important enough to mention it to Lady Huntingdon.[181] The latter part of 1772 was regarded by Wesley as marking a new phase in the intensity of the controversy, yet while the Countess was in Bath during the winter of 1772–3, she renewed contact with his brother Charles, who was described by Lady Gertrude Hotham as a 'sincere Trusty friendly creature apart from his doctrine'.[182]

---

[177] Fletcher to LH, 28 May and 10 Oct. 1777, A1/13(11, 12),CF; Patrick Streiff, *Reluctant Saint? A Theological Biography of Fletcher of Madeley* (Peterborough, 2001), 185–6.

[178] Seymour, ii. 201. Jonathan Scott met Fletcher in April 1777 and believed that he would now be 'found for ever in the *imputed* Righteousness of our divine Surety' (Scott to LH, 29 Apr. 1777, F1/389,CF). Glascott experienced hospitality from 'our good old friend at Madeley' when he visited the parish on his preaching tour in 1781 (Glascott to LH, 16 July 1781, E4/11(1),CF).

[179] The Earl was the father of Lady Glenorchy's friend, Lady Henrietta Hope, and had his seat at Ormiston.

[180] JW's Journal for 12 May 1772, *Works*, xxii. 322–3. Only a month before, however, Lady AE had expressed disapproval at Madan having preached against Wesley and quoted LH's own advice to the students to 'Preach the truth and error will fall to the ground' (Lady AE to LH, 21 Apr. 1772, F1/1599,CF).

[181] Lady AE to LH, 13 Nov. 1772, F1/1623,CF.

[182] JW to Mrs Turner, 18 Sept. 1772; JW to Mary Bishop, 4 Nov. 1772, Wesley, *Letters*, v. 340, 344; Lady G. Hotham to LH, 17 Apr. 1773, F1/215,CF.

Later that year Lady Huntingdon wrote to John Wesley in what were evidently friendly terms. Replying, Wesley spoke of her letter as 'the answer to many prayers'.[183] Yet two years were to pass without further signs of contact. At the end of June 1775, she received news of John's serious illness and wrote movingly to Charles of her concern: 'how does an hour of Loving sorrow swallow up the Just differences our various Judgments make', she wrote, 'and it is with pleasure that I find he remains in my heart as a friend.'[184]

This conciliatory letter coincided not only with another of Fletcher's attempts at reconciliation but with the first lull in the steady stream of polemical pamphleteering that had gone on since 1771, a lull that was to continue until Rowland Hill made a fierce attack on Wesley, two years later.[185] What is known of Lady Huntingdon's contacts with Wesley in these years, however, shows that it is impossible to match her attitudes to John Wesley with the ebb and flow of the controversy—another sign that the Connexion could no longer be regarded as part of the main stream of Calvinist evangelical attack. But though theological differences were not to the fore, organizational rivalry continued. In 1776 the *Gospel Magazine* carried a report that Wesley had spoken disparagingly of Trevecca and its students, and he had evidently followed this with a letter to Lady Huntingdon. Early in September she replied to him—in terms which were, for her, remarkably restrained—to deny that the Connexion was in competition with him in Cornwall, a Wesleyan heartland, and to stress that she had always warned the students to avoid attacks upon him. She remained, she said, his 'old and faithful friend' and what he should choose 'to say or think of their [the students] having me for their directress...I have no objection to'.[186] Wesley expressed himself satisfied with her reply but so seriously did he regard the rivalry in Cornwall that he asked her again to caution her students.[187]

[183] JW to LH, 16 Sept. 1773, Wesley, *Letters*, vi. 41–2.
[184] LH to CW, 28 June 1775, Meth. Arch. (LH), 81.
[185] Fletcher to CW, 8 Aug. 1775, Meth. Arch. (Fletcher), 52; Sangster, 'Rowland Hill', ch. 2 analyses the pattern of pamphleteering during the 1770s.
[186] LH to JW, 8 Sept. 1776, E4/3(2),CF.
[187] JW to LH, 15 Sept. 1776, E4/3(3),CF.

Two years later, on a visit to St Ives, he rejoiced that 'Those who styled themselves My Lady's preachers...are vanished away.'[188]

1777 saw a further stage in the controversy proper with a fresh onslaught on Wesley from the pen of Rowland Hill. Once again, this was a development with which Lady Huntingdon had no wish to be associated. She had already quarrelled with Hill himself, and Thomas Wills wrote in August that he was not surprised that the pamphlet had offended her. 'The Christian should repose in the spirit of meekness,' said Wills, 'as poor Mr. Wesley certainly does. I am called to bear my testimony against him at the moment but I pray to avoid all personal Rancour.'[189] Wills's remark is an apt description of the relationship that existed between Lady Huntingdon and John Wesley during the final years of their lives. Neither of them could compromise on essential doctrines or contemplate co-operation between their respective groups. But the very recognition that they must each go their own way served in itself to remove the former bitterness. Personality differences, once so significant, now mattered less and the two leaders may even have developed a certain respect for each other's integrity. There were occasions, during the latter part of the decade, when each dissociated themselves from the doctrines of the other, yet it seemed perfectly natural in 1779 for Wesley to write to Lady Huntingdon in the most courteous terms to enquire about the character of one of her former students. When Wesley visited Dublin in 1787, he commented on the mercy of God in providing 'such places as Lady Huntingdon's chapels for those delicate hearers who could not bear sound doctrine, if it were not set off with pretty trifles'.[190] If this did not suggest the closest cordiality between them, it was at least a recognition that she was on the side of the angels. The controversy had engendered too much suspicion and had taken up too much of their lives for them to go further than this. It was a measure of the gulf that still lay between them that

---

[188] JW's Journal for 28 Aug. 1778, *Works*, xxiii. 103–4.
[189] Wills to LH, 28 Aug. 1777, F1/1783,CF.
[190] Seymour, ii. 206.

Lady Huntingdon should have been surprised, as she was reported to have been, to be told that Wesley had died professing his sole dependence on the meritorious sacrifice of Christ.[191]

Although *The Times* reported, some months after Wesley's death, that one of Lady Huntingdon's preachers had given thanks for this deliverance,[192] this could not have been a reaction typical of many of the Connexion's ministers. What emerges clearly from the complex history of the 1770s and 1780s is that far from being a bastion of militant Calvinism, the Connexion, once it had made its initial stand against the Wesleyan Minutes, was content to abstain as much as possible from direct participation in the controversy. Its leaders were fully convinced in their theology and made little active attempt at reconciliation—unlike such of their lay friends as James Ireland and John Thornton who were both to press for moderation[193]—but they saw their task as the positive one of proclaiming their beliefs rather than of attacking those who dissented from them. Walter Shirley believed that the Connexion occupied a middle position between Wesleyans and extreme Calvinists, but it would be more accurate to say that it compassed within itself a variety of opinions. Among the ministers and students of the Connexion, clear differences are discernible. The early students, as noted, embraced a wide spread of theological opinion and their influence must have been felt within the Connexion for some time to come. William Ellis was described by one of his fellow students as tainted with Wesleyanism in November 1771; in March 1773 the moderate-minded Craddock Glascott, while acknowledging the faithfulness of another student, William Aldridge, yet found it necessary to ask for him to be replaced by a lively Calvinist.[194] After the controversy, young men of this kind

---

[191] Jackson, *Charles Wesley*, ii. 295.   [192] *The Times*, 15 June 1791.

[193] It was inevitable that Ireland's long friendship with Fletcher should make him anxious to secure the latter's reconciliation with LH. Thornton attempted to exert a moderating influence upon John Berridge when he belatedly entered the controversy in 1773 (Tyerman, *Fletcher*, 252).

[194] Henry Mead to LH, 16 Nov. 1771; Glascott to LH, 12 Mar. 1773, F1/140, 1636,CF.

ceased to be acceptable and the continuing danger was, as we have seen, that the students would apply their Calvinism to antinomian effect.[195]

The principal focus of this chapter has been on the role played in the controversy by the leaders of the two sides. It has been seen in passing, however, that congregations themselves could be influenced by, and have a bearing upon, the development of events and it is important to consider this aspect of the controversy in more detail. The difficulty lies in evaluating the extent to which flocks were actually aware of the doctrinal issues that so troubled their leaders. Attitudes are often only apparent when forcibly expressed, but it would be dangerous to assume that the absence of evidence of grass-roots theological opinion means that there was none. Some congregations were certainly aware of the issues at stake. We have already seen[196] how Glazebrook incurred the displeasure of a group within the congregation at Ote Hall in 1770 for failing to put sufficient stress upon the doctrine of imputed righteousness. Eyre's congregation at Busweal, Cornwall, in 1777 must have been as strongly Calvinistic for after he had disputed successfully on universal redemption with a Wesleyan who had come to the chapel for this purpose, he had been forced to clear the people from the building quickly for fear they would attack the unfortunate individual.[197]

It may be that those who have already gone through one change of religious allegiance in their lifetime (as the first generation members of evangelical congregations are likely to have done) are more prone to independent positions than those who remain in the religious environment in which they have been brought up. Certainly there is some evidence, within the congregations of the Connexion, of the existence of sub-groups holding their own distinct doctrinal positions, and it is these that make generalizations about the theology of congregations even more difficult than about that of the preachers. One student reported in 1776 that a part of the Norwich congregation was 'tinged with Sandimons [*sic*] notions', and another, in Devon in the same

[195] Above p.220. [196] Above p.240. [197] John Eyre to LH, 14 Jan. 1777, F1/376,CF.

year, spoke of the trials he had gone through with well-meaning Christians who had taken up an antinomian position.[198] The fact that the Connexion's chapels were as liable as Wesley's to disruption by followers of the hyper-Calvinist, William Huntington, is a sign both that some among their members rejected Huntingtonian excesses and that others found them attractive.[199] However carefully the leaders of the two sides defined their positions and the limits to which these could be taken, there was always the danger that ill-educated members of their congregations would carry them to excess. This was a danger which the Connexion's system of circulating rather than settled ministries could only partially offset.

It was precisely this independence of spirit within congregations that enabled the doctrinal controversy to affect them. When this happened, however, it might bear little relation to events at the centre and could involve other than purely doctrinal considerations. James Glazebrook provided an illustration of this during his time at Ashby when he stated that in spite of Wesleyan opposition he intended to begin preaching and let the Lord decide the issue.[200] What else could this mean, in practical terms, except to see which way the congregation went, and hence, which cause was a viable one? For on the size of the congregation depended the income available for the opening and then the upkeep of a chapel: if members fell away, then the building would not be completed or, if completed, the doors would have to be shut. There was a limit to the number of people in any area who would be influenced by evangelical preaching, and at least part of the purpose of all subsequent preaching was to prevent existing members being enticed away by other groups. It was always likely that a proportion of those awakened at any one time would subsequently be involved with other groups within the Revival, although this might be due as much to a greater attractiveness of preachers or regularity

---

[198] Thomas Molland to LH, 15 Oct. 1776, F1/367,CF.
[199] A good example of this was the chapel at Gainsborough, whose congregation was split by a Huntingtonian preacher in about 1780 ('A Brief Historick Record').
[200] Glazebrook to LH, 20 Jan. 1772, F1/167,CF.

of supplies as to any refining of doctrinal attitudes. Lady Huntingdon may have shared Wesley's belief that some parts of the country lay within the sphere of one of them rather than the other,[201] yet in practice, these were seldom clearly defined and the majority of areas were treated as common ground. Thus throughout the period warnings reached Lady Huntingdon of the dangers that threatened from the Wesleyans if supplies were not maintained. In 1788, a member of the Newark congregation reported to Lady Huntingdon that Wesley had built a new meeting house in the town, and that unless a good minister were sent, she would lose her interest there. His fears appear to have been justified, for in November 1789 Thomas Young informed her that some (apparently members, as well as casual hearers) had gone over to the Wesleyans.[202] Other examples are numerous: the chapel at Dudley, for instance, reported in 1789 that there had been a falling-off in numbers since Wesley had taken to sending his best preachers to the town.[203] Such instances far outweigh the few signs there are of co-operation between the groups.[204] The movement was not always away from the Connexion: twenty Wesleyans, for example, were reported to have joined the Norwich chapel in 1784.[205] There were also cases of individual preachers leaving Wesley. One such was the Mr Norman of Bradford-upon-Avon, who had been brought to Calvinism by attendance at the Bath chapel and whose subsequent preaching at Bradford was so successful that a chapel was built for him there; in April 1790 he applied for it to be taken into the Countess's Connexion.[206]

---

[201] This is implicit, for example, in JW's Journal for 3 July 1779, where students at Grimsby were condemned for encroaching upon established work rather than going 'where Christ has not been named' (*Works*, xxiii. 138).
[202] James Stevenson to LH, 28 Jan. 1788; Young to LH, Nov. 1789, F1/1982, 2111,CF.   [203] W. Jones to LH, 29 Sept. 1789, F1/862,CF.
[204] The Wesleyans at Swansea shared a room with the Connexion until as late as 1774, though this was evidently through convenience (or necessity) rather than from feelings of common interest (J. McBrom to LH, 12 Feb. 1774, E4/8(6),CF). Premises were also being shared at Monmouth, three years later, but this led to open conflict and the eventual expulsion of the Wesleyans in 1778 (Isaac Billings to LH, 13 Sept. and 10 Nov. 1777; E. and A. Bear to ?, 1778, F1/1787, 1799, 1824,CF).   [205] Norwich committee to LH, 27 Feb. 1784, F1/604,CF.
[206] Glascott to LH, 8 Apr. 1790; J. Jenkins to LH, 2 June 1790, F1/2127, 916,CF.

Although the controversy was conducted, for the most part, in an enclosed world of its own, its leaders were not entirely indifferent to the reactions of those outside. This manifested itself in two ways. The first was concern at the damage that the controversy could do to the public reputation of the Revival. 'Rather suffer in silence,' said Fletcher to Benson in 1771, 'than make a noise to cause the Philistines to triumph.' He himself was warned by Berridge, two years later, that he and Toplady were 'setting the Christian world on fire and the carnal world in laughter'.[207] There was reason for the anxiety, since the earlier phase of controversy had given fuel to the satirists of Methodism.[208] Against this, however, the combatants were anxious that their distinctive doctrinal positions should be understood. Shirley's *Narrative* expressed concern that people would suppose that all 'Methodists' shared the doctrines of the Wesleyan Minutes, and it appears that Lady Huntingdon sought to dissociate herself, before the bishops, from 'Wesley's doctrine of perfection as denied by our Church'.[209] The leaders were not successful, however, in making their differences clear, and there was confusion outside the Revival as to the distinctive doctrinal position held by each of the parties. In popular usage, all were 'Methodists'. In 1771, for example, Bishop Brownlow North spoke of 'the Doctrine of the Methodists such as reprobation, the irresistibility of Grace etc.',[210] and seemed unaware that these were doctrines which Wesley did not hold. For the great majority of those outside the Revival, whether sympathetic or antagonistic towards it, the doctrinal debates that mattered so deeply to its members must have passed either unnoticed or uncomprehended.

But if the world could ignore theology, theology could not forever ignore the world. To the general changes taking place within the social and industrial life of the country in

---

[207] Tyerman, *Fletcher*, 176, 284–5. There are other examples, from both camps, of this concern to avoid bringing the cause of religion into disrepute.
[208] *A Plain and Easy Road to the Land of Bliss* (1761) makes sport of the theological differences between Wesley and Whitefield–quoted in A. M. Lyles, *Methodism Mocked* (London, 1960), 117.
[209] (?) to the Bench of Bishops, n.d., E3/2(17),CF.
[210] Glazebrook to LH, 16 Dec. 1771, F1/153,CF.

the latter part of the eighteenth century, was added the spectacle of the French Revolution. Few could remain unmoved by the events in France, though sympathies were divided. Given the social origins of many within the Revival, it would have been surprising if notions of human rights and personal autonomy had not been attractive to some of its adherents, especially when Catholicism was among the targets of French revolutionary zeal. Indeed, there were frequent examples in the Wesleyan ranks of travelling preachers and ordinary laity who were delighted by news of the Revolution, at least in its earliest phase, before the Terror and de-Christianization. Many Calvinistic evangelicals and evangelical Dissenters also responded to the language of equality that it proclaimed. On the other side, there were many instances of the opposite viewpoint, reinforced by biblical injunctions on obedience to the civil power.[211]

The Church Evangelicals took a more solidly 'Tory' and establishmentarian view of the situation. Events in France had shown how closely the interests of Church and State were linked, and how an attack on one could threaten the whole social fabric. To challenge the parson within his parish—say, as to his views on justification or regeneration—now had implications that went beyond the purely theological and seemed to strike at the roots, not just of his personal authority, but at those of the system which he represented. Fears for property rights and the social order, combined with solidarity with their non-evangelical colleagues, all facing the same potential revolutionary threat, now made it essential for Church Evangelicals to keep their mission within the structures of the Church. The effect of this was to heighten their Anglican-consciousness and to widen the gulf between them and their Dissenting brethren. The more important division was thus no longer that between Calvinists and Arminians but between those in the Church and those outside it. This manifested itself in various ways. In 1795, for example, Church Evangelicals, despite their being closer to the theology of the London Missionary Society than to that of many of their

---

[211] Nancy Uhlar Murray, 'The Influence of the French Revolution on the Church of England and its Rivals, 1789–1802', D.Phil. thesis (Oxford, 1975), 216–19.

fellow Anglicans, still felt impelled, only a year after the latter's foundation, to establish a separate society (the Church Missionary Society) within the ranks of the Church.

Aside from these external pressures, the controversy had, by the end of the century, largely played itself out. Quite simply, there was very little left to be said. It had ended, not with the victory of one side over the other, but in the recognition that there can be no final answers to questions of this kind. The cause of truth, it became clear, was not to be served by the pitting of text against text and the construction of unanswerable logical systems, even if this had been possible. There could still be disagreement, but men no longer acted as though the holders of contrary opinions were damned to eternity. It was significant, for example, that the first issue of the *Evangelical Magazine*, which appeared in 1793 'on the lines of the *Gospel Magazine* but without acrimonious reflections' could speak of its potential readership as '30,000 Calvinists and many others savingly converted to God'. Similarly, Wesley's provocatively titled *Arminian Magazine* changed its name to *Methodist Magazine* within a few years of its founder's death. So far as the Connexion was concerned, all that the controversy had done had been to give it, for a brief period, a position of eminence within the ranks of Calvinist evangelicals—though at the cost of depriving it of the services of a number of valued friends, of distracting effort away from its primary concerns, and of lending theological fuel to the rivalry between chapels and congregations that was an inevitable feature of the Revival. When the century ended, as will be seen, it was with problems of organization and control, rather than theology, that the Connexion's leaders were forced to be concerned. The controversy, like all controversies, was undoubtedly a tragedy. But so significant were the issues with which it dealt that not to have debated them openly might conceivably be regarded as the greater tragedy still.

THE CONNEXION AND OTHER CALVINIST EVANGELICALS

Solidarity amongst Calvinist evangelicals in their initial reaction to the Wesleyan Minutes did not mean that harmony was maintained between them over the following years. The 1770s, indeed, witnessed the gradual estrangement of the Connexion from a number of groups to which it was doctrinally close. Of these, the most significant were the followers of George Whitefield. After Whitefield's sudden death in 1770 it was to be expected that Lady Huntingdon would play a part in the work of his former congregations. Whitefield had been her friend and supporter from early in the Revival, had preached for her when he could, and had been involved in some of her major initiatives, such as the founding of Trevecca College. He, in turn, had bequeathed his American Orphan House to her care. No individual took over Whitefield's role in respect of his congregations: instead, what became known as the Tabernacle Connexion remained under the control of the trustees to which it had passed at Whitefield's death. Between Lady Huntingdon and the trustees relations were at first of the closest kind. At the end of 1770, for example, the Tabernacle in Bristol was supplied by the student John Cosson, assisted by occasional visits from Walter Shirley, then serving in Bath.[212] There were other signs of close links between the work of the two connexions. In June 1771 Harmer supplied the Tottenham Court chapel for a month, prior to going on to serve Lady Huntingdon; later that year 'Christian friends in the late Mr. Whitefield's Connections' in Dursley, Gloucestershire, thanked Lady Huntingdon for letting Hawkesworth serve among them.[213] The Trevecca mission to the Georgia Orphan House was, at the start, a further bond between the two connexions, symbolized when a letter from William Piercy, leader of the expedition, was read aloud in the Moorfields Tabernacle in April 1773.[214]

The Tabernacle trustees later became drawn into the dispute that developed between Piercy and Lady Huntingdon over his stewardship of the Orphan House, but for the moment harmony between the trustees and the Countess

[212] Glazebrook to LH, 13 Dec. 1770; Mead to LH, 22 Dec. 1770, F1/114, 116,CF; Seymour, i. 215–16. The position of the Bristol Tabernacle was curious in that Whitefield had omitted references to it in his will. The trustees were prepared to befriend it, but not to regard it as part of their charge.
[213] Glascott to LH, 3 June 1771; J. Danclo to LH, 17 Nov. 1771, F1/125, 141,CF.
[214] J. Hunt to LH, 17 Apr. 1773, F1/214,CF; Welch, 166–7.

seemed set fair to continue. She stayed at the Tabernacle House in Moorfields during her visit to London in the summer of 1773;[215] a year later she sent Hawkesworth to supply for Andrew Kinsman, pastor of Whitefield's Tabernacle in Plymouth, in order to free Kinsman for service at Whitefield's London chapels.[216] It was in 1776 that this harmony was broken, apparently as a result of the perceived threat to the Connexion's work at Haverfordwest of the activities there of Rowland Hill and Captain Torial Joss,[217] and of moves by the Whitefieldite societies in Gloucestershire to ordain some of Lady Huntingdon's students without her consent.[218] The first hint of discord occurred at the end of October,[219] and quickly escalated into threats by Lady Huntingdon to take her dispute with them before the bench of bishops. Shirley thought this was an extreme reaction: although he did not condone what had happened, he reminded her (revealingly) that it was an offence only against a connexion, and not against Christ's Kingdom.[220] He was relieved when Lady Huntingdon decided not to go ahead with her protest, and he was not alone in wanting to make less of the incident than she did. In December, Glascott told her he was satisfied both as to the rectitude of Joss's conduct and that the Tabernacle trustees remained faithful friends; he had accordingly decided that to preach for them was not incompatible with service in her Connexion.[221] Seeds of suspicion, once sown in Lady Huntingdon's mind, were not easily extinguished, however.

---

[215] J. Harris to LH, 21 Aug. 1773, F1/243,CF.
[216] LH to Hawkesworth, 16 Sept. 1774, Seymour, ii. 174.
[217] Joss, 1731–1787, was a former sea captain who had become one of Whitefield's assistants in 1766, and itinerated regularly in Gloucestershire. The Whitefieldite societies in Gloucestershire went under the title of the Rodborough Connexion, reflecting the leading role of the Tabernacle in that town, founded in 1750 by a convert of Whitefield's, Thomas Adams. They came under the effective oversight of Rowland Hill after the deaths of Whitefield and Adams in 1770 (G. F. Nuttall, 'Rowland Hill and the Rodborough Connexion, *Transactions of the Congregational Historical Society*, 21/3 (1972)).
[218] Seymour, ii. 421; Shirley to LH, 14 Nov. 1776, F1/1734,CF.
[219] Shirley to LH, 28 Oct. 1776, F1/368,CF.
[220] Shirley to LH, 14 Nov. 1776, F1/1734,CF.
[221] Glascott to LH, 18 Dec. 1776 and 8 Jan. 1777, F1/371, 375,CF.

The assistance offered by the Tabernacle trustees in the planned establishment of a Connexional chapel in Mulberry Gardens, Wapping was interpreted as suspicious by Lady Huntingdon. Glascott assured her in January that this was not the case;[222] Berridge wrote in the same spirit in April, but by then a decisive split had occurred between the two connexions, and Lady Huntingdon's students had been withdrawn from service at the Tabernacle.[223] In October 1777 congregations in Wiltshire were said to face a choice between Mr Whitefield's preachers and those of Lady Huntingdon;[224] in the following month even the tolerant Glascott was suspicious of the trustees' intentions in respect of the Connexion's chapel at Norwich.[225]

The differences at Haverfordwest and with the Whitefieldites in Gloucestershire were to continue. In 1781 there was apparently a further attempt by the Gloucestershire Association to entice into its service students that the Countess had recently started sending to Cheltenham. In a letter about this to Alderman Harris of Gloucester, an old friend of Whitefield, Lady Huntingdon enclosed plans for a proposed agreement between the Gloucestershire Association and the Welsh Calvinistic Methodists. The first and fundamental article of this was that the Gloucestershire Association should give up 'all right, power or influence' in Haverfordwest.[226] Nothing, however, seems to have come of this, or of the further scheme of union between the Connexion and the Whitefieldites in which Berridge acted as intermediary in September 1788.[227] Once the breach had been made, it continued, and chapel rivalries entrenched the division. A Connexional chapel had already been built at Bristol before there was any hint of disharmony, but the reference in 1788 to a draining away of its congregation to the Bristol Tabernacle is a sign of what was probably frequent

---

[222] Glascott to LH, 8 Jan. 1777, F1/375,CF.
[223] Berridge to LH, 26 Apr. 1777, Seymour, ii. 422.
[224] J. Giles to LH, 8 Oct. 1777, F1/1790,CF.
[225] Glascott to LH, 8 Dec. 1777, F1/1806,CF.
[226] LH to Gabriel Harris Esq., Sept. 1781, Seymour, i. 434–8 and n.
[227] Berridge to LH, Seymour, i. 216–17.

competition between them.[228] A rather similar situation arose in Bath, where a new congregation was established in the early 1780s, following the secession of a group from Lady Huntingdon's chapel. This group applied to the Tabernacle trustees for support,[229] and it is likely to have been the successors of that congregation who were described in 1792 as 'followers of the late Mr. Whitefield'.[230]

Less easy to categorize is the situation of the chapel at Gloucester which was opened in 1788. This was the direct initiative of the Countess of Huntingdon, and the chapel was always to attribute its origin to her, yet it was soon being described in the city guide as 'used by followers of Mr. Whitefield'.[231] This may represent popular confusion, but it is just possible that it illustrates a softening of attitudes between the two connexions. If so, there may be parallels with the decision to join the Connexion made in 1790 by Dr Ford, who since 1777 had been one of the Tabernacle trustees.[232] But if there was a conciliatory spirit around the end of Lady Huntingdon's life, there was no question of the two groups merging. Indeed, a merger was unlikely, given that the Whitefieldites, being closer to Dissent and having fewer Anglican ties than the Connexion, had a different contribution to make to the course of the Revival.

The Whitefieldites, however, were not the only Calvinist group from whom the Countess's Connexion diverged. Most important among the others was that which formed round Rowland Hill, whose links with the Whitefieldites (in opposition to Lady Huntingdon) have already been mentioned. Lady Huntingdon had first made contact with Hill in 1767, while he was still an undergraduate, and she proved a powerful ally in the conflicts with his parents that his itinerant preaching occasioned. In the early 1770s, Hill appeared as the rising star of the new generation of evangelicals. He is recorded preaching for Lady Huntingdon, for the Tabernacle

---

[228] A. Gadd to LH, 7 July 1788, F1/740,CF.
[229] W. Tuck, *History of the Argyle Chapel, Bath* (Bath, 1906).
[230] *Bath Directory* for 1792.
[231] *Gloucester Guide* for 1792.
[232] Dr Ford to LH, 26 Feb. 1790, F1/2119,CF.

and the Lock, at Doddridge's old meeting house in Northampton, in Rocquet's Church in Bristol, and at a wide variety of other places.[233] His first conflict with members of the Connexion came in the August of 1771, when he was accused by the students of trespassing upon their preaching rounds in the Bridgwater area.[234] They also condemned him for the facetiousness he introduced into his preaching, an accusation that was to be repeated about Hill throughout his life. As yet this dispute did not affect Hill's position, and in May 1774 Shirley expressed the hope that Hill would preach for Andrew Kinsman in Plymouth, although there is a passing reference that June to 'Ro. Hill leaving the plan'.[235] The actual conflict seems to have occurred early in 1777: at the end of January, Haweis referred to 'R. H. ... a poor creature, vain of popularity & affecting it', adding also that, 'the conceite [*sic*] of the Revd Captains I pity'. Whatever the nature of their crime, Hill and Captain Joss were apparently associated in it together, but that this was something distinct from the Connexion's quarrels with the Tabernacle trustees was shown in Haweis's comment the following month that Hill and Joss were not important enough to lead a new sect.[236] There was still a danger that they might feed upon the Countess's societies, however, and Wills felt it necessary to inform her of Hill's presence in Cornwall in July. At the end of August Wills was shocked at the tenor of Hill's vehement contribution to the Calvinistic controversy. He compared Hill's verbal ferocity with Wesley's spirit of meekness, a striking example of the Connexion taking a more moderate approach than some of those whose theology it shared.[237]

Towards Hill, Lady Huntingdon's attitude remained rigid, in spite of attempts at a reconciliation by third parties. In August 1780 Peter Williams told her he hoped he would not

---

[233] Sidney, *Rowland Hill*, ch. 3.
[234] Rowley and Glazebrook to Hill, 15 Aug. 1771 and Hill's response, 23 Aug. 1771, E4/6,CF.
[235] Shirley to LH, 27 May 1774; E. Cosson to LH, 8 June 1774, E4/1(21); F1.298,CF.
[236] Haweis to LH, 30 Jan. 1777; Mr and Mrs Haweis to LH, (? Feb.) 1777, F1/1748, 1801,CF.
[237] Wills to LH, 3 July and 28 Aug. 1777, F1/1770, 1783,CF.

offend if he said he loved Hill and Joss, and he stated his wish that all the ministers of Christ were in closer connection. In the same month, Glascott was asked by the committee of the Norwich chapel whether they should invite Hill to preach during his projected visit to the city: he told them that this would be disagreeable to Lady Huntingdon, although his view was that it could cause little harm.[238] In 1781 Hill came to London in the hope of a personal reconciliation with Lady Huntingdon and the opportunity of preaching at Spa Fields, but in spite of the efforts of an unnamed correspondent, the Countess was not to be persuaded.[239] Indeed, although she was to contribute to the building fund for Hill's Surrey chapel in 1782, Hill himself continued to be regarded as a potential opponent.[240] Hill never became reconciled with the Countess during her lifetime, and was even to alienate himself from the trustees of Whitefield's chapels when, in 1786, he introduced an organ and the performance of oratorios into the Surrey chapel.[241] Hill was one of those proscribed in Lady Huntingdon's will from ever again preaching in her pulpits, though he may in fact have been allowed to do so.[242]

There were other individual preachers who contributed to the diversity of the Calvinistic wing of the Revival and with whom the Connexion's relations were mixed. One such was Henry Peckwell who, despite a period of service in the Connexion, never allowed Lady Huntingdon full control over the Westminster chapel which had been opened through his efforts. When his active Connexional involvement ended in the late 1770s, the chapel became an entity in itself, adding one more to the number of Calvinist evangelical pulpits in London. In 1784 Peckwell is recorded as having preached at Tottenham Court and at the Surrey

---

[238] Peter Williams to LH, 18 Aug. 1780; Glascott to LH, 12 and 22 Aug. 1780, F1/1856, 1853, 1857,CF. The Norwich example is a case of divisions being preserved at the centre, rather than at the grass roots.

[239] Seymour, ii. 317–18 claims that Hill preached at the reopening of both the Worcester chapel in 1815 and the Brighton chapel after its two enlargements in 1811 and 1822. [240] John Lloyd to LH, 3 Feb. 1784, E4/13(19),CF.

[241] Sangster, 'Rowland Hill', 159. [242] Seymour, ii. 208; i. 442, 394.

chapel. The interrelationship between the different causes in the metropolis could indeed be complex, with a good deal of fraternization as well as movement and division: for example, one man who had separated from the Connexion in 1783 subsequently preached at Westminster, at Rowland Hill's Surrey chapel and at Tottenham Court.[243] Similar mobility was shown by Thomas Wills, who after his dismissal from the Connexion in 1788 served for a while at the Westminster and Orange Street chapels before taking over the Silver Street meeting house on his own account.[244] Orange Street, indeed, had set the pattern for Calvinist evangelical chapels independent of any of the main groups. Toplady had leased it from a Huguenot congregation as a London preaching place for himself, while still retaining his parish of Broad Hembury. After his death in 1778, it continued on the same footing, being served by Richard Cecil, previously curate to Romaine, and by John Eyre, a former Trevecca student. During this period, its relations with the Connexion were apparently friendly. Wills is reported as preaching there in 1779. When its owners wanted to dispose of the chapel, Charles de Coetlogon, assistant chaplain at the Lock, sought permission to use it from the vicar of the parish, but when this was refused, it was fitted out with organ and reading desk, the liturgy was introduced, and it was used by Dissenters.[245] Its history is an involved one, but it serves to illustrate the complexity which the Revival introduced into religious life in London. Nor were chapels like this confined to London, for notice might be made in passing of the connexion of Calvinist evangelicals founded at his house by Philip Oliver of Boughton Lodge, Chester, in 1793. The direction of this group was taken over by Thomas Charles of Bala after Oliver's death and seems originally to have been conceived in terms of an Anglican ministry. By 1801, however, Charles was fearful that they would have to 'open

---

[243] Wills to LH, 2 Oct. 1783; W. Taylor to LH, 24 Mar. 1784, F1/1907, 1936,CF.
[244] Walter Wilson, *The History and Antiquities of Dissenting Churches in London*, (*London*, 1808), iii. 181.
[245] Ibid. iv. 22–3. Wills to LH, 16 July 1779, F1/1830,CF.

ye door wider at Boughton' because the English clergy's rigid attention to Church rules made them reluctant to provide help. Whether the Chester group had already received help from the Countess's Connexion is uncertain: in 1802 the arrival of Thomas Molland, who had been an early Trevecca student, was anticipated. By 1805 Trigo of the Connexion had become a frequent visitor.[246]

A word ought finally to be said about the followers of Lady Huntingdon's Scottish counterpart, the Viscountess Glenorchy. In general, relationships between the two women were harmonious and, since Lady Glenorchy's activities were mainly confined to Scotland, there was little reason for conflict between them. This did not, however, prevent suspicions when she did turn her attentions to England. In 1777 (a grim year for Calvinistic Methodist solidarity) Haweis felt it necessary to reassure the Countess that he felt that Lady Glenorchy's English initiatives ('setting up the Kirk in the West') in no way endangered their own activities. This was emphasized in 1780, when Lady Glenorchy requested that her newly founded chapel at Exmouth should be served by the ministers and students of Lady Huntingdon's Connexion. Ten years later Dr Ford was asked to preach at Lady Glenorchy's Hope chapel in Bristol, but there seem to have been few other contacts between the Connexion and the few Glenorchy chapels in England.[247]

It will be clear from this analysis that despite the brief period of leadership that the Connexion provided during the early stages of the Calvinistic controversy, it was far from representing the totality of Calvinist evangelicals, let alone from controlling that side of the Revival. In spite of the Connexion's size, and the prominence it enjoyed by virtue of its geographical spread, it by no means embraced all

---

[246] Chester City Record Office: Letters to John Walker of Boughton Lodge, Chester, MS CR47/1–81, especially Thomas Charles, 2 Mar. 1801 and 6 Apr. 1802; Mrs Olney, 19 Mar. 1805; J. Wilcoxan, 22 May 1805, CR47/5, 6, 41 and 72.

[247] Mr and Mrs Haweis to LH, (? Feb.) 1777; Dr Ford to LH, 26 Feb. 1790, F1/1801, 2119,CF; Seymour, ii. 72.

Calvinist evangelicals outside the Church of England,[248] and indeed alienated a number of the most prominent. Nor was the Connexion itself a monochrome organization, as its varied attitudes to the worship and disciplines of the Church of England showed. Indeed, it is probably truer to see the Connexion as a microcosm of the varied elements within Calvinist evangelicalism, rather than a unifying factor.

[248] The Connexion's relations with Church Evangelicals are discussed in the following chapter.

7

The Connexion, the Church of England and Dissent

By the end of the 1770s a chain of events was under way in London which was to lead, in the early part of 1782, to the formal secession of the Countess of Huntingdon's Connexion from the Church of England. The fact that this process was protracted over a period of some two to three years seems to suggest extreme reluctance on Lady Huntingdon's part to take a step that represented a fundamental change in the status of her Connexion. Before examining the events which led to secession, therefore, it is necessary to consider the strength of the Connexion's loyalties to the Church of England in the preceding period and, in particular, whether the two most obvious results of the separation—the licensing of major chapels and the institution of the Connexion's own ordination—were really as radical as they appeared to be.

Loyalty to the Church of England does not seem to have been a fundamental principle with Lady Huntingdon at any stage of her life. Membership of the Church clearly carried with it obvious advantages. It gave to her work a respectability that would have been denied to a movement within Dissent; it offered, through the Church's Articles and liturgy, a guarantee of doctrinal orthodoxy, the lack of which was so painfully obvious amongst certain sections of contemporary Dissent; it enabled her to seek the services of some of the best Evangelical preachers of the day; and it carried the possibility, however remote, of transforming the religious life of the nation at large. Yet these incentives, important though they all were, were only valid provided her work was not thereby hampered; she would remain within as long as there were not stronger arguments for being outside. As Lady Huntingdon's activities developed in the 1760s and 1770s her essentially pragmatic approach to the Established Church became more apparent, and her Connexion took on more and more of the features of a Dissenting body. A significant element in this development was, as seen, the foundation of Trevecca College. The persistent difficulties which Trevecca students encountered in securing ordination had a double effect; alternative forms of ministry had to be considered, and while these were being explored the Connexion gained the services of itinerant lay preachers who were to involve it, more and more, in the foundation and development of what were essentially Dissenting congregations.

EPISCOPAL ORDINATION FOR TREVECCA STUDENTS

The approach of Trevecca students to Anglican orders gives some indication of their and their patroness's attitude to the Established Church, though the picture is far from consistent in each particular case. In April 1769, for example, Cheek wrote to Lady Huntingdon that he himself had no particular feelings about orders, but that as the promise that he would be ordained had been the means of his admittance to the college, he would use all lawful means to achieve them.[1] Not all the students had the same idea about Lady Huntingdon's intentions for them, however; in the following month another student wrote of his relief that Lady Huntingdon had not, as he had feared, been angry with him for presuming to become a candidate for the ministry.[2] This cannot have implied that she expected her students to remain for ever as lay preachers. The Connexion never developed a system approximating to Wesley's full-time travelling preachers and part-time local preachers, and it was clear that no one could, or would, remain as an unordained student indefinitely. Ordination of some kind would have to follow eventually,

---

[1] Cheek to LH, 18 Apr. 1769, F1/59,CF. Cheek is probably the former Wesleyan Mosely Cheek, who subsequently became Minister of St Stephen's, Salford (Curnock, v. 29n; Wesley, *Letters*, iv. 318n).

[2] Mead to LH, 29 May 1769, F1/68,CF.

though Lady Huntingdon was understandably reluctant for this to happen too quickly. She could have no confidence that her students, once episcopally ordained (or, indeed, ordained to Dissenting congregations) would ever return to full-time service in her Connexion. Even if promises were made of future service, the men concerned had still to serve the curacies to which they had been ordained.[3]

The road to Anglican orders, however, was not an easy one, and some, even of those sympathetic to Lady Huntingdon's aims, believed from the start that it would prove impossible. In an undated letter, possibly written in May 1770, Edward Davies, rector of Bridgend, wrote of his pleasure in finding the 'wise and prudent Gospel Ministers deceived in their positive declaration that none out of your Ladyship's College should ever be ordained'.[4] This may refer to Pecore, one of the two students who joined the Bencoolen expedition early in 1770.[5] Lady Huntingdon's approach to Terrick, bishop of London, in support of the two students nominated to go to Bencoolen showed that she had few illusions about the chances of her students gaining ordination; indeed, she acknowledged that their association with her, as well as their limited formal education, might reduce their chance of success. Terrick assured her that there was no question of him being prejudiced, but he insisted on very complete testimonials before he would set aside his own normal requirement of twenty-one days' notice. As seen, Terrick did ordain Pecore—after what Lady Huntingdon acknowledged to be a 'tender' examination—but he refused the other student who was under the canonical age. Lady Huntingdon discouraged moves to appeal to the archbishop about the latter refusal. This, she said, would show disrespect to Terrick, although her concern may have been to avoid alienating the bishop who had been the first to ordain one of her students, rather than from any veneration for the episcopal office.[6]

---

[3] None of the Trevecca students who secured Anglican orders appears to have returned to full-time service in the Connexion (although a number gave support both to it and to Cheshunt College). [4] Davies to LH, n.d., F1/94,CF.
[5] See above, Ch. 5.
[6] LH to (? bishop of London) n.d.; bishop of London to LH, 3 Jan. 1770; LH to 'Revd. Sir,' n.d., E3/1, (7, 1, 10),CF.

Relations with the Church and Dissent 299

After Pecore there were very few students who are known for certain to have been successful in obtaining ordination during the 1770s. James Glazebrook, one of the original Trevecca students, did attain to the diaconate in 1771, although only after vigorous examination as to his theology and the nature of Lady Huntingdon's college. He had to wait until 1777 before being made priest.[7] His ordination in 1771 had brought the number of students ordained by then to three, though the identity of the third man is uncertain: it could possibly have been Cheek or else the John Williams who wrote to Lady Huntingdon in October 1770 of his kindly reception by diocesan officials and the bishop of Norwich, and of the bishop's promise to ordain him in December. Williams was still a deacon when he left de Courcy's curacy at Shrewsbury in January 1777.[8] Nothing had come of Mead's attempt at orders in 1769, nor of his further attempt in 1771, but he evidently was ordained by November 1772.[9] William Ellis may just possibly have gained ordination at the end of 1773,[10] though the evidence for this is inconclusive. There is uncertainty, too, surrounding the ultimate success of John Harris who informed Lady Huntingdon in September 1773 of his strange wish to settle, as a clergyman, with the independent congregation in Hull with which he had become associated. This attempt at orders failed, in spite of backing from Lady Smythe, wife of the evangelical Chief Baron of the Exchequer, and Harris evidently failed again in 1775 (this time with different

---

[7] Glazebrook to LH, 16 Dec. 1771, F1/153,CF, Seymour, ii. 86.

[8] Davies to LH, n.d.; J. Williams to LH, 25 Oct.1770; de Courcy to LH, 14 Jan. 1777, F1/1163, 1516, 1745,CF.

[9] The 1771 prospect of orders came through Mead's contacts at Brighton with Ashburnham, rector of Cuckfield (and brother of the bishop of Chichester) who wanted to employ him as his curate. Despite his brother's recommendation, the bishop was anxious to satisfy himself as to Mead's education and connections. This is presumably why the attempt failed (Mead to LH, 11 May 1771; Glascott to LH, 11 May and 3 June 1771; LH to Hawkesworth, 4 Nov.1772; LH to H. Harris, 18 May 1771; Harris to LH, 24 May 1771, F1/124, 1533, 125; G2/1(4),CF).

[10] The evidence in Ellis's case rests on a remark in September 1773 that Ellis wished to be in London by early October in order to prepare for ordination in December (which implies episcopal rather than Dissenting orders) together with an absence of any reference to him after that date (J. Harris to LH, 11 Sept. 1773, F1/247,CF).

aristocratic support), for in January 1777 he wrote that Lady Huntingdon's offer to help him to Oxford was probably the only way in which he would ever be ordained. This idea was not pursued, however, and August of the same year found him in Sweden seeking Lutheran ordination. This was a less remarkable move than it might appear, in view of the contacts known to have existed between Dr Wachsel, one of the ministers of the Swedish Church in London, and the Countess's Connexion.[11] There were evidently difficulties for Harris here too, and it is not clear what form of ordination (if any) he enjoyed as he continued to serve the Hull chapel in the 1780s.[12]

Harris's mention of Oxford was revealing, for it indicated the realization that a period at the universities might still prove essential for students wishing to be episcopally ordained, if for no other reason than to shed the stigma which attached to the alumni of Trevecca College. That Lady Huntingdon herself fully realized this is clear from Harris's remark and it was evidently a device that she herself suggested in the case of at least one other student. This was John Eyre, later to achieve prominence as a founder of the London Missionary Society and the first editor of the *Evangelical Magazine*, who had come to Trevecca in 1776 and after the usual employment as an itinerant preacher, went up to St Edmund Hall, Oxford, at Lady Huntingdon's desire and expense (though, apparently, with little personal inclination) in 1779. This had the required effect in a surprisingly short time, for Eyre was apparently ordained deacon and priest the same year[13]—a curious contrast to the case of

---

[11] Wachsel was at college in January 1774 and there are indications of contacts between him and students in London during this period (J. Lloyd to LH, 25 Apr. 1774; Mead to LH, 16 Aug. 1777; R. Kean to LH, 23 May 1775, F1/1688, 401; A1/12(30),CF).

[12] J. Harris to LH, 11 and 25 Sept. 1773; Lady Smythe to LH, 27 Sept. 1773; Kean to LH, 23 May 1775; J. Harris to LH, 20 Jan. 1777; Mead to LH, 16 Aug. and 1 Dec. 1777, F1/247, 251, 1659; A1/12(30); F1/380, 401, 417,CF.

[13] Eyre to LH, 29 Mar. 1776 and 30 Aug. 1779, F1/353, 446,CF. E. Middleton, *Biographia Evangelica or an Historical Account of the Lives and Deaths of the Most Eminent and Evangelical Authors or Preachers* (London, 1779–86), 153–5 has Eyre as a member of Emmanuel College, Cambridge, but there is no reference to his name in *Alum. Cant. Alum. Oxon.*, however, lists a John Eyre of Bodmin matriculating from

another student, Thomas Davies, who was advised, about the same time, that he would need to spend three to four years at Oxford if he hoped to be ordained at the end of it.[14] A year earlier, William Tyler had left Trevecca, after about five years as a student, to go to Magdalene College, Cambridge. The initiative, this time, was not Lady Huntingdon's—the suggestion came from Joseph Milner and support from the Elland Clerical Society—but he went with her full approval. Tyler was ordained in 1782.[15]

Lady Huntingdon's willingness to lose good men to the universities in this way is a further sign that she had few illusions about their chances of securing orders directly, and it was an acknowledgement that Trevecca had largely failed to secure one of the objects for which it had been founded. In 1770, as noted, she had assumed automatically that the bishops would be suspicious of her students. In 1773 she claimed to have it on good authority that the bishops had agreed together never to ordain anyone educated by her, whether at home or abroad (a reference to the Orphan House Academy in Georgia) or who had in any other way been associated with her, and that if any such did apply for orders, they were to disown, in the presence of three clergymen, all her principles and all future involvement with her.[16] There is no indication who this 'good authority' was, and no direct evidence of concerted action against her of this kind. There is certainly no suggestion that the men just discussed were forced to disavow her in the way described, and she would hardly have continued to be so keen to procure Anglican orders if it had really meant the renunciation of all that the

---

St Edmund Hall in March 1779, giving an age which corresponds with the date of birth quoted by Middleton. Middleton is the source for Eyre's rapid ordination (deacon by Bishop Lowth of London, and priest by Thurlow of Lincoln). There is manuscript evidence that he had already served one short curacy by August 1780 (Wills to LH, 2 Aug. 1780, F1/1852,CF).

[14] T. Davies to LH, 22 July 1779, F1/435,CF. In 1777 Harris thought it would take about a year and a-half (Harris to LH, 20 Jan. 1777, F1/380,CF).

[15] Seymour, i. 305–7. The first reference to him at college was in November 1773 (F1/258,CF). It cost the Elland Society £60 per annum to keep Tyler at Cambridge (George Burnett to Lord Dartmouth, Mar.1782, HMC (Dartmouth), iii. 256–7).

[16] LH to Piercy, 22 Sept. and 6 Oct. 1773, and n.d., A4/3(2, 3, 9 and 10),CF.

Connexion stood for. This is not to deny, however, a deep suspicion of evangelicals among the bishops, and signs at least of a common mind, if not of common action. After the young Rowland Hill had taken his Cambridge BA in 1769, he was refused the diaconate by no less than six bishops, including Edmund Law, the new bishop of Carlisle, who, while pleading his own recent admission to the bench and fear of counteracting the bishop of Ely (one of the others who had refused), did offer priest's orders once the first hurdle was overcome. When, at a further attempt, Hill was ordained deacon in 1773, Law was forced to withdraw his earlier offer, on the insistence of the Archbishop of York—an incident which could possibly have led to the report on the decision of the bishops which reached the ears of Lady Huntingdon at about the same time.[17] Belief that there was an agreed hostile episcopal policy towards the students was kept alive in the Connexion every time a student was refused ordination: in 1776, for example, after the rejection of John Clayton, Glascott concluded that 'the Bishops seem determin'd to reject them'.[18] In 1779, in the case of a student called Giles, it was even suggested that the fact of attendance at a Dissenting academy might count in his favour with the bishop 'as they are fond of ordaining those that have been Dissenters'. The plan (which Wills regarded as dishonest) was for Giles to preach at a Dissenting meeting in Kent on his way to London, and thus present himself as a Dissenter who had recognized the error of his ways. The ploy failed, as the bishop refused to ordain without testimonials, but it was significant that a Dissenting background should have been regarded as potentially less damaging to the chance of ordination than membership of the Countess's Connexion.[19]

Attaining ordination for the Countess's students depended not solely upon the attitude of the bishops, but upon the

---

[17] Edwin Sidney, *Life of the Rev. Rowland Hill* (5th edn., London, 1861), 82, 122, 136.

[18] Glascott to LH, 1 June 1776, F1/1729,CF. Clayton was later to enjoy a long and distinguished position within London Independency.

[19] Wills to LH, 7 and 16 July 1779, F1/1829–30,CF. The plan had been suggested by the London clergyman who wanted Giles ordained as his curate.

willingness of other incumbents to provide curacies and to sign the necessary documentation, the letters testimonial, and the certificate. One student who fell foul of this requirement was William Aldridge whose ordination was planned at the same time as that of James Glazebrook in December 1771. A title had been secured for him, evidently through the offices of John Fletcher, and the three clerical signatures necessary for his testimonials obtained by Edward Davies, rector of Coychurch, Glamorganshire.[20] In view of Glazebrook's acceptance at the same time, it was reasonable to suppose that Aldridge too would be lucky, until Morgan (the incumbent, presumably, of his home parish), refused at the crucial time to read in Church his *Si Quis*, or notice of intention for orders. Without Morgan's certificate that the notice had been read and no impediment alleged, the bishop refused ordination, an indication of how the perversity of an individual incumbent (who would not, by signing the certificate, have committed himself to any view as the suitability of the man concerned), could upset ordination plans at the last moment.[21] Testimonials, on the other hand, did imply a personal knowledge, and Edward Davies subsequently had to satisfy his bishop (Shute Barrington of Llandaff) who had issued a charge to his diocese against the presentation of sham titles and testimonials, that he really was acquainted with Aldridge's character and ability.[22]

Curacies might come from one of two very different sources: either from Evangelical incumbents wanting a like-minded assistant, or from absentees so indifferent to the

---

[20] Seymour, ii. 136; Fletcher to CW, 21 Sept. 1771, Meth. Arch.(Fletcher), 37; E. Davies to LH, 19 Nov. 1771; T. Davies to LH, 20 Nov. 1771, F1/142–3,CF. It was reasonable for Davies to help LH in this way since it was through her influence three years earlier that he had been presented to Coychurch by its evangelical patron, Lady Charlotte Edwin (E. Davies to LH, 25 Mar. 1768; J. Lloyd to LH, 2 Apr.1768, F1/26, 27,CF).

[21] Seymour, ii. 136. Glazebrook to LH, 19 and 24 Dec.1771; J. Cook to LH, 21 Dec. 1771, F1/155, 159, 158,CF. A major factor in the failure of Clayton's ordination attempt in 1777 was the refusal of the curate in the place where he lived to read the *Si Quis* (T. W. Aveling, *Memorials of the Clayton Family* (London, 1867), 33).

[22] E. Davies to LH, n.d., F1/1163,CF. At least one bishop at the time, presumably in an attempt to check the authenticity of the titles being offered, insisted upon the actual stipend being quoted in each case (Peckwell to LH, n.d., F1/1248,CF).

state of their parishes that they did not care who was left in charge. Lady Huntingdon encountered both situations and in this period probably had, overall, the possibility of as many titles as she had young men wanting them, although there was no guarantee that such offers would come at the right time. In September 1770, for example, Maxfield received a request for a curate from a parish whose elderly, non-resident incumbent had left the management of its affairs to the chief layman. This, Maxfield suggested, might provide a title for one of the students as well as an opening in the area.[23] In 1775 Lady Huntingdon was informed that the rector of Sleaford, Lincolnshire, was so desperate for a curate that he 'may even take a Godly man', though Lady Huntingdon's friend, who passed on this information, suggested that there might be hostility from the patron (the bishop of Derry, Lord Bristol) and some of the principal people of the parish.[24] Lady Huntingdon had received requests for curates even before the founding of Trevecca College. June 1764, for example, found her dealing with two such applications,[25] and it was perhaps natural that her patronage of ministers should have marked her out, in the eyes of many, as some kind of ecclesiastical clearing-house. This was particularly so in the case of those specifically wanting Evangelicals. The attempt, already mentioned, to secure Giles's ordination in July 1779 was on a title supplied by a Mr Bromley, minister of a City church and of the Portland chapel in London, who had asked for a Gospel curate and asked to hear him preach before he accepted him.[26] In other cases, the identity and motives of the applicant would be less clear, as in that of the West Country incumbent who asked Lady Huntingdon for a curate in January 1777. This time, although only two months earlier she had asked Richard de Courcy for a title for a student, there was apparently no other student then able to take advantage of the offer; instead, she proposed her former student, Williams, then

---

[23] Maxfield to LH, 30 Sept. 1770, F1/1511,CF.
[24] Lady Manners to LH, 14 Oct. 1775, F1/335,CF.
[25] LH to CW, 9 June 1764, Meth. Arch. (LH), 75.
[26] Wills to LH, 7 July 1779, F1/1829,CF.

about to leave de Courcy's curacy, having proved himself unsatisfactory.[27] Offers of curacies, it seems clear, had to come at exactly the right moment to be of use at all, and in spite of the number of requests she received, Lady Huntingdon still had, on occasion, to solicit them herself; in April 1779, for example, she wrote to Mr Beale, incumbent of Bengeworth near Evesham, and a friend of Wesley's as well as herself, to seek help in obtaining titles for two of her men.[28] In the last resort, of course, she could turn to those of her own ministers still holding livings, although titles from such quarters might prove of doubtful value: in 1777 she pressed Thomas Haweis for the curacy of his parish of Aldwincle, Northamptonshire, but although Haweis was anxious for a curate at the time, he suggested that a title from him would not only be refused but would be positively harmful to the man concerned.[29]

DISSENTING ORDINATION

If Anglican orders were difficult, or even impossible, to come by, what was the alternative? One answer was for students to serve without ordination, and this appears to have been accepted from an early stage in the college's life, even if not from the very start. Joseph Shipman, who had gone to Trevecca after his expulsion from St Edmund Hall, wrote to Lady Huntingdon that as he could not serve any of her institutions without the ordination of which he now despaired, he had thoughts of returning to trade 'as it would be distressing to serve only when a qualified minister is present'.[30] If this were really the situation when Shipman wrote, it very quickly changed and unordained students were soon employed, usually on their own, at all the Connexion's chapels and preaching places. What they were not allowed to do was to give the sacraments, and this, from the standpoint

---

[27] De Courcy to LH, 27 Nov. 1776 and 14 Jan. 1777, F1/1737, 1745,CF.
[28] LH to Beale, 6 Apr. 1779, G2/2(c),CF.
[29] Haweis to LH, n.d. and 10 Oct. 1777, F1/1190, 1793,CF.
[30] Shipman to LH, n.d., E4/5(11),CF.

of congregations, was the chief reason for wanting them ordained. No doubt this was an important factor with the students, too, but important also was the desire for some more secure and recognized position than the life of an itinerant lay preacher was able to offer. To these two factors was added, for Lady Huntingdon, the fear that if she did not secure ordination for the students herself, others would do so instead. This she used as an argument in her own cause. Thus in 1771, when seeking ordination for Cornelius Winter whom she hoped to send as a catechist to the Orphan House in Georgia, she warned Bishop Terrick that Winter would join the Dissenters if this was refused. This he subsequently did.[31] Similar arguments were used in 1776 when she persuaded the dean of Norwich, Philip Lloyd, to represent to the bishops her need for ordinations to offset the pressures which Dissenters themselves were now putting on students to join them; she had, she told Lloyd, got six young men at that moment who were still favourable to the Church services. The implication was that they would not always remain so.[32]

Dissenting ordination nevertheless remained an obvious alternative and it appears, in some cases, to have been sought without any prior attempt at episcopal orders. One instance was that of Thomas English who was itinerating from the college in 1773 and 1774 and who was ordained (by whom and when is not recorded) in time to participate in the ordination of another Trevecca student, Richard Herdsman, at South Petherton, in April 1775.[33] The attainment of Dissenting ordination, however, was by no means always easy. There must have been many Dissenting ministers who regarded the irregularity, enthusiasm, and educational limitations of the students with quite as much suspicion as did any of their Anglican counterparts;[34] and although others, along with the members of many Dissenting congregations, clearly looked upon the college as a useful source of

[31] LH to the bishop of London, 30 Aug. 1771, E3/1(5),CF.
[32] LH to the dean of Norwich, 23 July 1776; dean of Norwich to LH, 17 Sept. 1776, E3/2(9 and 10),CF.
[33] Seymour, ii. 294; J. Adams to LH, 20 Apr. 1775, F1/1714,CF.
[34] G. F. Nuttall, *The Significance of Trevecca College, 1768–91*, Cheshunt College Bicentenary Booklet (London, 1968), 7.

additional manpower, it was a different matter for the Countess to use Dissenting ordination (as she attempted to use Anglican orders) as an adjunct to the work of her own Connexion. Thus, despite efforts by Dissenters to entice her students from her, Lady Huntingdon occasionally experienced clear resistance from them when she sought Dissenting ordination for men intending to continue in the chapels of her Connexion. A prime example of this was the case of John Adams, a contemporary of English and Herdsman at Trevecca, who had apparently secured Lady Huntingdon's consent to his seeking Dissenting ordination. His plan, early in 1775, was for the ministers who had gone to South Petherton for Herdsman's ordination to stop off on their way back at Weymouth, where he was then serving, and ordain him.[35] In this he was disappointed, and in the following September he was still discussing ways in which ordination might be arranged. Again this came to nothing, and the problem was still unresolved more than a year later, in October 1776, when he wrote of fresh plans, and of the unrest at Weymouth occasioned by the repeated delays.[36] Ordination served both to unite congregations (who could then receive the sacraments without dependence on outside help) and to bolster the authority of the minister himself. The precise reason for Adams's difficulties is unclear. One minister named in connection with his several ordination attempts was Edward Ashburn (or Ashburner), one of those who had ordained Herdsman, who on occasion preached both at Connexional and Whitefieldite chapels.[37] Clearly he was sympathetic to the Revival, and it may have been either that he had difficulty in persuading others to join him in ordaining the Countess's students, or that it was impolitic for any to do so too often (a situation not dissimilar from that faced by clergymen over the signing of testimonials). Whatever the reason, Adams sustained a third disappointment, and it was not until the beginning of 1777

[35] Adams to LH, 20 Apr. 1775, F1/1714,CF.
[36] J. Adams to LH, 15 Sept. 1775 and 26 Oct. 1776, F1/1719, 1732,CF.
[37] E. Sheppard to LH, 12 Mar. 1777, F1/384,CF. Ashburn(er) had been strongly influenced by the preaching of James Hervey (John Brown, *Memoirs of the Life and Character of James Hervey* (Edinburgh, 2nd edn., 1809), p. iv).

that Lady Huntingdon appears to have made fresh plans for his ordination. At this point, Thomas Molland asked Lady Huntingdon for a similar opportunity for himself, now that he had given up thoughts of episcopal ordination.[38] Arrangements were made for both to be ordained at the end of June, but at the beginning of that month, the plan was abruptly called off. The objections from the Dissenters came so late, wrote Adams, that they appeared as a deliberate attempt to frustrate the whole plan. It is not clear what happened to change the position and enable both men to be ordained by Dissenters later that year.[39]

Adams's path to ordination had been exceptionally difficult, but he was not the only student to experience significant problems. Another was John Hawkesworth, who went to serve the Connexional chapel in Plunkett Street, Dublin, in April 1772. Lady Huntingdon agreed in October 1773 to his being ordained, though no moves were made on this, and she appears to have had some fear of losing Hawkesworth to the Dublin congregation once he was actually ordained to them. When he did finally achieve ordination in September 1774, it was to the Dublin congregation, but not in Dublin: the Irish Dissenting ministers, he warned Lady Huntingdon, were so hostile to the Connexion that they would never agree to do it, and he had to come over to Plymouth to be ordained by the Dissenter Andrew Kinsman at his Tabernacle there.[40]

Lady Huntingdon's concern at losing Hawkesworth is an indication of her ambivalent attitude towards Dissenting ordination: on the one hand it clearly enabled its recipients to exercise a more effective ministry, but it also enhanced the danger of their abandoning itinerancy and effectively being lost to the service of the Connexion. The practice of ordination to a particular congregation had a similar effect to that of Anglican titles (that is, ordination to a specific curacy), and threatened a similar restriction on future

---

[38] Molland to LH and J. Adams to LH, 2 Feb. 1777, F1/382, 1751,CF.

[39] Molland to LH, 26 May 1777; J. Adams to LH, 10 June 1777, F1/391, 1762; Aveling, *Claytons*, 37.

[40] LH to Hawkesworth, 29 July 1774, Seymour, ii. 173–4; LH to Hawkesworth, 16 Sept. and 2 Nov. 1774; Hawkesworth to LH, 7 Aug. 1774, G2/1(11 and 12); F1/318,CF.

freedom of action. It also increased the danger that, even if these men did not remain long with the congregations to which they were ordained, they would now be more liable to receive subsequent invitations from churches outside the Connexion. This ambivalence of attitude revealed itself in individual cases. Thus, in spite of the support which Lady Huntingdon gave Adams and Molland in their efforts to achieve ordination, she could still lament afterwards, 'that they should become so subjected to man, and to those obligations so fatal to their peace, as to [*sic*] narrow a sphere of action as theirs; and which must render a labourer in these days of evil but a miserable prisoner at best'.[41] The context of these remarks was a letter to another student, John Clayton, who had also just received ordination as a Dissenter, though by a rather different path. Clayton had made two serious attempts at episcopal ordination, in 1776 and 1777, but after his second disappointment had chanced (providentially as it might appear) to read Towgood's *Dissent from the Church of England Fully Justified*. This changed his theological position and he became the only one from Trevecca in this period known for certain to have chosen Dissenting ordination out of conviction rather than expediency.[42] Even so, he was left in no doubt by Lady Huntingdon that she regarded the threat to his liberty and usefulness as every bit as serious as that to Adams and Molland.[43] What no doubt made matters worse, in Clayton's case, was his then going as assistant to Sir Harry Trelawney, the eccentric evangelical Cornish baronet, who had himself been ordained a Dissenter in the April of 1777.[44] This re-emphasized the danger (shown the previous year by the ordination of students by the Whitefieldites)[45] that sheep-stealing could take place

---

[41] Aveling, *Claytons*, 37.
[42] Clayton to LH, 26 Sept. 1775; Glascott to LH, 1 June 1776, F1/332, 1729,CF; Aveling, *Claytons*, 33–4.   [43] Ibid. 35–9.
[44] Ibid. 41. Sir Harry Trelawny (1756–1834) was ordained as a Dissenter in 1777, having opened chapels at West Looe and Trelawny; preached, amongst others, for Lady Glenorchy. He had become a Unitarian by 1779; returned to the Church of England in 1781; ordained and held Cornish benefices for a period; became a Roman Catholic in 1810; and was ordained a Roman Catholic priest in 1831 (*Blackwell*).   [45] See Ch. 6.

between groups within the Revival, as well as from the ranks of traditional Dissent.

PLANS FOR CONNEXIONAL ORDINATION

In the face of this threat, and the difficulties and drawbacks inherent in both Anglican and Dissenting ordination, the one answer seemed to be for the Connexion to establish its own ordination. It was not until 1783, after the Connexion had formally seceded from the Church of England, that there took place in London what was described, in the account published afterwards, as the 'Primary Ordination' of the Countess's Connexion,[46] yet there is clear evidence that something of the kind was in Lady Huntingdon's mind nearly a decade earlier. The germ of the idea may even have come from Hawkesworth himself, for in July 1774 he suggested that as Dissenting ministers were reluctant to ordain except to a specific congregation, and as the Dublin congregation wanted to remain under Lady Huntingdon's patronage, the answer might be for him to be ordained to them.[47] This appears to have been the first occasion on which ordination was contemplated in respect of a congregation that intended to remain within the Connexion. It was a short step from Dissenters ordaining men planning to remain within the Connexion, to the latter starting to ordain their own brethren. Thus an ordained ministry would be perpetuated within the Connexion. Lady Huntingdon's thinking may well have run on these lines, although the details are uncertain and the picture has to be built up from a number of oblique references.

The first of these concerned the student John Meldrum, who in 1775 was serving a congregation at Laugharne, Carmarthenshire. Lady Huntingdon was told that he wanted, while remaining in connexion with her, to be ordained at the anniversary of the foundation of the college on 24 August.[48] If Lady Huntingdon had planned something

---

[46] *An Authentic Narrative of the Primary Ordination* (London 1784).
[47] Hawskesworth to LH, 'July', F1/1194,CF.
[48] Mary Butler to LH, 2 Aug. 1775, F1/1718, 1737,CF.

for her birthday, it does not appear to have been carried out; certainly there is no evidence of it and she is known to have stayed at Bristol throughout the month. Nevertheless, the reference is significant; the anniversary was just the sort of occasion she would have chosen, and the wording of the letter clearly implied that ordination was in her gift. Clearly it continued a possibility, for in October John Clayton, then at college, spoke of the students' day of fasting and prayer for a number of objects including 'the intended ordination', subsequently remarking that 'The ordination most people oppose'.[49] Whether it was this opposition that led to the abandonment of the scheme is not clear. The following June Glascott, writing as noted[50] of what appeared to him to be the determined opposition of the bishops to Trevecca ordinands, suggested that some sort of ordination for the students would be necessary, adding that 'I often wish the plan Your Ladyship had in agitation last winter had been put into execution.' The idea was evidently not dropped, for John Hawkesworth wrote in November of Lady Huntingdon's plan to get some of the students ordained. As he was anxious for one of them to serve with him in Dublin, it could not have been episcopal, and probably not Dissenting, ordination that he had in mind.[51] Again, this is followed by silence and there is no indication of any further thoughts until March 1778 when a meeting was held in London of some of the leading clergymen of the Connexion. This discussed what was termed 'the Irregular and the Students Plans' and the meeting will be considered again later for the light it sheds on the strength of Anglican loyalties among some of the Connexion's leaders.[52] The details are hazy, but the discussion apparently included plans for 'itinerant ordination', though there is no explanation of the term. There is no evidence, however, that these plans were put into effect,[53] and

---

[49] Clayton to LH, 20 Oct. 1775, F1/336b,CF.   [50] Above p.302.
[51] Hawkesworth to LH, 29 Nov. 1776, F1/369,CF.
[52] Wills to LH, 10 Mar. 1778, F1/1823,CF.
[53] There is, however, a significant gap in the Cheshunt archive in the 15 months following the London meeting; the F1 section, which is made up of two parallel chronological series, contains no items from this period.

it seems reasonable to suppose that the 1783 ordinations were, as claimed, the first to be held within the Connexion. Certainly they must have been the first performed by a clergyman. It is significant of the attitude towards ordination persisting in the minds of some of the Connexion, that Thomas Wills who took the service was described by the committee of Spa Fields chapel where it took place, as having 'performed the part of a Bishop so excellently well'.[54]

THE ACT OF TOLERATION

Apart from the institution of the Connexion's own ordination in 1783, the main effect of the Connexion's secession from the Church of England was apparently the decision to use the protection afforded by the Act of Toleration. This was by no means a new departure, however, and there is evidence that well before formal secession a considerable part of the Connexion's activities was being conducted under the protection of the Act. In this the Connexion was not unique within the Revival but was following parallel developments within Wesleyan Methodism. It is necessary to examine these developments and the legal background against which they came about.

The Toleration Act of 1689 had left unchanged legislation against Dissenters of the reigns of Elizabeth, James I, and Charles II, but it exempted from its penalties those who were registered by justices of the peace at general sessions, as having taken the oaths set out in the Acts of that year legalizing the Convention Parliament, and having made the Declaration against Transubstantiation and the Invocation of the Saints, contained in the Second Test Act of 1678. Specifically, the Act exempted from the penalties imposed by the Act of Uniformity 1662, the Five Mile Act 1665, and the Second Conventicle Act 1670, 'any preacher or teacher of any

---

[54] Spa Fields committee to LH, 10 Mar. 1783, D1/1, 23,CF. Tudor Jones sees significance in the fact that the Connexion omitted from its ordination services the second sermon (to the people) that was a normal feature of Dissenting ordinations (R. T. Jones, *Congregationalism in England, 1662–1962* (London, 1962), 227).

congregation of dissenting Protestants' who made the oaths and declarations and subscribed, with certain specified exceptions, to the Thirty-Nine Articles of Religion. The final section of the Toleration Act re-emphasized that no place of religious worship was permitted until it had been certified to the bishop or archdeacon, or to the justices of the peace at the general or quarter sessions, who were then required to register the same.[55] This meant that the earlier repressive legislation could be used against unregistered Methodist preaching houses which would, as well, be without the protection against popular disturbances which the Act offered to registered places.

The problem for the Methodists was that neither the earlier repressive legislation (aimed at groups believed to be separatist and seditious), nor the relief provided by the Toleration Act, were relevant to a new religious movement which used the Church of England liturgy and was instructed by its leaders to pay tithes without complaint. Thus it was unclear whether Methodists were subject to the penal statutes in the first place, and how far they qualified for the protection of the Toleration Act. This confusion over the legal position may have convinced some of Methodism's opponents that those who broke up Methodist meetings could do so with impunity. Wesley himself argued initially that the legislation was irrelevant, since Methodists were not Dissenters, nor were their meetings conventicles (which were defined in law as being for seditious purposes).[56] Moreover, he was at first reluctant to use the Toleration Act, believing this would lead Methodists to style themselves Dissenters. He discovered in 1750, however, that this need not be so. It was sufficient, he learned, to request justices to license a particular house 'for public worship' and a number of places were licensed in that form the same year.[57] Even

---

[55] See W. C. Costin and J. Steven Watson, *The Law and Working of the Constitution* (Oxford, 1961).

[56] David Hempton, *The Religion of the People, Methodism and Popular Religion, c.1750–1900* (London and New York, 1996), 146–7, 148, 149.

[57] JW to Mrs Gallatin, 19 July 1750, Wesley, *Letters*, iii. 42. The term 'Methodist' was seldom used in licence applications in the 1760s and 1770s; the terms 'independent', 'Protestant', and 'protestant dissenter' do occasionally appear (Rack, *Wesley*, 497).

so, use of the Act still seemed to imply dissent from the Established Church and Charles Wesley in particular showed growing concern, as the 1750s progressed, at the decision by a number of individual preachers to qualify themselves under it.[58] This was a step of arguably greater significance than the registering of preaching houses, as the Act specifically referred, as noted, to teachers 'of dissenting Protestants'. John Wesley gave official countenance to the licensing of preachers in what became known as the Large Minutes of 1763, though preachers were advised to license only under constraint and then as 'Methodist' preachers rather than Dissenters.[59] He continued, however, to be unenthusiastic about the licensing of preachers. In 1765 he wrote that possession of a licence was unlikely to deter determined rioters, and in 1768 (after the Methodists had been accused of inconsistency for licensing while still claiming to be members of the Church of England) he stated that most preachers were not licensed. Those who were licensed did not style themselves Dissenters unless forced to do so by the justices.[60]

The Large Minutes also repeated Wesley's advice on the method of applying for the registration of preaching houses, and the number of such registrations accelerated during the 1760s and 1770s.[61] Some areas ignored his advice to avoid denominational descriptions, but if any congregation which followed it was refused registration by justices for this reason, Wesley would always insist that justices had no such discretion: the Act simply stated that when a congregation had signified its place of meeting to the appropriate authority, 'the Register or Clerke of the Peace...is hereby required to register the same...'. This was a point on which he was still having to insist as late as 1790.[62] On the general principle of

[58] F. Baker, *John Wesley and the Church of England* (London, 1970), 173–4.
[59] Ibid. 197–8; Rack, *Wesley*, 497.
[60] JW to W. Orpe, 14 Dec. 1765; JW to T. Adam, 19 July 1768, Wesley, *Letters*, iv. 318; v. 98.
[61] Baker, *Wesley and the Church of England*, 198; Rack, *Wesley*, 499. With more property at stake than hitherto, there was more systematic registration of Methodist meeting houses from the 1780s (Hempton, *Religion of the People*, 156).
[62] JW to the bishop of Lincoln, 26 June 1790, Wesley, *Letters*, viii. 224, 230 n. In 1761 Lord Mansfield had appeared to muddy the waters by ruling that justices

registration, he appears to have remained undecided; in 1787, he concluded with his legal adviser that licensing would be in the best interests of all the chapels and the travelling preachers, yet in the following August he wrote that he did not require any of the preachers 'to license either themselves or the places where they preach'.[63]

The fact that some Methodist preaching houses could for a period remain unlicensed, and thus technically unlawful, showed that the legislation was not uniformly or rigidly enforced. If Wesley's chapels might get away with non-registration, therefore, so might Lady Huntingdon's, and an additional advantage in her case was her right, as a peeress, to the possession of private chapels, exempt both from episcopal jurisdiction and from the need to register under the Act. It was, of course, stretching these privileges to the limit to call 'private' a chapel which had been deliberately opened for public worship, and as early as 1756 George Whitefield had been advised that such a claim would not be accepted.[64] It did, nevertheless, remain unchallenged for nearly twenty years, and during the 1770s it was even suggested that the evangelical Earl of Dartmouth should use his position in the same way.[65] In this case, which concerned a church being built in Macclesfield for Rowland Hill's Cambridge contemporary, the Revd David Simpson, there was evidently no suggestion that a personal link need to be established between the Earl and the town. Lady Huntingdon's early chapels at Brighton, Bath, and Tunbridge Wells were built with houses attached—which did give some impression of their being intended for her personal use—but chapels were very soon being opened in places to which Lady Huntingdon had never been and to which she would probably never go. In such circumstances it would have been difficult to claim that these were private chapels, and in most cases no attempt appears to have been made to do so.

---

could not refuse to register a Methodist meeting house, but *could* then decide whether it qualified for relief under the Toleration Act (Hempton, *Religion of the People*, 148).

[63] JW's Journal for 3 Nov. 1787; JW to Sarah Mallet, 2 Aug. 1788, Curnock, vii. 339; Wesley, *Letters*, viii. 78.   [64] Seymour, i. 206–7.
[65] Lady Glenorchy to 'Rev^d. Sir', n.d. Congregational Library, II, a. 17—vol. I, (15).

There is no evidence of any formal decision to use the Toleration Act, yet the way in which much of the Connexion's work developed, in response to calls either from individuals or from churches and societies already in existence, meant that its members often found themselves operating in licensed places. In June 1771, Glascott wrote that a member of the Brighton society had licensed his house at Westham, north of Eastbourne, and had invited him there to preach;[66] two years later, when Aldridge went to Dover, the use of the licensed but disused meeting house was procured for him by those who had invited him to the town.[67] Others in the Connexion went further and refused to preach indoors unless the premises they used were licensed. One example of this was that of Mead and Glazebrook at Watchet in 1770, who insisted on preaching out of doors, even in December, until the room they had been offered was licensed.[68] Glazebrook continued to be scrupulous in this respect. In February 1772, after his ordination, he declined to speak in the laundry of Lady Huntingdon's house at Ashby-de-la-Zouch, then being fitted out as a chapel, on the grounds that this would constitute irregular preaching.[69] What the case of Watchet showed was that not only were members of the Connexion content to preach in licensed places, but that their arrival could be the cause of a licence application. A possible further instance of this was at Gainsborough in 1773, when a congregation formerly served by Wesleyans applied for the services of Lady Huntingdon's preachers. These were duly sent, and although the congregation continued in the same premises as before, they nevertheless felt the need to license them, later that year.[70] It was not necessarily admission to the Connexion which led to licensing in this case: there may have been some external threat, whether of a legal or popular nature, of which no record has survived, which made it expedient to seek the protection of the Act. What the incident shows, however, is that admission to the

---

[66] Glascott to LH, 3 June 1771, F1/125,CF.   [67] Seymour, ii. 131.
[68] Mead to LH, 22 Dec. 1770, F1/115,CF.
[69] Glazebrook to LH, 22 Feb. 1772, F1/173,CF.
[70] Lady Manners to LH, 7 Jan. 1773, F1/209,CF; A Brief Historick Record.

Connexion carried with it no automatic protection of the peerage.

There is no evidence that Lady Huntingdon was herself concerned, like Wesley, that her societies should avoid the appellation of Dissenters. The Gainsborough congregation, in their application, styled themselves 'Protestant Dissenters, commonly called Independents' and when, in 1776, a chapel had been built and a new licence was needed, they simply expanded this to 'Protestant Dissenters commonly called Independents...to make use of the new building called Lady Huntingdon's Chapel'.[71] Other congregations, however, were bothered at the designation they would have to adopt, and were plainly uncertain of the legal position. The Dover congregation found, when they wanted to prosecute those who were disturbing their worship in 1776, that their licence had been lost; a new one was needed, but they understood that this would have to be as Dissenters and that, they imagined, would deprive them of the services of all clergymen.[72] Protection from popular disturbance, indeed, may well have been a common motive for registration, although the provisions of the Riot Act, despite referring specifically to tolerated buildings, still applied whether the premises were operating lawfully or not. Glascott found this in Lincoln in 1774, when the congregation, like that at Dover, had lost the licence of the meeting house which it was using. Although prosecution of the rioters failed as there were only two persons named in the indictment, the judge was sympathetic towards the informants 'and frequently observed that if we had assembled together in a barn, they had no right to disturb us'.[73]

Lady Huntingdon's approach to licensing was essentially pragmatic. Some chapels, in fashionable centres, gained respectability from the use of her patronage and would have suffered from association with Dissent through the use of the

---

[71] Lady Manners to LH, 7 Jan. 1773, F1/209,CF. The applications are transcribed in the Gainsborough chapel book from the originals in the Lincoln Diocesan Record Office.
[72] William Atwood to R. Keen, 12 Mar. 1776, F1/1728,CF.
[73] Glascott to LH, 28 Mar. 1774, F1/284, CF. The Riot Act 1715 applied to gatherings of twelve or more, whereas the provisions of the Act of Toleration applied even to individual disturbers of worship.

Act. Here she was prepared to use her rights, and did so not only for her own chapels, but, in at least one case, that of Westminster chapel opened by Henry Peckwell in 1774, for a chapel with which she had no other legal links.[74] Outside such centres there was less call for this kind of respectability, and the protection of the Act seems generally to have been sought without hesitation. The picture is not uniform: the new meeting house at Mevagissey, Cornwall, for example, was under Lady Huntingdon's patronage when first opened in 1776, and the decision to license it, later that year, was regarded as an act of rebellion against her authority.[75] When Lady Huntingdon's patronage was used in such places, however, it was generally as a temporary expedient. In 1777, for example, Glascott reported that the chapel about to be opened at Ely was not yet licensed and therefore must, for the moment, remain under her patronage.[76]

RELATIONS WITH THE CHURCH OF ENGLAND

This consideration of the origins of Connexional ordination and licensing has touched in passing upon the relations of the Connexion with both the Established Church and traditional Dissent. Before turning to the events that led to formal secession, it is necessary to examine these relationships in a little more detail. Ordination attempts were an obvious source of contact between bishops and members of the Connexion and it was here, as has been seen, that episcopal hostility was sometimes felt. Bishops could bring pressure to bear at other times, however, and their known hostility could militate against the respectability that the Connexion was anxious to attain. An instance of this occurred at Chichester in 1774, where the bishop, William Ashburnham, clearly less sympathetic to the Revival than his brother, the rector of Cuckfield,[77] was known to be antagonistic towards the chapel then being built in the town. In this situation, it was

[74] Wills to LH, 10 Mar. 1778, F1/1823,CF.
[75] John Painter to LH, 24 Oct. 1776, F1/1731,CF.
[76] Glascott to LH, 18 Nov. 1777, F1/1802,CF.   [77] Above, n. 9.

felt that Lady Huntingdon's presence at the chapel opening would increase its respectability and thus offset the influence of the bishop.[78] More directly, bishops could, if they wished, bring pressure to bear upon clergy holding benefices or other appointments within their dioceses. They could, in the first instance, refuse to institute at all, and there was at least one diocese, as Dr Welch has shown,[79] which operated a black list of those prohibited from holding cures within it. After institution, an incumbent was subject to a mass of ecclesiastical regulations which, whether or not generally enforced, could still be used against him in the bishop's consistory court.[80] This applied particularly to clergy wishing to leave their benefices for periodic service at Connexional chapels. Absenteeism might not have been uncommon among eighteenth-century clergy, but there were still severe penalties for it (as well as injunctions in the Canons of 1604) and each bishop had full discretion to refuse the necessary licence. Thomas Pentycross, as rector of Wallingford, had an indication of the pressures a bishop could bring to bear in the running battle he had with his diocesan, Shute Barrington, from the moment of the latter's translation to Salisbury in 1782. Pentycross's weekday lecture was twice stopped by the bishop and then restricted to the four months in the year when it could be delivered by daylight; he was confined to his parish, he complained, more strictly than any other clergyman in the diocese; and he believed himself to be under continual threat of frivolous charges in the consistory court.[81]

---

[78] Peckwell to (? LH) n.d., F1/288(b),CF.

[79] E. Welch, 'Lady Huntingdon and Spa Fields Chapel', *The Guildhall Miscellany*, 4/3 (1972), 175–83. The diocese in question was Lincoln.

[80] The major legislation with regard to non-residence, tenure of farms by clergy, and clerical engagement in trade, dated from the reign of Henry VIII. The complexity of these provisions led, particularly at the end of the eighteenth century, to considerable confusion, and they were revised and re-enacted, together with those on the maintenance of stipendiary curates, in a new Act of 1817 (57 Geo. III Cap. 99).

[81] Pentycross to LH, 2, 16 and 21 Jan. 1784, and n.d., E4/13(6–9),CF. His experience was very different to that of John Newton at Olney, who wrote, 'except for about four days in three years, I know no more of a superior than if I was an archbishop myself' (B. Hindmarsh, *John Newton and the English Evangelical Tradition* (Oxford, 1996), 216).

Pentycross's conflict with his bishop had been direct and personal, but episcopal powers could also be used more generally. In 1777, Henry Mead, on taking up his duties at the (episcopal) Ram's Chapel in Hackney, turned down an invitation from Lady Huntingdon to combine this with occasional services at the Woolwich chapel, because of the bishop of London's expressed determination to expel from the Church all who preached in licensed places.[82] Even when clergy had given up ecclesiastical appointments they remained subject to episcopal authority, and to preach other than in a church (unless they decided to secede and license themselves as Dissenters) was a technical breach of the law. In general, little notice appears to have been taken of such irregularities, but the threat of action always remained. In 1780, Thomas Wills was informed of extensive enquiries being made into his background, degrees, and orders by the bishop of Chichester's surrogate; nothing appears to have come of this, but the fear had been of a citation against him for preaching at the Brighton chapel.[83]

Clearly, much depended on the attitude of the individual bishop, and alongside these examples of hostility can be set cases of helpfulness and tolerance. The friendly treatment which John Williams experienced in his ordination attempt in 1770 has been noticed, and even the rigorous examination to which James Glazebrook was subjected in 1771 was followed, he reported, not only with kindness from the bishop's chaplain, but with a cup of chocolate as well.[84] Glazebrook appears to have had a particularly winning way with bishops, and even when, in 1773, the bishop of Worcester advised him to leave his curacy at Rowley, Birmingham, because of his lack of a university education, the bishop (James Johnson) did so, it appears, with gentleness and a real desire to avoid distress.[85] Some bishops were not averse to a degree of public identification with the Connexion or its members. The wife and daughter of

[82] Mead to LH, 8 Oct. 1777, F1/1791,CF.
[83] Mrs Wills to LH, 15 Aug. 1780, F1/1854,CF.
[84] Glazebrook to LH, 13 Dec. 1771, F1/152,CF.
[85] Glazebrook to LH, 6 June 1773, F1/1645,CF.

the bishop of Lichfield, for example, attended the Brighton chapel in 1769, and the elderly Bishop Willes of Bath and Wells was present himself at the Bath chapel in the following year.[86] When Thomas Haweis sought his Cambridge doctorate in 1777, he had a particularly marked demonstration of public episcopal support. The attempt narrowly failed, owing solely, he believed, to his association with Lady Huntingdon, but his cause was, throughout, actively championed by his own bishop.[87]

Looking ahead to the 1780s and 1790s, it is impossible to detect any new pattern in episcopal attitudes that might be attributed to the Connexion's secession from the Established Church. There is no reason to think, for example, that Pentycross's hounding by Shute Barrington would have been any different, had the Connexion not seceded.[88] Events after secession, indeed, are curiously similar in this respect to those before. Bishop Ashburnham's hostility at Chichester is paralleled, in 1783, by that of the bishop of Hereford towards the chapel in his cathedral city,[89] while John Fletcher's comment in 1770 that his bishop had never taken action against him for his irregularity, was to be echoed by Glazebrook, thirteen years later, in regard to his bishop, Beilby Porteus of Chester.[90] Even the Bath chapel managed to maintain its appeal to bishops' families and in 1791 was counting that of Archbishop Markham of York among its frequent attenders.[91] By the end of the century, indeed, far from secession having made service from clergymen in the Connexion's chapels more difficult, Haweis wrote that such service normally passed without censure, since 'all persecution for religious offences is become so opposite to the spirit of the nation'.[92] There is, indeed, no

---

[86] De Courcy to LH, 8 July 1769; Shirley to LH, 19 Oct. 1770, F1/73, 1565,CF.
[87] Haweis to LH, 23 June 1777, F1/395,CF.   [88] Above p. 319.
[89] Mrs Paul to LH, 14 Oct. 1783, F1/559,CF.
[90] Tyerman, *Fletcher*, 168–9; Glazebrook to LH, 26 Sept. 1782, F1/1865,CF. It was Porteus's view, nevertheless, that it was impossible for a clergyman 'to divide himself between... the Church of England and the Church of Lady Huntingdon' (quoted in A. S. Wood, *Thomas Haweis* (London, 1957), 168–9).
[91] Haweis to LH, 9 Jan. 1791, F1/2163,CF.
[92] Haweis, *An Impartial and Succinct History of the Rise, Declension and Revival of the Church of Christ* (London, 1800), iii. 269.

reason to be surprised by instances of kindness at any point in this period; if the eighteenth-century episcopate were men of their time in rejecting enthusiasm and irregularity, so in general were they in rejecting persecution also. The bishops may, as a body, have felt it their duty to protect the Church from the dangers of the Revival, but as individuals they were fitted, most naturally, by their intellectual background and training, to a role of gentlemanly toleration.

It was the parochial clergy who came into more frequent contact with the Connexion, however, and instances of active opposition by them have already been described, both before and after secession.[93] But though there were frequent instances of clerical antipathy to the Connexion, there were still cases, albeit less numerous, of a more tolerant attitude. Sometimes such tolerance was evidenced by attendance at Connexional chapels, and when this did happen, the Connexion's friends were quick to comment. Dr Tavener, a prebendary of Canterbury cathedral, for example, was reported attending Tunbridge Wells chapel in 1771, and many clergy were noticed at Bath, five years later.[94] Other clergy went further and offered their pulpits to ministers of the Connexion, a facility which, from the beginning of the Revival, it had been important to obtain, as well as sometimes dangerous to grant. This was a more significant sign of support: an incumbent might, out of curiosity, attend preaching away from his parish, but he would hardly welcome the propagation of evangelical doctrines among his own people (with the consequent risk of his own shortcomings being exposed) unless he were reasonably sympathetic towards them. Thus Glazebrook was offered the pulpit of Hartshorne, Derbyshire, in 1772; Glascott preached in an unspecified Lincolnshire church in 1774; and Thomas Wills was informed in 1777 of four churches open to him in the Ashby area.[95] Even after Wills had personally seceded from

---

[93] Above pp. 112-14.
[94] Mrs Godde to LH, 6 Sept. 1771; Mrs Wills to LH, 18 Feb. 1776, F1/1548, 1725,CF.
[95] Glazebrook to LH, 15 Apr. 1772; Glascott to LH, 11 July 1774; Mrs Adams to LH, 14 Mar. 1777, F1/177, 308, 1755,CF.

the Established Church in 1782, and was thus disqualified from holding a benefice, he could still preach in church and was to do so at a number in London.[96] It would clearly be a mistake to depict the clergy as sharply divided between a handful of the converted and a great mass of indifferent and worldly men. There was clearly a large number of honest and sincere pastors, often closely in sympathy with the aims and doctrines of the Revival, who were yet outside its recognizable organization and whose names never enter into its annals. Who else were the Anglican clergy of the Northampton area who joined in religious meetings with James Hervey, and paid such effusive tributes to him at his death?[97] Who else were the three young clergymen with whom Glascott spent an agreeable hour at Kirklinton, Yorkshire, in 1781, or the many serious ministers in the area of neighbouring Almondsbury of whom he spoke at the same time?[98] With such men as these, the Revival struck a common chord. That this was not lessened by the passage of time was illustrated in 1790 by the reference to a Colchester clergyman who was 'a friend to the cause of God and our Connection in particular'.[99]

The Countess's approach to the Church of England in the 1770s was essentially pragmatic: she had no particular wish to leave the Church or to break its rules, but she would use irregular methods if the furtherance of the work demanded it. Amongst her followers, however, there were some less ready to compromise with Dissent, and their presence is an indication of the diverse organization the Connexion had already become. A prime example was that of Thomas Haweis. Haweis's original plan, after his conversion, and having decided on ordination, was to study with the young George Burnett (subsequently a founder of the Elland Clerical Society and a Churchman of 'invariable opposition to every

---

[96] The churches at which Wills preached included Cripplegate; St James's, Duke Street; St Luke's, Old Street; St Paul's, Shadwell; and St John's, Wapping (*Memoirs of the Life of the Revd Thomas Wills, by a Friend* (London, 1804), 233–5, 253, 256, 258).
[97] See, in particular, the anonymous *Life of the Reverend James Hervey* (Berwick, 1770). [98] Glascott to LH, 4 Sept. 1781, E4/11(6),CF.
[99] H. Atley to LH (stamped 20 Dec. 1790), F1/2160,CF.

other profession of Christianity')[100] under the Revd Thomas Adam of Wintringham.[101] At Oxford, to which in the event he was enabled to go, he formed about himself a religious group, and in this and in the importance he attached to the sacraments, he followed the traditions of an earlier generation of Oxford evangelicals.[102] Despite the hostility of his bishop, which was instrumental in driving him from his Oxford curacy, Haweis remained loyal to the Church of England: on at least two occasions, for example, he used his influence to keep John Newton in the Church and persuaded him to modify the expression of controversial views on Church government.[103] When in 1774 Haweis formally became one of the Countess's chaplains and agreed to itinerate for her, he attempted to stipulate that no minister of any other denomination be admitted to her pulpits, as he was by then concerned at the number of Trevecca students entering the Dissenting ministry.[104]

Haweis's regularity was more than an emotional attachment to traditional forms, and depended upon a thought-out belief in the rightness and value of the Anglican system. In 1777 he appears to have made a concerted attempt to preserve the Anglican features of the Connexion. In January he wrote to Lady Huntingdon deploring the growth of party spirit within the Revival and the movement towards Dissent. Of the Established Church he had, he said, become increasingly 'fixed in adherence to that mode of Church government and worship, where candour and moderation have opened the noblest door of Usefulness'.[105] Some weeks later, he repeated

---

[100] *Evangelical Magazine* (1793), 83.
[101] Adam (1701–84) was rector of Wintringham from 1724 until his death; he was an Evangelical staunchly loyal to the Church of England, who criticized JW's irregularity (*DNB*; Wesley, *Letters*, iii. 149). [102] Wood, *Haweis*, ch. 2.
[103] Haweis's action in declining the Olney curacy in 1764 in Newton's favour altered the latter's resolution to become a Presbyterian (Wood, *Haweis*, 100–1). Four years later Haweis and Madan persuaded Newton that publication of his views on the government of the Early Church would not come well from a minister of the Established Church (Newton to Lord Dartmouth, 25 Oct. 1768, HMC (Dartmouth), iii. 189).
[104] Wood, *Haweis*, ch. 5; LH to Hawkesworth, 2 Apr.1774, G2/1(10),CF.
[105] Haweis to LH, 30 Jan. 1777, F1/1748,CF.

his belief that greater tolerance was possible under the Anglican system than any other, and he argued that though bishops might not be essential to the True Church, there was scriptural authority for their role as overseers.[106] What Haweis wanted was a distinctively Anglican core to the Connexion, a group of chapels under the Countess's protection and served by clergymen, which would be unaffected (and untainted) by whatever went on in the rest of the Connexion. Haweis believed that to make three or four chapels (including Bath and Brighton) fully regular would not only benefit them but provide 'a sort of settled standard to rally under', and thus be of service to the whole Connexion.[107] Such places, he believed, would receive assistance from some of those Anglican Evangelicals now reluctant to involve themselves in the Connexion's irregularity, and Lady Huntingdon accepted the principle of such a group,[108] even if she doubted its practicability. At the end of June 1777 Haweis went to London to recruit clergy for the purpose, but although he wrote enthusiastically to Lady Huntingdon of promises obtained from Romaine and his curate Henry Foster, she remained doubtful whether he would gain sufficient support.[109]

Whether or not it was realistic to expect to find sufficient clergy to make his proposals work, Haweis was not alone in his wish for regularity. Henry Godde, a senior member of the Bristol chapel, wrote in July 1777, for example, that when they came to renew their tickets that Michaelmas, 'it would be well to have it [the chapel] quite in the regular Church order'.[110] At the end of that year, the Revd J. T. Jones, invited by Lady Huntingdon to exchange his curacy for the settled ministry of the Bristol chapel, expressed his willingness to serve her there, or at any other society served only by clergymen.[111] Clearly the unlicensed chapels were a group apart and

---

[106] Haweis and Mrs Haweis to LH, 12 (? Feb.) 1777, F1/1801,CF. Haweis's point about Anglican toleration was of course open to the objection that it was this very laxness which made the Revival necessary.

[107] Haweis to LH, n.d., F1/1192, 1191,CF.   [108] Ibid.

[109] Haweis to LH, 23 June 1777, F1/395,CF. LH to Wills and Mrs Wills, n.d. (but evidently from late June 1777), Congregational Library MSS, II. c. 7.

[110] Godde to LH, 31 July 1777, F1/398,CF.

[111] Jones to LH, 18 Dec. 1777, F1/1629,CF.

the distinction between them and the rest of the Connexion must have been significant, or secession would not have been the decisive step it was regarded as being. These chapels were not restricted exclusively to the ministrations of clergymen, however, and students appear to have been employed there at various times throughout the decade. There is concrete evidence of this at Brighton in 1779, where the congregation was promised one of the best ministers in season, and one of the best students out of it.[112] Wills believed that a student during the season would be improper,[113] but his attitude appears more akin to Godde's wish for regularity during a specific period, than to Haweis's desire for an exclusively Anglican ministry the whole year round.[114] Wills's approach to the Church of England was pragmatic like Lady Huntingdon's, and he and Haweis can thus be seen as representing the two opposite strands within the Anglicanism of the Connexion. This difference led to coolness between them in 1777, after Wills had allowed students to supply his Church at St Agnes.[115] That others shared Haweis's unease at the movement towards Dissent was shown during the meeting in March 1778 between Wills, Jones,[116] Peckwell, and Shirley, to discuss 'the Irregular and the Students Plans' and 'itinerant ordination'. The details of the proposals, as noted earlier,[117] have not been preserved, but they clearly occasioned strong reaction. Peckwell refused to comment on the proposed ordination, but he declared that he would have nothing to do with either of the other suggestions, even if this meant his leaving the Connexion. Walter Shirley also rejected the proposals for the students,

---

[112] Wills to LH, 18 Aug.1779, F1/1839,CF.

[113] Wills to LH, 29 Aug.1779, F1/1842,CF. Wills was doubtless more concerned with the superior abilities of an experienced minister than with the mere fact of ordination.

[114] Though students could preach at unlicensed chapels, Dissenting ministers were not in theory allowed to do so. When the newly formed congregation at Lewes (obviously not part of the inner circle) asked for an assurance that Dissenters would be allowed to preach, they were told by Peckwell that this would 'be inconsistent with the plan and the peace of the people' (Peckwell to LH (stamped 3 Mar.) F1/1246,CF).   [115] Wills to LH, 12 June 1777, F1/1763,CF.

[116] This was probably J. T. Jones rather than Herbert Jones who was to play a prominent part in the events leading to secession.   [117] Above p. 311.

though he promised the Connexion what assistance he could manage while not committing himself to the rigours of continual itinerancy. Augustus Toplady, who had also been invited to the meeting, declined even to attend.[118] As evidence of the general attitude to regularity of the Countess's clerical helpers, this is admittedly slender, certainly in comparison with the extended expressions of opinion by Haweis already noted. But it does reveal a latent opposition to the extremer forms of irregularity. Such views, as well as others more akin to those of Thomas Wills, were to emerge again during the events that led to secession, and it is these events which must now be considered.

THE SECESSION CRISIS

The dramatic extension of the Connexion's activities into many areas of the country during the 1770s was not paralleled immediately in London. To some extent this was surprising, given that it was towards fashionable centres that the Countess's attentions had first been directed. The desirability of having her own chapel in London was suggested to her in 1771 by Thomas Maxfield, who lamented the poor spiritual state of the Tabernacle and its preachers. Although he still had his own chapel in Moorgate, he suggested that Lady Huntingdon might be called to open a chapel of her own.[119] The idea of building a chapel in London evidently came under active consideration, for just a year later Lady Anne Erskine, expressing her own wish to see such a place, wrote enthusiastically about the suitability as a chapel of a place of entertainment called The Pantheon in Oxford Road.[120] Nothing came of this idea, despite Lady Anne's further hankerings after a London chapel in the following April,[121] but by the end of 1772 Lady Huntingdon had secured something of a toehold in the capital when, at the

---

[118] Wills to LH, 10 Mar. 1778, F1/1823,CF.
[119] Maxfield to LH, 21 Feb. 1771, F1/1528,CF.
[120] Lady AE to LH, 9 Feb. 1772, F1/1584,CF.
[121] Lady AE to LH, 14 Apr. 1772, F1/1597,CF.

departure for America of William Piercy, she assumed responsibility for his chapel in Woolwich Ropeyard.[122] Shortly afterwards Lady Huntingdon acquired an interest in some kind of wooden structure in the Mulberry Gardens at Wapping. An account for repairs done on the building is dated May 1773, although it was not until the following July that the Countess actually acquired the lease.[123] By October she was seeking further ground in Wapping for the erection of a large chapel, but this plan was evidently shelved: a further temporary structure was put up in 1774 and the opening of a permanent chapel in the Gardens did not take place until 1778.[124] Back in October 1773 Lady Huntingdon had referred to a large London congregation which she had been asked to supply, but there is no indication where this was, nor any evidence that it ever became more than a passing outlet for Connexional influence.[125] The same was true of the chapel in Princess Street, Westminster, which was taken over and opened by Henry Peckwell in May 1774. Although the Countess's preachers assisted at Westminster, her only official link with the chapel was in granting it her patronage, to prevent the need for recourse to the Act of Toleration.[126]

The Countess was thus still without a major chapel of her own in London when her eye lighted, in 1776, upon another building named The Pantheon, sited this time in Exmouth Market off Farringdon Road. This Pantheon, like the other, had apparently not proved successful as a place of

---

[122] Above, Ch. 6, n 209.   [123] John Groves's account for May 1773, A2/9(1),CF.

[124] LH to Hawkesworth, 13 Oct. 1773; W. Latimer's account for temporary carpentry work at Mulberry Gardens, Oct. 1774; Wills to LH, 7 Mar. 1778, G2/1(8); A2/9(5); F1/1822,CF. The curious anecdote recorded by Aveling, *Claytons*, 93–4 of the young John Clayton being sent from Trevecca to London to countermand orders she had given 'to commence the building of a large chapel, in the environs of the metropolis', may possibly refer to the earlier scheme at Wapping. Or it might relate to Seymour's story of an abortive plan for the purchase of a theatre at Richmond (Seymour, ii. 303).

[125] LH to Hawkesworth, 13 Oct. 1773, G2/1(8),CF. This may conceivably be the same as the chapel between Tottenham Court and Islington which was offered for her use at an unspecified date, probably in the early 1770s (John Weston to 'Revd Sir', n.d., F1/1276,CF).

[126] LH to Hawkesworth, 2 Apr. 1774; Wills to LH, 10 Mar. 1778, G2/1(10); F1/1823,CF.

entertainment, and the lease became available in the autumn of 1776. Walter Shirley doubted the value of a chapel so far from the fashionable parts of London,[127] but as Lady Huntingdon remained enthusiastic, he, Toplady, the former student Anthony Crole, and a layman, David Parker, met in November to discuss the possibilities of acquiring it. Toplady and Shirley reported separately to Lady Huntingdon, but their views were similar: the situation of the building was too remote to be certain of recouping the very heavy cost of adaptation, but close enough to Whitefield's Tabernacle to be a potential source of embarrassment. Either it could be licensed and operate on the 'Broad-Bottom Plan' operated by the Whitefieldite chapels, in which case its pulpit would be open to ministers of any denomination, including theirs, or be kept under Lady Huntingdon's patronage as an exclusively Connexional chapel, in which case it would be seen as in direct rivalry to the Whitefieldite Tabernacle.[128] Lady Huntingdon acceded to this advice, and it fell to others to have the building converted into a place of worship. According to Lady Huntingdon's own account, this was done at the personal expense of two evangelical clergymen, Herbert Jones, chaplain to the Misericordia Hospital, and William Taylor, then a chaplain to the Earl of Marchmont.[129] Initially, attempts were made to secure the protection of peerage for the chapel, but when these failed, it was licensed under the Toleration Act.[130] It is not clear why Lady Huntingdon did not bring the chapel under her own protection at this stage, an arrangement that would have been similar to that at Westminster. Certainly she appears to have maintained some interest in the chapel's fortunes and before it was opened had apparently requested Walter Shirley to preach there.[131] It was presumably problems over the status of the chapel which prevented the planned opening of the chapel by Romaine in June, and the ceremony was finally performed

---

[127] Shirley to LH, 28 Oct. 1776, F1/368,CF.
[128] Shirley to LH, 21 Nov. 1776, F1/1736,CF. Toplady's letter to LH (n.d.) is printed in Seymour, ii. 304–5.   [129] LH to ?, n.d., E3/2(16),CF.
[130] Ibid.   [131] Shirley to LH, 23 Apr. 1777, F1/388,CF.

on 6 July 1777, by the Revd John Ryland, a Baptist minister from Northampton.[132]

Northampton chapel, as the building was called, would possibly have occasioned no more opposition than any other evangelical chapel but for the peculiar financial arrangements surrounding the church of St James, Clerkenwell, in whose parish it was situated. This afforded its incumbent, William Sellon, no more than nominal stipend and preaching fees, and he had to depend for his income upon the other fees of his office and the voluntary subscriptions of his parishioners.[133] The existence of the Northampton chapel, offering Prayer Book services performed by clergymen, posed a direct threat to the latter of these two sources, a threat made yet more serious by the subsequent action of the proprietor in converting part of the land into a burial ground. This suggested that Taylor and Jones were seeking to deprive Sellon of burial fees as well.[134] Sellon was not slow to recognize the danger, and even before the chapel was opened appears to have sought recognition by the lessors of extensive claims to jurisdiction over the chapel. His demands included the nomination of ministers (with an annual payment for agreeing to nominate Jones and Taylor), and the right, when he chose, to pray, preach, and administer the sacraments there.[135] These demands were refused and Sellon, early in 1778, instituted proceedings against Jones and Taylor in the consistory court of the bishop of London, on the charge of holding Anglican services in his parish without the bishop's licence.[136] Events moved slowly: on 1 June, members of the chapel society and others launched a subscription to meet the costs of the action, and

---

[132] Haweis to LH, 23 June 1777, F1/395,CF; Welch,153; Middleton, *Biographica Evangelica*, 102.

[133] Welch, 153; Welch, 'Lady Huntingdon and Spa fields Chapel',177. William was the son of Walter Sellon, a former friend of LH, although a noted Arminian.

[134] LH to ?, n.d., E3/2(16),CF. She claimed that the proprietor's action was taken without the knowledge of Jones and Taylor.

[135] Seymour, ii. 307–8.

[136] The legal records are listed in Welch, 'Lady Huntingdon and Spa Fields Chapel'. The major documents have been transcribed in M. Francis, 'Selina, Countess of Huntingdon', B.Phil. thesis (Oxford, 1955), Appendix III.

the case itself was introduced by Sellon's proctor, three weeks later.[137] There the matter rested until the following February when judgement was given against Jones and Taylor who were ordered to pay costs and admonished not to preach in the chapel again without a licence.[138] Lady Huntingdon had been following these developments with concern,[139] and when the decision was announced was already clear in her mind on the action she would take. The news reached her in Bath on 15 February and on the 17th she set off for London to complete the arrangements for the purchase of the building. She realized that she was taking a major step, and she asked for prayers for what she described as a 'great event to our Church'.[140] On 25 February, she wrote to the bishop of London, Robert Lowth, to explain the action she was about to take. Jones and Taylor, she acknowledged, had acted precipitously in preaching without licence, but they were now faced with a choice between seceding from the Church, or leaving the congregation permanently in the hands of those Dissenting ministers who had been supplying the chapel since the verdict in the consistory court. To prevent so large a congregation being lost to the Church, she would take it under her protection and this, as she explained in a separate note to Sellon which she copied to the bishop, would do no more harm to his interests than had been done already. This claim rested on the assumption that the Northampton congregation would continue to attend the chapel even if it remained permanently in the hands of Dissenters.[141] Sellon's reply, dated 27 February, was uncompromising. He had been justified by the Court and would continue to take whatever steps were necessary to defend his rights.[142]

The chapel continued under Dissenters until early in March when it was announced that Lady Huntingdon had

---

[137] Northampton chapel account book, 1 June 1778, D1/2,CF. Francis, 'Countess of Huntingdon', Appendix III, Document 1.   [138] Ibid., Document 8.
[139] LH to Beale, 24 Jan. 1779, G2/2(A),CF.
[140] LH to Wills, 16 Feb. 1779, John Rylands Library, ENG. MS, 338.
[141] LH to the bishop of London, 25 Feb. 1779, E3/2, (3–4),CF.
[142] Sellon to LH, 27 Feb. 1779, E3/2(14),CF.

acquired the lease and that the chapel would be closed for further alterations until its reopening by Haweis, Wills, and Glascott on the 28th. Holders of tickets were invited to exchange them for new ones on application to Taylor at the chapel house. The latter was pointedly (and accurately) described as 'her Ladyship's House', for Lady Huntingdon had by now moved there from the apothecary's house in Titchfield Street where she usually lodged while in London.[143] The alterations included the provision of direct communication between the house and the chapel:[144] this was doubtless intended to emphasize the personal nature of the latter and its use by the Countess and her friends was to be stressed in evidence given at a subsequent stage in the legal process.[145] Sellon communicated the announced opening to the bishop, who then wrote forcibly to Lady Huntingdon about her decision to reopen the chapel 'as before'. This she was quick to refute, arguing that operation under her patronage was totally different and offered (as she still insisted) the one chance of preserving the chapel for the Church of England.[146] Lady Huntingdon was undeterred by the bishop's letter or Sellon's refusal to discuss the matter personally with her. The lease was finally signed on 22 March 1779, and the chapel, now more formally referred to as 'Spa Fields', was opened as planned on the 28th.[147]

Lady Huntingdon fully realized the threats that still lay ahead. On 6 April she found it noteworthy that no steps had yet been taken against her,[148] but she had not long to wait. Before the month was out, Sellon had instituted further proceedings in the consistory court, this time against Haweis who had officiated at the chapel since the opening. Haweis took his stand on the rights of peerage, arguing that the

---

[143] LH to ?, n.d.; Notice concerning the chapel opening, E3/2(16), (12),CF. Francis, 'Countess of Huntingdon', Appendix III, Document 5.
[144] Schlenther, 151; Welch, 155.
[145] Francis, 'Countess of Huntingdon', Appendix III, Document 5.
[146] Bishop of London to LH, 11 Mar. 1779; LH's reply, 19 Mar. 1779, E3/2 (7–8),CF.
[147] Francis, 'Countess of Huntingdon', Appendix III, Document 2; Welch, 156.
[148] LH to Mr Beale, 6 Apr. 1779, G2/2 (c),CF.

issue was beyond the competence of the court.[149] The court's principal, John Bettesworth, reserved judgement on this until June and Lady Huntingdon, on the legal advice she received, was confident of the outcome.[150] In this she was disappointed. On 4 June, Bettesworth held that the case was within his jurisdiction, and on the 12th, Sellon presented his case against Haweis for officiating in the chapel without a licence.[151] Haweis allowed the vacation to intervene and did not reply to Sellon's articles until November, still maintaining, when he did so, that he and the buildings were protected by rights of peerage.[152] It had been obvious that the action would take some time, and Lady Huntingdon was content to return to Bath early in July. Wills had by then taken over from Haweis, thus exposing himself to the possibility of similar proceedings, although, as he wrote to Lady Huntingdon on 16 July, when he too was preparing to leave, this now seemed unlikely.[153] He was succeeded by Glascott, against whom Sellon did decide to take action when the court was reconvened in November.[154]

Lady Huntingdon's first reaction to Bettesworth's ruling on admissibility had been that she would challenge it in the Court of King's Bench and, if necessary, in the House of Lords. She evidently abandoned this idea as the summer of 1779 progressed, and began to concentrate her thoughts upon the consistory court and the step she must take if the final verdict there went against her.[155] An issue of this magnitude could not be faced alone, and Lady Huntingdon called a meeting of ministers at Trevecca, although she had by then decided that if her rights were denied her, she would secede from the Church.[156] Lady Huntingdon returned to Spa Fields

---

[149] Welch, 'Lady Huntingdon and Spa Fields Chapel', 178–9. LH had hoped that the case would be settled on the first hearing (LH to Wills, 29 Apr. 1779, Congregational Library MSS, c. 7).
[150] LH to Mrs Wills, 11 May 1779, John Rylands Library, ENG. MSS, 338.
[151] Francis, 'Countess of Huntingdon', Appendix III, Document 1.
[152] Wills to LH, 16 July 1779, F1/1830,CF; Francis, 'Countess of Huntingdon', Appendix III, Document 2.
[153] Wills to LH, 7 and 16 July 1779, F1/1829, 1830,CF.
[154] Francis, 'Countess of Huntingdon', Appendix III, Document 6.
[155] LH to Beale, 20 Aug. 1779, G2/2(D),CF.
[156] LH to Mrs Wills, 3 Sept. 1779, John Rylands Library, ENG. MSS, 338.

in October, by which time she had, so she said, received support on the legal issue from an archbishop and from peers who were 'no friends to religion'.[157] The November session of the consistory court brought no more than the reply by Haweis and the commencement of the proceeding against Glascott, and there the matter rested into the New Year. The evidence produced by Sellon, when the Hilary term opened in January 1780, sought to cast further doubt on the claim that Spa Fields was a private chapel. Sellon emphasized, in particular, the size of the building (it was said to hold two thousand people, the majority of whom came in by the public entrance) and the fact that tickets were sold. He questioned whether Lady Huntingdon knew the names of those who had bought them.[158] In the following month it was suggested to Lady Huntingdon (by whom is uncertain) that a petition to the bishop of London by the inhabitants of the parish on the chapel's behalf might be beneficial. It fell to the chapel committee to put this in hand and one hundred and eighty-five signatures had been collected when the bishop asked to see the petition at the end of April.[159] There is no sign of this having had any effect, and events moved inexorably forward. Sellon presented his articles against Glascott on 20 April 1780,[160] and a month later judgment was given against Haweis who was ordered, like Jones and Taylor the year before, to pay costs and admonished not to preach there again without a licence.[161] Although the decision against Haweis had obvious implications for Glascott and any other clergyman whom Lady Huntingdon might choose to send, all was not necessarily lost. After the decision on Haweis she discussed a formal application for a ruling to the Lord Chief Justice, Lord Mansfield, although whether such an application was made is unclear.[162]

[157] Copy of LH to ?, 16 Oct. 1779, E3/3(1),CF.
[158] Francis, 'Countess of Huntingdon', Appendix III, Documents 3 and 4.
[159] Spa Fields minute book for 29 Feb., 25 Apr. and 2 May 1780, D1/1, 3, 5,CF.
[160] Francis, 'Countess of Huntingdon', Appendix III, Document 6.
[161] Francis, 'Countess of Huntingdon', 7; Welch, 'Lady Huntingdon and Spa Fields Chapel', 179.
[162] LH to 'Dear Sir', 29 May 1780, E4/10(8),CF. The decision against Haweis had not been entirely unexpected (LH to Wills, 12 May 1780, Congregational Library MSS, II, c. 7).

In any case, she seems to have taken a decision, shortly afterwards, to secede formally from the Church of England. An address to the archbishops and bishops of the Church of England was drawn up over the signatures of Wills, Taylor, and Glascott, and dated from Spa Fields on 30 June 1780. This asserted their previous belief in the legality of service in the chapels of the Countess, but that following recent decisions they were faced with the choice either of breaking the law or of abandoning their congregations. Since they could bring themselves to do neither of these things, they intended withdrawing from the Church of England, continuing 'to maintain her doctrines, though we cannot in all things submit to her discipline'.[163] Amongst the Countess's papers has survived, in her own hand, the draft of a formal note from Wills, Glascott, and Taylor to the Archbishop of Canterbury, seeking to call on him 'on particular business'. This and several drafts of a letter from the Countess herself to the Archbishop—on the subject of 'the late Sentence' and her reason for not appealing to the House of Lords—all appear to come from the same date, but none, clearly, could have been delivered.[164] When it came to the point, Lady Huntingdon had hesitated over so decisive a step and at the end of July was still debating the reasons she should give as 'the apparent cause of my departure from the Church'.[165]

These doubts may have stemmed from growing opposition among her friends to the idea of a general secession. Haweis left the Connexion at some point in 1780, claiming later that he had advised the Countess strongly against secession.[166] In July, Peckwell cautioned her against a move which, since the law did not recognize 'a third sect between the Establishment and Dissenters', must make the Connexion

---

[163] E3/3(10),CF. It was clearly not sent. An undated, later version exists, in the names only of Wills and Taylor, and in this form was printed in *An Authentic Narrative of the Primary Ordination* (London, 1784) (E3/3(11),CF). There is no evidence that this was submitted either (Welch,159).

[164] Note from Wills, Glascott, and Taylor to the Archbishop of Canterbury, n.d.; LH to the Archbishop, n.d., E3/3(9), E3/3(4-7),CF.

[165] LH to Mr Way, 25 July 1780, E3/3(2),CF.

[166] Haweis's MS Autobiography, quoted in Schlenther, 154; Wood, *Haweis*, 158, 168.

a wholly Dissenting body. This, Peckwell believed, would have harmful ramifications for the rest of the work: 'what has been winked at in Members of the Church of England, will not be tolerated in any mode of Dissension but that which is strictly legal.' The answer, since he had no doubt of Sellon's right to bar any but legally tolerated Dissenters, was to make Spa Fields on its own a regular Dissenting chapel.[167] Another minister opposed to a general secession was Pentycross who advised Lady Huntingdon against any precipitate step in regard to chapels '*properly* and *originally* protected by your Rank', none of which had yet been challenged.[168] James Ireland of Brislington and Henry Godde, two senior members of the Bristol congregation, were both said to be against such a move, and so were most of the Bath congregation.[169] In view of Pentycross's attitude, William Taylor thought it a strange choice of Lady Huntingdon to send him to plead the Connexion's cause to the Association of Welsh ministers at Llangeitho, Cardiganshire, in the middle of August. Taylor, by now fully integrated into the Connexion's ministry, was an advocate of secession, and doubted the need to involve the Welsh at all.[170] The attempt to win Welsh support, moreover, met with a mixed reaction. The Revd Peter Williams of Carmarthen, who had been an occasional preacher in the Connexion for some years, wrote after the Association to suggest that protected chapels should not be licensed unless challenged, and then privately, with no public declaration of independency. He summed up the views of his colleagues with the comment that it would be as easy to make the Pope a Lutheran as to persuade 'Mr. R——d [Daniel Rowland]' to accede to the proposals.[171]

Lady Huntingdon was unconvinced by these arguments, and resolutely believed that she was the object of a sustained attack. On 4 August she wrote that she was to be turned out of the Church, and insisted that she would take with her only

---

[167] Peckwell to LH, 31 July 1780, F1/469,CF.
[168] Pentycross to LH, n.d. (but evidently Aug. 1780), F1/1252,CF.
[169] John Lloyd to LH, 15 Aug. 1780, F1/472,CF.
[170] Taylor to LH, 16 Aug. 1780, F1/1855,CF.
[171] Williams to LH, 18 Aug. 1780, F1/1856,CF.

those who came entirely willingly.[172] A week later she wrote to her son in a similar vein, claiming that the choice was between shutting all her chapels or leaving the Church.[173] The issue had become one of principle. As she wrote to another correspondent, the advice on all sides, whether from 'courtier, politician, professor or infidel churchman', was to break the law but not to speak against it (that is, presumably, to continue as before at such places as Bath and Brighton, even though the Spa Fields decisions had cast doubt on the legality of so doing). But Lady Huntingdon had too much integrity (or too much pride) to do that. She would await the outcome of the next stage in the legal process, the hearing of Haweis's appeal in November 1780.[174] Thus, for a period, the matter was allowed to rest, though the report on 15 August of enquiries by the bishop's surrogate into Wills's activities at the Brighton chapel,[175] can have done little to convince the Countess that her other chapels would indeed remain unmolested. In early October she came up to London for a conference with Glascott, Wills, and Taylor about 'the important business we are engaged in'.[176]

Haweis's case continued after the hearing on 15 November, but petered out in the spring of 1781, his appeal to the Court of Arches not apparently having been pursued.[177] Haweis was no longer preaching at Spa Fields, so the outcome of his case was academic compared with that of Glascott who, with Wills, was the chapel's major supply. After the relative quiet of the winter of 1780–1, therefore, the Spa Fields committee were particularly disturbed to learn from Glascott on 2 April, of his fear of being silenced in the new term beginning at the start of May.[178] Glascott's subsequent letter to Lady Huntingdon has not survived, but seems to have been less pessimistic, for she commented, in sending it to Wills on 14 April, that Sellon must either have been

---

[172] LH to Hawkesworth, 4 Aug. 1780, G2/1(20),CF.
[173] LH to Lord Huntingdon, 11 Aug. 1780, E3/3(3),CF.
[174] LH to Beale, 13 Aug. 1780, G2/2(E),CF.   [175] Above p.320.
[176] LH to Wills, 26 Sept. 1780, John Rylands Library, ENG. MS. 338. D1/1, p. 7,CF.
[177] Francis, 'Countess of Huntingdon', Appendix III, Document 7; Welch, 'Lady Huntingdon and Spa Fields Chapel', 180.
[178] Spa Fields minute book, entries for 3 and 17 Apr. 1781, D1/1, 8,CF.

restrained by his bishop, or by some higher power.[179] When James Oldham, a member of the committee, went on Glascott's advice to seek an accommodation with Sellon, however, he found no such signs of moderation. Sellon maintained his original demand for unlimited access to the pulpit and in view of this, the committee secretary wrote to Lady Huntingdon, urging on her the need for immediate secession, although whether of the chapel, the whole Connexion, or just Glascott, was not made clear.[180] Lady Huntingdon, with the advice of the Bath committee, chose the third possibility, a sign of how much she had been influenced by the opposition to a general secession, expressed the previous summer. She urged that Glascott should secede privately in Cambridge. He was then to continue as before at Spa Fields, but with the omission from the liturgy of certain prayers, particularly that for the bishop. 'Mr. Wills to succeed him,' she continued, 'and as soon as cited take the same methods...without any public noise of any kind.'[181] Glascott, however, was reluctant to be alone in taking this step, and he declined immediate action in the hope of protracting the case for another term.[182] Glascott's reluctance is understandable for it is unlikely that he had the slightest wish to leave the Church. He was offered a living only four months later, and though he was to ask Lady Huntingdon's advice about accepting it, he had clearly been convinced for some time of the desirability of a parish for when, as he put it, 'the ship can no longer sail the open seas'.[183]

A further deputation from the committee saw Sellon early in May 1781, but when he stood firm on his claim to Spa Fields as a chapel of ease of the parish, they wrote a second time to Lady Huntingdon to urge secession.[184] Legal advice was obtained and it seemed for a time that Lady Huntingdon would now take the decisive step. By early June she was

---

[179] LH to Wills, 14 Apr. 1781, John Rylands Library, ENG. MS. 338.
[180] Spa Fields minute book, 19 Apr. 1781, D1/1, 8,CF.
[181] Copy of LH to Spa Fields committee, 22 Apr. 1781, E4/10(10),CF.
[182] Spa Fields minute book, following receipt of LH's letter of 22 Apr., D1/1, 9,CF.
[183] Glascott to LH, 20 Aug. 1781, E4/11(5),CF.
[184] Spa Fields minute book, entry for 12 May 1781, D1/1, 9,CF.

satisfied that there would be no problem in finding justices of the peace in Bath before whom individual declarations of secession could be made, and she was pursuing plans to license not only Spa Fields but Bath and Brighton as well.[185] Lacunae in the records conceal why, even at this stage, Lady Huntingdon drew back, and no further reference to secession has survived until the end of the year. During these months, Lady Huntingdon had reacted bitterly to Glascott's decision to accept a living;[186] and when the legal process ended at last in December with the silencing of the latter, this was, in one sense, academic. The implications, however, were far from academic, and the committee at Spa Fields was convinced that this would be the prelude to moves against others of their clergy.[187] Further citations were expected early in January, and Lady Huntingdon at once declared that if they came, she could not resist them.[188] This time she kept her resolution, and in the New Year wrote to urge Wills's secession. At a special meeting at Spa Fields on 7 January 1782, Wills declared to the committee his readiness to secede and the doctrinal grounds—his objection to the power of the bishops, to the thanksgiving prayer for the regeneration of the child in the service of baptism, and to the 'sure and certain hope' expressed by the Burial Service, whoever the person concerned may be—which had led him to regard himself as a Dissenter already. The committee were pleased to find such solid grounds for Wills's secession and that, as he had so far escaped the censure of the spiritual court, the step appeared one of conviction rather than necessity.[189]

---

[185] Copy of LH to Mr. G——[Glascott], 8 June 1781, E4/10(11),CF.
[186] Glascott, 9 Oct. and 8 Nov. 1781; LH to Glascott, 12 Oct. 1781, E4/11(8, 9), E4/10(18),CF.
[187] Spa Fields minute book, text of letter to LH of 22 Dec. 1781, D1/1,15–16,CF.
[188] LH to Piercy, 23 Dec. 1781, Seymour, ii. 311–12.
[189] Spa Fields minute book, entry for 7 Jan. 1782, and text of the committee's letter to LH of 8 Jan., D1/1, 16–17,CF. Wills focused on factors which led others to secede from the Church of England. Two of the elements in J. C Philpot's decision to secede in 1835, for example, were infant baptism ('when I knew the blessed Spirit had no more regenerated the child than He had regenerated the font'), and the use of the funeral prayers for those 'who I knew died under His eternal wrath' (J. H. Philpot, *The Seceders* (London, 1964), 94). Denial of baptismal regeneration was one of the principles of the Free Church of England, which formed in the

Thereafter events moved quickly: Wills was licensed as a Dissenter at the quarter sessions at Hicks Hall on 12 January, and on the same day added his signature to the committee's requisition to the bishop of London, registering Spa Fields as a Dissenting meeting house.[190]

It is difficult to assess just how significant these steps were seen to be. All they meant, in themselves, was that Wills was able to perform a truncated Anglican liturgy at Spa Fields without fear of reprisals in the ecclesiastical courts,[191] but he remained alone among the Countess's ministers in enjoying this privilege. Without other seceding clergy, the maintenance of preaching at Spa Fields promised to be as difficult as before. It was clear by February 1782 that a rapid rotation of ministers would be necessary, whenever Wills was away from Spa Fields, so that each man had moved on before judgement against him could be given.[192] Nevertheless, the steps taken on 12 January did mark a watershed, for they led both to fresh thoughts of a Connexional ordination and to plans for the Connexion's own confession of faith. The latter does not appear to have been considered during the earlier ordination speculation, but it was essential, as Lady Huntingdon wrote in February, before an ordination could take place.[193] Both of these factors (the needs of Spa Fields and the desirability of an ordination) made it important for at least one more minister to follow Wills's example, since Lady Huntingdon had evidently decided to follow the Dissenting practice of having ordinations performed by two ministers. In fact a whole year elapsed before another clergyman seceded. In April Lady Huntingdon complained that no other minister would secede: all, she believed, were seeking their own interests rather than the things of Christ.[194]

---

mid-19th century, following the case of the Revd James Shore, who (despite having seceded formally from the Church of England) was imprisoned for subsequently preaching as a Dissenter (Grayson Carter, 'The Case of the Revd James Shore', *Journal of Ecclesiastical History*, 47/3 (July 1996), 490 ff.).

[190] Spa Fields minute book, entries for 11 and 12 Jan. 1782, D1/1,17,CF. By a strange chance, it was after preaching at Spa Fields chapel in 1849 that James Shore was arrested. (Carter, 'James Shore', 491). [191] *Memoirs of Wills*, 88–9.
[192] LH to Wills, 12 Feb. 1782, Congregational Library MSS, II, c. 7. [193] Ibid.
[194] LH to Mrs Wills, 1 Apr. 1782, Congregational Library MSS, II, c. 7.

In July she reiterated her concern to Wills: 'I have wrote to Mr. Taylor to [? secede] Immediately or the dissenters will have all our congregations and students and you two upon our Plan ought to ordain till others so ordain'd by you Join in the same [? Ordinance].'[195]

Taylor, in one sense an initiator of the whole affair and one who had been a proponent of secession throughout, was an obvious choice for the second man. Why his secession was so long in coming is uncertain. His hesitation may have stemmed from the difficulty Lady Huntingdon experienced in agreeing the terms of his service in the Connexion. Taylor was anxious to ensure that if he deprived himself of the ability to hold an Anglican living, he could be certain of security of status and financial position inside the Connexion. Writing to Taylor in July 1782, Lady Huntingdon proposed making over the Tunbridge Wells chapel to him, under his full control, and not subject to a committee.[196] Taylor was not satisfied with this proposal, however, despite the easy access to the work in London which Tunbridge Wells afforded, and he demanded, instead, what appear to have been very similar arrangements in regard to the chapel and house at Bath. To this, Lady Huntingdon reacted strongly, apprehensive of the reaction this would occasion in Bath, and apparently fearful that Taylor planned to operate independently of her there.[197] Wills attempted in October to assuage her apprehension.[198] It was important that an arrangement with Taylor should be reached, for the plans for the ordination and Articles of Faith were well in hand.

---

[195] LH to Wills, 23 July 1782, Congregational Library MSS, II, c. 7; LH to Taylor, 19 July 1782, Seymour, ii. 146–7. The fate of Herbert Jones is uncertain. He expressed his determination to secede as early as 1780, when his request for preferment had been turned down by the bishop of London (Glascott to LH, 2 Aug. 1780, F1/1851,CF). Dr Schlenther may be correct in thinking that LH's diatribe in her letter to Wills of 8 Feb. 1782 was about Jones (Schlenther, 153; Congregational Library MSS, II, c. 7).   [196] Seymour, ii. 146–7.

[197] LH to Wills, 10 Sept. 1782, Congregational Library MSS, II, c. 7. LH was right in fearing resentment in Bath. In 1784 an anonymous correspondent complained that if it were true that Taylor was to be left the Bath chapel at her death, this would not be 'justice to the subscribers to the Building of the Gallery' who, had they known, would have left the entire expense to herself' (? to LH, Feb. 1784, E4/13(27),CF).   [198] Wills to LH, 10 Oct. 1782, F1/1868,CF.

Taylor's secession remained essential, even though hopes had arisen since the summer that the growing hostility which Pentycross was experiencing from his diocesan would persuade him to secede also.[199] Lady Huntingdon discussed the Articles and ordination plan with Wills, Taylor, and others, in Bath in October, and it may have been at this, or some subsequent meeting, that agreement was finally reached as to Taylor's future role. By the end of the year the problems had been solved, for on 16 January 1783 John Lloyd at Bath was able to rejoice at the news of Taylor's secession.[200]

Taylor's action was one more step along the Connexion's hesitant path to separation from the Church of England. Even after it, the Connexion had still not broken formally from the Church, although there was evidence, during the autumn of 1782, of the idea of a general secession being actively canvassed, once again. In October John Lloyd expressed to Lady Huntingdon 'his clearest Opinion that, without Secession, the Work here and elsewhere cannot but fall to the ground'; by December, Lady Huntingdon herself appears to have come round to the view that only a general secession would prevent confusion after her death.[201] What this meant in practice is far from clear: obviously not that some chapels and preachers were licensed, for this had been the case for some considerable time. If, on the other hand, 'general secession' implied all chapels and preachers being licensed, then that, equally obviously, was never fully achieved: all the chapels do appear to have been licensed eventually, but service by beneficed Anglican clergy continued, to the end of the century, a regular part of the

---

[199] See in particular, Pentycross to LH, 28 Aug. and 18 Sept. 1782; Lloyd to LH, n.d., F1/480; E4/13(1 and 26),CF.

[200] J. Lloyd to LH, 16 Jan. 1783, F1/1879,CF. The moment of Taylor's secession may have been delayed by his illness in November and December 1782 (see especially, Mrs Taylor to LH, 6 and 13 Dec. 1782; S. Phillips to LH, 9 and 18 Dec. 1782; Taylor to LH (marked 19 Dec. 1782), F1/1874, 1876, 496, 499, 1877,CF).

[201] Lloyd to LH (marked 17 Oct. 1782); Piercy to LH, 5 Dec. 1782, F1/488; A4/2(72–3),CF. It was later suggested that the problem which would face the Connexion after LH's death explained why the peerage question was not pursued to the House of Lords: there was little point in preserving the *status quo* if it depended solely upon the life of a woman in her late seventies (Plan of the Apostolic Society, 1787, C4/26,1,CF).

Connexion's ministry. It is thus difficult to say when the final breach was thought to have taken place. At the end of December 1782, the York congregation congratulated Lady Huntingdon on her separation from clergy who were 'blind to the world and...whose Doom stands in God's Booke',[202] although whether this refers to the events of the previous January or to some further, more decisive, step, later in the year, is not clear. There are, in any case, no further references of this kind prior to the plans for the ordination, which took place at Spa Fields on 9 March 1783. Six students were ordained by Wills and Taylor who, with the students, had previously subscribed to the newly-compiled Articles of Faith of the Countess's Connexion.[203]

Ordination itself was not necessarily an act of separation. Ordination had been considered before secession was even thought of, and the Lord Chief Justice (Lord Mansfield) had yet to make his celebrated comment to Charles Wesley that 'ordination is separation'.[204] Ordination was hailed, however, as the culmination of the events of the previous years. Pentycross, at the beginning of May, rejoiced 'that the Secession is now completed with Ordination',[205] while at the end of the month Taylor wrote that 'the glories of Secession brightens [*sic*] daily upon me'.[206] This did not mean that the remaining chapels were brought into line with Spa Fields immediately: Bath remained unlicensed until 1788.[207] But it was not illogical to regard the ordination as a major

---

[202] J. Beal to LH, 28 Dec. 1782, F1/503,CF.

[203] Taylor to LH, 31 *sic* Feb. 1783; Lloyd to LH, 30 Apr. 1783; Wills to LH, n.d.; Spa Fields minute book for 9 and 10 Mar. 1783, F1/1883, 1885, 1277; D1/1, 21–3,CF. All the ordinands are described as students in contemporary accounts though there is no evidence of one of them, J. A. Knight, ever having been to Trevecca. The public nature of the Connexion's first ordinations contrasts with the privacy with which Wesley's early ordinations were conducted (J. C. Bowmer, *The Sacrament of the Lord's Supper in Early Methodism* (London, 1951), 159).

[204] Quoted in Baker, *Wesley and the Church of England*, 273. Wesley had initially avoided ordination on the grounds that it would mean separation; when he was driven to it in the 1780s, he denied that it had that implication (Rack, *Wesley*, 506).

[205] Pentycross to LH, 8 May 1783, E4/13(2),CF.

[206] W. Taylor to LH, 31 May 1783, F1/1890,CF.

[207] Wells Diocesan Court Records (quoted in W. Tuck, *Notes on the History of the Argyle Chapel, Bath* (Bath, 1906)).

step.²⁰⁸ Once the sacraments were administered by those not episcopally ordained, it became difficult for members of congregations to remain in full communion both with the Connexion and the Church of England. This caused concern in some quarters. Within a fortnight of the ordination, John Lloyd spoke of those who 'quarrel with the means by wch yr Ladyship has lately so nobly endeavoured to make our Redeemer's praises more glorious', and in the following February a woman at Bristol declared she would attend preaching but not the sacraments, as she was 'no seceder'.²⁰⁹ Others, however, quickly accepted ordination as something natural to the Connexion. Five months before even the Primary Ordination had taken place, the Norwich congregation asked whether their current student, William Green, could be ordained there as a means of consolidating the chapel.²¹⁰ This request was not met and Green was one of the Spa Fields six in 1783. What appears to have been the next ordination, this time of thirteen students, took place at Spa Fields in 1784, but for a period the venue became more flexible: Bath was chosen in 1785, Trevecca in 1787, and Birmingham in 1790.²¹¹ At the college ordination fourteen students were ordained, bringing the total within four years to thirty to forty. This shows the limitations under which the Connexion must have laboured before it took this decisive step and of the highly significant role which those of its own ordaining quickly came to play in its life and ministry. Despite the instances of ordination away from the capital, however, the practice of ordaining in London seems to have become the norm: it was a conscious decision in 1796 to allow ordination elsewhere for those congregations unable to afford the journey to London.²¹²

---

²⁰⁸ LH herself regarded Wesley's 'ordination of bishops' as potentially far more divisive than the step she had taken (LH to Mr Carpenter, n.d. Meth. Arch. (LH), 133).
²⁰⁹ J. Lloyd to LH, 17 May 1783; Wills to LH, 24 Feb. 1784, F1/525, 1930,CF.
²¹⁰ Norwich committee to LH, 1 Oct. 1782, F1/482,CF.
²¹¹ Spa Fields minute book for 30 May 1784, D1/1,CF; LH to Carpenter, 31 May 1785, MS in the possession (in 1969) of the former Huntingdon chapel (latterly Trinity Presbyterian Church), Bath; LH to Bidwell, 10 Apr. 1787; Bradford to LH, 27 May 1790, B4/3. F1/913,CF.
²¹² Apostolic Society, minutes of the quarterly meeting on 6 Jan. 1796, C1/2,CF.

It is not difficult to see why Lady Huntingdon preferred multiple ordinations in a major chapel—with overtones of a cathedral ordination in the Church of England—to individual services before the congregations the men would be serving. The latter heightened the links between the minister and the specific congregation (something Lady Huntingdon was always anxious to avoid) and was more similar to Dissenting ordination. Although the committee at Spa Fields had been pleased to find doctrinal grounds for Wills's secession, Lady Huntingdon herself was anxious to prevent the Connexion appearing to be just another Dissenting sect. Separation from the Church was only 'upon ecclesiastick Laws and Bondages', she wrote in 1782, and insisted, in regard to the ordination service, that 'as ours is so different from the dissenters, the nearest the Church form the better'.[213] The committee reference to Wills in 'the role of a bishop' must thus have pleased her.[214] The continuing use of the term 'the plan of Secession' to describe the Connexion's system of rotating ministers and general organization, was itself significant of the role the Connexion saw itself performing: 'secession' emphasized its origins in the Established Church without implying so radical a breach as 'Dissent'. Thus in July 1784 Wills lectured on ministry to students at Trevecca 'with a particular reference to the Plan of Secession,' and then journeyed to Worcester where misgivings about 'Secession' had apparently been expressed. Here, it is interesting to note, the only member remaining unconvinced was one who wanted the establishment of a regular Dissenting ministry, a clear sign that concern was as much about future organization as about a separation now already in the past.[215] Three years later, the newly formed Apostolic Society defined its purpose as the continuation, after Lady Huntingdon's death, of the college founded by her for the education of young men 'according to the plan (of secession)'.[216]

---

[213] LH to Wills, 23 July 1782, Congregational Library MSS II, c. 7.   [214] Above p.312.
[215] *Memoirs of Wills*, 114, 116–17.
[216] Plan of the Apostolic Society, 17 Oct. 1787, C4/26,CF.

CLERGY AND THE CONNEXION AFTER SECESSION

With the major exception of Thomas Haweis, secession does not seem in itself to have marked a decisive change in the extent to which clergymen were willing or able to serve the Connexion. One reason for this was that a number of clergymen who had been associated with Lady Huntingdon in the earlier period had ceased to be actively involved in her work well before the separation took place. The earlier withdrawal of Townsend, Jesse, and de Courcy, for example, has already been mentioned.[217] There is no evidence of Romaine having preached for Lady Huntingdon after 1773; on the contrary, there are clear signs that relations between Romaine and the Connexion became strained from the mid-1770s.[218] Nothing came of Haweis's efforts in 1777 to persuade Romaine to be part of an Anglican cell within the Connexion, and Romaine's refusal to have anything to do with Lady Huntingdon's plans for Spa Fields led to the revocation of his appointment as one of her chaplains, shortly before the chapel's opening in March 1779.[219]

Berridge was another of Lady Huntingdon's earlier supporters who had apparently ceased to play any active part in the Connexion well before secession, and whose attitude to such services was thus unlikely to have been affected by the step she had taken. The reasons for Berridge's withdrawal (if, indeed, it was a conscious act) are uncertain. It seems unlikely that he would have been much concerned at the niceties of Church order, and there is evidence of his

---

[217] De Courcy remained in friendly contact with the Connexion, as evidenced by his recommendation of the master of the new Cheshunt College in 1792 (above, Ch. 5).

[218] Peckwell to LH, 5 May and 20 July 1774, F1/288 and 313,CF. There were also theological differences between Romaine and the Connexion (LH to Romaine, Sept.1776; Shirley to LH, 28 Oct. 1776, Bridwell Library MSS, 92; F1/368,CF).

[219] Romaine to LH, Feb. or Mar. 1779, E3/3(12),CF; Schlenther, 158 n. 95; Wills to LH, 13 Sept. 1783, F1/1904,CF. Although Romaine was removed from the work of the Connexion he remained in sympathy with its ultimate objectives. In 1791 he urged Haweis to accept the trusteeship of LH's chapels, bequeathed to Haweis at her death, arguing that he would himself have accepted the trust had the honour come to him. Romaine continued his refusal to preach for the Connexion, though Haweis was welcome in his pulpit (Wood, *Haweis*).

preaching (after the Connexion's secession) at Rowland Hill's Surrey chapel and Whitefield's old chapel in Tottenham Court Road.[220] Venn's position is also unclear. There is no record of his preaching for the Connexion after the secession, although he had done so as late as 1779,[221] which may imply a conscious withdrawal like that of Haweis. But there had been a break in his Connexional service prior to 1777,[222] and his subsequent disappearance may simply reflect the other pressures on his time. Like Berridge, he supplied the Surrey chapel occasionally in the 1780s.[223] Of Walter Shirley it can be said with some confidence that secession did not occasion a breach with the Connexion. He appears to have become less actively involved in its work as the 1770s advanced, but he did remain in contact after the separation had occurred: in 1784, for example, he was present at the ordination held in Spa Fields chapel.[224]

Other clergy clearly did not feel that secession prevented them preaching for the Connexion. Glascott had fallen from grace by accepting a living in 1781, but was restored to Lady Huntingdon's favour by early 1783, and combined service in the Connexion with the tenure of his living, at least as late as 1801.[225] There is no suggestion in Glascott's correspondence that this incurred episcopal displeasure. Pentycross came to a similar view about service in the Connexion, although for him the outcome was different, and the latter part of 1783 saw him being drawn temporarily towards secession by a combination of pressure from Lady Huntingdon and hostility from his bishop. The softening of the latter's

---

[220] Taylor to LH, 24 Mar. 1784, F1/1936,CF. The Surrey chapel was a proprietary chapel with Anglican trustees, but licensed under the Act of Toleration.
[221] John Lloyd to LH, 9 Nov. 1779, F1/451,CF.
[222] Wills to LH, 3 July 1777, F1/1770,CF.
[223] P. E. Sangster, 'The Life of the Revd Rowland Hill and his Position in the Evangelical Revival', D.Phil. thesis (Oxford, 1964), 167, 135.
[224] Spa Fields minute book, entry for 30 May 1784, D1/1, 26,CF. Dr Schlenther suggests that secession led Shirley to abandon his earlier thoughts of moving to a living in England, in order to facilitate service in the Connexion. But Shirley himself claimed in 1782 that he still wanted such a move (Schlenther, 154; Shirley to LH, 17 Sept. 1784, E4/1(24),CF).
[225] LH to Glascott, 12 Oct. 1781; Glascott to LH, 28 Jan. 1783; Glascott to Mr Kingston, 26 Mar. 1801, E4/10(18), F1/505, 2390,CF.

attitude towards him in 1784 (plus, some felt, the influence of Pentycross's Evangelical friends, the clergymen William Cadogan and Charles De Coetlogon) convinced him that he could remain in the Church 'with full liberty' to serve the Connexion. The recriminations from Lady Huntingdon at this decision were as bitter as those against Glascott, two years earlier.[226] For Pentycross, there was no reconciliation.

These men were not alone, however, in believing that service in the Church and the Connexion were not incompatible. In 1782 James Glazebrook, then minister of St James, Warrington, assured Lady Huntingdon that he anticipated no objections from his bishop to occasional service in the Connexion.[227] Similarly the Revd John Bradford, who began preaching for the Connexion in the early part of 1783 (and later seceded from the Church of England) saw no contradiction that December in applying for a lectureship at St George's-in-the-East while continuing to serve at the chapel in Mulberry Gardens.[228] Another group whose involvement with the Connexion was maintained after secession was that of the Welsh clergy. Despite the cautious reaction to the idea of secession which Lady Huntingdon had originally received from Wales,[229] the participation of Welsh clergy in the Connexion seems if anything to have increased over the following years. By the later years of the decade such prominent Anglican leaders of the Welsh revival as David Jones of Llangan, David Griffiths of Llwyngwair, and Thomas Charles of Bala were supplying regularly for the Countess at Spa Fields and, in some instances, at other of the Connexion's major chapels.[230] At the end of the century, Haweis recorded

---

[226] Pentycross to LH, 20 Nov. 1783; John Lloyd to LH, 15, 18 and 29 Nov. 1783; Pentycross to LH, 16 and 21 Jan. 1784, and n.d.; Lloyd to LH, 24 Feb. 1784 and n.d.; unsigned to LH, Feb. 1784; Thomas Piercy to LH, 5 Mar. 1784; Lloyd to LH, 9 Mar. 1784, E4/13 (5, 14, 15, 16, 7, 8, 9, 20, 25, 27, 30, 22),CF.

[227] Glazebrook to LH, 26 Sept. 1782, F1/1865. CF.

[228] J. Smith to LH, 12 Mar. 1783; Bradford to LH, 10 Dec. 1783, F1/513, 1919,CF. [229] Above p. 336.

[230] See in particular, Birmingham committee to LH, 30 Aug. 1787; D. Jones to LH, 8 Feb. and 2 Aug. 1790; D. Griffiths to LH, 25 Apr. 1789; T. Charles to LH, 15 July 1789 and to Lady AE, 25 Sept. 1792, F1/650, 882, 931, 2071,CF, Gloucester Record Office MS, D. 2538, 8/1/7. F1/2229,CF.

that it was by clergy 'especially from Wales' that the Connexion's major chapels were being served.[231]

The converse of clergy continuing to serve the Connexion was the ability of seceding clergy to preach in Anglican pulpits. Here local circumstances and attitudes were a major factor. Wills's biographer lists five separate London churches to which he was admitted after his secession, although when away from the capital Wills does appear to have experienced greater reluctance to allow him churches than he had done on preaching tours before.[232]

Despite the advantages that the Connexion gained from its continuing affinities to Anglicanism, there were some within its ranks who felt less kindly disposed towards the Church of their baptism. The Countess's friend John Lloyd, who in 1780 had been apprehensive about secession, soon became forceful in his condemnation of the Church: the consistory court was 'the Inquisitorial Court of Episcopacy', the bishop of Salisbury a 'Goliath the Second', and 'Prelacy and Precedency...one and the same thing'.[233] It was natural, in addition, that clergy who had seceded for the Connexion should be the more critical of the Church to which they had once belonged. Taylor commented caustically in October 1783 about the unreliability of Churchmen as supplies for the Connexion: they would only serve, he

---

[231] Haweis, *An Impartial and Succinct History*, iii. 260 ff. Parallel with Welsh assistance in England went harmonious relations between the Connexion's (limited) work in Wales and Welsh Evangelicals. In 1790 David Jones reported to the Countess that at the General Association of Welsh Methodists held in Glamorganshire at the end of May a resolution had been passed that 'The Welsh Association wish...to cultivate & maintain a christian & friendly Connection with the Right Honourable the Countess of Huntingdon: & that they wish to further & promote...her Ladyship's work at Swansea & everywhere else' (Jones to LH, 5 June 1790, F1/918,CF).

[232] When Wills visited Fishguard in 1780, he preached in the church but on his return four years later used the meeting house. He himself believed that many Pembrokeshire churches were closed to him that year through the efforts of Evangelical clergy (*Memoirs of Wills*, 24, 106–7).

[233] J. Lloyd to LH, 15 Aug. 1780 (marked 17 Oct.1782) and 15 Nov. 1783, F1/472, 488; E4/13(14),CF. It may have been the influence of Lloyd, who settled near Pentycross at Wallingford in 1783, which contributed to the vehemence of Lady Huntingdon's reaction to Pentycross's refusal to secede (J. Lloyd to LH, 24 Feb. and 1 and 9 Mar. 1784, E4/13(20–2),CF).

asserted 'when they please'.[234] Wills, too, was conscious of an essential difference between clergy who had seceded and those who had not: in 1786, for example, he was critical of a plan for the management of the Connexion which would have given clergymen who had not seceded authority over the Connexion's own ministers and committees.[235]

There was a conflict between those who rejoiced in the Connexion's separation from the Church of England, and those who wished to play down the significance of that step. The fall from Lady Huntingdon's favour of both Taylor and Wills in the final years of her life[236] left in the ascendancy men like Haweis, who returned to Connexional service at the end of the 1780s, and who was firmly in the latter camp.[237] Addressing the quarterly meeting of the Apostolic Society in October 1792 Haweis stated that the opening of chapels by the Connexion was not in opposition 'to other places opened for the Gospel, either by the church methodists or dissenters, but from a desire to give a more universal spread to the Gospel by steering clear of the rocks of Bigotry on either hand, the Church on one, and the stiff Dissenters on the other'. These were views which, being so well known, the Society decided not to publish 'as the Society had invariably discovered a firm attachment to the Church and shewn that they were not inimical to the dissenters'.[238] In matters of doctrine, the Connexion continued to affirm that secession had changed nothing. The printed account of the opening of Cheshunt College in the year after Lady Huntingdon's death took pains to point out that the Fifteen Articles were perfectly consonant with the doctrinal articles of the Church of England.[239] Doubtless there were those in the Connexion, as in Wesleyan Methodism, who saw affinity to the Established Church as a source of social respectability, and who were thus glad to minimize the breach which secession

[234] W. Taylor to LH, 9 Oct. 1783, F1/1910,CF.
[235] Wills to LH, 12 Oct. 1786, F1/1941,CF.   [236] See below, Ch. 8.
[237] Schlenther, 170.
[238] Apostolic Society minute book, entries for 3 Oct. and 3 Jan. 1793, C1/1, 128–9, 139,CF.
[239] *The Order observed at the Opening of the Countess of Huntingdon's College at Cheshunt, Hertfordshire* (1792).

represented.²⁴⁰ That desire to remain close to the Church continued. More than sixty years after the death of the Connexion's foundress, one of those embroiled in controversy over the source of legal authority in the Connexion and the college could still quote with satisfaction a statement of George Burder, one of the founders of the London Missionary Society, that the Connexion's particular strength lay in its being neither in the Church, nor wholly in dissent from it.²⁴¹

THE CONNEXION AND DISSENT

Just as there was no marked change, for better or worse, in the Connexion's relations with the Church after secession, so, with traditional Dissent, was there no sudden new relationship. Indeed, those Dissenters who were suspicious of the threat to their congregations posed by the Revival were unlikely to feel any more warmly towards a body that had now taken on more of their own organizational characteristics.²⁴²

The use of Dissenting meeting houses by Connexional ministers was often a point of contact, and instances became frequent with the general extension of the Connexion's activities in the 1770s. Among other clergy to enjoy this facility were Glascott at Lincoln in 1774 and Wills in Wales and the South-West in 1780 and 1781,²⁴³ but it was with the students that it happened most easily. The student Christopher Hull, for example, was welcomed by both Baptists and Independents when he visited Bromsgrove in 1771, and he spoke in the Baptist meeting.²⁴⁴ A meeting house at

---

[240] J. D. Walsh, 'Methodism at the End of the Eighteenth Century', in R. Davies and E. G. Rupp (eds.), *A History of the Methodist Church in Great Britain* (London, 1965), i. 309.
[241] J. Bridgman, *An Address to the Ministers, Deacons and Friends of the Countess of Huntingdon's Connexion and College* (London, 1857).
[242] On the Connexion's Articles, see Ch. 6 and Annex C.
[243] Glascott to LH, 28 Feb. 1774, F1/274,CF; *Memoirs of Wills*, 20 ff.
[244] C. Hull to LH, 16 Sept. 1771, F1/135,CF.

Wolverhampton was open to students in 1774; likewise, a former meeting house at Harwich in 1776, and various meeting houses in Cornwall in 1780.[245] From the use of meeting houses, it was but a short step for students to preach to Dissenting congregations and then to be invited to serve them. Lady Huntingdon soon experienced mounting pressures of this kind. Two independent congregations in Wiltshire asked for supplies in 1774; the student William Thresher received a call to Shaftesbury in 1777; and in the same year, another student, Richard Lane, received two calls, one of which, to Shiffnall, he wanted to accept.[246] A clear indication of the way the Connexion quickly came to be regarded as a source of manpower was provided, again in 1777, by the trust of a chapel built by a woman at Briston in Norfolk. This chapel, in whose foundation the Connexion had no apparent link, was nevertheless to be served by 'some other godly minister in the Connection of the Right Hon. Selina, Countess of Huntingdon'.[247] The pattern thus established appears to have been unaffected by secession, though the introduction of ordination in the Connexion may, as it had been hoped, have dissuaded some from leaving who might otherwise have gone. Thomas Suter, another student, is found at the Baptist meeting at Coleford in 1784 (though they were using him 'very ill') and Joel Knight, who had been ordained by Wills and who was acting as his assistant at Spa Fields, was invited in 1787 to leave Spa Fields for the congregation in Jewin Street.[248] Instances have already been quoted of established congregations who sought to join the Connexion, rather than to draw preachers away.[249] What all these examples show is that there were independent congregations who did not share the doubts about Trevecca of

---

[245] Shirley to LH, 12 May 1774; W. Dunn to LH, 8 July 1776; J. Painter to 'My Very Dear Friend' (Wills), 8 July 1780, F1/1692, 366, 458,CF.

[246] W. Parish to LH, 13 May 1774; W. Thresher to LH, 31 Jan. 1777; R. Lane to LH, 17 Feb. 1777, F1/291, 1749, 1752,CF.

[247] B. Cozens-Hardy, 'The Countess *versus* Methodism *versus* Independency', *Transactions of the Congregational Historical Society*, 21/3 (1972), 74–6.

[248] Suter to LH, 28 Feb.1784; Knight to the Deacons and Churchwardens in Jewin Street, 22 Aug. 1787, F1/605, E4/15(34),CF. Knight did not accept the invitation.   [249] Above pp. 71–2.

some of the Dissenting academies: the college might not produce scholars or theologians, but it did turn out ministers and it was in this that congregations were interested.

Against this pattern of co-operation with and from Dissenters, must be set some instances of opposition. The difficulties of some students in securing Dissenting ordination have been noted. Nor was the use of Dissenting meeting houses always forthcoming. Mead and Glazebrook, for example, were refused the meeting house at Ross in 1770, Crole was refused at Wareham in 1774, and Wills experienced rebuff, as well as welcome, in Devon in 1781.[250] Crole believed that his refusal had been due to the presence of Arians and Arminians, as well as Calvinists, within the Wareham congregation, and this gives a clue to the suspicion of the Connexion which some Dissenters felt. Dissent comprehended a wide variety of theological positions and included within its ranks some who rejected the enthusiasm of the Revival as forcefully as any latitudinarian bishop. The Countess's secretary, George Best, referred in 1789 to a Dissenting minister disliked by his fellows because his preaching was too like the Methodists. Eleven years earlier, the rational Dissenter, Kensick, spoke of 'the most rigid Calvinistical Connexion of the Countess which...few or no Dissenters join'.[251]

With the politically advanced sections of Dissent the Connexion had little sympathy or contact. A preacher who found himself with a congregation at Castle Donnington in 1794 which, he said, preferred Tom Paine to Jesus Christ, at once threatened to withdraw.[252] Even when there were no theological differences, Dissenters still had grounds for reserve. The closer the Connexion came to Dissent and the greater the sense of common purpose that they shared, the greater also the threat that each posed to the other. The chapel rivalry which coloured the Connexion's relations

---

[250] Mead and Glazebrook to LH, 15 Feb. 1770; Crole to LH, 13 July 1774, F1/87, 311,CF; *Memoirs of Wills*, 33, 35, 80.
[251] Best to LH, 2 July 1789, E4/4(17),CF; MS letter in the Wodrow–Kensick collection, Dr Williams's Library, London.
[252] J. Garrett to Lady AE, 27 June 1794, F1/1005, CF.

with the Wesleyans and other Calvinistic groups, applied just as much to Dissenting congregations—as shown in Wills's belief that the Connexion was always more likely to be successful in a new area than in one where Dissenters were already well established.[253] Thus there are signs of coolness from Dissenters at Lewes in 1774 and at Dorchester in 1775, and of outright hostility from 'bitter and persecuting' Dissenters at Kendal in 1783.[254] Dissenters, too, might resent the slur cast upon their preaching by the decision to open a Connexional chapel near their own: in June 1777, the Dissenting minister Dr Mays objected not only to the Mulberry Gardens chapel being built next to his own, but to the announcement by Peckwell that the Gospel had not been preached in the area for years.[255] What mattered most in the relationship of individual Connexional chapels with Dissenting ones, just as with Wesleyans or other Calvinist evangelicals, was the state of the congregations concerned, or the attractiveness of the preacher. Thus it was that the Connexion gained from a division in the meeting at Norwich in 1783, but lost members at Whitehaven, four years later, after the arrival of a new minister at the 'Seceder Meeting'.[256]

It was from Baptists, however, that opposition most consistently came, for the Connexion, despite its diversity of membership and outlook, remained consistently paedobaptist in theology. This very consistency of doctrine is a remarkable tribute to the centralized control of the Connexion. In spite of periodic pressure for believers' baptism, both from some ministers and from groups within congregations, the idea survived that anabaptist theology was inconsistent with Connexional membership. John Painter of Truro, a friend of the Countess who assisted in the organization of her work in his area, said as much in November 1783; earlier that year, William Taylor had automatically assumed that a woman

---

[253] Wills to LH, 28 Aug. 1777, F1/1783,CF.
[254] Peckwell to LH, 16 Mar. 1774; Molland to LH, 15 Apr. 1775; D. Gray to LH, 4 Dec. 1783, F1/281, 325, 579,CF.
[255] T. Gibbons to LH, 5 June 1777, F1/1761,CF.
[256] Norwich committee to LH, 2 May 1783; Whitehaven congregation to LH, 12 June 1787, F1/520, 634,CF.

member of the Spa Fields congregation who had sought rebaptism would wish to leave the chapel.[257] Throughout the period under consideration, the presence of Baptist doctrines within congregations led to division and Baptist preachers were seen as a threat. In 1765, Lady Huntingdon reported that Baptists were causing havoc in Sussex; in 1767 a division occurred over Baptist doctrines at Brighton and Ote Hall. Although peace was restored by the avoidance of controversial subjects by the ministers who preached there, the issue must have lingered on at Ote Hall: ten years later, there is a reference to 'about twenty to be dip'd next Sunday'.[258] In 1788, Brecon chapel reported the danger of some of their members joining the Baptists, and a year later there was a Baptist faction in the congregation at Ely.[259] The constant possibility of this within evangelical congregations, even Anglican ones, was shown at Reading, where William Talbot's congregation divided itself between the Connexion and the Baptists at his death.[260] Nor was this something which only happened from within, for there is evidence of deliberate opposition to the Connexion from the Baptists themselves. It was reported to Lady Huntingdon in 1787 that students from a Baptist academy were using their vacations to prey upon the congregation at Coleford, Gloucestershire. In 1788 John Williams, the master at Trevecca College, informed her that as the Baptists' annual association was to be held in their area, the following year, they were already preparing armour against them.[261] Against this background, instances of co-operation, such as Hull had experienced in 1771, were rare. One instance of collaboration

---

[257] J. Painter to LH, 17 Nov. 1783; Taylor to LH, 31 Feb. 1783, F1/570, 1883,CF.
[258] LH to Mrs Wadsworth, 27 Dec. 1765, Bridwell Library MS, 57; R. Hayman to LH, 14 Mar. 1767; Maxfield to LH, 15 Dec. 1767; Miss Scutt to LH, 1 Dec. 1777, F1/15, 1410; E4/2(16),CF.
[259] P. Valentine to LH, 15 Jan. 1788; J. Child to LH, 23 July 1789, F1/699, 2090,CF.
[260] C. Smyth, *Simeon and Church Order* (Cambridge, 1940), 2. Pentycross to LH, n.d., F1/1251,CF. Some Anglican Evangelicals continued to be drawn to adult baptism: as late as 1892 a group of laymen planning the foundation of a new parish in South Hertfordshire, seriously considered the provision of a baptistry for adult immersion in the new building (Christ Church, Little Heath MSS, B4).
[261] G. Dew to LH, 23 Dec. 1787; J. Williams to LH, 23 Aug. 1788, F1/697, 760,CF.

occurred in 1788 when the Birmingham chapel, which would otherwise have been unsupplied, received valuable help from an assistant at the Baptist meeting.[262] But this was unusual. The general pattern is of a more sustained and consistent opposition to the Connexion from Baptists than from any other section of Dissent.

CONCLUSION

The picture presented by the Connexion in the years after secession is far from consistent. It maintained, and continued to maintain, that it was not just another sect of Dissenters, but a distinct group placed between them and the Church. It was partly to this end that Lady Huntingdon attempted to preserve those features of the Connexion's activities, the use of the Anglican Prayer Book and itinerant rather than settled ministries, which most clearly marked the Connexion out from Dissent. Despite these efforts to remain distinct, however, it was clear that many did regard the Connexion in just the way it wished to avoid—that is, as one among a number of Dissenting bodies, one more to which congregations could turn for a supply of ministers, or to which ministers could apply for new spheres of work. Every time a minister or congregation passed into or out of the Connexion, this view was reinforced. The problem that confronted the Connexion was that the more this happened, the less the justification remained for its own continuation as a separate entity. The Connexion, like other groups of Calvinist evangelicals, served as a catalyst to late eighteenth-century Dissent: they raised new congregations, they revived Reformation doctrines in established congregations, and to all they were a source of fresh ministerial manpower. When these things had been achieved, however, the need for their continued separate existence was not always very obvious. By 1869 Robert Halley recorded that the majority of Calvinist

---

[262] J. Abson, on behalf of the Birmingham committee, to LH, 7 Jan. 1788, F1/698,CF.

evangelical chapels in Lancashire had become fully independent: this is no more than Haweis had predicted, nearly a century before. Some Dissenting congregations might be reduced by evangelical preaching, he wrote in 1777, yet the Dissenters still encouraged irregularity as they knew that they themselves would be the ultimate beneficiaries.[263] This, according to Halley, is what happened in Lancashire: the preaching of the Revival revived in men a desire for the doctrines of their ancestors without, necessarily, a continuing desire for the Revival's patterns of preaching and organization.[264] When Dissenters did come to recognize the value of some of the methods employed by the Revival, principally the use of itinerant preaching in the establishment and nurture of new congregations, it was to their own benefit that they applied them.[265]

It is an open question whether the eventual loss of the Connexion's distinctive features is a matter for regret. What is beyond question, in view of the trends already discernible within the Connexion, is that this would have happened anyway, with or without secession from the Established Church.

[263] T. and J. Haweis to LH, 12 (? Feb.) 1777, F1/1801,CF.
[264] R. Halley, *Lancashire, its Puritanism and Nonconformity* (Manchester, 1869), ii. 438, 432–3.
[265] D. W. Lovegrove, *Established Church, Sectarian People: Itinerancy and the Transformation of English Dissent, 1780–1830* (Cambridge, 1988).

8

The Connexion in the Last Years of Lady Huntingdon's Life

The years from the secession to Lady Huntingdon's death in 1791 were as active as any that had gone before, with the management of the Connexion if anything a more complex task than hitherto. This was the result, in part, of the events of the early 1780s, and the stimulus they gave to the expansion of the work. Secession itself enhanced the distinctive identity of the Connexion, and the sense that it was now a permanent part of the religious scene: if off-putting to some Anglican loyalists, this must have increased the overall attractiveness of the Connexion to many individuals and congregations. The availability of a growing cadre of ordained ministers may have eased the organizational task in some respects (particularly in maintaining the sacramental life of congregations) but it seems likely to have contributed also to the expansion of the Connexion. Such expansion might mean new congregations joining the Connexion, or existing congregations becoming more firmly established and demonstrating their increased self-confidence with new buildings. Either way, it added to the demands on Lady Huntingdon to ensure that the legal and financial implications of growth were properly assessed.

Through Lady Huntingdon's correspondence in the 1780s, in addition to the day-to-day issues involved in the organization of supplies,[1] runs a steady stream of plans for new chapels, building schemes, negotiations over terms for congregations joining the Connexion, and anxieties over

---

[1] 1788, for example, saw Birmingham unsupplied for a period, and Newark threatening to leave the Connexion if a better preacher were not sent within a fortnight (J. Abson to LH, 7 Jan. 1788; J. Stevenson to LH, 19 Apr. 1788, F1/698, 2007,CF).

The Countess's Last Years

debts and the means of meeting them. Two further London chapels were added to the Connexion in Lady Huntingdon's lifetime: Holywell Mount in Shoreditch in 1789,[2] and Sion Chapel, Whitechapel, in 1790.[3] Mention has already been made of the lengthy negotiations which took place in 1783 over the financial basis upon which the congregation at Rotherhithe might be admitted to the Connexion.[4] 1787, a year for which particularly full records have survived, saw Lady Huntingdon in correspondence about building projects as widely scattered as West Bromwich,[5] Woodbridge,[6] and Llangadog in Monmouthshire.[7] This was in addition to the five 'new and large' (but unnamed) chapels which she described earlier that year as having just been established.[8] West Bromwich raised such complex questions about the terms on which the new building would be assigned to the Connexion that at one stage the committee suggested they should be discussed directly with Lady Huntingdon.[9] Uncertainties over the basis upon which builder's bills had been incurred at Llangadog meant that arguments over the money were still continuing in 1790.[10] Monetary anxieties, indeed, provide a sub-theme of Lady Huntingdon's last years, as she faced the parallel demands of those congregations which believed they had a claim upon her, and the running costs of the college.[11] Lady Anne Erskine was available to share some of the work,[12] and the administrative burden was eased further by the recruitment of a secretary, George Best, in 1784.[13] Nevertheless the job of running

---

[2] Above, Ch. 4.   [3] Seymour, ii. 322–4.   [4] Above, Ch. 4.
[5] Beardmore to LH, 16 May 1787; West Bromwich congregation to LH (marked Nov. 1787), F1/627, 687,CF; F. W. Hackwood, *History of West Bromwich* (Birmingham, 1895), 81 ff.
[6] J. Beaumont to LH, 18 June and 11 Oct. 1787, F1/1947, 664,CF.
[7] H. James to LH, 15 Dec. 1787, F1/696,CF.
[8] LH to J. Bidwell, 10 Apr. 1787, B4/3,CF.
[9] Beardmore to LH, 16 May 1787, F1/627,CF.
[10] J. Williams to LH, 15 Apr. 1789; D. Jones to LH, 5 June 1790, F1/2070, 918,CF.   [11] Above, Chs. 4 and 5.
[12] For example, Haweis to Lady AE, 25 Nov. 1789, C12/7,CF.
[13] Taylor to LH, 18 Mar. 1784, F1/1934,CF. Best took on a direct role in running the Connexion, as witnessed by his trips to Birmingham in 1786 and to the college in 1789 (Wills to LH, 12 Oct. 1786; Best to LH, 2 July 1789, F1/1941;

the Connexion remained a substantial one for a woman entering her eighties.

Nor did her interest diminish in overseas ventures. She continued to be concerned over the fate of her American possessions, and in 1783 even considered going to live in America.[14] In addition, and as well as the missionary projects in which individual students were involved,[15] Lady Huntingdon took an interest in Continental Europe. Early in 1787 she was planning a visit to Germany;[16] by April this had become linked with the intention to establish a Connexional presence in Brussels. The circumstances of the Brussels scheme are shrouded in some mystery. On 10 April Lady Huntingdon wrote excitedly of the large chapel she had taken in Brussels, and of the six hundred Protestant families in that city to whom she saw the Connexion ministering.[17] She was, said a correspondent, 'going to attack the enemy in his strongholds'.[18] Wills was to go with her. But by the end of the month he was congratulating her on their deliverance from 'popish and hellish adversaries...from assassination, or Poison, and Death'.[19] According to Wills's biographer, what lay behind these events was a 'professed papist', Lord Douglass, who lived in Brussels, but who had secured Lady Huntingdon's favour when he visited London and professed conversion to Protestantism. It was he, according to this account, who invited Lady Huntingdon and Wills to establish a cause in Brussels; they missed the ship they had intended to take, and it was at this point that letters arrived claiming that the whole scheme was a plot to have them both assassinated. The sense of Divine providence underlying the sequence of events was then crowned by

E4/4(17),CF). Best's annotations on some incoming letters show how he acted as LH's adviser on matters of business, for example, identifying questions to be addressed before she should sign a chapel deed. On other occasions, like a good civil servant, he recognized decisions that LH alone could take: 'My Lady will please to answer this according to her own mind' (J. Dawson to LH, 2 Mar. 1790; R. Munn to LH, 16 Dec. 1789, F1/892, 875,CF).

[14] J. Williams to Best, 12 Jan. 1788, F1/1981,CF.   [15] Above, Ch. 5.
[16] LH to Carpenter, 10 Feb. 1787, and to Cromwell, 27 Feb. 1787, Meth. Arch. (LH), 135; A4/9(27),CF.   [17] LH to John Bidwell, 10 Apr. 1787, B4/3,CF.
[18] R. Herdsman to LH, 17 Apr. 1787, F1/621,CF.
[19] Wills to LH, 27 Apr. 1787, F1/622,CF.

the news of the sudden death of Lord Douglass on the very day Lady Huntingdon had set out.[20] This did not end Lady Huntingdon's interest in Continental mission, however. The possibility of supporting a Protestant congregation in Ostend had been raised at the same time as the Brussels venture, and was still being mentioned two years later. More strikingly, in the year before her death (and in the midst of the French Revolution) Lady Huntingdon speculated about establishing Protestant congregations in Paris and Madrid.[21]

Despite the growing confidence which characterized much of the Connexion's life during Lady Huntingdon's last years, there were losses also. On a personal level, Lady Huntingdon experienced the death of her last surviving son, Francis, in October 1789. She was also to quarrel with three clergymen, all seceders from the Church of England, who played a major part in the Connexion's work during the 1780s. The first casualty was Thomas Wills, who had been at the centre of the Connexion's affairs for nearly a decade when coolness set in between him and Lady Huntingdon late in 1787. The overt reason for his dismissal from the Connexion, which came finally in July 1788, was his opposition to the idea of the college being under the direction of laymen, which he believed implicit in the plan of the newly formed Apostolic Society.[22] Lady Huntingdon was certainly capable of taking disagreement with her plans in the most personal of ways,[23] but it seems unlikely that this was the

---

[20] *Memoirs of the Life of the Revd Thomas Wills* (London, 1804), 205–8. The author's dating does not tally with the manuscript evidence, but may otherwise be an accurate account. It is clear that Wills was less enthusiastic about the venture than LH, and it is not impossible that he made more dramatic the story of a plot (and of Douglass's death) than was justified (Wills to LH, 30 Apr. 1787, F1/624,CF).

[21] Samuel Beaufoy to LH, 27 Apr. 1787; Taylor to LH, 12 Nov. 1789, F1/623, 2109, CF; Schlenther, 172. LH was not alone in seeing events in France as opening the door for evangelism: in 1791 the Wesleyan Thomas Coke went to Paris to campaign for the city's conversion (N. U. Murray, 'The Influence of the French Revolution on the Church of England and its Rivals, 1789–1802', D.Phil. thesis (Oxford, 1975), 220.

[22] Spa Fields minute book for 7 July 1788, D1/1, 29,CF.

[23] Wills's biographer, possibly partisan, spoke in this context of her 'petulant and rather imperious disposition' (*Life of Wills*, 211). To counterbalance this picture, however, it is worth quoting the comment of the Unitarian Theophilus Lindsey,

whole reason for their split. The records of the Apostolic Society suggest that Wills had displeased her 'in some other matters';[24] these may have been doctrinal in origin, although personalities seem also to have been involved. There is evidence at Spa Fields during the 1780s of a division in the committee between those who welcomed due emphasis on the need for holiness in believers, and those who feared this would undermine a proper appreciation of the work of grace. Wills was favoured by the former camp; John Bradford, then apparently well established in Lady Huntingdon's regard, by the latter. William Taylor proved a false friend by showing Lady Huntingdon correspondence by Wills on this subject. This completed their alienation.[25] Wills's dismissal caused some stir in the Connexion, and both the resignation of a number of ministers and a fall-off in support at Bristol and Bath were attributed to it.[26] After his dismissal Wills preached at a number of evangelical chapels in London[27] before establishing a chapel of his own in Silver Street.[28] Hopes for a reconciliation were not to be realized,[29] and Wills was one of those proscribed in Lady Huntingdon's will from having any influence in the Connexion, or preaching in her chapels.[30]

The dismissal from the Connexion of William Taylor and John Bradford occurred over the next two years. The seeds

resuming contact with her two years earlier, that she had 'become more moderate towards those who held different opinions' (T. Belsham, *Memoirs of the late Revd Theophilus Lindsey* (London, 1873), 2 n.).

[24] C5/2,CF.
[25] *Life of Wills*, 200–20; LH to N. Rowlands, 25 July 1788, National Library of Wales Deposit 350A; Edmund Jones to LH (dated 9 Jan. 1788, but presumably 1789), Gloucester Record Office MS, D 2538, 8/1/2. Wills's printed farewell to the Connexion (which he was not allowed to preach) warned them against both 'Legality and Antinomianism' and spoke of 'my late heavy and unexpected trials' (*Farewell Address to the Congregations and Societies of the Countess of Huntingdon's Connexion* (London, 1788)).
[26] *Life of Wills*, 220–2; Abraham Gadd to LH, 12 Sept. 1788; James Jones to LH, 6 Dec. 1788, F1/766, 795,CF.
[27] For example, at Rowland Hill's Surrey chapel, and Toplady's old chapel in Orange Street.   [28] *Life of Wills*, 222–5.
[29] For example, Spa Fields minute book, entry for 8 Sept. 1790; JB Wildlove to LH, 6 May 1791, D1/1, 33; F1/2178,CF.
[30] Will of 11 January, 1790, transcribed in Francis, 'Selina, Countess of Huntingdon', B.Phil. thesis (Oxford, 1955).

of Taylor's fall lay in an accusation of adultery, made against him in October 1788, an allegation which appears eventually to have been substantiated. His work for the Connexion had finished by the start of 1790, but though some remained sympathetic towards him, there is no sense that he left on a tide of popular sympathy like Wills. What he did leave behind was a lengthy dispute over the monies which he claimed were owed him by the Connexion. This provoked even the generally tolerant Glascott to lament the 'immoderate' love of money, which had been a characteristic of him, even before his 'fall'.[31] Like Wills, Taylor was proscribed in Lady Huntingdon's will from playing any future role in the Connexion.

The seeds of Bradford's fall from favour appear to lie in the antinomianism with which he had periodically been charged over the previous years.[32] His apparent role in the doctrinal aspects of Wills's dismissal has already been mentioned; later in 1788 there were reports that his preaching was encouraging 'licentiousness'.[33] Possibly Lady Huntingdon decided over the following period that his reputation as a high Calvinist was making him a liability to the Connexion: certainly her coolness must have conveyed itself to him, for in February 1790 he asked Best to tell him honestly whether his services were still acceptable.[34] Bradford performed an ordination in May, but in early August Lady Huntingdon wrote criticizing his vanity and lack of judgement. It was a last warning: '... the first party or faction among the people that you make, ... no protection, but a certain separation from me, and all work in my hands finally!' Whatever Bradford's response to this, he got nothing further from the Countess; in late August he wrote that he assumed from her

---

[31] J. Sheppard and G. Ford to John Lloyd, 9 Oct. 1788; Haweis to Lady AE, 25 Nov. 1789; Haweis to LH, 6 Jan. 1790; N. Rowland to LH, 20 Feb. 1790; Taylor to Best, 5 Apr. 1790; Glascott to LH, 8 Apr. 1790; J. Jenkins to LH, 10 May 1790; Taylor to Best, 16 Nov. and 25 Jan. 1791, F1/772, C12/7 (transcript), F1/2115, 886, 2126, 2127, 911, 2157 and 2167,CF.

[32] This is the clear implication of J. Bridgman, *An Address to the Ministers, Deacons, and Friends of the Countess of Huntingdon's Connexion and College* (London, 1857), D3/2.   [33] Stephen Seager to LH, 3 Oct. 1788, F1/770,CF.

[34] Bradford to Best, 17 Feb. 1790, F1/885,CF.

silence that he was now dismissed.[35] A codicil to Lady Huntingdon's will in January 1791 added Bradford's name to the list of those proscribed from preaching.

Behind all these events lay the question of the organizational structure needed for the Connexion after Lady Huntingdon's death. The problem had been recognized for some years. When Lady Huntingdon was ill in 1767, for example, Lord Dartmouth had suggested that she leave her chapels to him, and that he should run them strictly according to her instructions.[36] There is a reference to an (unspecified) scheme for the future organization of the Connexion in 1774,[37] and mention has been made of the proposals, later in the 1770s, for the preservation of a distinct group of 'regular' chapels, and for arrangements in respect of itinerancy and ordination.[38] Nothing specific seems to have come from any of these initiatives, and the need for proper arrangements for the continuation of the work was being voiced again in 1780.[39]

Part of the problem appears to have been the difficulty of reconciling the personal ambitions of some ministers with the structure the Connexion had developed, which combined a degree of congregational autonomy with ultimate central control. Within such a structure there was little room for anything approximating to the independence and security of tenure that the Connexion's clergy might have enjoyed had they remained within the Church. Three factors had to be reconciled in any future organizational arrangements. One was the objection likely to be encountered from the more powerful chapel committees to any scheme which enhanced the direct influence over them of any individual minister. The vehemence of the reaction in 1784 to rumours that Taylor was to have control of the Bath chapel illustrated this.[40] Secondly there was the potential resistance of seceding clergy to

---

[35] Bradford to LH, 27 May and 20 Aug. 1790, F1/913, 937, CF; LH to Bradford, 6 Aug. 1790; William W. Horne, *Life of the Revd John Bradford*, (London, 1806), 109–11.
[36] H. Venn to LH, 18 Dec. 1767, F1/1411,CF.
[37] Glascott to LH, 25 July 1774, F1/1707,CF.   [38] Above, Ch. 7.
[39] Taylor to LH, 16 Aug. 1780, F1/1855,CF.
[40] ? to LH, Feb. 1784, E4/13(27),CF. This reaction showed that LH had been right to predict trouble, had she yielded to Taylor's bid for control over Bath in

proposals that gave authority in the Connexion to colleagues still within the Church. It was this which lay behind Wills's objection to Lady Huntingdon's suggestion in 1786 for the Connexion to be run by a trust including four non-seceding clergymen.[41] Thirdly there was the reluctance of some clergymen (including some still holding benefices, on whose services the Connexion remained crucially dependent) to allow an increased lay voice in the running of the Connexion. This was an important factor in undermining Lady Huntingdon's attempts to establish permanent organizational arrangements for the Connexion.

The idea of a trust was still in Lady Huntingdon's mind in 1788,[42] but it was a more sophisticated scheme that evolved in the course of the following year. The authors of this were a group, subsequently known as the London Acting Association, which Lady Huntingdon convened in November 1789, following her doctor's advice 'to retire and throw off the burden' of managing the Connexion. Initially the group was intended to comprise all the Spa Fields committee, representatives of the committees of the Holywell Mount and Mulberry Gardens chapels, and a small, mixed, group of Anglican, Dissenting and Connexional ministers. The Spa Fields committee subsequently withdrew from the group, however, apparently in irritation that they were not all invited to the next meeting.[43] The outcome of the work of the Acting Association[44] was the plan published in

---

1782. Above, Ch. 7. Tunbridge Wells congregation seems to have been more compliant and there appears to have been a sense in which he was given overall charge there (LH to Taylor, 19 July 1782, Seymour, ii. 147).

[41] Wills to LH, 12 Oct. 1786, F1/1941,CF.

[42] This is suggested by the letter to her of 11 Apr. 1788 from William Hodson, secretary of the Spa Fields committee, in which he advocated a three-man body consisting of Wills, Taylor, and a layman. The implication is that he had already been asked by her to play some part in such arrangements (E4/15(35),CF). By this date Wills was already under her displeasure, although not yet dismissed.

[43] Spa Fields minutes for 23 Nov. 1789, D1/1,30,CF. They were also annoyed not to receive from LH the description of the state and financial position of each of the chapels in the Connexion for which they had asked.

[44] Seymour records a report that the main drafting hand was that of William Platt, a former Trevecca student subsequently ordained as a Presbyterian and one of the founders of the London Missionary Society (Seymour, ii. 484; J. Morison, *The Fathers and Founders of the London Missionary Society* (London, n.d.), 295 ff.).

March 1790 for a general association to manage the whole Connexion. The plan envisaged the division of the Connexion into twenty-three districts,[45] each of which, outside London, would be under the control of a committee consisting of all the ministers operating within the district and two laymen from each congregation. The London Acting Association was to serve both as a district committee for London, and as a standing committee for the Connexion at large, receiving the quarterly reports of each district and transacting business between the annual meetings of the general association. The latter was to consist of the London Acting Association, a minister and two laymen from each district, and the trustees of the college.[46]

The Plan of Association (as it was called) was a bold exercise in conciliar government for an organization in which autocratic control had hitherto been the principal characteristic. Possibly the framers had in mind Wesley's Deed of Declaration, drawn up six years earlier to give legal expression to the Methodist conference.[47] That document similarly described a conciliar system, albeit one whose form had existed for the previous forty years. But there were respects in which the Connexion's scheme went much further. Wesley had provided for one hundred of the preachers (the Legal Hundred) to act as the supreme legislative body of Methodism, but there was no provision for a direct lay voice in the direction of its affairs, and nothing approximating to the recognized role for chapel committees implicit in the Plan of Association.[48] In a further important respect the

---

[45] The districts and the 63 named chapels of which they were made up, are shown in Annex B.

[46] The text of the plan is printed in Seymour, ii. 483–6 and E. Welch, *Two Calvinistic Methodist Chapels* (London, 1975), 92–5.

[47] F. Baker, *John Wesley and the Church of England* (London, 1970), 222–33; Maldwyn Edwards, 'John Wesley', in R. Davies and G. Rupp, (eds.), *A History of the Methodist Church in Great Britain* (London, 1965), i. 72; Rack, *Wesley*, 501–5. LH herself instanced the Association of Welsh Calvinistic Methodists in support of the idea (Seymour, ii. 486).

[48] In Wesley's view the preachers represented the laity at Conference, and there were no grounds for the latter to be present in person (J. D. Walsh, 'Methodism at the end of the Eighteenth Century', in Davies and Rupp (eds.), *History of the Methodist Church*, i. 282). JW had long vacillated between a collective leadership or

problem faced by the Connexion was different from Wesley's. For all Lady Huntingdon's autocratic instincts, she did not have the degree of pre-eminence that Wesley enjoyed. The corollary of that pre-eminence was a levelling effect within Wesleyanism and the blurring of distinctions among Wesley's followers.[49] It is difficult to see how anyone not ordained, let alone lacking Wesley's supreme ability to contain any challenge to his authority, could have achieved the position he did. Even so, there were challenges to the Deed (particularly over the choice of the one hundred)[50] and attempts after Wesley's death to impose a ministerial superstructure on top of the conciliar model implied by the Deed.[51] The Connexion, by contrast, if monarchial like Wesleyan Methodism, had long depended on an influential barony, even though individual barons might occasionally fall from grace. And it was the democratization implicit in the Plan of Association, particularly the substantial built-in majority it gave to lay representatives of congregations, which offended two of the currently most influential barons, Thomas Haweis and Lady Huntingdon's constant companion of the previous decades, Lady Anne Erskine.

It was the lay control of ministers which most disturbed Haweis when he saw the proposals in February 1790.[52] His dismay was possibly due as much to the fact that the plan was reminiscent of the role of the lay deacons in Dissenting churches (and thus emphasized the Connexion's affinities to Dissent), as to clerical *amour propre*. He remained adamant

---

the alternative of a single clerical leader (Rack, *Wesley*, 465, 495). The rights and influence of the laity in Wesleyan Methodism, as against the authority of the ministry, was an issue which was not resolved either by Wesley himself, or by the attempts at a settlement in the years immediately after his death. It continued an issue through much of the next century, involving a process of increasing rights for the laity and culminating in their admission to Conference in 1878 (J. Kent, 'The Wesleyan Methodists to 1849', in R. Davies, A. R. George, and G. Rupp (eds.), *A History of the Methodist Church in Great Britain* (London, 1978), ii. 214–16; H. D. Rack, 'Wesleyan Methodism 1849–1902', in R. Davies, A. R. George, and G. Rupp (eds.), *History of the Methodist Church in Great Britain* (London 1983), iii. 155–6).

[49] Walsh, 'Methodism at the End of the Eighteenth Century', in Davies and Rupp (eds.), *History of the Methodist Church*, i. 279.
[50] Baker, *Wesley and the Church of England*, 231.
[51] Walsh, 'Methodism at the End of the Eighteenth Century', 280.
[52] Haweis to LH, 27 Feb.1790, F1/2121,CF.

in his opposition, despite entreaties from Lady Huntingdon. In June he urged her to go back to the idea of a trust (consisting of non-seceding clergy) and threatened to leave the Connexion if the Plan of Association were persisted in.[53] Lady Anne, according to Seymour, took exception to a scheme that would have allowed her little say in the future management of the Connexion, and 'never let her Ladyship rest' until it was abandoned.[54] Other reactions were mixed. Amongst Lady Huntingdon's Welsh clerical supporters Thomas Charles thought the arrangements 'might be abundantly useful'[55] but Nathaniel Rowlands thought it impracticable to attempt to embrace the whole Connexion in one organizational structure.[56] Glascott's views are not recorded, though Haweis clearly expected that they would accord with his own.[57] Amongst congregations, views were also mixed, despite Lady Huntingdon's efforts to win support through a printed circular.[58] Swansea was unanimous in support; Faversham approved in principle, but was more concerned with establishing its own chapel; Morpeth was against anything novel; and Ote Hall was content to follow the lead of Brighton and Lewes.[59] Overall, Rowlands thought the congregations had been surprisingly cool towards the proposals.[60]

In the face of the opposition from Haweis and Lady Anne, Lady Huntingdon decided to abandon the plan. She may have hoped to reintroduce the proposals at a later date, but had taken no steps to do so before her death in June 1791. This left the Connexion with no formal system of government, and it came by default under the direction of the four individuals to whom Lady Huntingdon, in her will of January 1790, had bequeathed her houses and those chapels which

---

[53] Haweis to LH, 12 June 1790, transcript of MS in Mitchell Library, Sydney, C12/7,CF.   [54] Seymour, ii. 487.
[55] Charles to LH, (? 8) Mar. 1790, F1/890,CF.
[56] Rowlands to LH, 25 Sept. 1790, F1/939,CF.   [57] C12/7,CF.
[58] Seymour, ii. 486.
[59] J. Ford to LH, 5 July 1790; J. Child to LH, 23 June 1790; W. Honeywood to LH, 17 June 1790; T. Jones (Senior) to LH, 21 June 1790, F1/2136, 924, 921, 923,CF.   [60] Rowlands to LH, 25 Sept. 1790, F1/939,CF.

were her personal property.[61] The four devizees were Haweis, his wife, Lady Anne Erskine, and John Lloyd. The Haweises, at least, were unaware of the bequest before Lady Huntingdon's death, and it was a less than pleasant surprise to discover the obligations she had placed upon them.[62] The will had been drafted on the assumption that the Plan of Association would have come into effect as the framework within which the devizees' powers would be exercised. In fact, since the organization of preachers made no distinction between Lady Huntingdon's personal chapels and the rest, the devizees' influence in regard to the former came to embrace the whole of the Connexion.[63] It was agreed between the four that Lady Anne should take on the day-to-day and financial administration of the Connexion;[64] she appears to have slipped effortlessly into the role that Lady Huntingdon had established (and which she had had ample opportunity to study) so that Lady Huntingdon's death had the minimum of impact upon the life of the Connexion. Preachers wrote to her, as they had done to Lady Huntingdon, about the state of the congregations they served; chapels, in turn, wrote as before about the payment of ground rents, the maintenance of supplies or their desire for favoured preachers to remain with them longer or to be ordained.[65] Initially, therefore, Lady Huntingdon's Connexion had simply become Lady Anne's. Haweis, the longest surviving of the devizees, lived until 1820. Not until 1821 was a conference established for the Connexion, and there were those who believed with hindsight that this continuation of an autocratic system of government in the

---

[61] She possessed seven chapels at her death (Bath, Brighton, Hereford, Tunbridge Wells, and 'London'—probably Spa Fields, Sion, and Mulberry Gardens). The rest of the Connexion comprised places built or provided by others, and either transferred formally to the Connexion, or simply dependent upon its services (Seymour, ii. 492; Welch, 191).

[62] A. S. Wood, *Thomas Haweis* (London, 1957), 182.

[63] This is the interpretation argued in Bridgman, *Address*.

[64] Wood, *Haweis*, 183.

[65] For example, Child to Lady AE, 13 Aug. 1791; R. Bradley on behalf of Monmouth chapel to Lady AE, 4 July 1791; A. Gadd and J. Sevier to Lady AE, 15 Sept. 1791; I. Cresswell and J. Wilkes to Lady AE (stamped 22 Nov. 1791); Crowle society to Lady AE, 7 Dec. 1791, F1/2190, 2188, 2191, 2198, 2196,CF.

decades after Lady Huntingdon's death had, by denying the possibility of a say in its affairs to talented ministers and laymen, permanently weakened the Connexion's attractiveness and opportunities for growth.[66]

CONCLUSION: LADY HUNTINGDON'S ACHIEVEMENT

A year before her death Lady Huntingdon had written (characteristically) of her 'declining and evil days'.[67] Yet she could, if she permitted herself the indulgence, look back on a lifetime of remarkable achievement. In her salad days she had had the delights of fashionable eighteenth-century society at her feet, but they had not turned her head, even when life was at its rosiest. She had not shirked her duties as a wife and mother, but neither did she allow either the pleasures or the tragedies of her family life to turn her in upon herself, or blur her sense that she was called to fulfil a mission. She was not alone within the aristocracy in taking seriously the implications of her faith, but she had blazed a trail and was not deterred by the prospect of mockery or derision. There were clearly many in the upper levels of English society who were given confidence in the profession of their faith and a renewed sense of the obligations of their rank by the example and courage of Lady Huntingdon, as well as by the opportunities she provided for worship in congenial surroundings.[68] There were also many less fortunate, whose confidence in the goodness of God's creation was restored when their physical and spiritual needs were met by her ministrations.

---

[66] Bridgman, *Address*. The archives of Cheshunt College contain a bound volume of pamphlets representing a nineteenth-century dispute between the Revd John Thoresby and the trustees of the Connexion. Thoresby claimed that the bequest to the devizees was on the understanding that they would reintroduce the Plan of Association within a year or so, but that they had instead turned themselves into a trust. Thoresby claimed that this was against LH's intentions, and that the authority claimed by the trustees was illegal.

[67] LH to the Bath congregation, 19 May 1790, Seymour, ii. 486.

[68] In JW's phrase, noted above, '...delicate hearers, who could not bear sound doctrine if it were not set off with...pretty trifles!', Ch. 4, n. 90.

When she died at the age of nearly eighty-four, this woman, who in her youth had appeared delicate and prone to ill-health, had established a denomination bearing her name which was to survive as a separate entity well into the twentieth century. The identity of that denomination had been strengthened by formal separation from the Church of England; it had its own ordination, training college, and articles of religion. It had established a commanding and distinctive presence on the Calvinistic wing of the Revival, offering a home (in close proximity to the Church of England) for evangelicals drawn to a Calvinist theology whose needs, for whatever reason, were not met by the Church in the locality in which they lived. The lists in the Plan of Association showed that there were few substantial areas of the country in which the Connexion had not left some continuing mark. But Lady Huntingdon's influence was not to be measured only (or even chiefly) by the chapels that bore her name. Her preachers were a catalyst for revival amongst Churchmen and Dissenters in many places where the Connexion itself left no continuing presence. In her approach of using itinerant preaching within a connexional structure, she provided, like Wesley, a model for ordered Church growth that was to have a significant impact on Dissent in the last years of the century.[69] Most significantly of all, her college established the model of an evangelical seminary that was to be widely copied, as well as providing ministers for a large number of Anglican, Dissenting, and Calvinist evangelical congregations. The best of her former students were to play a major part in the evangelistic and missionary enterprises of the last years of the century, and the Connexion itself was poised to play a role in the early proselytization of Africa through its mission to Sierra Leone.[70]

---

[69] e.g. D. W. Lovegrove, *Established Church, Sectarian People* (Cambridge, 1988), 88–93. Dr Walsh describes the organizational legacy of Wesleyan Methodism as being the demonstrable effectiveness of itinerancy, within a connexional system that offered flexibility combined with strategic planning and control over orthodoxy. The same could be argued in the case of the Connexion also (Walsh, 'Methodism at the End of the Eighteenth Century', 295).

[70] Interestingly, Zachary Macaulay, as governor of Sierra Leone, was to write that the lives of 'Lady Huntingdon's Methodists...are very disorderly, and rank

All this amounted to a remarkable record, and it is not to diminish her achievements to set them against those of her contemporary, John Wesley. The Church that she left behind was certainly of a lesser order than his. As seen, the Connexion had no formal organizational structure to speak of. Nor did it compare in size. No lists of ministers have survived, but in the last years of Lady Huntingdon's life the names of some 30 to 35 individuals can be identified each year as actively involved in ministerial duties (although not all full time in the Connexion). That may well be an underestimate of the Connexion's available ministerial manpower: the influx of ordained men in the years after the Primary Ordination in 1783 would suggest a steadily rising overall figure. But even if there were a minister (or student) for each of the 63 chapels listed in the Plan of Association, the total would still be well short of the 188 lay preachers from whom Wesley had selected the Legal Hundred in 1784.[71] It is more difficult still to estimate the active membership of the Connexion, in order to compare with the 72,000 society members recorded by the Wesleyan conference in 1791.[72] On the evidence described,[73] of society members generally in double figures, the Connexion might at best have claimed a tenth of that figure. In 1800 Haweis estimated that the Connexion had 100,000 'members', a figure which must have been wildly out, even if he were describing attenders, rather than society members.[74]

antinomianism prevails among them' (G. O. Trevelyan, *The Life and Letters of Lord Macaulay* (Popular edn. London, 1889), 17).

[71] Baker, *Wesley and the Church of England*, 228. Wesley had some 400 preaching houses by 1784 (Rack, *Wesley*, 497).

[72] Walsh, 'Methodism at the End of the Eighteenth Century', 278. This was three times the number Wesley had estimated in 1767 (JW to R. Costerdine, 24 Nov. 1767, *Letters*, v. 66). [73] Above, Ch. 4.

[74] Thomas Haweis, *An Impartial and Succinct History of the Church of Christ* (London, 1800), iii. 260 ff. Haweis's figure would suggest more than a thousand worshippers at each chapel. The religious census of 1851 recorded 38,727 sittings at the (then) 109 chapels of the Connexion, compared with figures for Wesleyan Methodism of 1,447,580 sittings and 6,579 places of worship. This was not counting more than 4,000 chapels of other Methodist groups. These figures (source: R. Currie, A. Gilbert, and L. Horsley, *Churches and Churchgoers: Patterns of Church Growth in the British Isles since 1700* (Oxford, 1977), 216) are illustrative of the comparative stagnation of the Connexion in the nineteenth century, compared with other wings

Numbers were not everything. What differentiates Lady Huntingdon most from Wesley is the lack of what he so conspicuously possessed, a driving sense not only of his calling (Lady Huntingdon possessed that too), but of the path he was to take in furtherance of it. That in part explains why his connexion was established so much sooner than hers. Lady Huntingdon knew she was saved by grace, a brand plucked from the burning through no merit of her own. She knew that her duty was to share that conviction as widely as possible, whenever and wherever circumstances permitted, rather than by trying to implement any clearly thought out plan. Sometimes that spontaneity of response hit on initiatives of real worth, as in the founding of Trevecca, which was perhaps the only unique contribution that Lady Huntingdon made to the religious life of her time. At other moments it led her into sterile ground, like the efforts she expended on her American ventures, or the bitter and destructive doctrinal disputes of the 1770s. Seldom did she show the breadth and consistency of vision of which Wesley was capable. There was no parallel in Lady Huntingdon's thinking to Wesley's sense of a people raised up in pursuit of a Gospel holiness that affected every facet of their lives; to the breadth of his theology of salvation and of the Church; or to the catholicity of perspectives which led him to tackle the intellectual needs and bodily health of his followers, alongside the salvation of their souls.[75]

Nor, as it happened, did Lady Huntingdon's denomination enjoy the uniqueness of Wesley's. There was only one significant home for Arminian evangelicals, which in part explains the robustness of Wesleyan Methodism in the years after Wesley's death. But the Countess of Huntingdon's Connexion was only one of a number of Calvinist evangelical

of the Revival. They cast further doubt on Haweis's claims for the Connexion in 1800.

[75] Professor Ward argues that Wesley's failure to effect his planned reformation of Church and State in England led to that original objective being 'entirely forgotten, and dissolved historiographically into the founding legends of new or reconstituted denominations' (W. R. Ward, *The Protestant Evangelical Awakening* (Cambridge, 1992), 354). It is unlikely (certainly once she had embarked upon the active phase of her life) that LH ever thought of her mission in such grandiose terms.

groups: those who shared her theology might as easily hear it preached in the chapels of George Whitefield or Rowland Hill, in Dissenting congregations revivified by the Revival (perhaps by former Trevecca students), or even in the pulpits of the Church of England. Thus the Connexion was in an essentially vulnerable position as it entered the nineteenth century. Despite its name, which implied some cohesion and unity of purpose, and its broad connexional structure, there was less and less corporate reason for its continued existence. There was choice for individual Calvinist evangelicals as to which Church to attend (at least if they lived in the larger conurbations), and there was choice also for chapel committees as they surveyed the range of ministerial talent available to serve them. That the Connexion survived through the nineteenth century is probably due more to the needs and circumstances of the individual congregations of which it was comprised than to any unique contribution it was able to make, as a collective entity, to the religious life of the country. But that, perhaps, is all Lady Huntingdon would have wanted to achieve. The needs to which she gave her whole energies through a long and active life were those of individuals standing naked before God. Her calling was not to the development of theology or the evolution of new schemes of Church government, still less to producing some fresh insight into man's place in time or eternity. She had seen a need, and had responded to it, in the best way she could.

She would doubtless have wanted no other epitaph than that.

ANNEX A: STUDENTS OF TREVECCA COLLEGE

Trevecca students additional to those identified by Dr Nuttall. (The reference given by each name is the principal one establishing that person as a member of the college. All references are taken from the Cheshunt archives unless otherwise stated.)

William Aldington	F1/258a
Asher	E4/11(1)
John Bartholomew	F1/562
Bennett (of Grimsby)	F1/769
George Brown	Nottingham Guardian, 23 Oct. 1933
William Chiley	F1/969
John Cox	F1/1160
Samuel Davenport	F1/100
Joshua Denham (brother of Edmund)	Gloucester Record Office, D. 2538. 8/1, John Williams to Lady Huntingdon, 3 Apr. 1788.
Anthony Dickson	F1/562
Edwards	F1/1716
Feist	F1/706
J. Fletcher	F1/261
John Garrett	F1/2138
George Goodrick	F1/90
Hall	E4/11(4)
Harrison	F1/2076
Hayes	F1/1907
William Holland	F1/730
John Hornby	F1/713
Thomas Hull	E4/4(17)
Humphries	F1/1846
John James	F1/1964
William Kemp	C1/1, p. 84
Richard Lane	F1/223
Samuel Lloyd	F1/609
John McBrom	E4/8(6)
Mayer	F1/258a
John Mayes	E4/4(17)

G. Meller/Millar	F1/1229, 1807
Charles William Milton	F1/1972
William Morley	F1/1231
Thomas McKain/McRain	F1/738
Nicklin	F1/671
James Panton	F1/263
William Robertson	F1/2027
George Simmonds	F1/1980
Thomas Still	E4/4(17)
Sutherland	F1/2207
Taylor	F1/258a
Waite	F1/1464
Thomas Weston	F1/1964
Woodward	F1/562

(The student who appears as 'David' in Dr Nuttall's list was David Margate.)

STUDENTS KNOWN TO HAVE BEEN ENGAGED IN
PREACHING DURING 1777, 1783, AND 1787

1777: John Adams, Thomas Davies, Dunn, Eyre, Griffiths, Richard Lane, Leggatt, Molland, Newbon, Thresher, Matthew Wilks.

1783: Barnard, Beaufoy, Edward Burn, Anthony Dickson, Gray, Jenkins, Johnson, Kirkman, John Lloyd, Mills, Parsons, Satchell, Shuter, Thomas Thorn, Watkins, John Williams.

1787: Ellis, Green, Jenkins, Theo Jones, Milton, Morris, Munn, Nicklin, Daniel Rowland, Vaughan, Waring.

ANNEX B: THE PLAN OF ASSOCIATION (1790)

1. LONDON: Spa Fields, Mulberry Gardens, Sion, Holywell Mount
2. READING: Reading, Goring, Wallingford, Rickmansworth, Basingstoke
3. FAVERSHAM: Faversham, Dover, Milton, Tunbridge Wells
4. BRIGHTHELMSTONE (Brighton): Brighthelmstone, Lewes, Chichester, Ote Hall
5. ELY: Ely, Chatteris, Ramsey (Huntingdonshire), Peterborough
6. SUDBURY: Sudbury, Fordham, Woodbridge
7. BATH: Bath
8. BRISTOL: Bristol, Swansea
9. WINCANTON: Wincanton, a horse ride, Froome
10. ST COLUMB: St Columb, a horse ride, Star Cross
11. GLOUCESTER: Gloucester, Hereford, Coleford, Banbury
12. WORCESTER: Worcester, Evesham, Kidderminster
13. MONMOUTH: Monmouth, Broadoak, Langadock
14. BIRMINGHAM: Birmingham, West Bromwich, Handsworth, Edgbaston
15. WOLVERHAMPTON: Wolverhampton, Dudley, Bilston
16. ASHBY-DE-LA-ZOUCH: Ashby-de-la-Zouch, Ashbourn
17. WIGAN: Wigan
18. ULVERSTONE: Ulverstone, Whitehaven
19. NORWICH: Norwich
20. LINCOLN: Lincoln, Gainsborough, Newark
21. HAXEY: Haxey, Pinchbeck, Partney
22. YORK: York, Hull, Helmsley
23. MORPETH: Morpeth

A copy of the Plan in this form is preserved in the Cheshunt Archive as D3/2,CF. It is printed in Seymour, ii, 483–6n, and in E. Welch, *Two Calvinistic Methodist Chapels, 1743–1811* (London Record Society, 1975), 92–5 (in each case with some small discrepancies from the list as given here).

ANNEX C: THE ARTICLES OF THE COUNTESS OF HUNTINGDON'S CONNEXION*

WE BELIEVE

I. OF GOD

That there is but one living and true GOD, everlasting, without body, parts, or passions, of infinite power, wisdom, and goodness, the maker and preserver of all things, both visible and invisible. And in the unity of the Godhead there are three Persons of one substance, power, and eternity, the FATHER, the SON, and the HOLY GHOST.

II. OF THE SCRIPTURES

That it pleased God at sundry times and in divers manners to declare his will, and the same should be committed unto writing, which is therefore called the Holy Scripture; which containeth all things necessary to salvation. The authority whereof doth not depend upon the testimony of man, but wholly upon God its author; and our assurance of the infallible truth thereof is from the inward work of the HOLY GHOST, bearing witness with the work in our hearts.

III. OF CREATION

It pleased God, for the manifestation of his glory, in the beginning to create the world and all things therein; and having made man, male and female, after his own image, endued with knowledge, righteousness, and true holiness, he gave them a command not to

---

* Text as given in Seymour, ii. 440 n.–3n.

eat of the tree of knowledge of good and evil, with a power to fulfil it, yet under a possibility of transgressing, being left to the liberty of their own will, which was subject unto change.

IV. OF THE FALL OF MAN FROM ORIGINAL RIGHTEOUSNESS

Our first parents being seduced by the subtilty and temptations of Satan, sinned in eating the forbidden fruit, whereby they fell from their original righteousness, and became wholly defiled in all the faculties and parts of soul and body. And being the root of all mankind, the guilt of this sin was imputed, and the same corrupted nature conveyed to all posterity, descending from them by ordinary generation.

V. OF ORIGINAL SIN

Original sin standeth not in the following of Adam, as the Pelagians do vainly talk, but it is the fault and corruption of the nature of every man, that naturally is engendered of the offspring of Adam, whereby man is as far as possible gone from original righteousness, and is of his own nature inclined to evil, so that the flesh lusteth always contrary to the spirit; and therefore in every person born into this world, it deserveth God's wrath and damnation. And this infection of nature doth remain, yea, in them that are regenerated, yet without dominion; and although there is no condemnation to them that are in CHRIST JESUS, yet sin in them is evil as much as in others, and as such receives Divine fatherly chastisement.

VI. OF PREDESTINATION AND ELECTION

Although the whole world is thus become guilty before God, it hath pleased him to predestinate some unto everlasting life. Predestination therefore to life is the everlasting purpose of God, whereby (before the foundations of the world were laid) he hath constantly decreed by his counsel, secrets to us, to deliver from curse and damnation those whom he hath chosen in Christ out of mankind, and to bring them by Christ to everlasting salvation, as vessels made to honour. Wherefore they which are endued with so excellent a benefit of God, are called according to God's purpose by his Spirit working in due season; they through grace obey the call; they are justified freely; they are made sons of God by adoption; they bear the image of Christ; they walk religiously in good works; and at length, by God's mercy, they attain to everlasting felicity.

VII. OF CHRIST THE MEDIATOR

It pleased God, in his eternal purpose, to choose and ordain the LORD JESUS, his only begotten-Son, to be the Mediator between God and Man, the Prophet, Priest, and King, the Head and Saviour of his Church, unto whom he did from all eternity give a people to be his seed, and to be by him in time redeemed, called, justified, sanctified, and glorified. He therefore being very and eternal God, of one substance, and equal with the FATHER, did, when the fulness of time was come, take upon him man's nature, yet without sin, being conceived by the power of the Holy Ghost in the womb of the Virgin Mary; so that two whole, perfect, and distinct natures, the Godhead and the Manhood, were inseparably joined together in one person, without conversion or confusion; which person is very God and very Man, yet one Christ, the only Mediator between God and Man. This office of Mediator and surety he did most willingly undertake; which, that he might discharge, he was made under the Law, and did perfectly fulfil it by an obedience unto death; by which perfect obedience and sacrifice of himself on the Cross, which he through the eternal Spirit once offered up unto God, he hath fully satisfied divine justice, and purchased not only reconciliation, but an everlasting inheritance in the kingdom of Heaven, for all those whom the Father hath given him. To all of whom he doth, in his own time, and in his own way, certainly and effectually apply his purchased redemption; making intercession for them; and revealing unto them, through the Word and by his Spirit, the mysteries of salvation; effectually enabling them to believe unto obedience; and governing their hearts by the same Word and Spirit, and overcoming all their enemies by his Almighty power.

VII. OF THE HOLY GHOST

The Holy Ghost is the third person in the adorable Godhead, distinct from the Father and the Son; yet of one substance, glory, and majesty with them, very and eternal God, whose office in the

Church is manifold. It is he who illuminates the understanding to discern spiritual things, and guides us into all truth, so that without his teaching, we shall never be effectually convinced of sin, nor be brought to the saving knowledge of God in Christ. And his teaching, whether it be by certain means which he ordinarily makes use of, or without means, is attended with an evidence peculiar and proper to itself, therefore styled the demonstration of the Spirit and of power. By which Divine power he not only enlightens the understanding, but gives a new turn or bias to the will and affections, moving and acting upon our hearts, and by his secret energetic influence effecting those things which we could never attain or accomplish by our own strength. Nor is his guidance less necessary in our lives and all our transactions. Without his assistance we know not what to pray for, or how to pray aright. He confirms us in all grace, and he is the author of all holiness. It is he that assures us of our personal interest in Christ, and that sheds abroad the love of God in our hearts. He seals believers unto the day of redemption, and is himself the earnest of their future inheritance. He administers comfort to us in our temporal and spiritual distresses, by applying to our minds seasonable promises of God in Christ Jesus, which are yea and amen; and by receiving the things of Christ, and showing them unto us. Thus he encourageth and refresheth us with a sense of the favour of God; fills us with joy unspeakable, and full of glory; and is to abide with the Church forever.

IX. OF FREE WILL

The condition of man after the fall of Adam is such, that he cannot turn or prepare himself by his own natural strength and good works to faith and calling upon God; wherefore we have no power to do good works, pleasant and acceptable to God, without the grace of God by Christ preventing us, that we may have a good will, and working with us when we have that good will.

X. OF JUSTIFICATION

We are accounted righteous before God, only for the merit of our Lord and Saviour Jesus Christ, by faith, and not for our own works or deservings. Wherefore, that we are justified by faith only, is a most wholesome doctrine, and very full of comfort. And this is done by pardoning our sins, and by accounting our persons as righteous by imputing the obedience and satisfaction of Christ unto us, which is received and rested upon by faith, which faith we have not of ourselves, but it is the gift of God.

XI. OF SANCTIFICATION AND GOOD WORKS

They who are effectually called and regenerated, having a new heart and a new spirit created in them, are further sanctified, really and personally, through the virtue of Christ's death and resurrection, by his word and spirit dwelling in them; the dominion of the whole body of sin is destroyed, and the several lusts thereof are more and more weakened and mortified, and they more and more quickened and strengthened in all saving graces, to the practice of true holiness; and without which no man shall see the Lord. Works which are the fruits of faith, and follow after justification, though they cannot put away our sins, nor endure the severity of God's judgement, yet are pleasing and acceptable to God in Christ, and spring out necessarily of a true and lively faith; insomuch that by them a lively faith may be as evidently known as a tree discerned by the fruit.

XII. OF WORKS BEFORE JUSTIFICATION

Works done before the grace of Christ, and the inspiration of his Spirit, are not pleasant to God, forasmuch as they spring not of faith in the Lord Jesus Christ, neither do they make man meet to receive grace; yea, rather, for that they are not done as God hath willed and commanded them to be done, we doubt not but they have the nature of sin.

XIII. OF THE CHURCH

The Catholic, or universal Church, which is invisible, consists of the whole number of the elect that have been, are, or shall be, gathered into one, under Christ the Head thereof, and is the spouse, the body, the fulness of him that filleth all in all. The visible Church consists of all those throughout the world who profess the true religion, together with their children. To which visible

Church Christ hath given the ministry and ordinances of the Gospel, for the gathering and perfecting of the saints in this life, to the end of the world; and doth by his own presence and Spirit, according to his promise, make them effectual thereunto.

There is no other Head of the Church but the Lord Jesus Christ; nor can the Pope of Rome in any sense thereof, but is that Antichrist, the man of sin, and son of perdition, that exalteth himself in the Church against Christ, and all that is called God.

XIV. OF BAPTISM

Baptism is a sacrament of the New Testament, ordained by Jesus Christ, not only for the solemn admission of the party baptised into the visible Church, but also to be unto him a sign and seal of the covenant of grace, to be continued in the Church until the end of the world; which is rightly administered by pouring or sprinkling water upon the person, in the name of the FATHER, SON and HOLY GHOST. This sacrament ought to be administered but once to any person; and we also hold, that infants may and ought to be baptised, in virtue of one or both believing parents, because the spiritual privilege of a right unto and a participation of the initial seal of the covenant was granted by God to the infant seed of Abraham, which grant must remain forever, without the Lord's own express revoking or abrogation of it, which can never be proved from Scripture that he has done. Again, they that have the thing signified have a right to the sign of it; but children are capable of the grace signified in Baptism, and some of them (we trust) are partakers of it—namely, such as die in their infancy; therefore, they may and ought to be baptised. For these and other reasons, we believe and maintain the lawfulness and expediency of infant baptism.

XV. OF THE LORD'S SUPPER

The supper of the Lord is not only a sign of the love that Christians ought to have among themselves one to another, but rather it is a sacrament of the body and blood of CHRIST, and of our redemption thereby, called the LORD'S SUPPER, to be observed in his Church to the end of the world, for the perpetual remembrance of the sacrifice of himself in his death; the sealing all benefits thereof to true believers; their spiritual nourishment and growth in him; their further engagement in and to all duties which they owe unto him; and to be a bond and pledge of their communion with him and with each other as members of his mystical body. Insomuch, that to such as rightly and with faith receive the same, the bread which we break is a partaking of the body of Christ; and likewise the cup of blessing is a partaking of the blood of Christ; though in substance and nature they still remain bread and wine as they were before. Those, therefore, that are void of faith, though they do carnally and visibly eat the bread and drink the wine of the sacrament of the body and blood of Christ, yet are in nowise partakers of Christ, but rather to their condemnation do eat and drink the sign or sacrament of so great a blessing.

BIBLIOGRAPHY

PRINCIPAL MANUSCRIPT SOURCES

Bath Central Library, Bath: Letter of Lady Huntingdon to Mrs Barlow, 31 July 1756.

Center for Methodist Studies at Bridwell Library, Perkins School of Theology, Southern Methodist University, Dallas: letters of Lady Huntingdon.

Cheshunt College Foundation, Westminster and Cheshunt College, Cambridge: Archives of the Countess of Huntingdon's Connexion and College.

Cheshire and Chester Archives and Local Studies: MSS CR47/1–81, letters of John Walker of Boughton Lodge, Chester.

Congregational Library, Dr Williams's Library, London: Sir John Bickerton Williams collection, II a17.

Robert W. Woodruff Library, Emory University, Atlanta: John Wesley Collection.

Essex Record Office, Chelmsford: Accession no. 4497.

Gainsborough United Reformed (John Robinson Memorial) Church: 'A Brief Historick Record of Events Relating to the Independent Church Assembling in Caskgate Lane Chapel'.

Gloucestershire County Record Office, Gloucester: Ebley Chapel Records, D. 2538 8/1.

Huntington Library, San Marino, California: Hastings MSS.

John Rylands Library, Manchester: letters of Lady Huntingdon— ENG. MS 338; 346/185a.

Leicestershire Record Office: Hastings family papers.

Methodist Connexional Archives, John Rylands Library, Manchester: Letters of Lady Huntingdon, John Fletcher, and Benjamin Ingham; Letters to Charles Wesley.

National Library of Wales, Aberystwyth: Trevecka Letters; Diary of Howel Harris; MSS 350A, 1086C, 7005C, 9231C.

West Sussex Record Office, Chichester: NC/C3/2/1—Society Book of the Countess of Huntingdon's Chapel, Chichester.

PRIMARY PRINTED SOURCES

An Authentic Narrative of the Primary Ordination [of the Countess of Huntingdon's Connexion] (London, 1784).

Berridge, John, *A Letter of the Revd John Berridge, giving an Account of his Life* (1758).

Byrom, John, *The Private Journals and Literary Remains of John Byrom*, ed. R. Parkinson (Chetham Society, Manchester, 1854–7).

Chesterfield, 4th Earl of, *Letters of Lord Chesterfield to Lord Huntingdon*, ed. A. Francis Steuart (London, 1923).

Cottingham, J., *A Funeral Sermon for Lady Huntingdon* (1791).

Dartmouth, 2nd Earl of, *Manuscripts of the Earl of Dartmouth* (Historical Manuscripts Commission, London, 1887–96).

Doddridge, Philip, *Calendar of the Correspondence of Philip Doddridge*, ed. G. F. Nuttall (London, 1979).

Evangelical Magazine (London, 1793–).

Extracts of the Journals of Several Ministers of the Gospel, in a Series of Letters to the Countess of Huntingdon (Preface by T. Pentycross) (London, 1782).

Fletcher, John, *Works* (London, 1825).

Foote, Samuel, *The Minor* (London, 1760).

Gillies, J., *Historical Collections Relating to Remarkable Periods in the Success of the Gospel* (Glasgow, 1754).

Gospel Magazine (London, 1766–).

Harris, Howel, *Memoirs of Howel Harris from Papers Written by Himself* (Trevecka, 1791).

—— *Howel Harris, Reformer and Soldier*, ed. T. Beynon (Caernarvon, 1958).

—— *Howel Harris's Visits to London*, ed. T. Beynon (Aberystwyth, 1960).

Hastings, R. R., *Report on the Manuscripts of the late Reginald Rawdon Hastings Esq.* (Historical Manuscripts Commission, London, 1928–47).

Haweis, Thomas, *An Impartial and Succinct History of the Rise, Declension and Revival of the Church of Christ, from the Birth of our Saviour to the Present Time* (London, 1800).

Hervey, James, *A Collection of the Letters of the Revd James Hervey... To which is Prefixed an Account of his Life and Death* (London, 1760).

—— *Sermons and Tracts* (Collection published in 1761, with a memoir of his life).

—— *Eleven Letters... to... John Wesley; Containing an Answer to that Gentleman's Remarks on Theron and Aspasio* (London, 1765).

—— *The Works of... James Hervey, with a Particular Account of the Life, Character and Writings of the Author* (Newcastle upon Tyne, 1789).

—— *Original Letters of the Revd James Hervey from the Originals in the Collection of the Revd R. H. Knight, present Rector of Weston Favell* (1829).

Hill, Richard, *Pietas Oxoniensis: Or, A Full and Impartial Account of the Expulsion of Six Students from St. Edmund Hall, Oxford* (London, 1768).

Hill, Richard, *A Conversation between Richard Hill, Revd Martin Madan and the Superior of a Convent of English Benedictine Monks at Paris, Relative to Some Doctrinal Minutes Advanced by the Revd Mr J. Wesley Held There on July 13, 1771, in the Presence of Thomas Powis and Others* (London, 1772).

Horne, William W., *Life of the Revd John Bradford* (London, 1806).

Lindsey, Theophilus, *Letters of Theophilus Lindsey*, ed. H. McLachlan, (Manchester, 1920).

Lyttleton, 1st Baron, *Memoirs and Correspondence of George, Lord Lyttleton*, ed. R. Phillimore (London, 1845).

Maxfield, Thomas, *A Short Account of God's Dealings with Mrs Elizabeth Maxfield* (London, 1778).

Penrose, John, *Letters from Bath, 1766–67, by the Rev. John Penrose*, ed. B. Mitchell and H. Penrose (Gloucester, 1983).

Pierce, Samuel Eyles, *A True Outline and Sketch of the Life of Samuel Eyles Pierce, Written by Himself* (London, 1824).

Priestley, Joseph, *Autobiography* (Bath, 1970).

Roberts, G. M. (ed.), *Selected Trevecka Letters* (Caernarvon, 1956 and 1962).

Shirley, Walter, *A Narrative of the Principal Circumstances relative to the Revd Mr. Wesley's late Conference held in Bristol, August the 6th, 1771, at which the Revd Mr. Shirley, and Others, his Friends, were Present* (Bath, 1771).

Some Account of the Proceedings at the College of the Right Hon. The Countess of Huntingdon, in Wales Relative to those Students called to go to her Ladyship's College in Georgia (London, 1772).

Wesley, Charles, *The Journal of the Revd Charles Wesley*, ed. Thomas Jackson (London, 1849).

Wesley, John, *The Letters of the Rev. John Wesley, A. M.*, ed. J. Telford (Standard edn., London 1931).

—— *The Journal of the Rev. John Wesley, A. M.*, ed. N. Curnock (Standard edn., London, 1938).

—— *The Works of John Wesley*, Bicentennial edn., ed. R. P. Heitzenrater and F. Baker, vols. xx–xxiii (Nashville, 1991–5); ed. F. Baker, vols. xxv–xxvi (Oxford, 1980–2).

Wills, Thomas, *Farewell Address to the Congregations and Societies of the Countess of Huntingdon's Connexion* (London, 1788).

Wills, Thomas, *Memoirs of the Life of the Revd Thomas Wills, by a Friend, Published under the Full Patronage of Mrs Wills* (London, 1804).
Winter, Cornelius, *Memoirs of the Life and Character of... C. Winter* (Bath, 1808).
Woodforde, James, *The Diary of a Country Parson, 1758–1802* (Oxford, 1978).

SECONDARY SOURCES

Abbey, C. J. and Overton, J. H., *The English Church in the Eighteenth Century* (London, 1887).
Alumni Cantabrigiensis, ed. J. and J. A. Venn (Cambridge, 1922–54).
Alumni Oxoniensis, ed. J. Foster (Oxford, 1886–91).
Anon., *The Life of the Revd James Hervey* (Berwick, 1770).
Aveling, T. W., *Memorials of the Clayton Family* (London, 1867).
Baker, Frank, *John Wesley and the Church of England* (London, 1970).
—— 'Thomas Maxfield's first sermon', *Proceedings of the Wesley Historical Society*, vol. 27.
Bebbington, D. W., *Evangelicalism in Modern Britain: A History from the 1730s to the 1980s* (London, 1989).
Belsham, T., *Memoirs of the late Reverend Theophilus Lindsey, M. A.* (London, 1873).
Benham, D., *Memoirs of James Hutton* (London, 1856).
Bennett, R., *The Early Life of Howel Harris*, trans. G. M. Roberts (London, 1962).
Best, G. F. A., *Temporal Pillars: Queen Anne's Bounty, the Ecclesiastical Commissioners and the Church of England* (Cambridge, 1964).
Bickerstaff, M., *Our Children's Heritage, Being a Short History of the Calvinistic Methodists* (Caernarvon, 1934).
Bogue, D. and Bennett, J., *History of Dissenters from the Revolution in 1688 to the Year 1808* (London, 1808–12).
Bolam, G. C., Goring, J., Short, H. L., and Thomas, R. (eds.), *The English Presbyterians from Elizabethan Puritanism to Modern Unitarianism* (London, 1968).
Bonarjee, P., *The History of the Countess of Huntingdon's Church, Brighton* (1934).
Bossy, J., *The English Catholic Community, 1570–1850* (London, 1975).
Bowmer, J. C., *The Sacrament of the Lord's Supper in Early Methodism* (London, 1951).

Bridgman, J., *An Address to the Ministers, Deacons and Friends of the Countess of Huntingdon's Connexion and College* (London, 1857).
Brown, F. K., *The Fathers of the Victorians* (Cambridge, 1961).
Brown, J., *Memoirs of the Life and Character of James Hervey* (Edinburgh, 2nd edn. 1809).
Caplan, N., 'Outline of the Origins and Early Development of Nonconformity in Sussex, 1603–1803' (1961), MS in Dr William's Library, London.
Carter, G., 'The case of the Revd James Shore', *Journal of Ecclesiastical History*, 47/3 (July 1996).
Coppedge, A., 'John Wesley and the Doctrine of Predestination', Ph.D. thesis (Cambridge, 1976).
Cozens-Hardy, B., 'The Countess *versus* Methodism *versus* Independency', *Transactions of the Congregational Historical Society*, 21/3 (1972).
Crowe, I., 'Methodism and its Critics in Eighteenth Century Bath', M. Litt. thesis (Bristol, 1991).
Currie, Robert, Gilbert, Alan, and Horsley, Lee, *Churches and Churchgoers: Patterns of Church Growth in the British Isles since 1770* (Oxford, 1977).
Davies, R., *Methodism* (London, 1963).
—— and Rupp, E. G. (eds.), *A History of the Methodist Church in Great Britain*, i (London, 1965).
—— George, A. Raymond, and Rupp, E. G. (eds.), *A History of the Methodist Church in Great Britain*, ii and iii (London 1978, 1983).
Dallimore, A., *George Whitefield*, (London, 1970, 1980).
Downey, J., *The Eighteenth Century Pulpit* (Oxford, 1968).
Elliott-Binns, L. E., *The Early Evangelicals* (London, 1953).
Evans, R., 'The Eighteenth Century Welsh Revival, with its Relationship to the Contemporary Evangelical Revival', Ph.D. thesis (Edinburgh, 1956).
Everitt, Alan, 'Nonconformity in Country Parishes', *Agricultural History Review*, 18 (1970), Supplement.
Forsaith, P. S., 'Wesley's Designated Successor', *Proceedings of the Wesley Historical Society*, 42/3 (1979).
Francis, M., 'Selina, Countess of Huntingdon', B.Phil. thesis (Oxford, 1955).
Garlick, K. B., *Mr. Wesley's Preachers, 1739–1818* (World Methodist Historical Society, London, 1977).
Gibbons, T., Jerment, G., and Burder, S., *Memoirs of Eminently Pious Women* (London, 1815).
Gillies, J., *Memoirs of the Life of... George Whitefield* (London, 1772).
Gledstone, J. P., *George Whitefield, M. A., field preacher* (London, 1902).

Gray, J., *Johnson's Sermons: A study* (Oxford, 1972).
Green, V. H. H., *The Young Mr. Wesley* (London, 1961).
—— *John Wesley* (London, 1964).
Gunter, W. Steven, *The Limits of 'Love Divine'* (Nashville, 1998).
Haig, A., *The Victorian Clergy* (London and Sydney, 1984).
Halley, R., *Lancashire, its Puritanism and Nonconformity* (Manchester, 1869).
Harding, A., 'The Anglican Prayer Book and the Countess of Huntingdon's Connexion', *Transactions of the Congregational Historical Society*, 20/12 (1970).
Hempton, D., *The Religion of the People: Methodism and Popular Religion* c.1750–1900 (London and New York, 1996).
Hindmarsh, B., *John Newton and the English Evangelical Tradition, Between the Conversions of Wesley and Wilberforce* (Oxford, 1996).
Hobhouse, S., *William Law and Eighteenth Century Quakerism* (London, 1927).
Hull, J. E., 'Lady Huntingdon and John Wesley', Ph.D. thesis (Edinburgh, 1959).
Jago, J., *Aspects of the Georgian Church, Visitation Studies of the Diocese of York, 1761–1776* (Cranbury, NJ, 1997).
Hutton, J. E., 'The Moravian Contribution to the Evangelical Revival in England, 1742–55', *Historical Essays by Members of the Owens College, Manchester*, ed. T. F. Tout and J. Tait (London, 1902).
Jackson, T., *The Life of the Revd Charles Wesley, M. A.* (London, 1841).
Jay, W., *Memoirs of the Life and Character of the Revd Cornelius Winter* (London, 1806).
Jones, M. H., *The Trevecka Letters* (Caernarvon, 1932).
Jones, T. S., *The Life of Willielma, Viscountess Glenorchy* (London, 1822).
Jones, R. Tudor, *Congregationalism in England, 1622–1962* (London, 1962).
Knox, R. A., *Enthusiasm: A Chapter in the History of Religion* (Oxford, 1950).
Lane, M., *Purely for Pleasure* (London, 1966).
Laqueur, T. W., *Religion and Respectability: Sunday Schools and Working Class Culture* (New Haven and London, 1976).
Lawton, G., *Shropshire Saint, a Study of Fletcher of Madeley* (London, 1960).
Lindstrom, H., *Wesley and Sanctification* (Upsala, 1946).
Lovegrove, D. W., *Established Church, Sectarian People: Itinerancy and the Transformation of English Dissent, 1780–1830* (Cambridge, 1988).
Lowther Clarke, W. K., *A History of the SPCK* (London, 1959).

Lyles, A. M., *Methodism Mocked: The Satiric Reaction to Methodism in the Eighteenth Century* (London, 1960).
Lyons, N., 'Satiric Techniques in "The Spiritual Quixote"', *Durham University Journal* (1974).
MacDonald, J., *Memoirs of the Revd Joseph Benson* (London, 1822).
McGonigle, H. B., 'John Wesley, Evangelical Arminian', Ph.D. thesis (Keele, 1994).
Mather, F. C., 'Georgian Churchmanship Reconsidered: Some Variations in Anglican Public Worship, 1714–1830', *Journal of Ecclesiastical History*, 36/2 (April 1985).
Matthews, A. G., *The Congregational Churches of Staffordshire* (London, 1924).
Middelton, J. W., *The Ecclesiastical History of the First Four Decades of the Reign of George III* (London, 1822).
Middleton, E., *Biographia Evangelica, or an Historical Account of the Lives and Deaths of the Most Eminent and Evangelical Authors or Preachers, both British and Foreign, in the Several Denominations of Protestants, from the Beginnings of the Reformation, to the Present Time* (London, 1779–86).
Morison, J., *The Fathers and Founders of the London Missionary Society* (n.d.).
Murray, N. U., 'The Influence of the French Revolution on the Church of England and its Rivals, 1789–1802', D.Phil. thesis (Oxford, 1975).
New, A. H., *The Coronet and the Cross* (London, 1857).
Nightingale, A., *Lancashire Nonconformity* (Manchester, 1892).
Norman, E. R., *Church and Society in England, 1770–1970* (Oxford, 1976).
Nuttall, G. F., *Howel Harris, the Last Enthusiast* (Cardiff, 1965).
—— 'The Students of Trevecca College', *Transactions of the Hon. Society of Cymmrodorion* (1966–7).
—— *The Significance of Trevecca College* (Cheshunt College Bicentenary Booklet, London, 1968).
—— 'Rowland Hill and the Rodborough Connexion, 1771–1833', *Transactions of the Congregational Historical Society*, 21/3 (1972).
—— 'Methodism and the Older Dissent: Some Perspectives', *Journal of the United Reformed Church History Society*, 2/8 (1981).
—— 'Howel Harris and the "Grand Table": A note on Religion and Politics', *Journal of Ecclesiastical History*, 39/4 (1988).
Ollard, S. L., *The Six Students of St. Edmund Hall, expelled from the University of Oxford in 1768* (London, 1911).
Outler, A. C., *John Wesley* (New York, 1964).

Peaston, A. E., *The Prayer Book Tradition in the Free Churches* (London, 1964).
Philpot, J. H., *The Seceders* (Banner of Truth, London, 1964).
Piggin, S., *Making Evangelical Missionaries, 1789–1858* (Abingdon, Oxford, 1984).
Podmore, C. J., 'The Fetter Lane Society, 1739–40', *Proceedings of the Wesley Historical Society*, 47/5 (May 1990).
—— *The Moravian Church in England, 1728–1760* (Oxford, 1998).
Pratt, J. (ed.), *The Life and Remains of the Revd Richard Cecil* (Edinburgh, 1854).
Rack, H., 'Religious Societies and the Origins of Methodism', *Journal of Ecclesiastical History*, 38/4 (1987).
—— *Reasonable Enthusiast: John Wesley and the Rise of Methodism* (London, 1989).
Reynolds, J. S., *The Evangelicals at Oxford, 1735–81* (Oxford, 1953).
Ritson, J., *The Romance of Primitive Methodism* (London, 4th edn., 1909).
Rupp, E. G., *Religion in England, 1688–1791* (Oxford, 1986).
Sackett, A. B., 'John Wesley and the Greek Orthodox Bishop', *Proceedings of the Wesley Historical Society*, 38/3 and 4 (1971–2).
Sangster, P. E., 'The Life of the Revd Rowland Hill and his Position in the Evangelical Revival', D.Phil. thesis (Oxford, 1964).
Schlenther, B. S., *Queen of the Methodists: The Countess of Huntingdon and the Eighteenth Century Crisis of Faith and Society* (Durham, 1997).
Sell, A. P. F., *The Great Debate: Calvinism, Arminianism and Salvation* (Grand Rapids, Mich., 1983).
Seymour, A. C. H., *The Life and Times of the Countess of Huntingdon* (London, 1839).
Sidney, E., *Life of the Rev. Rowland Hill* (5th edn., London, 1861).
Simon, J. S., *John Wesley and the Religious Societies* (London, 1921).
Smyth, C., *Simeon and Church Order* (Cambridge, 1940).
Snape, M. F., 'Anti-Methodism in Eighteenth-Century England: The Pendle Forest Riots of 1748', *Journal of Ecclesiastical History*, 49/2 (1998).
Streiff, P., *Reluctant Saint: A Theological Biography of Fletcher of Madely* (Peterborough, 2001).
Stromberg, R. N., *Religious Liberalism in Eighteenth-Century England* (Oxford, 1954).
Sykes, N., *Church and State in England in the Eighteenth Century* (Cambridge, 1934).
—— *From Sheldon to Secker* (Cambridge, 1959).
Taylor, J. H., 'The Survival of the Church Meeting', *Transactions of the Congregational Historical Society*, 21/2 (1971).

Taylor, R. V., *Biographia Leodiensis* (London, 1865).
Taylor, S., 'Church and State in the mid-Eighteenth Century: The Newcastle Years, 1742–1762', Ph. D. thesis (Cambridge, 1987).
Thomson, D. P., *Lady Glenorchy and her Churches* (Crieff, 1967).
Townsend, W. J., Workman, H. B., and Eayrs, G. (eds.), *A New History of Methodism* (London, 1909).
Treffry, R., *Memoirs of the Revd Joseph Benson* (London, 1840).
Tuck, W., *Notes on the History of the Argyle Chapel, Bath* (Bath, 1906).
Tyerman, L., *The Oxford Methodists: Memoirs of Messrs Clayton, Ingham, Gambold, etc.* London, 1873).
—— *The Life of the Revd George Whitefield* (London, 1876/7).
—— *The Life and Times of the Revd John Wesley* (London, 1880).
—— *Wesley's Designated Successor: The Life, Letters and Literary Labours of J. W. Fletcher* (London, 1882).
Tytler, S., *The Countess of Huntingdon and her Circle*, (Cincinnati, n.d.).
Valentine, B. H., *The Story of the Beginnings of Nonconformity in Arundel* (Harpenden, c.1925).
Virgin, P., *The Church in an Age of Negligence: Ecclesiastical Structure and Problems of Church Reform, 1700–1840* (Cambridge, 1989).
Walsh, J. D., 'The Yorkshire Evangelicals in the Eighteenth Century', Ph. D. thesis (Cambridge, 1956).
—— 'The Origins of the Evangelical Revival', in G. V. Bennett and J. D. Walsh (eds.), *Essays in Modern Church History in Memory of Norman Sykes* (London, 1966).
—— 'Methodism and the Mob in the Eighteenth Century', *Studies in Church History* (1971).
—— 'The Cambridge Methodists', in P. Brooks (ed.), *Essays in Christian Spirituality, Essays in Honour of Gordon Rupp* (London, 1975).
—— 'Methodism and the Local Community in the Eighteenth Century', *Vie Ecclésiale, Communauté et Communautés* (Paris, 1989).
—— 'Joseph Milner's Evangelical Church History', *Journal of Ecclesiastical History*, 10/2.
—— Haydon, C., and Taylor, S. (eds.), *The Church of England, c.1689–c.1833: From Toleration to Tractarianism (Cambridge, 1993)*.
Ward, W. R., 'The Religion of the People and the Problem of Control, 1790–1830', *Studies in Church History*, 8.
—— *The Protestant Evangelical Awakening* (Cambridge, 1992).
Warne, A., *Church and Society in Eighteenth Century Devon* (Newton Abbot, 1969).
Watts, M. R., *The Dissenters, from the Reformation to the French Revolution* (Oxford, 1978).

Wearmouth, R., *Methodism and the Common People of the Eighteenth Century* (London, 1945).
Welch, E., 'A Forgotten Thread in Congregational History: The Calvinistic Methodists', *Transactions of the Congregational Historical Society*, 21/4 (1972).
—— 'Lady Huntingdon and Spa Fields Chapel', *The Guildhall Miscellany*, 4/3 (1972).
—— *Two Calvinistic Methodist Chapels* (London Record Society, 1975).
—— *Cheshunt College: The Early Years* (Hertfordshire Record Society, 1990).
—— *Spiritual Pilgrim: A Reassessment of the Life of the Countess of Huntingdon* (Cardiff, 1995).
Whitehead, J., *The Life of the Revd John Wesley* (London, 1793–6).
Whittingham, R. (ed.), *The Works of the Revd John Berridge, With an Enlarged Memoir of his Life* (London, 1838).
Wilson, W., *The History and Antiquities of Dissenting Churches in London* (London, 1808).
Wood, A. S., *Thomas Haweis* (London, 1957).
—— *The Inextinguishable Blaze* (London, 1960).

INDEX

All London churches, chapels, societies, and other institutions are listed under 'London'.

Abraham, William 223, 224
absenteeism by clergy 7–8, 319
Adam, Thomas (of Wintringham) 324
Adams, John 104, 222
   ordination 307–8, 309
Adams, Thomas 288 n. 217
Addington, Dr 72
Aldington, William 214
Aldridge, William 105, 187 n. 75, 232 n. 363, 280, 316
   early preaching experience 202
   ordination attempt 303
Aldwincle 55
Allen (applicant to the Connexion) 84
Almondsbury 323
America, mission in 206–11, 287, 373
Angmering 51, 153
antinomianism 220, 247–9, 255, 282, 362 n. 25, 372 n. 70
anti-slavery 14, 209 n. 219
Apostolic Society 152 n. 470, 215, 219, 345, 350
   established 225
   plans for Cheshunt college 227–8
Arianism 11
Arminian Magazine 286
Arundel 51, 110, 153
Ashburn(er), Edward 307
Asburnham, Bishop William 318

Ashburnham (rector of Cuckfield) 299 n. 9
Ashby-de-la-Zouch 69, 126, 139, 144, 282
   LH bears cost of building work 73
   LH's house at 163
Augmentation Fund 170

Ball, Hannah 159
Banbury 77, 104
   chapel debt 167
Baptists 5, 71, 130, 351, 352, 356
   opposition to the Connexion 354–5
Barlow of Bath 85
Barnard, Samuel 225
Barnard, Thomas 25
Barry, Edward 189
Bartholomew, John 84
Barton-upon-Humber 118, 153 nn. 476 & 479, 155
Basingstoke 71
Bath 168, 202
Bath, Argyle chapel 76
Bath LH chapel 95, 127, 142, 155, 172
   founded 51–2
   social composition of committee 78
   chapel school 99, 120–1, 150–1
   assistant minister at 107
   disturbances at 115, 116–7
   singing master 122, 146

Bath LH chapel (*cont.*)
  week-night meetings 128
  Holy Communion 133, 135
  love feasts 136
  informal worship 137 n. 391
  publication of chapel tunes 145
  singers 146
  organs 148
  funded by LH 156
  outgoings 162
  support for other chapels 171
  JW preaches at 236
  Wesleyan sympathies at 239
  episcopal and clerical attendance at 321, 322
  resistance to Taylor taking control 341
  licensed 343
  ordination at 344
  chapel owned by LH 369 n. 61
Bath, LH's house at 225 n. 334, 315
Bath, Whitefieldite congregation 290
Baxter, Richard 191
Beale, Reverend (of Bengeworth) 305
Beaumont, Jonathon 75
Beaufoy, Samuel 65, 72, 134, 167
Bedford 72
Bell, George 233–4
Bencoolen 205–6, 298
Benezet, Anthony 209 n. 219
Benson, Joseph 212–13, 219, 238
  dismissed from Trevecca 262
Berkhamsted 104, 107 n. 228

Berridge, John 80–1, 91, 142 n. 413, 284
  conversion and contacts with LH 43–4
  on ministerial training 176
  consulted on plans for Trevecca 178
  enters controversy 280 n. 193
  and the Tabernacle Connexion 289
  weakening Connexion links 346–7
Best, George 94, 353, 359
  and Trevecca 215, 225, 226
  takes possession of Cheshunt House 230
  involvement in decision-taking 360 n. 13
Bettesworth, John 333
Birmingham 89, 95, 99, 107, 145, 358 n. 1
  committee alarmed at responsibility for building costs 74, 96 n. 168, 157
  loss of hymn books 147–8
  LH supplies plate 157
  collections 165
  new gallery 162
  appeal for financial support 168
  ordination at 344
  assistance from Baptists 356
Bligh, Captain 211
Bolney 50
Bowen, Hannah 211, 222, 223 n. 311
Bowen, Owen 195 n. 128
Bowlling, Mrs 223 n. 311
Bradford, John 94, 95, 165, 254, 348
  dependence on LH 101

address to New Brunswick 210
dismissed from the Connexion 363–4
Bradford-upon-Avon 72, 283
Brecon 98, 128, 137 n. 387, 201 n. 162, 202, 214
chapel rent 163
conflicts with Wesleyans 258
Baptist faction 355
Bretby 52
Bridgewater 89, 91, 202, 259, 291
Brighton 94, 127, 128, 153, 172, 292 n. 239
chapel founded 48–9
love-feasts 136
children's work 150
catchment area 156
funded by LH 156, 164
LH's house at 163, 225 n. 334, 315
support for other chapels 171
student preachers at 202, 326
enlarged chapel opened 235
bishop attends 321
Baptist split 355
chapel owned by LH 369 n. 61
Bristol, Lord 304
Bristol:
  Baptist Academy 177
  Clerical Education Society (1795) 177 n. 16
  Education Society (1770) 177
Bristol, Hope chapel 294
Bristol, LH chapel 91, 126, 130, 137 n. 388, 344
  collections 165
  LH supplies Communion vessels 157
  funding of clerical supplies 161
  sale of tickets 166, 325
  support for other chapels 170, 171
  proposal for a settled ministry at 325
Bristol Tabernacle 287, 289
Briston 352
Broadstairs 101
Bromley, Reverend 304
Bromsgrove 351
Brown, George 187, 189, 195
Brown, John 266 n. 132
Brown (of Plymouth) 186
Brussels 360–1
Buchan, Lady 198, 267 n. 132
Buckingham, Duchess of 34
Builth 201 n. 162
Bull, William 86
Burder, George 351
Burge, John 85
Burn, Edward 192, 193, 232 n. 363
Burnett, George 177, 323–4
Busweal 281
Butler, Bishop 11
Byrom, John 33, 37

Cadogan, William 230, 348
Caldwell, Robert 106
Calvinistic controversy of 1740 30–1
Cambuslang revival 16 n. 25, 125
Cannon, Thomas 167–8
Cardiff 243
Carmarthen 186
Cart, Elizabeth 24 n. 18
Carteret, Lord 34
Case, John 157–8, 224

Castle Donnington 114, 353
Catterick 150
Cecil, Richard 245 n. 52, 293
charity schools 14
Charles, Thomas 229, 293, 348
   supports the Plan of Association 368
Chatham 167
Chatteris 75, 154–5
Cheek, N. Mosely 187 n. 75, 189, 232 n. 363, 297, 299
Chelmsford 65, 154
Cheltenham 86
Cheshunt college 151, 226–30
Chester 293
Chesterfield, Lord 36, 52
Cheyne, Dr 23 n.13, 35
Chichester 73, 153, 155
   start of ministry in 67, 115
   chapel rules 119, 123, 127, 134
   receives funds from LH 157
   chapel rent 163
   episcopal opposition 318–19
Childham 65
children's work 149–51
Christian Perfection 250–1
   Maxfield and Bell affair 233–4
   evidence of the doctrine at Brighton and Bath 238–9
   students' suspicion of 264
Church Missionary Society 286
Churchey, Walter 214, 261
Clark, Samuel (of South Petherton) 159
   recommends students to college 186, 187, 189
Clarke, Samuel 11
Clayton, John 69, 85–6, 110 n. 244, 141, 232 n. 363

   on life at Trevecca 87, 221, 311
   shares authority in college 214
   ordination attempts 302, 303 n. 21, 309
clerical incomes 8
Clifford 201 n. 162
Clifton, religious colony at 47
de Coetlogon, Charles 293, 348
Coke, Thomas 361 n. 21
Colchester 323
Coleford 137, 139, 157, 220, 352
   threats from Baptists 355
Connexion, see Countess of Huntingdon's Connexion
Conyers, Richard 179
Cook, Joseph 88 n. 133, 207, 208, 209 n. 218
Cook, Captain 210
Coram, Thomas 24
Corfe 113, 140
Cornwall 66, 69, 80, 89, 352
Cornwallis, Archbishop 198–9
Cosson, Elizabeth, see Hughes, Elizabeth
Cosson, John 187 n. 75, 207, 208, 209 n. 218, 261
   supplies Bristol Tabernacle 287
Countess of Huntingdon's Connexion:
   opening of first chapel 48–9
   expansion in Sussex 50–1
   initiation of Connexion work 62–73
   field preaching 67–8
   financing and building chapels 73–7
   social origins of congregations 77–8

clergy in the Connexion
    79–83, 161
  recruitment to the
    Connexion 83–6
  student preachers 86–8,
    158–9
  organisation of preachers
    88–98
  horses 91–2
  accommodation for
    preachers 92–3
  committees 99, 118–21
  itinerancy 102–5
  settled ministries 105–9
  popular opposition 109–17
  authority within
    congregations 117–23
  trustees 121–2
  societies 124–30
  sacraments 131–5
  love feasts 136
  Prayer Book 136–40
  clerical dress 140–1
  hymns 142–9
  music for hymns 145–6
  organs 149
  children's work 150–1
  size and spread of
    congregations 152–3
  numbers in congregations
    and societies 154–5
  catchment areas 155–6
  source of finance 163–72
  tickets 165–6
  theology 254–6
  role in Calvinistic
    controversy 257–74
  doctrinal position of
    congregations 281–2
  rift with the Tabernacle
    Connexion 289
  ordination in the Connexion
    310–12, 340–1, 343,
    344–5
  secession 335–7, 342–3, 345
  Articles of Faith 341–2, 343,
    350
  as middle ground between
    Church and Dissent
    350, 351
  relations with Dissenters
    351–6
  resistance to anabaptist
    theology 354–5
  plans for future organisation
    364–9
  impact and influence 371–4
Coughlan, Lawrence 182 n. 47
de Courcy, Richard 58–9, 209,
  230, 263 n. 120, 299, 304
Cowper, William 61 n. 232
Coychurch 242, 303 n. 20
Creaton Clerical Education
  Society 177 n. 16
Cregrina 201 n. 162
Crickhowell 201 n. 162
Crole, Anthony 87, 197 n.
  141, 230, 353
  preached against 113, 140
  involved in initial
    consideration of Spa
    Fields 329
Cwmyoy 201 n. 162

Dartford 155
Dartmouth, Earl of 315, 364
Davenport, Samuel 187 n. 75,
  189
Davies, Edward 59 n. 229,
  241–2, 298, 303
Davies, Howel 16, 59 n. 229
Davies, Thomas 264 n. 123,
  301
deism 10–11
Derbyshire 68
Derbyshire, John 195
Devizes 98
Devon 66, 353

Dissenters:
  and the Evangelical revival 20
  charities 75
  using the Prayer Book 140
  ordination 306–8
  grant use of meeting-houses to the Connexion 351–2
  opposition to Connexion 353–4
Dissenting academies 5, 72, 173, 184, 302
  producing ministers 174–5, 188 n. 83
  breadth of curriculum 191 n. 101
  evangelical academies 200, 227 n. 341
Ditchling 50, 153
Doddridge, Philip 20 n. 33, 33, 40 n. 103, 44
  Northampton academy 173
Dorchester 70, 89, 96, 135, 156
  cost of building 75
  opposition at 112
  society 126, 155
  rivalry with Dissenters 354
Dover 71, 76, 141, 162, 316
  press-gang 92
  changing attitudes to LH 101–2
  resistance to Prayer Book 138
  numbers of communicants 155
  new chapel in 1787 167
  licensed 317
Drummond, Robert, 9 n. 10
Dublin 73, 130, 142
  weekly collections 165
  Hawkesworth serving 308, 310
Dudley 67, 283

Douglass, Lord 360–1
Dunn, William 103, 111, 113, 185–200
Dupont, Matthew 151
Dursley 287
Dyer (of St George's, Southwark) 144

Easterbrook, Joseph 180, 186
Eccles, Charles Stuart 207, 208
Edinburgh 240, 256
Edwards, John 85, 86, 122 n. 304
Edwin, Lady Charlotte 303 n. 20
Elland Clerical Society 60, 177, 182, 194, 301
Ellis, Robert 106
Ellis, William 159, 187 n. 75, 280, 299
Ely 318, 355
English Evangelical Academy 200, 227 n. 341
English, Thomas 306, 307
Erasmus, Bishop 182 n. 47
Erskine, Lady Anne 94, 96, 116, 198, 277, 359
  wants a London chapel 327
  resistance to Plan of Association 367–8
  devizee of LH's chapels 369
Evangelicals in the Church of England 19, 285–6
Evangelical Magazine 286, 300
Evangelical Revival 14–20
Evesham 95, 107–8, 155
Exeter, bishop of 40
Exmouth 294
Eyre, John 94, 102, 182, 186, 204, 281
  background 189
  officiates at opening of Cheshunt college 230

Index 401

serves Orange Street chapel 293
Oxford and ordination 300–1

the Fall 243–4, 246, 255
Faversham 368
Feathers Tavern Petition 11
Ferrers, 2nd Earl 21
Ferrers, 4th Earl 46, 51 n. 172
Ferring 51
final perseverance 252, 254
Fletcher, John 96, 135, 202, 237, 238
  first links with LH 44–5
  accepts presidency of Trevecca 178
  involved in college planning 179–80
  links with St Edmund Hall students 182
  and the college syllabus 189–91, 196, 198
  resigns presidency of Trevecca 213, 263–4
  influence over the students 219, 220–1
  and Calvinistic preaching 253
  attempts peace-keeping between LH and JW 258, 259–60
  on Benson's dismissal from Trevecca 262
  vindication of the Minutes 268, 269–70, 271
  Second Check to Antinomianism 273
  deteriorating relations with LH 273–4
  Third Check to Antinomianism 275–6
  reconciliation with LH and others 276–7
  worried at impact of controversy 284
  no difficulties with bishop 321
Fletcher, John (of Gainsborough) 118
Fishguard 349 n. 232
Foote, Samuel 247
Ford, Dr 290, 294
Foster, Henry 325
French, Thomas 205
French Revolution 285
Frome 85, 92, 101, 154
Furley, Samuel 237

Gainsborough 74, 77, 118, 158, 160
  society 126
  purchase of hymn books 147
  receives funds from LH 157
  prefers Connexion preachers to Wesley's 254
  Huntingtonian split 282 n. 199
  premises licensed 316–17
Germany 360
Gibbons, Dr Thomas 248
Gibbons, William 187 n. 75, 191, 216
Giffard, Dr Andrew 185
Giles, J. (student) 302
Glascott, Cradock 74, 96, 112, 125, 154, 280, 316
  pattern of involvement in the Connexion 55–6, 79
  preaching tour in 1781 68
  acceptance of living 100, 339
  attitude to itinerant ministry 103
  experiences opposition 110–1, 113

Glascott, Cradock (*cont.*)
  at Hatherleigh 145
  receives funds from LH 160
  seeks students for Trevecca 184
  proposals for examining potential students 192
  views on students 194, 195
  spends time at Trevecca 216 n. 263
  on the Minutes of 1770 267, 269
  on the Tabernacle Connexion 288, 289
  and Rowland Hill 292
  favours Connexion ordination 311
  and the early history of Spa Fields 332–4
  involved in moves towards secession 335, 337–8
  Connexion links after secession 347
  on William Taylor 363
  thought to support Haweis over Plan of Association 368
Glazebrook, James 147, 185, 186, 187 n. 75, 188, 232 n. 363
  offered settled ministry in Connexion 100, 161
  experiences violence 112
  ministry at Ashby 126, 139, 144, 282, 316
  itinerant preaching 140, 202, 204, 316, 322, 353
  ordination 158, 159, 299, 320
  recruited for Trevecca 179
  offered mastership of Cheshunt college 229
  theology 239–40, 259, 261
  well-treated by bishops 320, 321, 348
Glenorchy, Lady Willielma 59, 86, 309
  financial support for LH 164
  self-examination 253
  and JW 256–7, 262–3
  activities in England 294
Gloucester 150, 290
Gloucestershire Association 289
Gold, David 84
Goode, Mrs A. E. 236
Goode, Henry 325, 336
Goodrick, George 187 n. 75
Goodwin, John 241
Gospel Magazine 263, 271, 286
Gosport academy 227 n. 341
Grantham 74, 163
Graves, Richard (*The Spiritual Quixote*) 114
Gravesend 162
Green, Thomas 104
Green, William 344
Griffiths, David 348
Grimsby 283 n. 201
Grove, Thomas 86
Guernsey 137 n. 387
Gye of Bath (printer) 148

Halburton 76
Hall (student) 93
Halle 16
Hampshire 84
Harman, Richard 50, 159
Harmer, J. 287
Harris, Alderman Gabriel 289
Harris, Howel 16, 38, 50, 178, 206 n. 201, 222
  first links with LH 32–3, 37
  jealous of Whitefield 39
  conversion 140
  vision of a 'School of the Prophets' 173

Index

on letter-learning 176
complains about the
  students 203, 219, 220
influence over the college
  216–17
breach with LH 217
at 1764 conference with LH
  and JW 235
theology 244 n. 49, 247
on JW 259
college witch-hunt against
  261
Harris, John 64, 103
  ordination attempts 102,
    299–300
Harris, Thomas 178
Hart, Richard 59 n. 229
Hartshorne 322
Harwich 76, 93, 113, 352
Hastings, Lady Anne 46
Hastings, Lady Betty 22, 23,
  182
Hastings, Lady Frances 22, 46
Hastings, Henry 22
Hastings, Henry (son of LH)
  46
Hastings, Lady Margaret 22,
  26, 30 n. 44, 47
Hatherleigh 145
Hatton 59 n. 229
Haverfordwest 134, 288, 289
Haweis, Judith (née Townsend)
  57
Haweis, Thomas 79, 166, 214,
  305
  background and early links
    with LH 54–5, 324
  as composer 146
  Tahiti mission 210
  episcopal support 321
  loyalty to the Church of
    England 323–5, 335
  and the early history of Spa
    Fields 332–4

sees the Connexion as
  middle ground 350
resistance to Plan of
  Association 367–8
devizee of LH's chapels
  369
estimate of the size of the
  Connexion 372
Hawkesworth, John 142, 232
  n. 363
helps the Tabernacle
  Connexion 287, 288
ordination 308, 310, 311
Haxey 90, 106
Hay-on-Wye 201 n. 162, 261
Heathfield 153
Heckmondwike 175
Henderson, John 212 n.
  240
Henfield 50
Herdsman (or Hurdsman),
  Richard 107, 199, 200
  ordination 306, 307
Hereford 97, 122, 165, 170,
  201 n. 162
  legal dispute at the chapel
    214, 215
  LH's house at 225 n. 334
  episcopal opposition 321
  chapel owned by LH 369 n.
    61
Herefordshire 64, 152, 202
Herrenhaag, 27
Hervey, Lady Caroline 242
Hervey, James 44, 124, 323
  catechising children 149
  Vindication of *Theron and
    Aspasio* 240
  on predestination 244–5
  antinomianism 248
  final perseverance 252
Hewer, William 187 n. 75,
  205–6
High Wycombe 150

Hill, Richard 56, 241, 265, 266
   Paris *Conversation* 272–3
   response to Fletcher's *Second Check* 274
Hill, Rowland 18, 81, 122 n. 304, 315, 374
   conversion and contact with LH 56–7
   use of the Prayer Book 139
   moderate Calvinism 248
   attacks on JW 278, 279
   rift with LH 288, 290–2
Hill, Thomas 207, 209 n. 218
Hodson, William 169, 365 n. 42
Hogg, James (*The Private Memoirs and Confessions of a Justified Sinner*) 248
Holland, William 121
Holmes, John 112
Honeywell, John 103
Hope, Lady Henrietta 277 n. 179
Hopetown, Earl of 277
Hornby, John 170
Hotham, Sir Charles 49 n. 158, 50
Hotham, Lady Gertrude 49, 277
Hoxton academy 188 n. 83
Hughes, Elizabeth 208, 220
Huguenots 15 n. 23
Hull 102, 122, 137 n. 387, 299
Hull, Christopher 89, 187 n. 75, 197 n. 140, 351
Huntingdon 72
Huntingdon, Francis, 10th Earl of 36, 45–6, 148, 163, 238 n. 27, 361
Huntingdon, Selina, Countess of:
   early life and marriage 21
   conversion 24–6
   early contacts with the Wesleys 28–9, 31–2
   and the Moravians 30, 41 n. 109
   and the first Calvinistic controversy 31
   early influence on the Revival 32–4
   Jacobite links 34
   widowed 37
   assumes major role in the Revival 39, 40–5
   start of chapel building 48
   develops her work in the 1760s 48–61
   control over the Connexion 93–4, 96, 98–102
   loved and loathed in the Connexion 99–100
   attitude to religious societies 125
   and Holy Communion 132
   composes hymns 142–3
   financial position 163, 225 n. 334
   breach with Howel Harris 217
   influence over students 217–19, 221 n. 300
   co-operation with JW 234–5
   relations with CW 238
   reaction to the Minutes of 1770 257–8, 262–3, 264–5
   suspicious of the Wesleys 258
   decision to leave off controversy 271–2
   later relations with JW 278
   relations with Whitefieldites 287–90
   attitude to the Church of England 296, 297

Index

active to the end of her life 358–60
considers living in America 360
European interests 360–1
achievements 370–4
Huntingdon, Theophilus, 9th Earl of 21, 26–7, 37
Huntingdonshire 152
Huntington, William 282
Hupton, Job 199
Hurdsman, Richard, *see* Herdsman
Hurstpierpoint 50
Hutchings, John 38 n. 92
Hutchins, Richard 38 n. 92
Hughes, Elizabeth 208
Hughes & Walsh 147, 148

Idle academy 227 n. 341
Illingworth, Revd Dr 229 n. 351
imputed righteousness 248, 255
Ingham, Benjamin 18, 24, 27, 30 n. 44, 47
Ireland, James 266, 269, 270, 280, 336
Isle of Purbeck 89
Isle of Wight 67, 169

James, John 209–10
Jane, Joseph 54
Jenkin, Jenkin 225
Jernegan, William 224–5
Jesse, William 58, 235
Johnson, Bishop James 320
Jones, David (of Llangan) 69, 171, 186, 216 n. 263, 348
Jones, Griffiths (of Llanddowror) 16, 63
Jones, Herbert 329, 330–1, 341 n. 195
Jones, John (of Birmingham) 215, 230

Jones, J. T. 325, 326
Jones, Thomas (of St Edmund Hall) 125, 207
Joss, Torial 288, 291

Ken, Bishop 28 n. 33
Kendal 167, 354
Kensick (Dissenter) 353
Kent 95
Kidderminster 157
Kingswood School 180, 196, 212, 214
Kinsman, Andrew 86, 288, 291, 308
Kirklington 323
Kirkman, Thomas 230
Knight, J. A. 343 n. 203, 352

Lakenheath 162
Lane, Richard 352
Large Minutes of 1763 314
Laughton 51
Law, Bishop Edmund 302
Law, William 13, 26, 37
latitudinarianism 12
Leggett, Richard 85
Leicestershire 111
Leigh, Edmund 194
letters testimonial 303
Lewes 73, 74, 76, 153, 156, 368
  support for other chapels 171
  rivalry with Dissenters 354
  licensing of preachers and preaching houses 313–15, 316, 317–18
Lincoln 102, 111, 115, 127, 317, 351
Lincolnshire 68, 90, 111, 125, 152
Lindsey, Theophilus 25 n. 24
  Sunday school 150
  on Trevecca 197

Lindsey, Theophilus (*cont.*)
  on LH at the end of her life
    361 n. 23
Little Gidding 149 n. 453
Llanbedr 201 n. 162
Llandovery 186
Llanedy 194
Llanelli 225
Llangadog 157, 359
Llangrwyney 201 n. 162
Lloyd, John (friend of LH)
    145–6, 342
  role at Bath chapel 95
  attends Wesley's conference
    269
  hostile to Church of England
    344, 349
  devizee of LH's chapels 369
Lloyd, John (student) 65
Lloyd, Philip (dean of
    Norwich) 306
London 327
  Clerical Education Society
    177 n. 16
  Essex Street (Unitarian)
    chapel 125
  Fetter Lane society 27, 29
  Finsbury dispensary 171
  Foundry society 30, 166,
    233
  Greenwich Tabernacle 260
  Hackney academy 227 n.
    341, 228 n. 342
  Holywell Mount chapel,
    Shoreditch 108, 169,
    359, 365
  Hoxton academy 227 n.
    341, 228 n. 342
  Jewin Street congregation
    352
  Lock Hospital 42 n. 120,
    291
  Moorfields Tabernacle 45,
    260
  Mulberry Gardens chapel,
    Wapping 120, 144, 170,
    348, 365
    effect of paid seats 166
    offered assistance by
      Tabernacle trustees
      289
    original buildings 328
    rivalry with Dissenters 354
    owned by LH 369 n. 61
  Orange Street chapel 293
  Pantheon, Exmouth Market,
    see Spa Fields
  Pantheon, Oxford Road 327
  Portland chapel 107, 304
  Northampton chapel, *see* Spa
    Fields
  Ram's Chapel, Hackney 320
  Rope-Makers Alley chapel
    239, 275 n. 170
  Rotherhithe 72, 137, 165,
    359
  St George's-in-the-East 348
  St George's, Southwark 144
  St James, Clerkenwell 330
  Silver Street chapel 139,
    293, 362
  Sion chapel, Whitechapel
    359, 369 n. 61
  Spa Fields chapel 80, 99,
    101, 119, 120, 122,
    assistant minister at 107,
      123
    committee 120, 158
    society 126–7
    purchase of hymn books
      147
    Sunday school 151
    collections 165
    receives appeals for
      financial help 168,
      169, 170
    location for ordinations
      210, 343, 344

links with Apostolic
    Society 228
'Prophets School' attached
    to 231
origins 328–32
LH moves into chapel
    house 332
legal moves against 330–9
licensed 340
Baptist convert at 355
theological divisions within
    the committee 362
and the London Acting
    Association 365
chapel owned by LH 369
    n. 61
Spitalfields 73
Swedish congregation 300
Tottenham Court Road
    chapel 45, 260, 292,
    293
Union Street chapel,
    Whitechapel 157
Wapping, *see* Mulberry
    Gardens
Westminster, Princess Street
    chapel 144, 170, 292,
    293, 318
West Street chapel 31
Woolwich 105, 128, 133,
    320, 327
London Acting Association, *see*
    Plan of Association
London Missionary Society
    211 n. 230, 285, 300, 351,
    365 n. 44
Longtown 64
Lowth, Bishop 301 n. 13, 331,
    332, 334
Lutherans 300
Lyme Regis 128, 155

McAll, Robert 94, 96, 138,
    139

Macaulay, Zachary 371 n. 70
Macclesfield 315
Madan, Martin 42, 49, 52, 54,
    142 n. 413
    at Bristol conference in 1764
        235
    Paris *Conversation* 272
    preaches against JW 277 n.
        180
    influences Newton to stay in
        the Church 324 n. 103
Madeley 179, 180
Madrid 361
Magdalene College,
    Cambridge 301
Maidstone 96, 137 n. 387,
    138, 156
Manchester 67
Manners, Lady 77
Mansfield, Lord 314 n. 62,
    334, 343
Margate 138
Margate, David 209
Markham, Archbishop 321
Marlborough 127–8
Marlborough academy 227 n.
    341
Marlborough, Duchess of 34
Markfield 35
Matthews, James 182, 183, 184
Maxfield, Thomas 80, 239,
    253, 274–5, 304
    encouraged by LH 33, 101
    seeks students for Trevecca
        183–4
    and Christian Perfection
        233, 234 n. 8
    suggests Connexion
        presence in London
        327
Mays, Dr 354
Mead, Henry 186, 187 n. 75,
    232 n. 363, 297 n. 2, 320
    ordination 158, 299

Mead, Henry (*cont.*)
  itinerant preaching 202, 204, 316, 353
  chosen for American mission 207, 208
Meldrum, John 310
Melksham 103
Methodist Magazine 286
Mevagissey 218
Midhurst 111, 113, 115, 153
Midlands 67, 152
Milgrove, Benjamin 146, 239
Mills (student) 70
Milner, Joseph 230, 301
Milton, Charles William 209–10
Milton (Kent) 164
Moira, Elizabeth, Countess of 22, 46
Molland, Thomas 104, 112, 126, 232 n. 363, 294
  publishes pamphlet 159
  supervisory role in college 213, 218
  ordination 308, 309
Monmouth 98, 115, 283 n. 204
Moor (of Newgate) 59
Moravian Brethren 15, 27, 29–30
Morgan, William 149
Morley, William 167, 189, 194
Morpeth 120, 152, 368
Mott, Martha 28
Mumbles, the 225

New Brunswick 209
New Forest 89
Newark 78, 106, 123,
  opposition at 112
  chapel building 121
  society 126
  threat to leave the Connexion 153 n. 476, 283, 358 n. 1

Newell (Vice-Chancellor of Oxford) 241
Newman's *Apologia* 249
Newport Pagnell academy 86 n. 120, 227 n. 341
Newton, John 61, 71 n. 47, 86 n. 120, 125 n. 321, 183, 241
  on parish ministry 105
  children's work 149
  links with JW 237
  untroubled by his bishop 319
  Haweis's influence keeps him in the Church 324
Nicholl, James 192
Nicholson, Isaac 230
Nisbet, Charles 266 n. 132
Norman (of Bradford-upon-Avon) 283
nonjurors 7
non-residence by clergy 7–8
North, Bishop Brownlow 195, 284
Northampton 124, 291
Northamptonshire 111, 322
Norwich 105, 130, 292
  cost of chapel building 76
  opposition at 117
  committee 119
  disputes with Shirley 121, 123
  communicant numbers 134, 155
  use of the Prayer Book 138
  funding of clerical supplies 162
  theological differences within the congregation 281
  joined by Wesleyans 283
  threat from Tabernacle Connexion 289
  want student ordained 344

benefit from divisions in the
   Dissenters 354
Nottingham 65
Nottinghamshire 90
Nova Scotia 170, 209

Okeley, Francis 103, 175, 178
Oldham, James 338
Oliver, Philip 293
Olivers, Thomas 189 n. 86,
   269, 270, 271 n. 150
organs 148
Orphan House, Savannah
   206–9, 306
Orton, Janet Payne 49 n. 158
Ostend 361
Ote Hall chapel 71, 91, 98,
   130, 185, 240
   established 49
   and the Plan of Association
      153, 368
   funded by LH 156
   Baptist split 355
Oundle 111
Owen, Edward 269
Oxford 300
Oxford Holy Club 17, 124
   and children 149

Paine, Tom 353
Painter, John 354
Paris 361
Parker, David 329
Parsons, Edward 205
Partney 70, 167, 203–4
patterns of Anglican worship
   9, 131
Pease (student) 94
Peckwell, Henry 67, 68, 73,
   74, 271, 292
   regarded as a prize 81
   sphere of influence 95, 159
   encounters opposition 111,
      115

proposes hymn collection
   144
declines presidency of
   Trevecca 213 n. 245
Anglican loyalties 326,
   335–6
Pecore, G. 187 n. 75, 205–6,
   298
peerage, rights of 45, 315,
   317–18, 342 n. 201
Pembrokeshire 89
Pentycross, Thomas 71, 91,
   126 n. 321, 248 n. 60
   development of links with
      Connexion 81–2
   reaction to his dismissal
      99–100
   relations with his bishop
      145, 319
   curate funded by LH 160
   and secession 336, 342, 343
   rift with LH 347–8
Perry, Thomas 100
Pershore 113
Peterborough 203–4
Petworth 65, 133, 153
Phillips, David 67
Phillips, Samuel 193 n. 110,
   214, 221
Philpot, Joseph 177 n. 15, 339
   n. 189
Pierce, Samuel Eyles 104 n.
   212, 187, 193 n. 114
Piercy, William 106, 122 n.
   304
   preaching tour in 1781 68
   leader of the Orphan House
      expedition 207, 208–9,
      287
Plan of Association 93 n. 154,
   152–4, 365–8
Platt, William 192, 230, 365 n.
   44
pluralism 8

Plymouth 94, 288, 291, 308
Porter, Edward 87, 204
Porteus, Bishop Beilby 321
Powell, Mrs Averina 223, 224, 230
Power, Ann 164
Powis (or Powys), Thomas 266, 272 n. 159
Powley, Matthew 59 n. 229
predestination 244–6, 253, 255
Presbyterians 12
press-gang 92
Preston 77
Price, John 211
Priestley, Joseph 85
Putsham 70

Quakers 5, 37–8

Raikes, Robert 150
Rankin, Thomas 207
Ratby 35
Reading 97, 133, 146, 355
reformation of manners 14
religious societies 13, 124
Restoration Settlement 6–7
Richards, Lewis 207, 209 n. 218
Rickmansworth 72
Ringmer 50, 153
Riot Act 1715 317
Ripon, dean of 115
Roberts, Daniel 187 n. 75, 207
Robinson, Robert 143
Robinson, Thomas 230
Roby, William 193 n. 113, 199, 232 n. 363
Rodborough Connexion 288 n. 217
Romaine, William 52, 254, 267, 293, 325
  first links with LH 42
  critical of Christian Perfection 234
  attacks JW 263
  reconciliation with Fletcher 276
  intended to open Spa Fields 329
  cooling relations with Connexion 346
Romaine, Mrs William 272
Roman Catholics 6
Ross-on-Wye 64, 353
Rottingdean 50
Rouquet, James 59 n. 229, 291
Rowlands, Daniel 16, 336
Rowlands, Nathaniel 160 n. 518, 368
Rowley, Adam 187 n.75
Ryland, John 237, 330

St Agnes 66, 134
St Bees Theological College 174
St Columb 152
St Edmund Hall, Oxford 212
  expulsion of the six students 181–2, 189, 240–1
St Ives, Cornwall 279
Sandemanians 281
Scott, James (of Heckmondwike) 175
Scott, Jonathon 277 n. 178
Scott, Thomas 249
Sellon, Walter 238, 240 n. 36, 241, 248, 263, 267
Sellon, William 330, 331, 332, 333, 334, 337–8
Seymour, A. C. H. 1, 3–4
Shaftesbury 352
Sheppard, Edward 59 n. 229, 79, 239, 242, 252 n. 79, 277
Shiffnall 352
Shipman, Joseph 182, 183, 184, 242, 305
Shirley, Walter 51 n. 171, 86, 95 n. 162, 122 n. 304

early involvement with LH's work 53-4
ends active participation in the Connexion 80
attitude to rioters 116-17
disputes over his role at Norwich 121, 123
organisation of chapels 127, 129, 136
edits Connexion hymn book 143-4
favours theological moderation 242, 249, 272, 274, 280
on Christian Perfection 251, 256, 264
and final perseverance 252
on JW 259
role in the Calvinistic controversy 266-70, 271, 273
reconciliation with Fletcher 277
supplies Bristol Tabernacle 287
moderating influence on LH 288
Anglican loyalties 326-7
involved in initial thoughts of acquiring Spa Fields 329
Connexion links after secession 347
Shirley, Mrs Walter 129, 242
Shore, James 340 n. 189 & 190
Shute Barrington, Bishop 303, 319, 347-8
Sierra Leone 371
Simeon, Charles 229
Simpson, David 315
Simpson, William 119-20
Singleton 65
Si Quis 303

Slaughter, Richard 159
Sleaford 106, 153 n. 479, 304
Smisby 125
Smythe, Lady 299
Socinianism 11
Societas Evangelica 75, 228 n. 342
Society for Promoting Christian Knowledge (SPCK) 13, 23, 35, 183
Society for Propagating the Gospel (SPG) 13
Somerton 156
South Petherton 107, 145, 154, 306, 307
Sowden, Joseph 106
Spa Fields chapel, *see* London
Spencer, Edward 59 n. 229, 267
Staffordshire 125
Stamford 74, 75, 76, 111, 115
Star Cross 138, 139
stillness 29
Stourbridge 67, 163
Stowbridge 114
Strafford, Countess of 23
Surrey chapel 139, 292, 293, 347
Sussex 65, 84, 114, 140, 153, 155
development of work in 49-51
organisation of preaching in 95
violent opposition 111
Baptist threats in 355
Suter, Thomas 97, 193 n. 113, 204-5, 352
Swansea 96, 148, 228, 283 n. 204
plans for college at 224-5
congregation supports Plan of Association 368
Sydling 70

Tabernacle Connexion 267,
    287–90
  fear that Spa Fields would
    rival 329
Tahiti 211
Talbot, William 355
Taunton 76, 242
Tavener, Prebendary 322
Taylor, David 28
Taylor, Bishop Jeremy 13, 26
Taylor, William 120, 141
  first links with LH 82
  sphere of influence 95
  at Wallingford 145
  receives funds from LH 160
  acquisition of Northampton
    chapel 329
  proceedings against 330–1
  involved in moves towards
    secession 335, 336, 337
  secedes himself 341–2
  takes part in Primary
    Ordination 343
  critical of non-seceding
    clergy 349–50
  role in Wills's fall 362
  is himself dismissed 362–3
Taylor, Mrs William 101
Teignmouth 66
Tenby 115
Terrick, Bishop 205–6, 298,
  306
The Whole Duty of Man 13
Thorresby, John 370 n. 66
Thornton, Henry 231
Thornton, John 58 n. 221, 86
  n. 120, 144, 164, 179
  moderating influence on the
    controversy 280
Thresher, William 92, 352
Thurlow, Bishop 301 n. 13
Toleration Act 1689 6, 312–13
Toplady, Augustus 142 n. 413,
    293, 327
  attacks Arminianism 241
  declines to join deputation
    to Wesleyan conference
    267
  reconciliation with Fletcher
    276
  involved in initial thoughts
    on acquiring Spa Fields
    329
Torbay 66
Townsend, Joseph 57–8, 80,
    240, 241, 256
Travelling Fund 67, 168–71
Tregunta 178
Trelawney, Harry 309
Trevecca college 62, 297
  Easter Communion at 135
  origins and precedents
    173–8
  choice of location 178
  building work 179–80
  plan of study 179, 189–91
  opening 184
  recruitment, origins, and
    examination of students
    183–9, 191–3
  probationary periods 193–4
  students' abilities 196–9
  length of course 199–200
  student involvement in
    preaching 200–5
  foreign missions 205–11,
    287
  authority in 211–19
  theology 219–20, 239, 261,
    264–5
  life at 220–4
  last days 224–30
  ordination at 344
Trevecka settlement 178, 216,
    236
Trigo (Connexion minister)
    294
Trinity, disputes over 11, 140

Truro 354
'Tunbridge Town' 111
Tunbridge Wells 128, 129,
    160, 164, 236
  chapel opened 52–3
  employs a clerk 122
  payment to ministers 162 n.
    528
  LH's house at 163, 184, 315
  support for other chapels 171
  clergy attendance at 322
  offered to Taylor 341
  chapel owned by LH 369 n.
    61
Twycross, Isaac 214
Tyler, William 301

Upton 243
Usk 201 n. 162

Venn, Henry 52, 80, 122 n.
    304, 142 n. 413, 177, 241
  enters LH's circle 43
  influences Shirley's
    conversion 53
  on Whitefield's death 260
  weakening Connexion links
    347
Venn, Mrs Henry 237
Venn, John 43 n. 125
Village Itinerancy 228 n. 342

Wachsel, Dr 300
Waite (student) 187 n. 75
Wales, Prince of 34
Wallingford 94, 145, 248 n.
    60, 319
Walpole, Horace 51
Walsall 107, 116
Walsh, Father 272–3
Ward, Nathaniel 84–5
Wareham 353
Warrington academy 222 n.
    307

Warrington, St James 348
Warwick 72
Watchet 316
Watkins, Jane 223 n. 313
Watts, Isaac 20 n. 32
Waugh, Michael 211
Weatherill, Thomas 231
Webster, Dr (of Edinburgh)
    257
Wednesbury 135
Welsh Calvinistic Methodists
    16, 366 n. 47
Welsh clergy 83, 336
  assist Connexion after
    secession 348–9
Wesley, Charles 314
  and the Moravians 30
  relations with LH 41–2, 235,
    238, 258, 259, 261
  breach with LH 268
  contact with LH renewed
    277
Wesley, John:
  and William Law 13 n. 21
  and Jeremy Taylor 13 n. 21,
    14 n. 22
  start of preaching 18
  walk out from Fetter Lane
    29–30
  resort to the courts 116–17
  and religious societies 124
  and Holy Communion 131,
    132, 134 n. 372
  on LH's hymns 143, 259,
    260
  and Trevecca college
    anniversaries 184 n. 59,
    257
  attitude to Trevecca 190,
    203, 236, 278–9
  co-operation with LH and
    Whitefield 234–6, 237
  attitude to predestination
    245–7

Wesley, John (*cont.*)
    Minutes of 1770 251, 257
    and Lady Glenorchy 256–7
    critical of LH 259–60
    tribute to Whitefield 260
    later relations with LH 278, 279–80
    attitude to the Toleration Act 313–15
    and Methodist ordination 343 n. 204
    Deed of Declaration 366, 367
Wesley, Susanna 126 n. 321
West Bromwich 76, 157, 359
Westerham 156
Westham 113, 316
Weymouth 89, 112, 155, 307
White, William 159, 207, 208, 214–15
Whitefield, George 45, 125 n. 320, 128 n. 339, 143, 192
    conversion 17
    role in the first Calvinistic controversy 31
    contacts with LH 32, 38, 40
    preaches for her at Brighton 49
    opens Tunbridge Wells chapel 53
    and religious societies 124
    and Holy Communion 131–2
    bequeaths American estates to LH 163, 206
    on academic training 176
    opens Trevecca college 184
    co-operation with LH and JW 235–6, 237
    reactions to his death 260
Whitefield's Trustees, *see* Tabernacle Connexion
Whitehaven 97, 155, 163, 354
Wigan 75, 137 n. 387, 168

Willes, Bishop 321
Williams, John (first master at Trevecca) 180–1, 211–12, 213
Williams, John (last master at Trevecca) 187 n. 78, 215
    on the students' abilities 197, 198, 204, 209 n. 222
    on threats from the Baptists 355
Williams, John (student) 299, 304–5, 320
Williams, Peter 186, 291, 336
Williams, William (of Pantecelyn) 195, 215, 216 n. 263
Wills, Thomas 66, 67, 82–3, 116, 123, 302
    preaching tour in 1781 68, 112, 114, 353
    role in organisation of preachers 95
    and Holy Communion 134, 135
    use of Prayer Book 139
    establishes Augmentation Fund 170
    on the value of Trevecca 196
    encourages meekness in controversy 279, 291
    service in London 293
    takes part in the Primary Ordination 312, 343
    episcopal enquiries about him 320
    churches open to him 322–3, 349
    pragmatic approach to the Church of England 326
    and the early history of Spa Fields 332–3
    involved in secession 335, 337, 338, 339–40, 345

resists giving authority to
    non-seceding clergy 350
on rivalry with Dissenters
    354
and the Brussels venture 360
dismissed from the
    Connexion 361–2
Wiltshire 289, 352
Wincanton 133 n. 369, 152,
    167
Winter, Cornelius 134, 269,
    306
Woodbridge 75, 359
Wolverhampton 71, 89, 352
Worcester 105, 155, 161, 292
    n. 239
  make-up of congregation
    71, 77
  desire a settled ministry
    106, 108
  use of Prayer Book 137
  expectation of financial help
    from LH 157
  interest payments 163
  misgivings about secession
    345
Worcestershire 64
Wren, William 84
Wynn, Sir W. W. 39

Young, Thomas 106, 283
York 157 n. 499, 343
Yorkshire 68, 90

Zanchius, Jerome 241
Zinzendorf, Count 27